Texas Government

McGRAW-HILL BOOK COMPANY
New York
St. Louis
San Francisco
Düsseldorf
Johannesburg
Kuala Lumpur
London
Mexico
Montreal
New Delhi
Panama
Paris
São Paulo
Singapore
Sydney
Tokyo
Toronto

SEVENTH EDITION

Texas Government

STUART A. MacCORKLE
Former Professor of Government and
Director of the Institute of Public Affairs
The University of Texas at Austin

DICK SMITH
Late Emeritus Professor of Government
Tarleton State University

JANICE C. MAY
Assistant Professor of Government
The University of Texas at Austin

Commissioner,
Texas Constitutional Revision Commission

TEXAS GOVERNMENT

This book was set in Times Roman by Black Dot, Inc.
The editors were Stephen D. Dragin and John M. Morriss;
the designer was Barbara Ellwood;
and the production supervisor was Leroy A. Young.
The drawings were done by ANCO Technical Services.
Kingsport Press, Inc., was printer and binder.

Library of Congress Cataloging in Publication Data

MacCorkle, Stuart Alexander, date
    Texas government.

    Includes bibliographies.
    1. Texas—Politics and government. I. Smith,
Dick, date   joint author. II. May, Janice C.,
joint author. III. Title.
JK4825 1974.M3   320.4'764   73-18021
ISBN 0-07-044322-X

Contents

List of Maps

Preface

Texas political institutions may appear to some to move at a glacial pace, but the authors are in a position to attest to the contrary after reviewing the past five years of Texas politics. Changes are occurring, and the future promises an even greater acceleration.

Those familiar with previous editions of this textbook will find Chapters 1, 7, and 20 virtually rewritten and many additions and deletions made in others. The changes include a summary of the revised Texas penal code, election law reforms, new developments in Texas political-party battles, the public school financing crisis, proposals for judicial reform, a fresh look at the Texas constitution, revenue sharing, ethics and politics, new labor laws, citizen communication with legislators, governing metropolitan Texas, the strong executive model, and new labor laws. Moreover, all chapters have been updated and some have been rearranged to incorporate new ideas. Also, the Appendix has been drastically cut.

Throughout the book a special effort has been made to relate the material to the Texas constitution, which at the time of writing was undergoing its most extensive and intensive study since 1875. Also, we have tried to answer not only the "what" but also the "how" and the "why" of political decision making. To be an effective leader or follower, the citizen must know how his state and local governments operate, who holds power and how it is exercised, how political values are developed and what effect they have upon political behavior, and how forces of localism and centralization interact in the federal system. As was true of earlier editions, no attempt has been made to espouse any particular political philosophy.

The authors are deeply grateful to those individuals and organizations mentioned in the prefaces of other editions and to all who aided with the current enterprise. Among those to whom we are particularly indebted are James W. McGrew, Executive Director, and Glenn Ivy, Research Director, of the Texas Research League; James F. Ray, Executive Director, and George D. Braden, Consultant to the Texas Constitutional Revision Commission; Philip W. Barnes, Acting Director, Texas Advisory Commission on Intergovernmental Relations; W. Page Keeton, Dean of The University of Texas Law School; Emmette S. Redford, Professor of Government at The University of Texas at Austin, and the eight graduate students who, in the spring of 1973, participated in the seminar on state administrative structure and the Texas constitution at the Lyndon B. Johnson School of Public Affairs, The University of Texas at Austin; Mary Louise Nelson and Tanya Reischman, librarians at the LBJ School; Lynn F. Anderson, Director of Conferences and Training, the LBJ School, and Associate Professor of Finance, The University of Texas at Austin; Jim Hutcheson, Assistant Counsel, the Texas Civil Judicial Council; Jim Sanders, Director, Texas Legislative Reference Library; John E. Bebout, Program Director, Institute for Urban Studies, University of Houston; W. James Kronzer, Jr., of Kronzer, Abraham and Watkins, Houston; Colin J. Carl, Assistant Attorney General; Anna Merle Danz, Senior Library Assistant, Bureau of Business Research, The University of Texas at Austin; Lawrence McBride, student at The University of Texas and of Texas government; and Holly McCall, typist. Our appreciation also goes to staff members of the Texas Legislative Council, the Texas Employment Commission, and the Planning Division of the Governor's Office for their kind assistance. Finally, the junior author wishes to acknowledge her debt to her husband, Francis B. May, for his incredible patience, support, and understanding.

Stuart A. MacCorkle
Dick Smith
Janice C. May

Chapter 1

An Introduction to the State of Texas and Its Political System

This is a book about Texas government and politics, or to use the language of systems analysis, the Texas political system.[1] It is impossible to understand the Texas political system without also knowing something about the contextual variables or the environments in which the system operates. Political decision making in Texas is greatly influenced by such factors as the geography, economy, population, and culture of Texas as well as by the Federal Union of which Texas is a member. The Texas political system in turn has an impact upon all these factors. For these reasons, we begin our study with an introduction to the State of Texas, emphasizing major contextual variables that interact with Texas government and politics.

[1]For a discussion of political system analysis, consult David Easton, *A Systems Analysis of Political Life*, John Wiley & Sons, Inc., New York, 1965. For an application of systems analysis to Texas government and politics, see Dan Nimmo and William E. Oden, *The Texas Political System*, Prentice-Hall, Englewood Cliffs, N. J., 1971.

THE MEGASTATE

Texas is one of the megastates, a term used by Neil Peirce to describe the ten most populous states in the American Federal Union.[2] The nine other great states are New York, Massachusetts, New Jersey, Pennsylvania, Ohio, Illinois, Michigan, Florida, and California.

It is not surprising that, on some counts at least, Texas should qualify as a megastate. Texas is the second largest state in area, encompassing 267,339 square miles or one-seventh of the land and water area of the United States. (Alaska is the largest state.) The tourist may be interested to know that Texas is 801 miles long from north to south and 773 miles from east to west; and that "Texas has the largest all-paved, toll-free state highway network in the United States."[3] Texas is also the home of the famous King Ranch which covers 865,000 acres. In comparison with other states, Texas has the largest number of counties (254), one of which is larger than the state of Connecticut. The enormous expanses of Texas suggest regionalism; and in fact, there are many regions, of which the precise number and character vary with the classifier.[4] Politically, attempts have been made to divide Texas into several independent states.[5]

In 1970, the population of Texas reached 11,196,730, making Texas the fourth most populous state, exceeded only by California, New York, and Pennsylvania in that order. It is predicted that Texas will soon surpass Pennsylvania to become number three.

Texas is larger in area and population than the majority of independent nation states of the world today. Texas was, of course, an independent nation from 1836 to 1845, after her revolt from Mexico and before her annexation by the United States. Many observers have commented upon the great sense of state pride among Texans. This may no doubt be traced in part to the heritage of independence among the nations of the world.

Texas is also a leading urban and metropolitan state. In 1970,

[2]Neil Peirce, *The Megastates of America: People, Politics, and Power in the Ten Great States*, W. W. Norton & Company, New York, 1972. Peirce's thesis is that the ten great states form a distinct entity, bound together by common ties of metropolitanism, political prowess, economic resources, and culture.

[3]*Texas Almanac, 1972–73*, p. 350, A. H. Belo Corporation, Dallas, 1972.

[4]Many examples may be given. Texas has been divided into twenty-one economic and twenty-four state planning regions. Texas contains twenty-four Standard Metropolitan Statistical Areas. Texas is the crossroads of four major physiographic subdivisions of North America and is commonly divided into eight geographic regions: East Texas, Central Texas, West Texas, the Panhandle, South Texas, the Gulf Coastal Plain, Trans-Pecos, and North Texas.

[5]The most recent attempt was made by the late V. E. "Red" Berry, state Senator from San Antonio. He proposed legislation in the 1967 legislature which would have divided Texas into a North and a South Texas in the hopes that the fun-loving southerners would legalize pari-mutuel betting, his major or only campaign plank.

Table 1   1970 Federal Census Rankings of Ten Largest States Showing the Relative and Absolute Change from 1960

1970 rank	State	1970 population	Change 1960–1970 Percent	Change 1960–1970 Number	1960 rank
1	California	19,953,134	27.0	4,235,930	2
2	New York	18,190,740	8.4	1,408,436	1
3	Pennsylvania	11,793,909	4.2	474,543	3
4	TEXAS	11,196,730	16.9	1,617,053	6
5	Illinois	11,113,976	10.2	1,032,818	4
6	Ohio	10,652,017	9.7	945,620	5
7	Michigan	8,845,083	13.4	1,021,889	7
8	New Jersey	7,168,164	18.2	1,101,382	8
9	Florida	6,789,443	37.1	1,837,883	10
10	Massachusetts	5,689,170	10.5	477,592	9

Source: U.S. Bureau of Census 1970 Data on Resident Populations. Table prepared for the Texas Urban Development Commission, 1971.

8,920,946 Texans lived in urban places or almost 80 percent (79.7 percent to be exact) of the total population; and 73.5 percent lived in Standard Metropolitan Statistical Areas (SMSAs).[6] Texas ranks eleventh in urbanization but has more SMSAs (twenty-four) than any other state. The Houston SMSA is one of the fastest growing areas in the United States, the center of an impressive industrial and space research complex.

Texas is a megastate for economic reasons. Texas is the nation's foremost producer of oil and natural gas. In 1970, Texas accounted for approximately 35 percent of the nation's crude oil production.[7] Texas is also the number-one state in oil refining and petrochemicals (chemicals made from petroleum products).

Texas is a top-ranking agricultural state, having more farms and farm acreage than any other state. Texas leads in head of cattle and feedlots; and is number one in "sheep and goats, wool, mohair, cotton, cottonseed, grain sorghums, cabbage, carrots, onions, watermelons, castorbeans, and guar."[8]

Texas is also a financial power of some note. Texas has more

[6]The SMSA is a statistical term employed by the Federal Office of Management and Budget (OMB), formerly the Bureau of the Budget. The SMSA is always coterminous with one or more county boundaries for ease in gathering statistics. The SMSA is named for the central city or cities included within it. In order to qualify as an SMSA, the area must contain at least one city with a minimum population of 50,000 or twin cities with a combined population of 50,000 or more. Contiguous counties are included only if they are socially and economically integrated with the central city as determined by criteria specified by the OMB. See Chapter 20 for more information.

[7]*Texas Almanac, op. cit.,* p. 399. The figure is an estimate.

[8]*Ibid.,* p. 414. For the student interested in guar, it is a leguminous plant, like clover or alfalfa, used for paper sizing.

commercial banks than any other state although this is largely a consequence of the law banning branch banking. In 1969, Texas banks ranked fifth in total assets or liabilities. One of the nation's twelve Federal Reserve Banks is located in Dallas.[9] Texas also ranks high in shipping, served by thirteen principal ports, led by Houston, which usually ranks second or third in the nation by annual volume of tonnage.

Texas is a megastate politically in relation to national politics in several important respects. In 1972, Texas cast twenty-six electoral votes for President, the fourth largest bloc in the electoral college and a sizable proportion of the 277 needed to win. Texas has given the nation two Presidents, Dwight D. Eisenhower and Lyndon Baines Johnson. Texans elect twenty-four members of the U.S. House of Representatives in addition to two U.S. Senators to Congress. In the 93rd Congress (1973–1974), four Texans were chairmen of major House standing (regular) committees: Wright Patman, Banking and Currency; George H. Mahon, Appropriations; Olin E. Teague, Science and Astronautics; and W. R. Poage, Agriculture. Patman is also chairman of the Joint Economic Committee. The late Sam Rayburn from Texas was U.S. Speaker longer than any other person. The late Lyndon Johnson was regarded by many as the most powerful Senate Majority Leader of all time. Before his defeat in 1970, Senator Ralph Yarborough served as chairman of the Senate Labor and Public Welfare Committee. John Tower, U.S. Senator from Texas since 1961, is the ranking minority member on the Senate Banking, Housing, and Urban Affairs Committee. Lloyd Bentsen, elected Senator in 1970, is a member of the powerful Senate Finance Committee. These are just a few of the men who have ably represented Texas in Congress throughout Texas history.

CHANGING ENVIRONMENTS

The position Texas now holds as a leading urban, industrial megastate in the Federal Union has been of relatively recent origin. Many of the developments have occurred only since 1950, following World War II. For example, Texas was a rural state until the 1950 census. The numerous changes and their pace have had important consequences for the Texas political system and will be briefly reviewed.

Texas Economy and Social Factors

There are myriad interrelationships between a state's economy and its politics. For one thing, the economy provides the tax base. In general, a

---

[9] *Ibid.*, p. 433. Texas has a total of 1,183 national and state banks.

poor state is less capable of providing the money to support governmental services, such as education and highways, than a rich state. For another, a host of interest groups arises to promote by political action their economic well-being, including farm, business, labor, and professional groups.

Some specialists in state politics argue that a state's economy is the most important factor determining its politics and policies. In one massive statistical analysis, it was argued that a state's economic development (as measured by income, industrialization, education, and urbanization) is more important than its political system (as measured by apportionment, voter turnout, partisanship, and interparty competition) in explaining the differences among the states in expenditures on selected programs, such as education, health, and welfare.[10] This argument has been disputed.[11] Nonetheless, few would question the importance of economics in politics, particularly in Texas.

Agriculture　Agribusiness, as agriculture is now called, continues to be an important sector of the Texas economy, accounting for $7.3 billion in 1971. But it is no longer the mainstay of the economy as it was earlier in the nineteenth and twentieth centuries. Only a fraction of the labor force is now employed in farming (5.7 percent); and during the past ten years, farm employment declined by 31 percent while at the same time nonfarm employment rose by 40 percent.[12]

Industry　The most important single factor in Texas accounting for the change from an agriculturally based economy was the discovery of great oil fields. A date famous in Texas history is 1901 when Spindletop, the state's first great gusher, blew in near Beaumont, and the first of the big oil booms was underway. Later, in 1930, a seventy-year-old independent operator, C. M. "Dad" Joiner, discovered oil in Rusk County in East Texas. The East Texas Oil Field turned out to be the biggest in the entire country until recent discoveries in Alaska.

Oil production led to oil refining and to the petrochemical industry; and Texas soon dominated in both industries. The oil refining and petrochemical industries are concentrated along the Gulf Coast from Corpus Christi to the Louisiana border. In this area are produced "40 percent of every basic petrochemical, 80 percent of the synthetic rubber,

[10]Thomas R. Dye, *Economics, Politics and the Public: Policy Outcomes in the American States*, Rand McNally & Company, Chicago, 1966.

[11]For example, see Ira Sharkansky and Richard I. Hofferbert, "Dimensions of State Policy," in Herbert Jacob and Kenneth N. Vines (eds.), *Politics in the American States*, 2d ed., pp. 315–353, Little, Brown and Company, Boston, 1972.

[12]Joe B. Harris, *Urban Texas: Past—Present—Future, A Report Prepared for the Texas Urban Development Commission*, p. 19, Arlington, Tex., 1971.

and 10 percent of the sulphuric acid" in the United States.[13] In fact, the largest concentration of refinery facilities in the entire world is here. Houston dominates among the cities in the area. The oil capital of the world, Houston is the national headquarters of Exxon and other oil companies and is first in the nationwide distribution of natural gas as well as the manufacture of oil field equipment. Houston is served by the Houston ship channel, which has made Houston one of the major ports in the United States, as we have seen. Now there is talk of superports along the Gulf Coast.

Insofar as manufacturing in general is concerned, Texas ranks eighth among the states. From 1960 to 1970 there was a significant increase in manufacturing employment, which rose by nearly 50 percent. Employment in durable goods manufacturing (furniture, machinery, etc.) increased almost 75 percent. Despite the importance of manufacturing, however, more workers are employed in wholesale and retail trade in Texas than in manufacturing. Also important, though employing fewer people than trade and manufacturing, are services (hotels, garages, etc.) and government.[14]

Labor Unions   Texas lags well behind other states in the percentage of the nonagricultural labor force in labor unions. Only 523,000 workers or 14.4 percent of the nonagricultural labor force are in unions, placing Texas forty-fourth among the states in this regard.[15] Several factors are important in explaining this ranking. For one, the Texas legislature has passed anti-labor union legislation, which reflects a hostile attitude toward unions in Texas. Texas is a right-to-work state where it is illegal to require a worker to belong to a union in order to be hired or retained in his job. But perhaps the most important explanation lies in the difference in the character and timing of industrialization in Texas. Unlike the Northern and Northeastern states where industrialization occurred much earlier, "industrialization in Texas has not been a story of mass-production industries employing large percentages of unskilled, immigrant labor"; rather, Texas industrialization "has been distinguished by its relatively high ratio of skilled to unskilled, white-collar to blue-collar, native-born to non-native, non-white personnel."[16]

---

[13]*Texas Almanac, op. cit.*, p. 452.

[14]In 1971, 703,900 persons were employed in manufacturing; 948,300 in trade; 694,000 in government; and 602,000 in services. See Stanley Arbingast, "Texas Manufacturing, 1971," *Texas Business Review*, pp. 33–38, February, 1972.

[15]U.S. Bureau of the Census, *Statistical Abstract of the United States: 1972*, 93d ed., p. 242, U.S. Government Printing Office, Washington, D.C., 1972.

[16]James R. Soukup, Clifton McCleskey, and Harry Holloway, *Party and Factional Division in Texas*, p. 43, University of Texas Press, Austin, 1964.

The character of Texas industrialization has placed several barriers in the path of unionization. First, the white-collar worker, particularly professional and scientific trained personnel, is much harder to organize than the semiskilled or unskilled blue collar worker. And Texas has had a great number of the white-collar workers. Second, the youth of Texas industries has made it much easier to turn to automation, and automation has reduced the number of workers to be organized. Third, we must consider the absence of the millions of European immigrants who came to this country in the early twentieth century. Unions played an important role in assimilating them into American society and raising their economic status. This role has been unnecessary in Texas where industrialization came after mass immigration.

The politics of a state is influenced by labor unions. In the Northern and Northeastern states where unions have been strong, they have been a dominant force in state politics. Michigan is a good case in point. In Texas, the unions have scarcely even approached the level of domination although their political influence has grown over the years. Labor unionism has become respectable, and labor representatives are invited to serve on civic and political councils.

Personal and Family Income Despite the dynamic Texas economy, Texas is not a rich state when compared with the others by such measurements as per capita or median family income. It is true that the total amount of personal income in Texas is high. In 1970 it was $39.7 billion, the fifth largest in the nation; but Texas has a large population. When the personal income is divided by the total population, Texas ranks only thirtieth (1970) or thirty-first (1971).[17] Per capita income (which is what we were measuring) has been climbing. In 1960, the Texas figure was $1,924, which was 86.9 percent of the national average. In 1970, it was $3,515, or 89.9 percent of the average. The growth was 82.7 percent during the decade.[18]

The median family income in Texas in 1970 was $8,489 whereas the national average was $9,867. It may be less surprising to learn, then, that Texas has more poor persons, as defined by Federal standards, than any other state.

Texas Population and Related Social Factors It has often been said that the greatest resource a state can have is its people. No one would question that the number and characteristics of the people are important in understanding Texas and its politics.

[17]*Statistical Abstract, op. cit.*, p. 319.
[18]Harris, *op. cit.*, p. 21.

Population Growth   We have already stated that Texas climbed from sixth place to fourth among the states in population between 1960 and 1970. The rate of increase was 16.9 percent, which was greater than the 14.2 percent experienced by the nation as a whole; and the net gain of 1,616,553, was the third highest in the nation, exceeded only by that of California and Florida. However, sixteen states registered a higher growth rate than Texas, topped by Nevada's impressive 71.3 percent increase; also, Texas's growth was less than anticipated. A reason for the latter was the decline in fertility rates, a decline experienced nationally. The decline in natural increases (the number of births minus deaths) was offset somewhat by a larger migration to Texas from other states from 1960 to 1970 than during the prior decade. Migration accounted, however, for only about 12 percent of the population increase in Texas.[19]

Urbanization and Metropolitanization   The most important single fact about the population growth in Texas is that it has been urban and metropolitan growth. The change from a rural to an urban and then a metropolitan state has been recent and dramatic. In 1900 Texas was 80 percent rural; in 1970 it was 80 percent urban. And, as we noted earlier, Texas first became an urban state in 1950. It may be hard to believe but 90 percent of the population growth between 1960 and 1970 occurred in the SMSAs of the state. Furthermore, 85 percent of the increase took place in the state's four largest SMSAs—Houston, Dallas, San Antonio, and Fort Worth.[20] Each of the central cities in these SMSAs deserves a separate chapter. Suffice it to say that Houston's 1.2 million people make it the sixth largest city in the United States, the first Southern city to pass the million mark, and its growth rate from 1960 to 1970 was a spectacular 31.4 percent. Dallas with a population of 840,000 has grown at a 24.7 percent rate during the same period.

Within the SMSAs, the national pattern of growing suburban areas surrounding the central city can be seen in Texas. The suburban cities in the Dallas area, for example, including Arlington, Irving, Garland, Mesquite, and Richardson, grew over 100 percent during the past decade.[21] However, in sharp contrast to the national trends, the central cities in the largest SMSAs in Texas have also gained population.

Concomitant with metropolitan growth has been the decline of population in the non-SMSAs or the small town and rural areas. No less than 146 of the state's 254 counties lost population during the past decade.

[19]Benjamin S. Bradshaw and Dudley L. Poston, "Texas Population in 1970," *Texas Business Review*, pp. 97–109, May, 1971.
[20]*Loc. cit.*
[21]Harris, *op. cit.*, p. 44.

This amounted to about one-half of the land mass of the state. For example, most of the Panhandle counties lost population, as did most counties in the Texas southern high plains and northeast Rio Grande plain.

Age and Sex   The Texas population has paradoxically become both older and younger. The median age dropped from 27.0 years in 1960 to 26.4 years in 1970, but the number of persons over 75 increased almost 32 percent. Also, the number of children under four years of age declined.[22] The age of the population is important in determining governmental service needs, such as education and health care, and the capacity of the population to bear tax burdens.

A dramatic turnabout occurred in the ratio of males to females in the Texas population between 1950 and 1970. In 1950, males outnumbered females by 15,000; but by 1970, females outnumbered males by 238,200, and now constitute a unique majority-minority. Together with the population changes, changes have occurred in the place of women in Texas society. One of the most important changing roles has been as a participant in the labor force.[23] From 1940 to 1970 the female component of the Texas labor force increased from 22.1 percent to 36.0 percent. Wages and salaries also increased. However, the status of women has not improved so rapidly as the status of men; and women's relative status has declined in that sense.

Texas women have recently formed a new group for political purposes. The Texas Women's Political Caucus with local chapters was organized in 1972. There is a national organization as well. In addition, there are numerous other women's groups whose objectives include political goals. Sexism has become a household word with many of these women.

Ethnicity and Race   The Texas population is composed of three major ethnic and racial groups: Anglos or whites, including persons not of Anglo-Saxon or British stock; blacks or Negroes; and persons of Spanish heritage or Mexican Americans. The Anglos are clearly the dominant group, accounting for about 70 percent of the population; the blacks make up about 12 percent; and the Mexican Americans about 18 percent. See Table 2.

Differences among the three major groups are very apparent from

[22]*Executive Budget, 1974–75 Biennium—State of Texas, Preston Smith, Governor of Texas*, p. 46, Austin, 1972.

[23]Rosemary Santana Cooney and Dudley L. Poston, Jr., "Texas Population in 1970: The Changing Status of Women," *Texas Business Review*, pp. 64–68, March, 1973.

Table 2 Tri-ethnic Population Distribution in Texas in 1970

Ethnic-Racial group	Number	Percentage
Total population	11,196,730	100.0
White*	7,717,382	68.9
Negro	1,419,677	12.7
Spanish American	2,059,671	18.4

*The number of Spanish American persons has been subtracted from the total number of "Whites and others" given in the original table.

Source: Summary: Selected Demographic Characteristics from Census Data—Fourth Count, Office of Information Services, Office of the Governor, Austin, August, 1972.

the statistics collected by the U.S. Bureau of the Census. Tables 3, 4, and 5 highlight some of the major ones: education levels, family income, and occupation. Whites have higher education levels with only about 22 percent completing less than nine years of schooling. In contrast about 44 percent of the blacks and 62 percent of the Mexican Americans have less than nine years of education. Family income statistics also show that the whites dominate. About 60 percent have incomes over $6,000 whereas the percentage of blacks with these incomes is half that (30 percent) and the Mexican-American figure is about 40 percent. It is very interesting that the income levels of Mexican Americans are higher than those of blacks whereas their education levels are lower. The figures on occupational distribution also reveal a higher proportion of whites in the more prestigious jobs and a preponderance of blacks (65 percent) in the semiskilled positions with the Mexican Americans close behind (44 percent).

Among other statistics of interest not shown in the tables is that of

Table 3 Tri-ethnic Population in Texas by Education Completed in 1970 in Percentages

Ethnic-Racial group	Less than 9 years	9–11 years	High school	1–3 years college	4 years college
Total population	30.2	22.4	25.1	11.4	10.9
White*	22.2	23.5	27.7	13.4	13.0
Negro	43.6	26.3	19.5	5.9	4.7
Spanish American	61.9	13.4	15.2	5.3	4.2

*The number of Spanish-American persons has been subtracted from the total number of "Whites and others" given in the original table.

Source: Summary: Selected Demographic Characteristics from Census Data—Fourth Count, Office of Information Services, Office of the Governor, Austin, August, 1972.

Table 4   Tri-ethnic Population in Texas by Family Income Distribution in 1970 in Percentages

Ethnic-Racial group	Less than $1,000	$1,000–1,999	$2,000–2,999	$3,000–3,999	$4,000–5,999	$6,000–9,999	$10,000–14,999	$15,000 or more
Total	8.5	9.2	7.3	6.9	12.8	23.9	18.6	12.9
White*	7.3	7.9	6.5	5.8	11.3	24.1	21.2	15.8
Negro	14.7	14.6	11.0	10.0	16.8	21.3	8.8	2.8
Spanish American	9.7	9.4	8.9	10.4	18.2	25.3	12.5	5.5

*The number of Spanish-American persons has been subtracted from the total number of "Whites and others" given in the original table.

Source: Summary: Selected Demographic Characteristics from Census Data—Fourth Count, Office of Information Services, Office of the Governor, Austin, 1972.

Table 5   Tri-ethnic Population in Texas by Occupation in 1970 in Percentages

Ethnic-Racial group	Professional, technical	Managers & administrators	Clerical & sales	Craftsmen & foremen	Semi-skilled	Farm workers	Experienced unemployed
Total population	13.9	8.6	24.4	13.8	32.1	3.8	3.3
White*	16.4	10.4	27.8	14.5	24.6	3.5	2.7
Negro	6.8	2.0	10.2	8.3	64.8	2.5	5.4
Spanish-American	7.2	4.8	18.3	14.3	44.2	6.3	4.8

*The number of Spanish-American persons has been subtracted from the total number of "Whites and others" given in the original table.

Source: Summary: Selected Demographic Characteristics from Census Data—Fourth Count, Office of Information Services, Office of the Governor, Austin, August, 1972.

median family income. In 1970, the figure for blacks was $5,333 and of Spanish Americans, $5,897. In contrast, the median family income of the total population was $8,489 and for "whites and others" (which includes Spanish Americans) $8,923.[24]

The generally disadvantaged position of the two minorities has contributed to political demands on their part, which have accelerated in recent years. In terms of political organization, the Mexican Americans have been the more active of the two. In the last edition of this textbook, we described the election in 1963 of a Mexican American, Juan Cornejo, as mayor of Crystal City, a municipality of some 10,000 people located southwest of San Antonio. This was such a political precedent that it rated notice in the *New York Times*. Crystal City had always been governed by Anglos, and the methods Cornejo used in gaining control appeared to set a pattern for more organized Mexican-American political action in the future. Cornejo's campaign mobilized the tripartite forces of the Political Association of Spanish-speaking Organizations (PASO), the Teamsters Union, and ethnic political appeals. PASO was formed as an offshoot of the 1960 "Viva Kennedy" movement, which first taught many Mexican Americans the nuances and problems of running political campaigns. PASO was more politically active than the older League of United Latin American Citizens (LULAC), formed after World War I, and the GI Forum, formed after World War II. Since the 1962 Crystal City election, the political pace has quickened considerably. Several new and much more militant groups have been formed. Two of the most important are the Mexican American Youth Organization (MAYO) and La Raza Unida. La Raza, formed in 1970, has been characterized by militant rhetoric but conventional political action. Candidates for local and district office have run on the La Raza Unida ticket without much success. In 1972 candidates also ran for statewide office, and the number of votes received by the gubernatorial candidate was impressive.

Independent organizations of blacks have been less visible statewide although, as is true of Mexican Americans, quite prominent on various campuses and in municipal campaigns. History was made in the 1960s by the election of the first blacks to the Texas legislature during this century. Barbara Jordan of Houston was the first black woman state Senator in Texas history and became the second black woman to be elected to Congress when she won her race in 1972. (Shirley Chisholm of New York was the first black Congresswoman.)

---

[24]*Summary: Selected Demographic Characteristics from Census Data—Fourth Count*, p. 3, Office of Information Services, Office of the Governor, Austin, August, 1972. The data presented in this source were not complete enough to segregate the family median income of Anglos from that of Mexican Americans.

The emphasis upon the three ethnic-racial groups in this section should not obscure the fact that many other peoples have settled in Texas and have left their mark on the state. At the 1968 Texas Hemisfair, one of the most popular exhibits was the Institute of Texan cultures, which featured the contributions of about twenty-six different ethnic groups. The institute has since become a permanent part of The University of Texas system.

Texas Culture

There are about as many definitions of culture as there are anthropologists in whose scholarly realm the concept dwells. We will say that Texas culture refers to the dominant behavioral patterns or life-style of Texans. Although today Texans are Americans first and Texans second (well, maybe), Texas as a state has definitely possessed an identity separate from that of other states. Texas is known around the world, which is not true of most of the states in the Union. The Texas identity suggests a distinct subculture within the American culture. However, the exact components of this subculture are not readily identified or, at least, they are the subject of considerable dispute. Texas seems to evoke, or should we say, provoke, different images in different observers. On the one hand, we read about the "Super Americans" whose materialistic desire to make money from oil, cattle, cotton, or whatever overrides other values; we read about superprovincialism and conservativism that stifle new ideas and retain antique institutions; we read that Texas is a state of intellectual depression where culture in the sense of the classics and the arts is bought for display rather than lived or enjoyed for itself; we hear charges of racism, sexism, poverty, rampaging "law 'n order" Rangers; and so on.

On the other hand, we read about significant strides in public and higher education; of a dynamic economy; of a growing cosmopolitanism; of articulate political leaders; of progress among the minorities; of significant contributions to the arts and humanities; of innovations in community, regional, and state planning; of strong religious beliefs and values; and so on.

Culture, however described, will have an impact on politics, but it is not always clear what it is. Directly tying culture to politics is a new concept called "political culture."[25] In general it refers to people's political orientations, including their attitudes and feelings, their beliefs, and their evaluations with respect to government and politics. The

[25]For a summary of political culture as it applies to the states, see Samuel Patterson, "The Political Cultures of the American States," *Journal of Politics*, pp. 187–209, February, 1968.

concept holds great promise for understanding the political system of Texas and the other states, but to date it has not been fully developed. However, a three-fold classification of state political cultures by Daniel Elazar has been widely hailed as a good beginning for further research.[26] The three cultures are (1) the moralistic; (2) the individualistic; and (3) the traditionalistic. Briefly summarized, the moralistic culture is characterized by a belief in broad popular participation in government. Government is expected to serve the public interest. Public service is valued, and everyone is encouraged to contribute toward attaining the goals of the commonwealth. The individualistic culture is more akin to capitalism or free enterprise in its emphasis upon politics as a competitive enterprise in which people pursue their self-interest. Government, it is believed, should be limited in order that free enterprise and individual freedom can flourish. The traditionalistic culture is more elitist in character than the others. Government is controlled by a few ruling families or an Establishment. Popular participation is discouraged; and government is limited for fear of upsetting the status quo.

Elazar places Texas in the individualistic and traditionalistic categories. Although we lack empirical proof that this characterization is an accurate one, there is some support for it. First, traditionalism might be seen in the small electorate and largely one-party system with conservative domination. The discrimination against blacks in the past (for example, by the white primaries to be discussed in a later chapter) suggests similarities with the traditionalistic cultures of the Deep South. Second, there are several patterns that suggest an individualistic culture. Texas has had its share of political scandals in which individuals have used government for their own private economic gain. Also, the frontier tradition lends itself well to individualism in politics as does the Protestant religion, which is dominant in Texas, by stressing the work ethic. The emphasis upon self-reliance and self-help may explain in part the relatively ungenerous government programs toward the poor in Texas.

Nonetheless, several cultural patterns of political importance are not readily subsumed under the two categories suggested by Elazar. Agrarian radicialism in Texas of which we will speak in later chapters has had an influence on Texas politics. A strong fundamentalism within the dominant Protestant religion has influenced policies, such as prohibition and gambling. (It was not until 1971 that mixed drinks were legal in Texas.) A certain element of lawlessness combined with a desire for law

---

[26]Daniel Elazar, *American Federalism: A View from the States*, Thomas Y. Crowell Company, New York, 1966.

and order both stem at least in part from experiences on the frontier.[27] And there are other patterns.

Federalism

We have saved until last the most important environmental variable that affects the Texas political system. This is federalism. The fact that Texas is a member of the Federal Union, the United States of America, is elementary but nonetheless of overriding significance in explaining Texas politics and government.

Federalism is a difficult term to define, some would say impossible, but let us describe it as one form of political organization based on territory. It is marked by a distribution of power between a central government which governs the entire territory and regional subunits (called states in the United States) which govern subdivisions of the territory. Each unit enjoys a measure of legal independence, and neither the central government nor the regional subunit governments can eliminate one another. The division of power is determined by a constitution which, in order to be formally amended, requires the participation of the member governments. In the United States, the local governments are legally "creatures" of the state governments and are unrecognized by the U.S. Constitution which established federalism. But in practice, the local governments are considered to be members of the Federal Union as the third of three levels of government—national, state, and local.

For Texas there are many consequences of her membership in the Federal Union. In addition to the political to which we will turn in a moment, there are others. For one, Texas enjoys membership in a common market characterized by the free flow of goods, people, and ideas across state boundaries. Also, Texas shares the same language, basic constitutional law, customs, and other legal and cultural traditions of citizens of the United States. For better or worse, Texans are deeply affected by the decisions of national institutions—economic, educational, religious, social, or whatever as well as political.

Modern technology has been a principal force changing federalism in the United States. It has helped foster by such means as a national communications and transportation network a greater similarity and uniformity among the American people and their institutions. Nonetheless, the states differ from one another. In short, diversity exists alongside

---

[27]For a brief summary of cultural and historical influences, see Clifton McCleskey, *The Government and Politics of Texas*, 4th ed., pp. 15–18, Little, Brown and Company, Boston, 1972.

uniformity. The diversity justifies or at least continues to nourish the roots of federalism, which owes its origins to the desire to bring the people of the several states together into a common union for the pursuit of common goals while at the same time allowing state independence and differences and government close to the people.

Federalism is a complex and fascinating subject, one which would require a separate volume at the very least to do it justice. Only a few features of federalism as it affects Texas will be singled out for comment in the following sections.

U.S. Constitution   The U.S. Constitution, which established federalism in the United States, has greatly affected Texas political decision making. A factor of untold importance is that the U.S. Constitution is the supreme law of the land. The Texas constitution explicitly recognizes this in Section 1 of Article I:

> Texas is a free and independent State, subject only to the Constitution of the United States.

The U.S. Constitution requires state legislators, executives, and judges to take an oath or by affirmation to support the Constitution. It also states that state judges are bound by the Constitution, notwithstanding anything to the contrary in state laws and constitutions. There is no doubt whatsoever, therefore, that the Texas constitution and laws are inferior to the U.S. Constitution and also to U.S. laws and treaties, both of which are also included in the "supremacy clause" of Article VI of the U.S. Constitution.

In the past as well as in the present, Texas political decision making has been greatly affected by the U.S. Constitution and by its interpreters. In modern times, the impact has been of unusual importance in the field of civil rights. Although the student will have to read a constitutional law book to learn the full story, a few illustrations will serve to show the influence of the U.S. Constitution upon Texas.

1. Reapportionment   The U.S. Supreme Court in 1962 began what has been been called the reapportionment revolution, which resulted in redistricting of the Texas legislature and congressional districts to conform to the "one man–one vote" principle.

2. Public School Desegregation   In 1954 and 1955, the U.S. Supreme Court declared racial segregation of the public schools unconstitutional. Texas, which maintained segregation by constitutional and statutory law, was forced to desegregate.

3. *Suffrage* The U.S. Supreme Court and other Federal courts have issued numerous judgments striking down Texas voting laws. Among the most recent decisions, the courts have held unconstitutional the Texas poll tax as a requirement for voting, the annual voter registration law enacted to replace the poll tax, and party financing of primaries.

4. *Criminal Justice* The U.S. Supreme Court has broadened the interpretation of the Fourteenth Amendment to bring almost all criminal procedures of state courts under the Constitution. Many of the cases have concerned Texas. In 1972, the Texas death penalty statute was held unconstitutional; and in 1973, the criminal abortion law.

The civil rights decisions we have been discussing have been based primarily upon the Fourteenth Amendment. There are many other provisions of the U.S. Constitution that concern the states. Some flatly prohibit the states from engaging in certain kinds of activities, such as entering into a treaty, alliance, or confederation with a foreign nation; others require cooperation, such as the extradition or interstate rendition clause; still others grant privileges and guarantees, such as the obligation of the national government to guarantee to every state a republican form of government; and so on. One of the most important of all the provisions is the "reserved powers" clause of the Tenth Amendment under which all powers not delegated to the national government are reserved to the people or to the states. One of the consequences of this clause is that states have powers unless they are denied; and in writing state constitutions, to which we will turn in Chapter 2, a basic principle is that the state legislature has power unless the state constitution denies it in some manner.

Cooperation in the Federal System Modern scholars of American federalism have stressed the concept that from the beginning of our nation all levels of government have cooperated to administer programs and policies of concern to the American people.[28] According to these scholars, federalism has been characterized by the sharing of responsibilities and functions rather than by separate and individual administration by different levels of government. This concept has been called "marble cake" federalism to distinguish it from the "layer cake" variety in which each layer or level of government administers acts separately.

In Texas innumerable programs have involved the cooperation of all levels of government. Some of the most important, which will be

---

[28]Two leading scholars and their books emphasizing this concept are Morton Grodzins, *The American System*, Rand McNally & Company, Chicago, 1966; and Elazar, *op. cit.*

discussed in this textbook, include: (1) education; (2) welfare; (3) highways; and (4) comprehensive state, regional, and local planning.

Fiscal Federalism   A special kind of cooperation among governments in the federal system has been the sharing of financial resources. States have long aided their local governments by grants-in-aid, by collection of local taxes, and by sharing of revenues. Also from the beginning of the U.S. Constitution, in fact even before its adoption, the national government has assisted other governments. The best known of the early national grants was the land-grant program for education. In the twentieth century, the national government has turned mainly to Federal cash grants for specific purposes, conditioned upon the acceptance by the states or local governments of certain requirements or "strings." Usually, the states or local governments have had to match the Federal grant in some proportion. These grants grew substantially during the depression years of the 1930s and then positively skyrocketed during the 1960s. In 1973, approximately $38 billion was budgeted by the Federal government for grants of this type.

A fiscal development that promises to be far-reaching in its impact occurred in 1972. Under the leadership of President Richard Nixon, Congress adopted a new program of general revenue sharing by enacting the State and Local Fiscal Assistance Act of 1972. General revenue sharing is designed to give the states and local governments more flexibility in the expenditure of Federal money than the Federal grant-in-aid program. The original concept called for "no strings" in the spending of the money; but Congress did not go this far except to allow the states to spend their share on any program they chose. The local governments were limited to seven high "priority" programs, capital expenditures, and financial administration. (The law will be discussed in Chapter 11.)

President Nixon signed the new law in Independence Hall in Philadelphia to emphasize his conviction that revenue sharing was a historic turning point in federalism. The President said that the law would start power flowing back to the states and local governments from Washington, D.C. More spending decisions would be made by governments closest to the people.

Concurrently with general revenue sharing, there has been a cutback in Federal grant-in-aid programs. The states have more responsibility than ever before to take up the slack if certain programs are to be continued.

Modernizing the States   The 1972 general revenue sharing act was just one of many new developments concerning federalism. Both Presidents Lyndon Johnson and Richard Nixon have emphasized the need to strengthen the states and local governments as partners in the federal system. In addition to various Congressional laws and executive orders encouraging the states and local governments, there have been other pressures to modernize. The reapportionment revolution, to which reference was made, has been very important in this regard. Whatever the cause, a modernization movement gained momentum in the 1960s and has continued in the 1970s. We are witnessing a revival of the states and a trend away from "maligning" them.[29]

THE TEXAS POLITICAL SYSTEM

The Texas political system has been greatly influenced by the changing environments or contextual variables we have been describing. Nonetheless, it also appears to be true that Texas politics and government are not changing as rapidly as the other variables. In other words, there is a political lag. In comparison with other states, Texas government continues to be less dynamic than its economy, for example. The Texas state government stands lower than the other states on a variety of indicators often used today to compare the performance of states. Before we turn to them, let us hasten to add that Texas stands high on many counts, but politically there have been shortcomings as well as strengths.

Let us take the three branches of Texas government first. On a recent scale, the Texas legislature ranked thirty-eighth among the states. (See Chapter 7.) In another study, the Texas governor ranked fiftieth or last. (See Chapter 8.) On a legal professionalism scale, the Texas courts ranked forty-second and on court organization twenty-fifth.[30]

Some of the low rankings can be traced to the Texas constitution, which is the sixth longest in the United States and one of the most restrictive and antiquated. (See Chapter 2.)

With respect to government programs and policies, Texas ranks low on an innovation index designed to determine which states adopt new programs first.[31] Texas ranked forty-fourth among forty-eight states on the index. (Alaska and Hawaii were excluded.) In terms of total general expenditures per capita Texas ranked forty-sixth in 1968.[32] Texas usually ranks among the lowest fourth on social programs. In a recent year, Texas placed thirty-eighth on welfare, forty-third in health and hospitals,

[29]One recent book in which the states are defended is Ira Sharkansky, *The Maligned States: Policy Accomplishments, Problems, and Opportunities*, McGraw-Hill Book Company, New York, 1972.

[30]Kenneth N. Vines and Herbert Jacob, "State Courts," in Jacob and Vines, *op. cit.*, pp. 292, 290.

[31]Jack L. Walker, "Innovation in State Politics," in Jacob and Vines, *ibid.*, p. 358.

[32]Ira Sharkansky, "State Administrators in the Political Process," in Jacob and Vines, *ibid.*, p. 254.

thirtieth in higher education, and thirty-eighth in local public schools.[33] Texas ranks high on certain other kinds of programs, among which are highways and state prisons.

The low Texas program rankings can be traced in part to the tax system. Texas is one of the states with a low tax effort. Tax effort is defined as the ratio of general revenues to personal income or general revenues expressed as a percentage of personal income. In 1972, Texas ranked forty-ninth on tax effort.[34] Texas is one of a handful of states not to have the personal income tax or the corporate income tax.

Yet, there is no doubt but that the Texas political system is changing. This will be clearly apparent in virtually every chapter of this book. We conclude this introductory chapter with a brief look at two of the most important areas of change either consummated or under way.

First, the 1973 Texas legislature passed numerous reform laws. For example, majority rights were conferred upon eighteen to twenty year olds, and the penal code was revised for the first time in 117 years. Many of the reform laws concerned the legislature itself. The immediate impetus for them was the Sharpstown bank and securities scandal of 1971, which will be described in Chapter 7. The scandal lowered public confidence in the legislature and in state government generally. Suffice it to say that following the conviction for bribery of the speaker, the speaker pro tem, and the speaker's principal aide, there was a tumultuous primary and general election. Candidates campaigned on a reform platform; and the voters turned out of office many high executive officials and many legislators. In 1973 Texas had a new governor, lieutenant governor, speaker, and attorney general as well as a majority of new members of the legislature. The legislative reforms enacted into law will be discussed in Chapter 7.

Second, the voters in 1972 approved an amendment to the Texas constitution that set up machinery to overhaul the Texas constitution. For the first time in almost 100 years, the voters approved of a constitutional convention, although unlike all the others in Texas history, the 1974 convention will consist entirely of members of the Texas legislature. Revision of the Texas constitution has involved numerous groups and individuals throughout the state and has led to new research and new interest in all phases of state and local government.

All in all, these are exciting times to be studying Texas government and politics.

[33]Peirce, *op. cit.*, p. 519.
[34]*Executive Budget, op. cit.*, p. 49.

Chapter 2

The Texas Constitution

Texas has followed the tradition inaugurated about two hundred years ago by the original thirteen states of having a written constitution that establishes government, broadly defines its powers and the manner of their exercise, and guarantees basic rights of the people. The state constitutions preceded the adoption of the United States Constitution and were a very significant contribution to the art of government.

CONSTITUTIONAL PRINCIPLES

The Texas constitution has been called the "people's document."[1] In legal and political theory the people of Texas are the source of political authority in Texas. They have drawn up the constitution to create government, which is their servant, existing by their grace and consent.

[1]George D. Braden, *Citizens' Guide to the Texas Constitution*, p. 9. Prepared by the Institute for Urban Studies, University of Houston, for the Texas Advisory Commission in Intergovernmental Relations, Austin, 1972.

The Texas constitution implicitly and explicitly expresses this theory of popular sovereignty.[2] For example, the preamble reads:

> Humbly invoking the blessings of Almighty God, the people of the State of Texas, do ordain and establish this Constitution.

And Section 2 of the Texas Bill of Rights states:

> All political power is inherent in the people, and all free governments are founded on their authority, and instituted for their benefit. The faith of the people of Texas stands pledged to the preservation of a republican form of government, and, subject to this limitation only, they have at all times the inalienable right to alter, reform or abolish their government in such manner as they think expedient.

The similarity of Section 2 to the Declaration of Independence of 1776 is striking. It is clear that Texas government rests upon the consent of the governed.

The theory that the Texas constitution was written by the people and is superior to the government it creates has also led to special procedures for drafting and revising the constitution. Particularly important in this regard is the constitutional convention, another contribution of the original thirteen states to the art of government. First used successfully in Massachusetts in 1780, the convention consists of a body of delegates elected by the voters for the special and only purpose of drafting a new constitution or making lesser revisions in the existing document. The constitution or revision is then submitted to the voters for their approval. By 1972 about 224 of these conventions had been held in the United States.[3]

The constitutions of the State of Texas have all been drafted by constitutional conventions. The present constitution does not provide for a convention of the type described above, but by interpretation conventions may be held. The attorney general has ruled that the voters must approve a call by the Legislature for a convention although others have argued that popular approval is not required.[4]

---

[2]A readable copy of the Texas constitution has been recently published by the Texas Advisory Commission on Intergovernmental Relations and the Texas Legislative Council. An outline of the Texas constitution appears in the Appendix of this book. Article I of the Texas constitution contains the Texas Bill of Rights. For an expression of popular sovereignty in addition to the preamble and Section 2 of Article I, see Section 3, Article I, which recites the philosophy of the social contract, with roots in the seventeenth century.

[3]*The Book of the States 1972–73*, p. 10, Council of State Governments, Lexington, Ky., 1972.

[4]See John P. Keith, *Methods of Constitutional Revision*, pp. 24–25, Bureau of Municipal Research, University of Texas, Austin, 1949.

The Texas constitution is the highest state-made law, taking precedence over statutory laws enacted by the legislature, executive orders, city ordinances, and the like. However, as noted in Chapter 1, the United States Constitution, laws, and treaties are superior to the Texas constitution. The Texas constitution is also the state's fundamental law. It provides the basic framework for government and is sometimes referred to as the basic rules for making rules in Texas. What is fundamental or basic is not self-evident, but there is certain core material that goes into all state constitutions.[5]

The Texas constitution is similar to other state constitutions and to the United States Constitution insofar as adherence to certain basic political principles is concerned. These include *separation of powers* among the three branches of government—legislative, executive, and judicial.[6] *Checks and balances*, which may be regarded as both complementary and contradictory to separation of powers, are also provided for. An example is the governor's veto whereby the executive exercises a legislative power. *Bicameralism* is another principle observed in the U.S. and state constitutions except for Nebraska. *Limited government*, which is a corollary of constitutionalism as practiced in the United States, is also universal. All states and the United States have *Biils of Rights*, a major purpose of which is to limit government. Then there is *republican government* or government by representatives of the people. Under the Texas constitution the voters elect their key governing officials and vote on amendments to the Constitution. Article VI is devoted entirely to the suffrage and elections. Unlike the U.S. Constitution, however, the Texas constitution and most other state constitutions provide for numerous elective offices and for popular votes on constitutional amendments, thereby providing for the principle of the *long ballot*.

When measured by adherence to fundamental principles of government, the similarities of the state constitutions outweigh their differences; and this is also generally true when state constitutions are compared with the U.S. Constitution. Nonetheless, when attention is paid to the myriad variations in principles and their application, no two state constitutions are alike, and regional differences are prevalent. The differences may be traced to the environmental diversity that still exists among the states and regions despite modern centralization. The differences are best understood by looking at each state's history, for state constitutions are

---

[5]For a good discussion of this point, see Frank P. Grad, "The State Constitution: Its Form and Function for Our Time," *Virginia Law Review*, pp. 928–973, June, 1968.

[6]Article II of the Texas constitution expressly provides for separation of powers. The following three articles, III, IV, and V, establish the legislature, the executive, and the courts, respectively.

products of history and reflect the experiences of the people. A brief glance at Texas history will be useful for understanding the Texas constitution.

HISTORICAL DEVELOPMENT

Texas can boast of a colorful and unique history under six flags and seven constitutions.[7] At one time part of French territory Texas has been a colony under both Spain and Mexico, an independent republic, a state in the Union, a state in the Confederacy, and then following the Civil War, once more one of the states of the United States of America. During this period, the most important cultural influence upon the Texas constitutions was American despite the experiences under Spanish and Mexican rule. The Anglo-American settlers of Texas, who were primarily from the Southern states, carried American political ideas with them; and when they got the chance to set up their own constitutions, they followed American principles. Generally speaking, the history of Texas constitutions from the time of the republic has not been one of radical change. But changes have, of course, occurred. The influence of the Jacksonian principles of government affected the 1845 state constitution in particular; the Reconstruction influenced the temporary constitutions of that period; and then reaction to the Reconstruction has had a lasting and generally deleterious impact on the present Constitution adopted in 1876.

Constitution of 1827 under Mexico

From 1787 until 1821 (at which time Mexico won its independence from Spain), Texas was one of the four Spanish provinces—Texas, Coahuila,

---

[7]The student will find many good sources of material on Texas history and the Texas constitution. A good single volume on Texas history is Rupert N. Richardson, Ernest Wallace, and Adrian N. Anderson, *Texas: The Lone Star State*, 3d ed., Prentice-Hall, Englewood Cliffs, N.J., 1970. For documents from 1833 to 1869, see Ernest Wallace and David Vigness (eds.), *Documents of Texas History*, Steck Company, Austin, 1960. Among other books not otherwise cited in this chapter are Eugene C. Barker, *Mexico and Texas*, P. L. Turner and Co., Dallas, 1928; J. L. Clark, *A History of Texas*, D. C. Heath and Company, Boston, 1939; Seth S. McKay, *Making the Texas Constitution of 1876*, University of Pennsylvania Press, Philadelphia, 1924; Seth S. McKay, *Seven Decades of the Texas Constitution*, Texas Tech Press, Lubbock, 1942; C. W. Ramsdell, *Reconstruction in Texas*, Columbia University Press, New York, 1910; John Sayles, *The Constitutions of the State of Texas*, 4th ed., E. H. Cushing, Houston, 1893; and Henderson K. Yoakum, *History of Texas*, Steck Company, Austin, 1935. Among the numerous articles on the Texas constitution only a few will be mentioned: Howard A. Calkins: "The Need for Constitutional Revision in Texas," *Texas Law Review*, May, 1943; J. William Davis, "The Abortive Movement for Constitutional Revision, 1957–1961," in Fred Gantt, Jr., Irving O. Dawson, and Luther G. Hagard, Jr. (eds.), *Governing Texas*, Thomas Y. Crowell Company, New York, 1966; Page Keeton, "The Methods of Constitutional Revision in Texas," *Texas Law Review*, October, 1957; Samuel Dale Myers, Jr., "Mysticism, Realism, and the Texas Constitution of 1876," *Southwestern Political and Social Science Quarterly*, September, 1928; and A. J. Thomas, Jr., and Ann Van Wynen Thomas, "The Texas Constitution of 1876," *Texas Law Review*, October, 1957.

Nuevo Leon, and Santander—which comprised the Eastern Interior Province of New Spain. At the head of these provinces was the commandant general who exercised both civil and military jurisdiction from his headquarters in Monterey. The immediate civil head of the Province of Texas was the governor, whose capitol was at San Fernando de Bexar (San Antonio). With the launching of the national Mexican Constitution in 1824, which provided for a federal government, Texas and Coahuila were united to form a single state. It was not until 1828, however, under a state constitution promulgated in 1827, that a real government was organized for Texas. This constitution provided for a representative form of government, but it was highly unsatisfactory to the Texans, for they were allotted only two of the twelve members of the unicameral legislative body and had little influence with the provincial governor.

The union of Texas and Coahuila was supposed to have been temporary, but the central Mexican government made no move to separate them, and Texas lived under the constitution of 1827 for nine years. In the meantime, the unrest that finally culminated in the Texas revolution was growing. In 1832, a convention was held at San Felipe de Austin which discussed the colonists' grievances and the possibility of separation from Coahuila. It drew up a petition to this effect, which, for some reason, was never presented to the Mexican government. The next year, 1833, another convention met at the same place. The delegates prepared a list of grievances and proposed a constitution for the State of Texas. Stephen F. Austin was selected to present the petition personally to the central government at Mexico City. Almost every request of the colonists was granted except that of separate statehood. Finally, in 1835, a third convention at San Felipe, while not declaring Texas independent from Mexico, set up a provisional government and called another convention for March 1, 1836, at Washington-on-the-Brazos.

Constitution of the Republic of Texas, 1836

On March 2, 1836, the delegates to this convention made a formal declaration of independence from Mexico and soon thereafter drew up a constitution for the Republic of Texas. Since a federal system was not applicable to Texas, a unitary government was established, with separate legislative, executive, and judicial departments. In general, the constitution was a composite of sections from the Constitution of the United States and those of several different states. It provided for a bicameral congress, a president, both elected by direct popular vote, and an appointed judiciary. The county, as organized in the Southern states of the United States, was set up as the major unit of local government and has remained so ever since.

Until the new constitution could be ratified by the voters, the convention set up a government ad interim, with David G. Burnet as president. It was not until after the victory of the Texan army at the Battle of San Jacinto in April and the signing of the Treaty of Velasco on May 14 that steps could be taken to establish the permanent government. President Burnet called a general election for September, 1836, to ratify the constitution and to elect the officers of the new republic. At the same time the voters were to pass on the question of annexation of Texas to the United States. Favorable majorities were received for both the constitution and annexation, and Sam Houston was elected president. The new congress met on October 3, 1836, and on October 22, Houston was inaugurated.

The United States government was in no hurry to act on the question of annexation because of the growing conviction of the North that no more slave territory should be added to the Union. Furthermore, annexation would be likely to cause war with Mexico. In 1845, however, a joint resolution of the United States Congress offered statehood to the nine-year-old republic.[8]

President Jones of Texas called a convention of elected delegates for July 4, 1845. This convention approved the offer of annexation and drew up a proposed state constitution. In October, 1845, the voters approved the actions of the convention, and in December, the United States Congress accepted the constitution, declaring that Texas should be admitted to the Union. In February of 1846, the Republic of Texas came to an end, and officers of the new state government, who had already been elected as provided by the new state constitution, took office.

State Constitutions of 1845 and 1861

The state constitution of 1845, which served Texas for fifteen years, not only is the best one the state has had, but is considered one of the best state constitutions of that time. It was simple, avoided complexities, and provided for appointment of the judges and all state officers except the governor, lieutenant governor, and members of the legislature. In 1850, influenced by the ideas of Jacksonian Democracy, the voters approved an amendment which provided that the judges and most of the administra-

---

[8]One provision of this document which has been of untold importance to Texas in later years concerned the public lands. In return for assuming the debt of the Republic, which amounted to nearly 8 million dollars, the state was to retain the entire public domain of the Republic.

tive officers were to be elected. This constitution served Texas until the state withdrew from the Union in 1861 to join the Confederacy.

In February of 1861, an extralegal convention, meeting in Austin, repealed the ordinance of annexation and declared that Texas was a separate, sovereign state. The actions of this informal body were soon approved by the voters, and the convention reassembled on March 2 to seek admission into the Confederate States of America and to amend the state's fundamental law. Practically all provisions of the constitution of 1845 were left unchanged, the chief difference being the substitution of the "Confederate States of America" for the United States of America." This constitution remained in effect until the defeat of the Confederacy and the appointment by President Andrew Johnson of A. J. Hamilton as provisional governor in June, 1865.

Reconstruction Constitutions, 1866 and 1869

Governor Hamilton had to establish a new state government in its entirety. He appointed new state and local officials, issued a proclamation for assessing and collecting taxes, and set in motion the reconstruction plan of President Johnson. The first step was the registration of voters, followed by election of delegates to a constitutional convention. This convention met in Austin in February, 1866, declared the ordinance of secession null and void, and acknowledged the supremacy of the United States. In accord with the President's reconstruction plan, all debts made by Texas during the war as well as the state's share of the debt of the Confederacy were repudiated, and slavery was prohibited.

A new constitution, which was basically the constitution of 1845, was presented to the voters, who approved it in June, 1866. A newly elected legislature met on August 9, and shortly thereafter the new governor, J. W. Throckmorton, was inaugurated. On August 20, President Johnson proclaimed the insurrection at an end.

Governor Throckmorton, though hampered by the presence of Federal troops who were not inclined to submit to civil authority, made steady progress in restoring order in the state. In the Congressional elections of 1866, however, the radical Republicans gained control of the Congress and proceeded to upset President Johnson's plan of reconstruction by passing their own reconstruction acts in the spring of 1867.

The results of these acts were that the reconstructed Texas government was set aside, military rule was established, Negroes were enfranchised, and the leading whites were disfranchised. The governor and all other civil officers were removed by the military authorities, and former Governor E. M. Pease was appointed provisional governor.

Another convention was soon called to write another new constitution, which was ratified in 1869.

The constitution of 1869 made only a few changes in the general organization of the government and in general was not a bad document, though poorly drafted. Certain provisions, however, especially those concerning education, were highly unpopular. The continuation of the office of state superintendent, first provided in the constitution of 1866, and the authorization of a compulsory school-attendance law were deeply resented by the frontier-minded Texans as unwarranted invasions of individual liberty. Another unpopular feature concerned the conduct of elections. All were to be held at the county seat, rather than in precincts, between 8 A.M. and 4 P.M. for four consecutive days. This provision for a central polling place caused considerable hardship to those living any distance from the county seat.

The first elections under the new constitution were supervised by the military. Many of the leading Democrats, mostly former Confederates, native Texans, and other old-time residents, were still not allowed to vote. For these reasons the Democratic party did not enter a candidate for the governorship. E. J. Davis, a member of the radical wing of the Republican party, was elected, along with a legislature which was friendly to him. After the legislature met in February of 1870, there followed a period of corruption unequaled in the history of Texas.

The Davis administration has been characterized as one of boundless extravagance, lawless despotism, and disregard for every principle of personal and political liberty.[9] Although this may be an exaggeration, there is no question but that the period was a trying one for Texans. Extravagant and corrupt public expenditures resulted in an increase of taxes on real property to the verge of confiscation. The corruption and misrule, combined with a serious economic depression, soon resulted in a demand for a drastic revision of the constitution and the return of the state to Democratic control. Protest meetings of leading citizens of both parties were held in Austin in 1870 and 1871, but nothing could be done until the Federal limitations on voting in the South were removed. In the first statewide election after this was done, a Democratic delegation was sent to Congress. In 1872, the radical Republicans in the state legislature were decisively defeated, and the new legislature was overwhelmingly Democratic. In 1873, the Democrats regained control of the governorship and all other elective state offices. Although Davis contested the election, the new governor, Judge Richard Coke, was inaugurated in January of 1874. That same year, after the legislature had increased the size of the

---

[9]Eugene C. Barker (ed.), *History of Texas*, p. 512, P. L. Turner and Co., Dallas, 1929.

supreme court so the governor could appoint new members and some of the old ones were removed, the Democrats regained control of the state's highest court.

Now having rid themselves of the radical Congressmen, state legislators, governor, and supreme court judges, the Democratic party was determined to dispose of the last vestiges of the extravagant and inefficient Reconstruction government in Texas—the constitution of 1869. Instead of calling a convention to draw up a new constitution, however, the legislature decided on the more economical method of having the fundamental law revised by a joint commission of the legislature. The revision was completed in the spring of 1874 and approved by the Senate, but the House of Representatives refused to adopt it, since they considered the method by which the proposal was drawn up undemocratic.

The following year the legislature decided to submit the question of calling a convention to the voters. In the summer of that same year the voters approved the resolution and elected delegates—three from each of the state's thirty senatorial districts. Seventy-five of the delegates were Democrats, and fifteen (six of whom were Negroes) were Republicans. There were forty-one farmers and twenty-nine lawyers. On the whole they represented the "old-time Texans," rather than the group which had so nearly ruined the state under the Reconstruction administration of Governor Davis.

The convention met in Austin in September of 1875 and set about the task of framing a new constitution. The strongest single influence at the convention was the Texas Grange, to which about half the delegates belonged. The Grange was a farmers' organization which was interested not only in governmental reform but also in economy in government. Their slogan of "retrenchment and reform" was the guiding principle of the convention and resulted in provisions decreasing salaries of state officials (some to as little as $2,000 a year), shortening the terms of office, and severely limiting the powers of the legislature, the governor, and the local governments.

The convention adjourned in November, 1875, and the new constitution was approved by the electorate in February of 1876. For over nine decades this document—the constitution of 1876—has been the fundamental law of the State of Texas.

Constitution of 1876, the Present Constitution

The constitution of 1876 is longer and more detailed than the ones which preceded it. Matters which were formerly left to the discretion of the legislature were now embodied in the constitution, and owing to the experience under the Reconstruction governments, many specific restrictions, especially with regard to taxing, borrowing money, and passing laws dealing with localities, were placed on the legislature. The per diem of the legislators was reduced from $8 to $5 for the first sixty days of a regular session and to $2 for the remainder. As might be expected, the powers and duties of the governor were limited and were set forth in detail. He was given no control over the other state officers or over local officials, and his salary was reduced from $5,000 to $4,000. Six other executive officers were provided, all of whom, except the secretary of state, were to be elected. Their salaries were likewise meager, $2,500 being the maximum.

Under the Reconstruction government, the court system had been severely criticized because the judges were appointed by the governor and many of them had been quite incompetent. Accordingly, the new constitution provided that all judges were to be elected by popular vote, with terms of two to six years. There was also a general reduction in salaries. Justice of the peace courts, county courts, and district courts were provided. For appellate courts a dual system was set up. A supreme court was to review civil cases only. A court of appeals was set up for criminal cases and certain classes of civil cases.[10]

Reaction from the constitution of 1869 was also evident in the suffrage provision. Registration of voters was not permitted, precinct elections were again provided, and in cities only taxpayers could vote to issue bonds or spend public money.

Further reaction was seen in the provisions concerning education. The legislature was forbidden to pass a compulsory school-attendance law. The office of state superintendent was abolished, and no provision was made for local school taxes. Separate schools were required for Negroes and whites. The 3,200,000 acres of land which had previously been set aside for a state university was reduced to 1 million, and no tax could be levied or appropriations made by the state for buildings at the state university.

With regard to the financial support of public schools, the constitution was more generous. The legislature was empowered to levy a poll tax of $1 for the schools and to contribute not over one-fourth of the general property and occupation taxes for educational purposes. As a permanent endowment, some 45 million acres of public lands were given to the schools.

Several of the important miscellaneous provisions of the new

[10]A constitutional amendment in 1891 established a court of civil appeals to relieve the supreme court of some of its burden. Other courts of civil appeals have been added since then. The old court of appeals was made the court of criminal appeals with jurisdiction over appellate criminal matters only.

constitution were the setting aside of 3 million acres of public lands for the erection of a new capitol at Austin, the retention of the provisions in the constitution of 1845 prohibiting the forced sale of homesteads, and permitting separate ownership by women of all property owned before marriage or acquired afterward by gift or inheritance.

A leading Texas historian has said:

All in all, the constitution complied with public opinion quite faithfully. Biennial sessions of the legislature, low salaries, no registration requirements for voters, precinct voting . . . a homestead exemption clause, guarantees of a low tax rate, a more economical school system with schools under local control, a less expensive court system, popular election of officers—all of these were popular measures with Texans in 1876. The constitution was a logical product of its era. It was to be expected that men who were disgusted with the vagaries of a radical regime would design a government that was extremely conservative. Furthermore, low prices, low wages, and hard times generally had created a demand for the severest economy in government.

As a pattern of government for the period in which it was made, the constitution was fairly adequate, but as an enduring fundamental law it had many unfortunate features.[11]

The group of men who drew up this constitution were in a disgruntled mood. They seemed to be mad at all government and at theirs in particular. Although we can understand this attitude, especially since they were just emerging from a period of misrule and were still in the midst of a serious economic depression, it did not make for a good atmosphere in which to draw up a new fundamental law for the state. The delegates were interested mainly in tailoring the new constitution to the needs of that particular time in the history of Texas, and in 1875–1876, Texas was an entirely different world from that of today.[12]

Texas in 1875–1876

In 1876, there were only 150 counties which held elections on the adoption of the constitution. Half of what is now known as West Texas was still unorganized territory. The cities of Amarillo, Lubbock, Midland, and Odessa did not even exist. The total population of the state was a little

[11]Rupert Norval Richardson, *Texas, the Lone Star State*, pp. 296–297, Prentice-Hall, Englewood Cliffs, N.J., 1943.

[12]Many of the data in the following discussion of Texas in 1875–1876 have been taken from a paper read by S. S. McKay before the Citizens Committee on the Constitution which met in Austin in January, 1949.

over 800,000. In 1875, there was not a single municipality with as many as 15,000 people, and the rural population outnumbered the urban 14 to 1.

At the time the constitution was drawn up, a bushel of sweet potatoes cost 50 cents. A milk cow and her calf could be bought for from $12 to $15. Common beef cattle sold for $5 or $6 per head. Sheep were $1 each, and hogs from $2.50 to $3. Butter cost 12 cents per pound. Chickens were 15 cents each. Eggs were 12 cents per dozen.

The state was still paying for the passage of immigrants across the Atlantic Ocean and across the United States to their homes in Texas, where there was still some 88 million acres of public lands available for settlement. The Old Chisholm Trail and a few other cattle trails existed, but it was not until forty years later that there was a single mile of hard-surfaced state highways.

When the constitution was written, the average annual salary of public-school teachers was $212, and Texas was spending annually less than $1/2$ million dollars for all phases of education. Total state expenditures were a little less than 2 million dollars. In 1875, there were only about 160,000 public-school pupils in the state, and there was not a single state-supported institution of higher learning.

The general economy of the state was also completely different. For example, the oil and gas business in Texas was of no importance until twenty-five years after the adoption of the present constitution. The great petrochemical industry, which is so important in the Texas economy, was not even dreamed of in 1875, and there was practically no manufacturing business. Except for geography, the Texas of today bears little resemblance to the Texas of 1875.

100 YEARS OF AMENDMENTS

When we consider the differences between Texas in 1876 and today, it is not surprising that the Texas constitution has been amended over two hundred times. It has been necessary to amend for many reasons but essentially because the 1876 document was not designed for the long run but for the immediate future. Frequent amendment has been facilitated by the framers' provision for a relatively easy amendment process in Article XVII of the document.

Amendment Procedures

Proposal   The first step in the amendment procedure consists of initiation or proposal by two thirds vote of the *entire elected membership of each house of the legislature*. Prior to 1972, amendments could be proposed only at the regular biennial sessions. At present, as a result of an amendment approved in November, 1972, they may be proposed at any session. However, the proposed amendment must be included within the governor's call for the special session in order to be considered by the legislature.[13]

A proposed amendment is always introduced in the form of a joint resolution. If first presented in the House of Representatives, it is known as House Joint Resolution (HJR) No. ——— (1, 2, 13, 105, or whatever). If originating in the Senate, it is called SJR No. ———. Since the majority required for adoption is two-thirds of the total membership of each chamber, this means that at least 100 representatives and 21 senators must declare themselves as favoring the proposal.

Although the governor often signs joint resolutions proposing amendments to the Texas constitution, he is not required to do so. He may not veto them, since the amending process is not a legislative but a constituent function, a reflection of the supremacy of the constitution. The constitutional requirement that all legislative acts that have passed the legislature must be submitted to the governor for his approval is, therefore, not applicable here.

Ratification: Publicity The second step in the amendment process consists of approval or ratification of the amendment by a majority of voters voting on the amendment. To the end that the voter be informed, the constitution requires that publicity be given to each amendment.[14] An amendment approved by the voters at the November, 1972, general election requires that a brief explanation of each amendment be prepared by the secretary of state and approved by the attorney general. It must be published "together with the date of the election and the wording of the proposition as it is to appear on the ballot" two times in each newspaper in Texas "which meets requirements set by the legislature for the publication of official notices of officers and departments of the state government." The first publication must appear about two months before an election ("not more than 60 days nor less than 50 days before the date of the election") and the second, one week after the first. The legislature fixes the standards for the rate to be paid the newspapers. The rate "may not be higher than the newspaper's published national rate for advertising per column inch." The entire text of each amendment must be posted by

[13]See HJR No. 68, 62nd Legislature, Regular Session, 1971.

[14]*Ibid*. The original provisions of the amending article, Article XVII, provided that the proposed amendment must be printed once a week for four weeks, beginning at least three months before the election, in a newspaper in each county in Texas. The newspapers usually placed the amendments in the legal or classified ad sections where it was both difficult to find and to read them. However, the complexity of most amendments would preclude their being understood by many voters in any event.

the county clerk at the county courthouse at least "30 days" before the election.

Ratification: Election   The people vote on the proposed constitutional amendments at either a regular or a special election. The legislature decides which to use; and if a special election is the choice, sets the date. The wording in which a proposal will be presented to the voters is also determined by the legislature and is supposed to give a clear idea of its scope and character. The order of the proposition on the ballot is drawn by lot by the secretary of state. Each proposition is submitted to the voter by printing the words "FOR" and "AGAINST" on the left side of it as it appears on the ballot. The voter pulls the proper lever, punches the proper hole with his stylus, or marks an "X" in the square beside the "FOR" or "AGAINST," depending upon whether a voting machine, voting device, or paper ballot is used.

Promulgation   Only a simple majority of those actually voting on the amendment is required for adoption. Seventeen days after the election the returns are opened and officially counted by the secretary of state in the presence of the governor and attorney general. If the amendment has received a majority of votes cast on it, the proposal is considered adopted. The governor then issues a proclamation saying that the amendment is now a part of the constitution.

The Amendment Story

"The story of amendments to the Constitution of 1876 is a story of relatively large numbers."[15] Beginning with the first legislature after the adoption of the 1876 constitution, proposals for amendments have been introduced in each legislature. By 1972 a grand total of 335 had received the necessary two-thirds vote for submission to the people out of approximately 3,000 joint resolutions introduced. Of these 212 had won approval by the people.[16] The number of amendments submitted to the voters has been increasing each decade since 1940. Between 1961 and 1970, 84 amendments were submitted to the voters of which 56 were adopted. An extrapolation based on the fast and furious pace of the past twenty years indicates that by the year 2001, 345 amendments will have

---

[15]Braden, *op. cit.*, p. 13.

[16]Information on the votes has been secured from the secretary of state's office and the Texas Legislative Reference Library. Three amendments approved by the legislature were not submitted to the voters.

been adopted![17] In contrast, the U.S. Constitution has been amended only 26 times in about 190 years.

A recent analysis of amendments from 1951 to 1972 supports the findings of other research that the legislative article (Article III) and fiscal provisions account for the most amendments.[18] Actually, every article except the one on impeachment has been amended at least once. The prohibitions against debt and against spending or lending money to any individual, group, or corporation have proved unrealistic and unworkable time and time again. The numerous constitutional funds, because they usually contain myriad details, and other earmarked expenditures have caused frequent amendment. The specific salary limits for government officials have accounted for 10 percent of all amendments during the entire life of the Texas constitution of 1876. Numerous restrictions on counties, as well as on other local governments, have accounted for about one-third of the amendments from 1951 to 1972. Federal government actions of one sort or another have resulted in several amendments, most notably in welfare. Well over half of all amendments from 1951 to 1972 were amendments to amendments.

The 1972 study of amendments also revealed that the costs incurred by the state for publishing amendments and by counties for holding elections were considerable. The cost of publishing amendments from 1951 to 1971 amounted to $2,491,467 or about $19,000 an amendment. The range for each amendment was from $6,818 to $39,500. The costs of holding elections were estimated at about $6,500,000. Combining the figures, each amendment approved cost the taxpayers about $95,744.

The frequency of amendment places a heavy burden upon the voter. Not only are there many trips to the polls, but the ballot is frequently long. As many as sixteen propositions have been voted upon at a single election; in 1972, there were fourteen. Only a minority of voters bothers to make the effort. An average of 32 percent of the registered voters participated from 1951 to 1971. Only 16 percent voted in special elections. In fact, only 6.7 percent turned up at one special election. A small minority, then, makes the decisions affecting the future of Texas.

The voters have approved most of the amendments submitted to them. The approval rate from 1951 to 1971 was 72 percent. However,

---

[17]Janice C. May, *Amending the Texas Constitution: 1951–1972*, pp. 1, 19, Texas Advisory Commission on Intergovernmental Relations, Austin, 1973.

[18]*Ibid.* The information in the text on the subject of amendments from 1951 to 1972 is drawn from this source. Research covering earlier years shows that the constitution has had to be amended for such purposes as correcting errors in the judicial article, overcoming the reactionary educational provisions, providing for retirement systems, and so on.

there was a significant difference between the approval rate at general elections (82 percent) and special elections (51 percent).

Those who have studied the U.S. Constitution will recall that it has been adapted to change by many methods but particularly by judicial interpretation. In contrast, the Texas constitution has been changed principally by amendment.

AN APPRAISAL OF THE TEXAS CONSTITUTION

The amendments story suggests that the piecemeal amendment process has not produced the ideal constitution for Texas. Although effecting needed improvements in the judicial, education, and other articles, the amendments have not reached the root of the problem: the original constitution of 1876. The basic structure of government generally remains intact; instead of replacing provisions that breed amendments, amendments are continually added, primarily in legislative, fiscal, and local government areas; also, amendments have required other amendments, often to clarify confusions of earlier ones. With a constitution closer to the model of fundamental law, most of the amendments could have been avoided while at the same time the public interest could have been adequately protected.

The amendments story reveals many but not all the reasons why the Texas constitution has had its share of criticisms. Most critics single out the following general shortcomings of the Texas constitution.

Age

While age alone does not make a constitution ready for the scrap heap, witness the U.S. Constitution, the age of the Texas constitution is relevant. The constitution was oriented toward rural needs and was framed by delegates attempting to resolve the problems of their day. It was also framed during a period of intense distrust of government, not only in Texas and other southern states reacting to the Reconstruction, but in the rest of the country as well.[19] The period from 1860 to 1899 produced the most and the longest state constitutions.[20]

Length

The length of the Texas constitution is an obvious target of critics. The Texas document is the sixth longest state constitution and over five times

---

[19]Braden, *op. cit.*, p. 13.

[20]Robert B. Dishman, *State Constitutions: The Shape of the Document*, rev. ed., p. 2, National Municipal League, New York, 1968.

as long as the U.S. Constitution. Containing over 50,000 words and 212 amendments, it is much more a code of laws than an organic document limited to fundamentals. However, it is what makes the constitution so long that is important—the restrictions, statutory detail, poor draftsmanship, and the like.

Restrictions

The restrictions placed by the framers of the 1876 document in order to make government weak, frugal, and honest have resulted in shackling the state and local governments.[21] They are hampered in their task of resolving problems of concern to all Texas in the modern age. Furthermore, the fiscal and other restrictions have not worked as intended; they have been constantly evaded by amendments and other means.

Statutory Detail

A reason for the length of the Texas constitution is that it contains myriad provisions more appropriate for the statute books. These have been commented upon throughout this chapter. Statutes, unlike properly drafted constitutions, are designed for the daily operation of government and are more temporary, easier to change, and much more detailed.

Draftsmanship

A common failing of state constitutions is their poor draftsmanship. The Texas constitution is in dire need of codification, simplification, and abbreviation. For example, sections on the same subject are scattered throughout the constitution; numbering of sections and subsections is not orderly; language is often excessively wordy; confusion abounds. In one instance a single sentence contains 765 words![22]

Intergovernmental Relations

A criticism of the Texas constitution particularly appropriate to modern federalism is that it has been an obstacle to effective relations among the many governments in Texas. The Texas constitution provides the framework for intergovernmental relations whereby the local, state, and national governments may work toward common goals in Texas. But

---

[21]See Dick Smith, "Constitutional Revision in Texas, 1876–1961," *Comment*, Institute of Public Affairs, University of Texas, Austin, 1961; and Dick Smith, "Constitutional Revision: Attempts to Unshackle Texas," *Comment*, 1969.

[22]Braden, *op. cit.*, p. 62. The sentence is in Section 12 of Article IX.

restrictions, particularly of a fiscal and local governmental nature, have impeded cooperation. Also state constitutions have been blamed for hamstringing state and local governments and thereby encouraging the transfer of governmental responsibilities to the national government where action is more likely to resolve problems. In other words, state constitutions have been regarded as a cause of the increase in the functions of the national government. Critics urge that the state constitutions be modernized in order to allow local and state governments to be more effective partners in the federal system.

PROGRESS TOWARD CONSTITUTIONAL REVISION

The Texas constitution presents a paradox: on the one hand it has been excessively changed; on the other it has been changed very little. The point is that although there have been many amendments, the Texas constitution has not been revised in a comprehensive manner or given an overhaul. Incremental change by amendments has not really changed the basic nature of the document.

Advocacy of constitutional revision of a comprehensive nature began even before the ink had dried on the document of 1875. The first governor to serve under the constitution, Richard Coke, was one of many governors to propose revision. The question of calling a constitutional convention for the purpose of revision has been before the legislature many times. Two resolutions passed, one in 1917 and another in 1919. There is some mystery about the 1917 proposal. It passed the legislature and was sent to Governor James E. Ferguson, but final disposition is not certain. It was probably vetoed, but there are no official records to show what took place. The proposal in 1919 was referred to the people for approval but was defeated by a vote of 71,376 to 23,349, with only 10 percent of the qualified voters voting on the proposition. Later, in 1949, Governor Beauford Jester formed an informal citizens committee for revision, but nothing came of its recommendations; and the untimely death of Governor Jester ended the project.

Modern Revision Movement

A nationwide movement toward state constitutional revision dates from 1950 with the greatest spurt of activity occurring in the 1960s. From 1950 to 1970, 80 percent of the states had taken some kind of official action to revise their constitutions.[23] In fact, more official moves to revise state

[23]Albert L. Sturm, "Effective State Governments Need Modern Constitutions," *National Civic Review*, p. 65, February, 1971.

constitutions have taken place in more states in the past ten years than in any other decade in the nation's history. The movement owes a great deal to reapportionment, a subject of Chapter 5 of this book, and to urban industrial changes discussed in Chapter 1.

1957–1961   The first of the modern attempts to revise the Texas constitution dates from 1957. The legislature, responding to appeals from the League of Women Voters of Texas and other interested groups, adopted a concurrent resolution directing the Texas Legislative Council to make a study of the constitution to determine whether it was an appropriate document of government for the twentieth century. The resolution also authorized the establishment of a Citizens Advisory Committee of eighteen members, six each to be appointed by the governor, the lieutenant governor, and the speaker of the House. Although no appropriation was provided, considerable preliminary work was done, and an interim report was made to the legislature in 1959. The report recommended that the legislature appropriate $150,000 to the Legislative Council for the purpose of a professional and thorough study of the constitution. It also recommended that the study when completed be widely disseminated by a public relations campaign. A particularly interesting recommendation was that a continual review of the need for constitutional change be institutionalized.

The legislature responded with only a $50,000 appropriation in 1959. The Legislative Council, partly as a result of this small sum and the time constraint of having to report by 1961, simply analyzed each section of the constitution as to its original intent and its present significance, following which it made recommendations. The report of the council held that, while some sections of the constitution could be clarified, simplified, or eliminated, there was no need for a new constitution as the present constitution, despite its age and alleged deficiencies, was still a sound document that reflected the government philosophy of the people of Texas.[25]

1966–1969   The next effort at revision was launched at the State Democratic Convention in September, 1966, by Governor John Connally. The governor strongly urged the legislature to submit to the voters the question of calling a constitutional convention, saying that the people of Texas had no more compelling need than to overhaul the outdated features of their governmental machinery. He later repeated the request

---

[24]The Citizens Advisory Committee on the Revision of the Constitution, *Interim Report to the 56th Legislature and the People of Texas*, Texas Legislative Council, Austin, 1959.

[25]Texas Legislative Council, *Constitutional Revision*, 3 vols., Austin, 1960.

for a constitutional convention in his opening message to the 1967 legislature. The legislature balked at the convention idea, but the House of Representatives under the leadership of the speaker, Ben Barnes, passed a simple resolution setting up a twenty-five–member commission to study and make recommendations. The commission submitted its report to Governor Connally in December, 1968.[26] The proposed constitutional changes in the report, which was in the form of a new constitution, were introduced as a joint resolution in the 1969 legislature; but the resolution died in committee.

The 1967–1968 commission was not, however, a failure. For the first time since the adoption of the 1876 constitution, a constitutional revision commission had actually been created, had actually worked, and had actually drafted a revised constitution. Also, for the first time, as a result of momentum created by the commission, a somewhat comprehensive, although nonsubstantive, revision was accomplished in 1969 with the removal of fifty-six obsolete provisions, including one entire article. This reduced the length of the constitution by 10 percent.[27]

1971 to the Present The revision movement took a new and unexpected turn in 1971. The legislature, with scarcely any fanfare, passed a proposed amendment which would authorize the legislature to serve as a constitutional convention in 1974. It also provided for the establishment by the legislature of a constitutional revision commission in 1973 to study the need for revision and to make a report by November 1, 1973. Further, the amendment stated that the "Bill of Rights of the present Texas constitution shall be retained in full."[28]

Groups interested in the passage of the amendment and in good government formed a new organization called the Citizens for Texas. They conducted a campaign for adoption of the amendment. The Institute for Urban Studies at the Universities of Houston and Arlington as well as the Texas Advisory Commission on Intergovernmental Relations, a new state agency established in 1971, and the LBJ School of Public Affairs at the University of Texas contributed research efforts on revision while the campaign for the amendment was in progress. Leading public figures, including the incoming governor, lieutenant governor, speaker, and attorney general, all endorsed the proposal for revision.

In a historic action, the voters approved the amendment at the

[26]Constitutional Revision Commission, *Report to the Members of the 61st Legislature*, Austin, 1968.

[27]See John E. Bebout and Janice C. May, *The Texas Constitution: Problems and Prospects for Revision*, Texas Urban Development Commission, Arlington, Tex., 1971.

[28]HJR No. 61, 62nd Legislature, Regular Session, 1971.

November, 1972, general election. The vote was 1,549,982 for and 985,282 against. For the first time since 1875 the voters had endorsed revision and thereby lent legitimacy to the movement.

Preparations for legislation to carry into effect the amendment were underway even before the voters had acted. Bills were prefiled and later introduced in the 1973 legislature based on recommendations of the Texas Advisory Commission on Intergovernmental Relations. The legislature acted relatively promptly on the legislation before them. SCR No. 1, which set up a thirty-seven–member constitutional revision commission, was passed early in February; and in accordance with its provisions the members were appointed on February 24. The resolution provided that the members should be as nearly as possible representative of the citizens of Texas in terms of geography, race, sex, social groups, ethnic groups, and so on. The appointments were made by a six-member committee composed of the governor, the lieutenant governor, the speaker, the attorney general, the chief justice of the Texas supreme court, and the presiding judge of the court of criminal appeals. Four of the six votes were needed for appointment. The chairman and vice chairman of the committee were designated at the same time as the appointments. Former chief justice of the Texas supreme court, Robert Calvert, was named chairman and former vice chairman of the state Republican party, Mrs. Malcolm Milburn, was named vice chairman.

The commission was given until November 1, 1973 to report its recommendations to the legislature. Copies of the report were to be made widely available to the citizens and public libraries by December 31. In addition the commission was to provide information, briefings, and other appropriate support to the constitutional convention, including legal drafts of any proposed constitutional changes.

The commission was directed to encourage "the maximum participation at the grass roots level by scheduling and holding open public hearings in a minimum of six geographic areas of the state" and to set up citizen advisory committees in each of the areas. The commission took its mission seriously and held nineteen public hearings throughout the state from April through June and assisted over forty citizen committees. These were highly significant steps for Texas and probably unprecedented for any constitutional commission anywhere. In addition, all meetings and all public records were open to the public.

All these provisions were designed to bring the public into the constitutional revision process at every step.

The commission members were appointed to hold office until sixty days after the convening of the constitutional convention in order to render advice and assistance. The legislature appropriated $900,000 for the work of the commission. Each member received $50 per diem and expenses. A professional staff was appointed.

During the 1973 regular session of the Texas legislature, a ten-member joint committee composed of five representatives and five senators was directed to make plans for the convention. Before expiring at the end of the session, the committee recommended that the House chamber be the convention site. The 1973 legislature also appropriated $2 million for the convention; and the House and the Senate each appointed an interim committee to make convention plans with the assistance of the House and Senate Administration Committees.

The convening of the Texas legislature as a constitutional convention in January, 1974, was another historic event. The Texas legislature has been amending the Texas constitution with the concurrence of the voters for years, but this was the first time it had been authorized to revise or rewrite the entire constitution or to sit as a convention. The legislature as a constitutional convention has been rarely seen in this century, but it is not unknown. Texas has been innovative in providing that the legislature shall sit as one body rather than two, in designating a special session for the purpose of revision, and in requiring a two-thirds vote for the adoption of proposals.[29]

The amendment creating the constitutional convention of 1974 provided that it was to sit until dissolved by a two-thirds vote or until May 31, 1974. However, the convention could be extended another sixty days beyond May 31 by a two-thirds vote. The convention was authorized to submit a new or revised constitution, could decide whether to submit the revisions in a single package or in alternate sections, and was empowered to set the date of the election at which the proposals would be acted upon by the people.

Roadblocks to Revision

Many roadblocks have obstructed constitutional revision in the past.[30] For one thing, the interest groups, who have worked so hard to get their pet proposals protected in the constitution, have not viewed possible changes with indifference.

Objections have been made to the procedure by which revision proceeded in 1973 and 1974. It is argued that if the constitution is the people's document, superior to the legislature, then the traditional kind of convention composed of delegates elected by the voters, including other

[29]Bebout and May, *op. cit.*, pp. 36–43.
[30]See Smith, *op. cit.*

than legislators, should be the body to write the constitution. However, as a practical matter, it must be kept in mind that the people do not literally govern in a representative democracy. They elect those who do. The legislature is in many ways more representative of the people than a convention, which is likely to attract delegates from the more prestigious occupations and higher income and education levels. They may be less politically attuned to the people's wishes than the legislators. Another objection to the legislature as a convention is image. The legislature does not fit the myth of a body of statesmen drawing up a new constitution. Legislators look like politicians, not James Madisons. (But then James Madison was a politician also.)

The problem of public apathy has been mentioned in many discussions of constitutional revision. There is also the fear of the unknown. And there is considerable public ignorance of what constitutional revision is all about.

Roadblocks to revision no doubt exist. Yet, it is well to recall the words of John E. Bebout, national authority on state constitutional revision. He has said that there really is no failure in revision efforts. The fact that little revision occurs in the first attempt is not so important as the fact that revision is underway. In other states so-called failures have been followed by later successes and a new state constitution. This may well be the Texas story.

Chapter 3

Texas Laws Governing Parties and Elections

The Texas constitutional principle of government by the consent of the governed leads naturally to the institution of elections, a major means by which the people hold their government responsible. In modern times, elections have been inextricably joined with political parties. In fact, parties have sometimes been defined entirely in electoral terms—as organizations to win or mobilize votes. The parties perform numerous electoral functions, including the nomination of candidates for public office, campaigning for candidates, administering primary elections in Texas, and in general publicizing the election process.[1]

In the United States, legal regulation of elections and parties has traditionally been the primary responsibility of the states. State laws, for example, have a great deal to do with the election of the President and Vice President, a subject one would normally think would be a respon-

---

[1]For a discussion of party functions, see Frank J. Sorauf, *Party Politics in America*, Little, Brown and Company, Boston, 1969.

sibility of the national government.[2] Until the Civil War, the states were virtually free to make any election regulations they chose with some exceptions in congressional elections. Passage of the Fourteenth Amendment and the Fifteenth Amendment (Negro suffrage) following the war ultimately provided the constitutional base for considerable national regulation. Suffrage amendments have been relatively frequent in the twentieth century, with passage of the Seventeenth Amendment (popular election of Senators), the Nineteenth (woman suffrage), the Twenty-third (District of Columbia voting for President and Vice President), the Twenty-fourth (ban on the poll tax in Federal elections), and the Twenty-sixth (lowering of the minimum voting age to eighteen years of age).

The trend is clearly away from state domination over parties and elections except for the actual administration of the laws. Increasing nationalization of voting standards was very evident in the 1972 presidential election. As every college student knows, the Twenty-sixth Amendment enlarged the electorate to include eighteen to twenty-year olds in states not allowing this age group to vote prior thereto. In addition, Congress, by the 1970 Amendments to the 1965 Voting Rights Act, has suspended for five years all literacy tests in all the states having them; and in presidential elections, has abolished durational residence requirements and required absentee voting and absentee registration.[3] To cap it off, the U.S. Supreme Court, in the case of *Dunn v. Blumstein*, ruled out durational residence requirements in all elections, although a state could require voters to register in advance of an election, thirty days being an acceptable number for this purpose.[4] The net result of the national rules and regulations was the largest expansion of the electorate since woman suffrage in 1920. Furthermore, in Texas, the size of the electorate was influenced by Federal court decisions holding unconstitutional several state laws between 1970 and 1972, including the annual registration requirement with the January 31 deadline, the ban on aid to illiterates in the voting booth, and the requirement that minors and students register where their parents resided. These will be discussed later in the chapter. Finally, although not bearing upon the 1972 presidential election, the U.S. Supreme Court had also ruled out property or tax paying qualifications in certain local bond and tax elections.[5]

---

[2]The U.S. Constitution in Section 1 of Article II provides that the President and Vice President shall be elected by electors appointed in the manner determined by each state legislature.

[3]84 Stat. 314.

[4]405 U.S. 330 (1972).

[5]See *City of Phoenix v. Kolodziejski*, 399 U.S. 204 (1970), and *Cipriano v. City of Houma*, 395 U.S. 701 (1969).

VOTING REQUIREMENTS IN TEXAS

Voting Qualifications and Disqualifications

Texans who wish to participate in Texas elections must meet three general qualifications:

1 United States citizenship
2 Residence in the state and in a county[6]
3 Age of eighteen years or older

These qualifications have been set by the Texas constitution as modified by the U.S. Constitution, laws, and court rulings.[7] The residence requirement must be distinguished from the unconstitutional durational residence prerequisite for voting held unconstitutional by the U.S. Supreme Court. The requirement that so far is constitutional is determinative residence—that is, the state of Texas can still require the individual to belong to or have an attachment to a given place in the state although Texas may not set a time period for establishing residence, which is the essence of the durational residence requirement. The question of determinative residence has been of great concern to minors and students in Texas. A 1971 law required minors to register and vote in their parent's place of residence unless they were or had been married or had had their disabilities of minority removed. This law was declared unconstitutional by a Federal district court; the state did not appeal it.[8] Two other cases have been brought to question the constitutionality of Texas law that requires students to intend to reside in their college or school communities indefinitely after completing their studies in order to register there.[9] In one case the Federal district court held the law unconstitutional and in the other it was sustained.

The Texas constitution bars three groups of persons from voting:

1 Paupers supported by the county
2 Idiots and lunatics

---

[6]It is possible to vote for President and Vice President in Texas without actually residing in the state. Texas laws allow former residents to vote absentee up to two years, provided voting eligibility has not been established in another state. See Texas Election Code, Art. 5.05b. The 1970 Amendments to the 1965 Voting Rights Act passed by Congress also requires the states to provide for absentee voting.

[7]The qualifications and disqualifications for voting are defined in Article VI of the Texas constitution. The constitution is unusual in setting forth the disqualifications first and then the qualifications.

[8]*Ownby v. Dies*, 337 F. Supp. 38 (1971).

[9]*Wilson v. Symm*, 341 F. Supp. 8 (1972). In this case the students lost. In *Whatley v. Clark and Bullock*, an unreported case, they won.

3 Felons with such exceptions as the legislature chooses to make.[10]

The constitutional disqualification with respect to paupers is not currently being enforced, and in any event, appears to be unconstitutional. The disenfranchisement of felons is being challenged in other states and may have to be altered to some extent at some future date in Texas. The disqualification of persons adjudged mentally incompetent appears constitutional although the language is archaic.

The Texas constitution also requires the ownership or rendition of property to vote on local bond issues and expenditure of funds where a referendum is called for. As indicated earlier, this kind of provision has been thrown out as unconstitutional in other states, but the Texas supreme court upheld the Texas requirement in a 1971 case.[11]

Registration

In Texas a voter must register before he is allowed to vote. Registration consists of identifying oneself and indicating one's voter qualifications before a registration official in person or by mail or by agent. The registration officials (county tax assessor-collectors in Texas) then prepare registration lists of qualified voters for use at the election.

In 1902, the Texas constitution was amended to require Texas residents between twenty-one and sixty years of age to pay a poll tax as a condition of voting. One of the reasons for the amendment was to set up a registration system. Voters who paid the poll tax in effect registered every year and were placed on poll tax lists which served as registration lists. The lists also contained the names of persons who were exempt from the poll tax but required to secure exemption certificates during the same time and in the same manner as poll-tax payers. The poll-tax system was the Texas voter registration system from 1902 until 1966. In 1964, the Twenty-fourth Amendment to the U.S. Constitution banned the poll tax as a voting requirement in Federal elections; and then, in 1966, the U.S. Supreme Court held it unconstitutional in Texas state and local elections as well.[12]

---

[10]The legislature has provided that felons may vote provided their rights have been restored by a full pardon or by other means.

[11]*Montgomery Independent School District v. Martin*, 464 S.W. 2d 638 (1971).

[12]The case in which the Texas poll-tax requirement for voting was declared unconstitutional was *U.S. v. Texas*, 384 U.S. 155 (1966). For a discussion of the Texas poll tax, see Dick Smith, "Texas and the Poll Tax," *Southwestern Social Science Quarterly*, September, 1964. For a discussion of the poll tax as a registration system, see Janice C. May, "The Texas Voter Registration System," *Public Affairs Comment*, Institute of Public Affairs, University of Texas, July, 1970.

The Texas legislature enacted a voter registration law in 1966 following Federal court decisions. It was patterned very closely after the old poll-tax system in that voters had to register annually during the former payment period from October 1 through January 31. Then this law was held unconstitutional by a three-judge Federal district court in 1971.[13] Specifically, two features of the 1966 law were struck down: (1) annual registration; and (2) the January 31 deadline for registration. Texas was the only state to have these provisions. The district court was persuaded that they disfranchised about 1.2 million Texans and unconstitutionally burdened their fundamental right to vote.

The Texas legislature in 1971 rewrote the registration law, adding important provisions and deleting others. The new law is among the most enlightened in the nation insofar as voter convenience and encouragement of voting are concerned. The highlights of the new system will be briefly reviewed.

1. Initial Registration The voter initially registers in person or by mail; or he may be registered by his spouse, parent, or child, provided they are qualified voters of the county.

2. Permanent Registration Based on a Three-year Cycle The voter's initial registration is good for as long as he remains qualified and votes in a primary or general election once every three years. Each time he votes in a primary (either the first or second) or the general election his registration is automatically extended for another three years. If he fails to vote during this time, he will be notified by mail of the pending cancellation of his registration unless he returns the notice, declaring his desire to remain registered, and is qualified to vote.

3. Year-round Registration The voter may register at any time during the year although he may not vote in a given election unless he has registered at least thirty days prior thereto.

4. Encouragement of Registration It is the declared purpose of the statute to register as many qualified persons as possible. To that end the registrar must deputize qualified citizens without discrimination on the grounds of race, creed, color, or national origin or ancestry. The deputies are expressly authorized to go to residences or anywhere else in the county to register voters. A sufficient number of registration places are to be established throughout the county as well.

[13] *Beare v. Smith*, 321 F. Supp. 1100. The attorney general appealed the decision to the U.S. Court of Appeals of the Fifth Circuit in April, 1971.

5. Purging of the Records Before the 1971 law, keeping the registration rolls clear of the disqualified or deceased was accomplished almost entirely by the annual registration requirement—that is, every year the records were compiled anew. Under the 1971 law the records are purged monthly by the receipt of official records of persons disqualified by reason of felony conviction, mental incompetency, or death. Registrars are required to subscribe to a special postal service by means of which a monthly check on postal patrons who move is possible; however, the provision has been observed in only one or two counties.

6. Administration The responsibility for administration of the law is mainly vested in the county tax assessor-collector, an obvious carry-over from the days when the poll tax was a voting requirement and used as a voter registration system. The secretary of state, who was designated the chief election officer of the state in 1967, continues in this role under the new law. However, he provides services rather than supervision.

The 1971 law is too new to be fully evaluated as to its effectiveness. However, it is clear that the number of registered voters reached a record high in 1972 with approximately 5.2 million persons on the rolls. This is well over one million more than the next best year, 1970. However, the impact of the 1971 law cannot be isolated from the effect of the Twenty-sixth Amendment and other changes made by Federal rules.

TEXAS ELECTIONS

Primary Elections

Primaries were at one time regarded as private affairs run by the political parties in the manner of a private club from which blacks and others could be excluded with impunity. It has now, however, become settled law that party primary elections are public functions subject to constitutional and statutory regulation, at least insofar as necessary to protect the right to vote.[14] The Texas Election Code defines a primary election as "an election held by the members of an organized political party for the

---

[14]Many of the major cases involving the white primary have concerned Texas. In *Nixon v. Herndon*, 273 U.S. 536 (1927), and *Nixon v. Condon*, 286 U.S. 73 (1932), the U.S. Supreme Court held unconstitutional state laws barring blacks from participating in primaries or giving state party committees this power. In *Grovey v. Townsend*, 295 U.S. 45 (1935), a Democratic party rule barring blacks was upheld. In *Smith v. Allwright* 321 U.S. 649 (1946), the Grovey decision was reversed. The Smith case was influenced by *United States v. Classic*, 313 U.S. 299 (1941), a key case in the development of suffrage law. The U.S. Supreme Court held that primaries were elections within the meaning of the Constitution and the right to vote threat could be protected. Another case in which a Texas white primary was declared unconstitutional was *Terry v. Adams*, 345 U.S. 461 (1953). It concerned a preprimary.

purpose of nominating the candidates of such party to be voted for at a general or special election, or to nominate the county executive officers of a party" (Art. 13.01). The basic purpose of the primary is to *nominate* for public office candidates from whom the voters will choose at the general election.[15]

Texas primaries were first required by law in 1903, a law revised extensively in 1905 (Terrell Election Law). For some thirty years prior to 1973, Texas required all parties whose candidate for governor at the last general election received 200,000 or more votes to hold primaries. Parties receiving 2 percent of the total vote, provided it was under 200,000, were to choose between primaries and conventions. The other parties had to use conventions. Under the current law, primary elections are now required only of parties whose candidate for governor polled 20 percent or more of the votes at the last general election. Parties whose gubernatorial candidate received between 2 percent and 20 percent of the vote must hold conventions. Other parties must make their nominations by conventions.

Until the Republican party began to offer some real competition to the Democrats, the Democratic party primary was the *de facto* general election in Texas—that is, the winner of the Democratic primary won the general election by default in the absence of competition. Even today this is still true for many positions on the ballot, particularly at the district and county level. Largely for this reason, Texas law requires that the primary winner must have received a majority of the votes, not simply a plurality. If a majority is not obtained in the first primary, a second or runoff primary must be held between the two candidates receiving the most votes in the first primary. The two-primary system is found almost exclusively in the Southern states where the one-party system has dominated.[16]

Primaries in Texas are administered by the political parties. The Republicans and the Democrats each hold their own although they may occupy the same building. Candidates who wish to get on the ballot file with party rather than state officials.[17] The financing of the primaries was

[15]It may be noted that party primaries may also be held for municipal offices although none has been. Texas Election Code, Art. 13.55.

[16]The absolute majority was also designed to prevent black candidates from being elected. Clifton McCleskey, *The Government and Politics of Texas*, 4th ed., p. 49, Little, Brown and Company, Boston, 1972.

[17]In order for a candidate's name to appear on the primary ballot as a candidate for any county or precinct office or district office including only one county, he must submit a written request to the county chairman before the first Monday in February. Such requests may, with the consent of the person concerned, be made by petition of any twenty-five qualified voters in the county. Candidates for nomination to state offices and district offices encompassing more than one county file their requests for a place on the primary ballot. No person who advocates the overthrow of the government by force may have his name printed on the ballot of either a primary or an election. Candidates must file an affidavit that they will support and defend the Constitution and laws of the United States and Texas. Furthermore, candidates of political parties opposing representative government are barred.

strictly up to the parties before 1971. No public funds were appropriated or even constitutional for this purpose. The county executive committee, to be described later in this chapter, would estimate the cost of the primary and apportion the expenses among the candidates except for those for whom the fee had been set by statute. The assessments varied among the candidates according to the salary of the public office for which they were running. The assessments could get quite high. One district judge in Tarrant County was assessed $8,900.

A Federal district court held the primary financing system in Texas unconstitutional in 1970, a ruling upheld by the U.S. Supreme Court in 1972.[18] The Texas Legislature responded with a new law in 1971, which was also declared unconstitutional.[19] Finally, the McKool-Stroud Primary Financing Law of 1971 was enacted. Based on recommendations of the secretary of state, it provided for a filing fee schedule and state appropriations of over $2 million.[20] The law was only temporary, however, and expired in January, 1973.

The 1973 legislature also enacted temporary legislation providing for the financing of the 1974 primaries and appropriated $3.8 million for this purpose. Contributions from the parties and a fee schedule were expected to supplement the state appropriation. A permanent law regarding the financing of primaries is, at the time of writing, still to be passed.

General Elections

The general elections in Texas are held in the even year on the first Tuesday after the first Monday in November, a date originally selected by Congress for Congressional elections. Beginning in 1974 Texas will join those states separating the election of governor and other high state officials from the election of President. The voters approved a constitutional amendment in 1972 giving to these state officials a four-year term beginning with the 1974 election year. This means, obviously, that the elections of state officials will fall in the off year, not the year the President is elected. Five states hold elections for statewide offices in the odd years when no Congressional elections are held; this completely separates the state from the national elections.

The administration of the general elections is a state function although almost all the actual work is performed by county officials. In

---

[18]*Carter v. Dies*, 405 U.S. 134.

[19]*Johnston v. Luna and Bullock*, 338 F. Supp. 355 (1972). On January 27, 1972, the U.S. Supreme Court denied a motion to stay the order of *Johnston v. Bullock*.

[20]An effort by the secretary of state to fund the primaries without an appropriation was held unconstitutional by the Texas Supreme Court in *Bullock v. Calvert*, 480 SW 2d 367 (1972). The Texas Supreme Court did, however, rule unconstitutional a 1916 case, *Waples v. Marrast*, 108 Tex. 5, 184 S.W. 180 (1916), which had stipulated that state funds could not be used for primary election expenses.

other words, election administration is decentralized. The secretary of state, who is the state's chief election officer, issues guidelines, offers help, and is a depositor of records. He also canvasses certain votes. He may use a mandamus procedure against errant officials but has not availed himself of the power.[21] The county commissioners court, among its other duties, authorizes expenditures for the conduct of elections, appoints election judges, selects the voting method—machines, paper ballots, or devices—and canvasses the vote. The county election board which is composed of the county clerk, the county sheriff, the county judge and the chairmen of the major parties' county executive committees has the formal responsibility for handling election supplies. Actually, the county clerk performs most of the duties; and in addition, administers the absentee voting for general elections and nonmunicipal special elections, and canvasses the county vote for district and state offices prior to their transmittal to the secretary of state's office. The county clerk is the most important single county official in charge of election administration.

To appear on the general election ballot as the candidate of a political party it is necessary to be certified as the winner of the party primary or the choice of the party convention by the appropriate party official. The secretary of state submits to the counties the names of certified candidates for state and district offices; the county clerk certifies the others. Independent candidates must also be certified before being placed on the ballot; this requires a petition signed by qualified voters who have *not* participated in any party primary or convention. The number of signatures varies with the office: for a statewide office it is 1 percent of the votes cast for the winning candidate for governor at the last election; for a district, it is 3 percent of the vote cast for governor in the district; and for a county or precinct office, it is 5 percent. But "the number of signatures required on an application for any district, county or precinct office need not exceed five hundred" (Art. 13.50 of the Texas Election Code).

The general election ballot is of the party column type. At the top of the ballot are the names of the political parties, independents (if any), and a write-in column. The names of the candidates appear below the party or other labels in vertical columns. The law spells out the order in which the offices are printed on the ballot. Proposed constitutional amendments, if any, are on the bottom of the ballot. The party column ballot facilitates straight ticket voting; and to make it even easier, a special box or lever is provided so that one "X" or pull of the lever or punch of the stylus will count as a vote for all the candidates of a given party. To split the ticket,

---

[21]For a discussion of the administration of Texas election laws, see the following two publications of the League of Women Voters of Texas: *Election Laws in Texas: The Battered Ballot*, Dickinson, Tex., 1971; and *Election Laws in Texas: Politics, Parties and Primaries*, Dickinson, Tex., 1971.

that is, to vote for candidates of different parties, the voter must vote on each office separately.

When the voter goes to the polls, he presents his registration certificate or makes affidavit of its loss. The voter then picks up his ballot or goes into a voting-machine booth. If ballots are used, voting booths must be provided in cities of 10,000 population or more. In smaller communities there must be a guardrail so that no one can approach within 6 feet of the voter.[22] The voter selects the candidate for whom he wishes to vote by placing an "X" in the square beside the candidate's name although any ballot is supposed to be counted if the intention of the voter is clearly evident.

In the top right-hand corner of each ballot there is a small perforated tab bearing a number identical with one in the left-hand corner of the ballot. After marking the ballot, the voter writes his name on the reverse side of the tab, tears it off, and deposits it in a locked box. The ballot is then folded and placed in another locked box. All ballots and tabs are kept for specified periods, cannot be examined except upon court order in election contests, and must eventually be destroyed.

To win in the general election a candidate need poll only a plurality of votes—that is, the most regardless of whether they add up to a majority. The Monday following the election the county commissioners court canvasses the vote. The county judge delivers certificates of election to the winners of county and precinct offices. The county clerk forwards the election returns for state and district officers, including presidential electors, to the secretary of state for canvassing. The governor then signs and delivers certifications of election to the winners. Recounts may be ordered when the vote is close and the outcome could be changed and for other reasons.[23] However, a deposit of $10 for each precinct is required of the challenger and is forfeited if the outcome is not changed after the recount.

Special Elections and Local Elections

Both the state and local governments hold special elections. At the state level they include elections called to vote on constitutional amendments not submitted at the general elections and to fill vacancies in the office of U.S. Senator or U.S. Representative or for a state legislator. Local units of government hold general elections to elect members of city councils or

[22]The courts have held that failure to provide them does not render the election void. The law's purpose is to secure secrecy of the ballot, and so long as this is done and no injury results from their not being used, the election is valid. Although the law should be enforced, said the court, failure to do so would not invalidate the election. *State v. Fletcher*, 50 S.W. 450 (1932).

[23]Grounds for a recount and the procedures are spelled out in the Texas Election Code, Art. 9.38a.

commissions, depending upon the election date set by the charter or other law. Most independent school districts are required to hold elections for school board members the first Saturday in April, either in the odd or even year. Special elections may also be held by various local units of government for purposes of voting on a referendum of one sort or another—local liquor option, school bonds, county bonds, and the like.

Except for some local elections, the rules regarding the administration of special elections are generally the same as for general elections. One important exception is that the ballot is nonpartisan, and a candidate for an office in which there is a vacancy need not be certified by a party. Also in these elections to fill vacancies the filing fee is set by law at a relatively low figure, running from $10 to $1,000. A majority vote is required to win; hence, a second election may be necessary.

Absentee Voting

Texas law permits absentee voting in person or by mail in any election for reasons of illness, planned absence from the polling place on election day, and for religious belief. Sick and disabled voters may receive their ballots by mail within the county of their residence. Voters absent from the county may vote by mail provided they make application from outside the county of their residence. If, however, they expect to be within the county during the period of absentee voting, they are required to vote in person at the county clerk's office.[24]

The period of absentee voting begins on the twentieth day preceding the first primary (or the tenth day preceding the runoff primary) or the general election and ends four days before the given election. Applications for absentee ballots may be made as much as sixty days before the election, but the ballot will not be mailed and one cannot vote in person before the regular absentee voting period.

Voter Turnout

Texas has had a poor voter participation record in comparison with other states, even in the South, where participation has lagged behind that of other regions. Taking as a measuring rod the potential electorate, Texas ranked forty-fourth among the states in the 1964 presidential election and

---

[24]An applicant for a mailed ballot must enclose his registration certificate, and if ill or disabled, a doctor's certificate to that effect. A 1973 law provides for a permanent disability certificate that avoids the necessity of securing a new one every year. When the ballot is received, it is marked in the presence of a notary public and returned to the county clerk, who must receive it before 1 P.M. on the day of the election. The votes are counted on the day of the election by a canvassing board or three members appointed by the county judge for elections and by the county executive committee of the party for primaries.

forty-eighth in the 1968 election, the latter ranking including the District of Columbia.[25] The national averages in the past twenty years have hovered between 50 and 60 percent whereas in Texas they have been around 30 to 40 percent. The turnout for Congressional, state, and local elections, and for primaries is even less, often much less.

The reasons for the low turnout have been the subject of considerable scholarly consideration for a number of years. Recent research tends to emphasize the importance of Texas laws, particularly the registration laws. It is true that a considerable number of Texas election laws have been restrictive and primarily for that reason have been declared unconstitutional. Among these were laws requiring white primaries from which blacks were excluded and the payment of a poll tax in order to vote. Also held unconstitutional were limitations on voting by military personnel[26] and the ban on assisting illiterates in the polling booth.[27] Furthermore, many provisions concerned with voter registration have been struck down.

Social-economic factors—including income, occupation, race—and political factors, such as the extent of party competition, are also important as explanatory variables. Low-income, black, blue-collar, various ethnic groups, less well educated, and similar groups vote less than do the higher-income, white Anglo-Saxon Protestants, managerial and professional, and college-educated people.[28] A state like Texas with a one-party tradition, a relatively low family median income, an average education level, and a minority population of about 30 percent (blacks and Mexican Americans) would tend to score lower on participation than other states.

PARTY MEMBERSHIP AND ORGANIZATION

Party Membership

In Texas, party membership is determined by voting in the party's primary, if one is held, or participating in the convention of a party not

[25]U.S. Department of Commerce, Bureau of the Census, Current Population Reports, *Population Characteristics*, p. 4, Series P-20, No. 177, Dec. 27, 1968.

[26]For many years the Texas constitution, reflecting the fear of control of the civil government by the military, has had a prohibition against voting by members of the Armed Forces. Originally the constitution of 1876 prevented all members of the Army and Navy Reserves from voting. In 1932 an amendment allowed members of the National Guard and Reserves to vote. Another provision allowing persons who were already residents of the state before entry into the Armed Forces to vote in the county of their former residence but still denying suffrage to other regular members of the Armed Forces was adopted in 1954. In 1965 this was declared unconstitutional by the United States Supreme Court as a violation of the Fourteenth Amendment. The provision was then removed from the constitution by amendment in 1965.

[27]*Garza v. Texas*, 400 U.S. 998 (1971).

[28]Among the numerous studies, see Angus Campbell et al., *The American Voter*, John Wiley & Sons, Inc., New York, 1960; Robert E. Lane, *Political Life*, The Free Press, New York, 1959; and Lester W. Milbrath, *Political Participation*, Rand McNally & Company, 1965.

holding primaries. From then until the end of the voting year, which begins March 1 and ends the following February, the voter is eligible to participate in only one party. This rule is applied to participation in conventions, holding party office, and running for public office on the party's ticket as its nominee. It is actually a misdemeanor to engage in the activities of another party, including voting in the runoff primary if the voter voted in the first primary held by another party.

One means of limiting participation in the political party is to close the party primary to outsiders or nonmembers. Texas like most states has a closed primary system, but in practice the Texas primary is similar to the open primary in which the voter is permitted to select the party primary of his choice without questions asked. In Texas, any registered voter may participate in the primary of any party he chooses. The methods used to close the primary are imposed after he has made his selection. One is the party pledge that is required by statute to appear on every ballot. It reads as follows:

> I am a________________[name of party] and pledge myself to support the nominee of this primary. [Article 13.11 of the Texas Election Code.]

The Texas courts have held the pledge unenforceable upon voters although it has been held to restrict the activities of party officers and candidates for public office.[29] A proposal that would more effectively close the primary would be to adopt *party registration*. Found in twenty-two states, the voter is required to declare his party affiliation at the time of registration.[30] Then, when he presents himself at the primary, he receives only the ballot of the party for which he has declared. If he is an independent, he cannot participate in any primary.

In an effort to make party membership more meaningful to the average member and the party more responsible to its members, the Texas legislature enacted a law in 1971 requiring parties to file with the secretary of state "a set of specific, detailed, and written party rules for the conduct of its conventions, executive meetings, and any other party meetings" (Article 13.43b of the Texas Election Code). Failure to comply with the regulations will result in the omission of the party's candidates on the general election ballot. For the amateur in politics, the rules ought to facilitate participation. Strange as it may seem, there were literally no published party rules before the statute.

---

[29]O. Douglas Weeks, "The Texas Direct Primary System," *Southwestern Social Science Quarterly*, September, 1932.

[30]National Municipal League, *Elections Systems Project*, p. 18, New York, Mar. 2, 1972 (mimeographed).

Party Conventions

It is common to classify party organization as temporary and permanent. Temporary organization, as the name suggests, functions only for a short time whereas permanent organization is continuing in nature. The party primaries and conventions make up the temporary organization; committees and their chairmen constitute the permanent.

All parties in Texas used to nominate their candidates for public office by conventions composed of delegates elected or appointed to represent various geographical or other divisions of the party. Today, only small or new parties nominate by convention with one important exception: all parties supporting presidential candidates nominate their candidates for presidential and vice presidential electors at a state convention.

(a) Precinct Conventions   The point at which the average citizen makes the greatest impact upon the organization of his party is at the precinct convention, the smallest and basic building block of the party organization. For parties holding primaries, the convention is held on the same day as the party primary, and all voters who participated in the party's primary are eligible.[31] Given to the voter at the primary, the ticket of admission to the precinct convention is a special certificate containing the name of the party. (The registration law of 1971 provided for *permanent* certificates not designed for party identification at primaries.) In addition to presenting his certificate of party affiliation, the voter signs a roster at the precinct convention at the head of which reads:

> I swear that I have not voted at a primary election or participated in a convention of any other political party during this voting year. [Article 13.01a (4). Texas Election Code.]

The precinct conventions can be held at any time between 2:00 and 9:00 P.M. at a place determined by the county executive committee. Rural precincts often hold theirs in the afternoon whereas the city precincts hold theirs in the evening following the close of the primaries at 7:00 P.M.

The precinct conventions are normally presided over by the precinct chairman although any qualified member of the convention can do so. The principal task of the convention is to select delegates to the county or district convention, which is held the following Saturday. Precinct conventions also frequently adopt resolutions of one kind or another with

---

[31]The law distinguishes between parties holding primaries and those holding conventions. The discussion in the text refers to the former only.

the hope of influencing the party platform of the state and national party. The Democrats in 1972 were operating under new rules that required the delegates selected to the next level of conventions to be reflective of the presidential preferences of the members and to be representative of various groups in the population, including a fair number of women, blacks, Mexican Americans, and young people. An important development was the general abandonment by the Democrats of the unit rule under which a majority of the precinct convention members would bind all its members and precinct votes to the choice of the majority, freezing out the minority from any representation or voice.[32] The Republicans have not observed the unit rule in their conventions in contrast to the practice of the Democrats.

(b) County and District Conventions   The Saturday following the precinct conventions, delegates elected by the precinct conventions assemble at a place determined by the county executive committee for the county convention. The county chairman serves as temporary chairman of the convention; the delegates elect their permanent chairman. District conventions are held in lieu of county conventions "whenever the territory of a county forms all or part of more than one senatorial district" [Art. 13.34 (a) of the Texas Election Code]. Currently, this applies to the state's three largest counties. The county and district conventions are fairly large. One delegate for every twenty-five votes cast or major fraction thereof for the party's gubernatorial candidate at the last general election is the basic formula for apportioning delegates. The main task of the county and district conventions is to select delegates to the state convention. The number from each county or district is determined by the state executive committee within the framework of the election code that requires a number ranging from one delegate for every 300 votes cast for the party's candidate for governor to one for every 600 votes. The county and district conventions may also adopt resolutions.

(c) State Conventions   Every two years in the even year a state convention, which may be called the regular convention, is held on the third Tuesday in September. Known as the governor's convention in the Democratic party, it is the highest party authority in the state. The delegates assembled in the convention canvass the returns of the primaries for state offices, frame and adopt the state party platform, and

---

[32] However, even under the new rules it was possible for 70 percent of the delegates to cast for their choice all the votes to which the precinct was entitled. The rule was called the "70 percent unit rule."

select the members of the state executive committee of the party. The convention may also in the presidential year review the decisions of the state convention that meets in June, which will be described below. Canvassing the returns of the primaries is merely routine inasmuch as this has already been done by the state executive committee. The convention does, however, certify the returns to the secretary of state who, in turn, sends to the county clerks the names of the successful candidates so that they can be placed on the ballot for the general election.

In addition to the regular convention every two years, parties hold a second party convention on the second Tuesday after the second primary in June in presidential election years. The delegates selected by the county conventions serve as delegates to this convention as well as to the later September convention. A primary purpose of the June convention is to select delegates to the party's national convention at which the presidential and vice presidential candidates will be selected. The convention also selects the party's nominees for presidential and vice presidential electors. For these reasons the June convention is called the "presidential convention."

The number of delegates from Texas to the national party conventions is determined by the national party. In 1972 the Democrats were allotted 130 and the Republicans 52. As was true of the precinct and county conventions of the Democratic party, the 1972 state convention selected delegates in accordance with state and national rules which required apportionment on the basis of presidential preference among the delegates and fair representation of various groups within the general population.

Because of its potential influence in national politics, factions of the party will try to control the June convention. In the Democratic party the governor will be especially active, for control of the state's delegation to the national convention may well give him a strong voice in determining the presidential and vice presidential candidates of his party. The governor usually leads the delegation. The Republicans have not yet captured the governorship; but when they do, it is likely that their governor will act similarly.

As has been mentioned, a function of the state convention is to select the list of candidates for the position of presidential and vice presidential elector. This list may be changed by the September convention. In 1960, for example, two candidates for electors nominated by the Democratic party state convention in June were replaced because they declared their refusal to cast their electoral votes for the Democratic nominees for President and Vice President, should the state voters elect them. The September convention selected two replacements who pledged their support of the party's nominees.[33]

Party Committees

Frequent references have been made to party committees during the discussion of party organization. These committees and their chairmen represent the permanent organization of the party and are essential cogs in the machinery.

(a) Precinct Chairman   The precinct chairman is elected at his party's primary for a two-year term. A majority vote is required to win the office so that a second primary may be necessary. The precinct chairman serves as a member of the county executive committee; and, if a Democrat, is normally appointed to serve as precinct election judge not only at the Democratic primary but also at the general and special elections held by the county. Much of the success of the party depends upon the precinct chairman who is expected to serve the party between elections, whipping up support, helping to raise money, encouraging candidates, and so on. However, these functions are rarely performed in Texas.

(b) County Chairman and the County Executive Committee
The county chairman of the party is elected at the party primary for a two-year term, and he, too, must receive a majority of votes, which may necessitate a runoff. He is chairman of the important county executive committee, which, as indicated above, is composed of the precinct chairmen of the county. The importance of the county executive committee and especially the chairman who usually does the real work of the committee, can scarcely be overemphasized. Although having other duties, his most important task is to administer the party primary election. For this reason it is easy to see why local party members are anxious to elect a chairman who is fair, honest, and impartial.

The responsibility for administering the party primary means that the county executive committee will receive applications and petitions to place names of candidates for county and district offices on the ballot; they collect fees from the state, county, and candidates; they will provide the voting machines, devices, or ballots; they will have the ballots printed

---

[33]Similar action had taken place in the Democratic conventions of 1944 and 1948 and had been upheld by the Texas supreme court, which said, in effect, that electoral candidates could be selected by either convention and that what the presidential convention did could be reviewed and changed by the regular party convention in September.

and distributed if paper ballots are used; they will buy election supplies, select the polling places, appoint the primary election judges to conduct the primary in every voting precinct, and canvass the returns. The results of the primary election are certified to the county clerk. The returns for state and district officers are certified to the state executive committee.

(c) District Executive Committee   Party organization also includes the district executive committee. The composition of this committee varies with the number of counties and parts thereof located within a state senate district. For example, if the district is composed of more than one county, the county chairman of a county located wholly within the district will be an ex officio member of the district committee. Chairmen of precincts located within parts of counties in a single district will elect one of their number to serve on the district committee. The district executive committee is not so important as other party committees and never meets except to fill vacancies after the primary in nominations for district offices.

(d) State Executive Committee   The state executive committee, which is at the apex of the party's permanent state organization, is composed of one man and one woman from each of the thirty-one state senatorial districts plus a chairman and a vice chairman, one of whom must be a man and one a woman. The State Democratic Executive Committee is frequently referred to as the SDEC. All members of the committee are selected at the regular state convention in September. At the convention the delegates from each senatorial district hold a caucus and select their members. The list is then combined for official approval by the convention.

Custom gives the successful gubernatorial nominee of the Democratic party a vote on the membership of the SDEC. If he states that a certain member is "personally obnoxious" to him, that person will ordinarily be removed and another, more suitable to the governor, substituted. The chairman and vice chairman, by courtesy, are usually selected by the successful gubernatorial nominee, although in 1972 the vice chairman was selected by the delegates. The governor is able to control the official party membership while he is in office by controlling the SDEC. The control will extend to the state conventions, both the governor's and the presidential, which are so important to his political fortunes.

The state executive committee has general charge of the affairs of the party. It also has considerable duties to perform in relation to the primary. The laws prescribe that it meet before the first primary to select

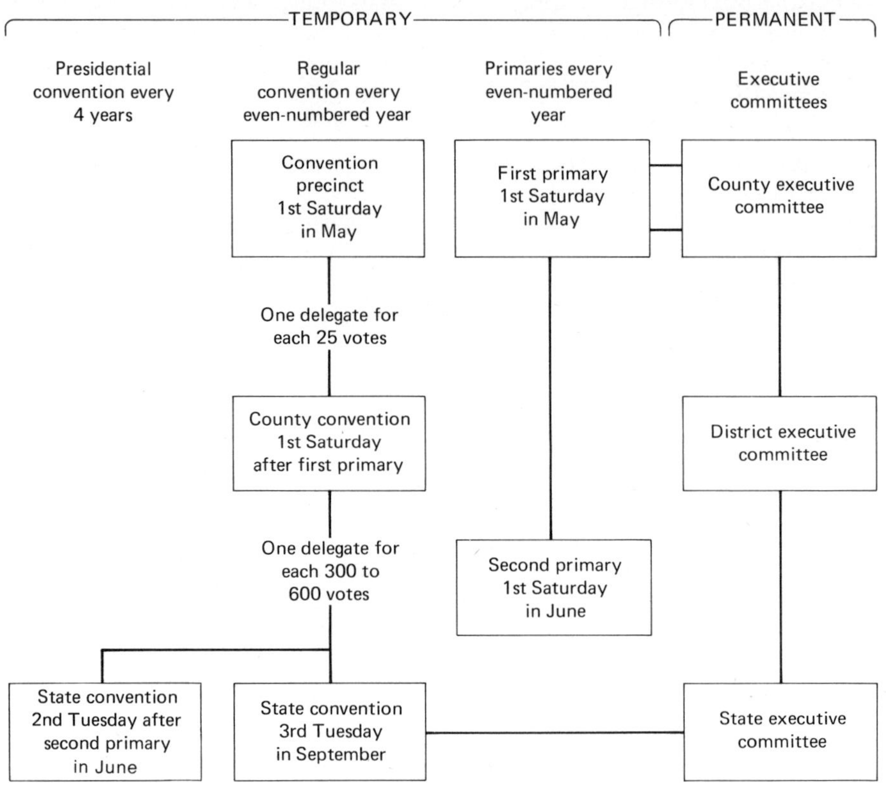

the city for the state convention and certify to the county chairmen the names of all candidates for nomination to state offices. After the first primary, the committee meets again and canvasses the returns for state and district offices. When there is no majority, the two highest candidates for each state and district office are certified to the county chairmen for the second primary. A third meeting is required after the second primary to canvass the returns, which are certified to the state convention. Special meetings of the committee may be called by the chairman at any time.

Of considerable importance is the committee's power to make the temporary roll of the state convention. It may hold hearings on contested delegations before the convention meets, deciding which of the groups shall be seated temporarily. Of course all decisions concerning contested delegations must be approved on the floor of the convention itself, but even so, those who have been seated temporarily by the committee can often have great influence on the ultimate control of the convention.

The actual work of the committee is carried on by a paid executive director who is ordinarily a close political associate of the governor in the Democratic party or the gubernatorial nominee in the Republican party. The director and his assistants serve as general coordinators of party affairs, raise money, issue press releases, and help in party organization. They work very closely with the governor, if Democratic, and with the gubernatorial or other nominees to high offices, if Republican. The close ties with the governor in the Democratic party may cause friction within the party around primary time, for the governor may use the committee as his personal machine, and other candidates or factions of the party resent it. In presidential election years, the committees of both parties usually work rather closely with their respective national committee.

SELECTED ISSUES

Election laws invite controversy. The rules may very well affect election outcomes by working to favor one side or the other. Of many election and party issues, a few will be selected for comment to close this chapter.

Party Registration

Although an issue at least since the 1940s, party registration has not yet been adopted in Texas. The support for party registration has come mainly from liberal Democrats who argue that Republicans crossing over to the Democratic primaries defeat liberal candidates. Former Senator Ralph Yarborough, following his defeat in the 1970 Democratic primary by Lloyd Bentsen, made this charge; but other liberals have also urged party registration. Bills have been introduced in the Texas legislature to set up the system. Arguments for party registration stress the concept of party responsibility which was discussed at the beginning of the chapter. Arguments against party registration emphasize the importance of free choice, the privacy of the ballot, and the special problems in a largely one-party state where to be barred from voting in the major party effectively disenfranchises the voter in many races where there are no opponents in the general election.

Unitary Primary

Under a unitary primary all parties would hold their primary in the same location, at the same time, and with the same election officials using the same election supplies. It is argued that state financing of primaries will be prohibitively expensive unless the primaries are combined to save money from duplications of supplies, employees, and so on. It is also argued that present laws barring participation in more than one party at a time will be more easily enforced under a unitary primary system. On the other side fears have been expressed by Republicans that the Democrats would actually be administering the Republican primaries in a state where the vast majority of public election officials are Democrats. Some Democrats are afraid that their Republican support would be less. The Texas legislature has so far failed to enact bills providing for the unitary primary system. In 1973, Texas was one of only three states requiring the primary method of nominating candidates for public office without at the same time providing for the unitary primary.

Regulation of Campaign Financing

The number-one election issue is perhaps that of proper regulation of campaign contributions and expenditures. Never an easy question to resolve, the issue has turned out to be extremely troublesome in modern times.

Democracy presupposes political campaigns, and political campaigning has become tremendously expensive. Informed sources have said that a hotly contested campaign for a major statewide office will cost the backers of each candidate at least 1 million dollars. Other estimates have gone as high as $2^{1}/_{2}$ million. Even candidates for local offices may spend several thousand dollars. And most of the expenditures are perfectly legitimate. Candidates must use the radio and television, and this is very expensive. A thirty-minute statewide television broadcast with total coverage and promotion can cost as much as $40,000. Newspaper advertising, posters, circulars, letters, postage, clerical assistance—these all add up fast. For example, to produce and send a first-class letter to every family in Texas would cost approximately $300,000. A single billboard in a large city rents for about $550 a month.[34] Candidates for statewide offices travel widely, visiting as many different sections of the state as possible, often using sound trucks to attract crowds. Public relations men must be hired. Campaign headquarters in the larger cities must be maintained. All this takes vast amounts of money. Actually, no one knows how much, for the laws requiring the reporting of campaign expenses have been almost a farce, and probably not more than half of what is actually spent is reported. Also many contributions are made by way of services (*e.g.,* free use of airplanes and automobiles, clerical assistance, space for headquarters, campaign workers, etc.). Then too,

[34]Jim Wright, "Clean Money and Congress," *Harper's*, April, 1967.

campaigns for important offices such as governor, lieutenant governor, and United States Senator have become almost a continuous process. It is not at all unusual for public officials or their organizations to be subsidized on a regular monthly payment basis by individuals and special interests so that the office holder may have sufficient funds for more or less constant political activity.[35] So we do not know, and under the laws we cannot be certain, how much political campaigns cost in Texas—but the expenditures are necessary, for there have been no instances in recent Texas political history where a candidate who ran a "poor boy" campaign won a major statewide office.[36]

State regulation of party finance ordinarily takes the form of limiting the amounts spent; requiring publicity concerning amounts, sources, and purposes of expenditures; and limiting the size of individual contributions. In most instances, the laws have been unrealistic and largely ignored. Texas laws have generally followed the pattern of other states. However, widespread dissatisfaction with campaign practices and a wave of reform resulted in a substantial revision of the laws by the 1973 legislature.[37]

Campaign Manager Texas laws require candidates for public office and political committees, including those formed to support or defeat a "measure," such as a constitutional amendment, to appoint a campaign manager. The written appointment must be filed with the appropriate authority (for example, the secretary of state for candidates and committees concerned with statewide offices or issues) before money may be received or spent. The candidate may appoint himself as manager, and assistant managers may be appointed for counties. Only candidates and managers may spend campaign money except where the law expressly determines otherwise.

Expenditures and Contributions Campaign expenditures and contributions are strictly regulated. Money may be spent for only eleven purposes, which are enumerated in the law; and any others are declared unlawful. Contributions may be made by individuals only for lawful purposes. Campaign funds from corporations and labor unions are forbidden, and nonpolitical clubs or associations are forbidden to use contributions by corporations or labor unions for political expenditures. No individual acting in his own capacity (other than the candidate) may

[35]Richard Morehead, "Long, Costly Grind Ahead," *The Dallas Morning News*, June 4, 1967.
[36]William H. Gardner, "The Costly Campaigns," *The Houston Post*, Mar. 18, 1962.
[37]House Bill No. 4, providing for revision of the campaign laws, was one of the speaker's nine reform bills in the 1973 legislature. See Chapter 7.

spend more than $100 for all purposes. He may, however, give his services and necessary expenses provided he is not paid by others or, if reimbursed, it must be from lawful campaign funds. Out-of-state contributions over $500 require special reporting.

Reports   Candidates and political committees and their managers must keep accurate records of expenditures and contributions on forms prescribed by the secretary of state and make sworn statements as to their accuracy. However, unopposed candidates are exempt from many of these regulations. The full names and addresses of everyone who contributes or loans over $10 or who receives over $10 must be included in the reports with the dates of the transactions. Candidates must include in their reports the names and addresses of supporting political committees and their campaign managers. Persons who contribute over $100 are responsible for seeing that their contribution is reported by the candidate or committee.

Periodic reports (thirty-one to forty days before the election; seven to ten days before; and one month after the election) must be filed with the appropriate authorities, such as the secretary of state for statewide candidates and campaign committees. In runoff elections, the reports are due one week before and one month after the election. Reports must also be filed yearly by candidates and committees who have surpluses or debts after the election until they have been disposed of. The records are open to public inspection for two years.

Political Advertising   No political advertising can be lawfully accepted for printing or broadcasting unless accompanied by the full name and address of the person placing the ad and that of the candidate or political committee, if any, who has authorized it.

Remedies and Penalties   A host of enforcement provisions are included in present law, involving both civil and criminal penalties and new watchdog commissions. The provisions apply to individuals, candidates, managers, political committees, corporations, labor unions, and all others mentioned in the laws. Some violations allow civil suits in which the opposing candidate receives double the amount of the unlawful expenditure or contribution from the offending candidate or committee. In these cases, the state may receive triple the amount. In addition, any citizen can apply for an injunction in a state district court to enforce the law. The criminal penalties, which may involve a fine or a term in the penitentiary or both, apply to corporations and other groups as well as to individuals and candidates.

Election Commissions[38]   The 1973 law adopted a new approach to enforcement of campaign laws in Texas by establishing county and state election commissions. The county commissions are composed of the county chairmen of the two major parties (those receiving the most votes) and the senior district judge of the county. The state commission is composed of the chairmen of the state executive committees of the two major parties, the chief justice of the supreme court, the presiding judge of the court of criminal appeals, one justice of a court of civil appeals appointed by the chief justice of the supreme court, one district judge appointed by the court of criminal appeals, two county party chairmen of the executive committees of the two major parties, and the secretary of state. The commissions have authority to investigate upon request or upon their own initiative violations of the law and to initiate appropriate action, which may involve submission of the information to the district attorney of the district having jurisdiction for prosecution.

Presidential Primaries

In 1972 twenty-two states and the District of Columbia held presidential primaries of one sort or another to elect delegates to the national party conventions and to give in most instances some indication of the party members' preference for President. Texas is not among these states. Instead, delegates are selected by the state convention. For several sessions the Texas legislature has had before it bills to establish presidential primaries. The reforms introduced by the Democrats in their convention procedures in 1972 may diffuse some of the sentiment for the primaries. However, there are those who think primaries are inevitable.

---

[38]After the following paragraph was written, the Texas attorney general ruled that the election commissions were unconstitutional. The judges on the commissions were in a position to prejudge election cases that might come before them in court. See Att. Gen. Op. H-117 (1973).

Chapter 4

The Texas Political Party System

Texas political parties, although not established by the Texas constitution, are nonetheless an integral part of the fundamental structure of the Texas political system. Parties perform significant functions in Texas. Already we have seen that parties are inseparately linked with elections. Among their other functions, parties act as agents of political socialization—that is, they help to educate people about politics and to assimilate them into the political system and the larger society of which it is a part. Perhaps the most important concept for illustrating the potential value of political parties is that of party responsibility. In theory at least, parties make it possible for the people to control their government. Competing parties nominate candidates who support a given program for government; the voters select the candidates who support the program they prefer; the winning candidates carry the program into effect; then, the candidates go back to the people for approval or rejection with competing parties offering alternative candidates and programs.

Party responsibility has never been fully implemented in the United States, but various laws promote it, for example, the Texas laws limiting participation in a party to its members. One of the many barriers to realization of party responsibility in the state of Texas is the absence of a two-party system. Studies in which state parties are compared on the basis of their number and degree of competitiveness place Texas among the one-party Democratic states.[1] It is common knowledge, of course, that the Democrats have dominated Texas politics for years. In 1972 all statewide offices were held by Democrats, all but 4 of the 24 seats in the U.S. House of Representatives, all seats but 3 of the 31-member Texas Senate, and 17 of the 150-member Texas House of Representatives. One of the two U.S. Senators was a Democrat. The *Texas Republican Citizen*, a party newsletter, claimed only 89 of the 4,500 elected office holders in statewide, district, and county offices.[2] The Democrats have also won all but five presidential elections during the past 100 years or so, losing in 1872, 1928, 1952, 1956, and 1972.

The consequences of having a one-party system in Texas are important to explore. Although research has been undertaken on the impact of different kinds of party systems in general, many questions remain unanswered, particularly on the impact of the Texas parties. The late V. O. Key, a native Texan, and others have argued that the absence of regular two-party competition tends to produce a lower voter participation rate, less awareness of real issues, and in general less rationality in political choice. In terms of policy, the haves are favored over the have-nots.[3] The Key thesis has been disputed, but a few recent studies show that party competition and high turnout at the polls tend to make a difference insofar as policy is concerned, most particularly in education and welfare.[4]

The Texas party system, although dominated by the Democrats, has undergone numerous changes in its history. Trends underway indicate even greater changes for the future. A brief review of Texas political party history will provide a useful vantage point from which to view the current political scene.

POLITICAL PARTY HISTORY

Early Politics: 1845–1873

At the time Texas entered in the Union in 1845, there were no political parties. Only personal followings of political leaders, such as Houston

---

[1]See Austin Ranney, "Parties in State Politics," in Herbert Jacob and Kenneth N. Vines (eds.), *Politics in the American States*, 2d ed., p. 87, Little, Brown and Company, Boston, 1971.

[2]"Capitol A," by Jim Berry, *Austin American*, Feb. 24, 1973.

[3]V. O. Key, Jr., *Southern Politics in State and Nation*, chap. 14, Alfred A. Knopf, Inc., New York, 1949; Fred I. Greenstein, *The American Party System and the American People*, 2d ed., chap. 5, Prentice-Hall, Englewood Cliffs, N.J., 1970.

[4]Ira Sharkansky and Richard I. Hofferbert, "Dimensions of State Policy," in Jacob and Vines, *op. cit.*, p. 338.

and anti-Houston men, provided political organization. Efforts to organize the Democrat and Whig parties finally bore fruit in 1856 at which time the Democrats were established to counter, successfully it turned out, the sudden rise of the Know-Nothing party. This party, a nativist, anti-Catholic, and anti-immigrant group, got its name from members of secret societies who refused to answer questions.[5] The Whigs never really got off the ground and disbanded in 1854 in Texas and elsewhere, although they had drawn votes in three presidential elections prior thereto. As the Civil War approached, the Democrats split into the Unionists led by Sam Houston and the states' rights factions. The secessionists won out, and war terminated normal party politics.

After the war, the Democratic party revived to become the chief reliance of the white citizenry. However, from the beginnings of Congressional Reconstruction in 1866, the radical Republicans were in control of the South. A repressive regime ensued which disfranchised many whites, enfranchised Negroes, and afforded full opportunity to "carpetbag" and "scalawag" Republicans to organize the Negroes into state and local Republican party units which could control government at all levels. By 1874, however, after several elections and bitter struggles between the two parties, marked by much fraud and intimidation, the Democrats were generally successful in getting full control, and a new era in politics began.[6]

Agrarian Politics: 1874–1899

This new period, which extended to around the turn of the century, was not an easy one. It was marked by the prolonged aftermath of Reconstruction, two depressions which extended through most of the 1870s and 1890s, the growing pains of an essentially pioneer state—the western half of which was in the process of being settled—prolonged agricultural discontent, and the beginnings of industrialism with its accompanying problems of governmental controls, particularly in the areas of railroads and corporations. The politics of the period was, therefore, turbulent.

Although the Democratic party became dominant at the end of Reconstruction and thereafter usually won elections, until 1900 it had to contend with sizable Republican votes in presidential elections and with formidable competition at the state and local levels from the Greenback party from 1878 to 1884[7] and the People's or Populist party all through the

---

[5]In 1855 the Know-Nothing party elected about twenty representatives and five senators to the Texas legislature, Rupert N. Richardson, *Texas, the Lone Star State*, 2d ed., p. 129, Prentice-Hall, Englewood Cliffs, N.J., 1958.

[6]*Ibid.*, pp. 127–132, 207–211, 214.

[7]Roscoe C. Martin, "The Greenback Party in Texas," in Frank Carter Adams (ed.), *Texas Democracy*, 4 vols., Vol. 1, chap. 5, Democratic Historical Association, Austin, 1937.

1890s. These parties stemmed, respectively, from two organizations which strenuously defended the cause of the depressed farmers and frontiersmen and voiced the general agricultural discontent, namely, the Grange and the Farmers' Alliance, which were more pressure groups than parties. The Greenback party advocated "cheap money," the adoption of an income tax and other tax reforms, regulation of railroads, and retrenchment in state government. It reached its crest in the state election of 1882, when a Greenback-Republican coalition polled 102,501 votes for its candidate for governor as opposed to 150,891 for the Democratic candidate. After 1884 the Greenback party disappeared in Texas, but the agricultural discontent continued and produced in the 1890s the larger Populist party.

The Republican party survived during this period, partly dominated and supported by Negroes. It polled large presidential votes but was of little consequence in state politics. It could not hope to win, but it could at times serve in shifting the balance one way or the other between the Democrats and Greenbackers or Populists, none of whom was averse to having Negroes vote in local situations if their votes were needed to win.

In the interim between the heyday of the Greenbackers and the full flowering of the Populists, the Democrats, under the liberal leadership of James Stephen Hogg, whom many consider Texas's greatest governor, introduced some notable reforms. Hogg served as state attorney general from 1887 to 1891 and as governor from 1891 to 1895. During this time Texas was having her initial experiences with industrialization and the operation of newly emerged "trusts" and "malefactors of great wealth." Through suits, Hogg regained for Texas over a million acres of land illegally obtained by the railroads and drove forty "wildcat" insurance companies from the state. In the legislative field, he sponsored antitrust and railroad commission measures and a number of other regulatory laws. After retirement, he became a staunch supporter of William Jennings Bryan and a forerunner in Texas of the progressivism later espoused by Woodrow Wilson. Although a reformer, Hogg steered clear of the more radical ideas of the Populists and at the same time fought reactionary Democrats and Republicans. Even though he stood for liberal reforms, he helped to establish the middle-of-the-road tradition that characterized the Democratic party in Texas in later years.[8]

The Populist party gave the Democrats very serious opposition during most of the 1890s. In 1894 and 1896 it reached the zenith of its strength. In the first of these years, in coalition with the Republicans, it almost equaled the Democratic vote for governor, and in the later year it polled on its own a vote that fell only 60,000 short of the Democrats' for

[8]Robert C. Cotner, *James Stephen Hogg*, University of Texas Press, Austin, 1959.

the same office. In these and later elections, the Republicans abstained from naming state tickets and aided the Populists. The policies of Hogg and his successor, Culberson, did not go far enough to suit the Populists, who wanted government ownership of the railroads, abolition of national banks, and more aids to the farmers. With the adoption by the national Democratic party in 1896 of some of the ideas of the Populist party—including its principal demand for cheap money—and the nomination of Bryan, its candidate for President, the back of Populism was soon broken. The return of prosperity after 1897 aided in the process. The party had practically disappeared by the election of 1902.[9]

Democratic Party Domination: 1900–1950

The turn of the present century ushered in a new period of Texas politics, characterized by the complete dominance of the Democratic party. It had always been the majority party except during the Civil War and Reconstruction interval, but it had usually been confronted with more or less serious opposition from Whigs, Know-Nothings, Republicans, Greenbackers, and Populists. Although factionalism had split the Democratic party occasionally, the usual area of conflict had been more interparty than intraparty, with final settlement of basic issues in the general election. Also, in most elections the issues of slavery, secession, war, Reconstruction, and control of government and the problems of serious economic depressions and pioneer adjustment were important. Strong personalities had played a part, but issues also were highly significant.

Now, in the early twentieth century, the Democratic party suddenly found itself without rivals.[10] Prosperity had returned and was destined to continue for a long time. What panics and economic crises occurred were short-lived and of limited extent until the Great Depression of 1929. Thus the rampant agrarianism of the last three decades of the nineteenth century, with its tendency to breed radical minor parties, disappeared. Without this divisiveness to play upon, the Republican party became practically a cipher in state and local politics, and even its Presidential vote dwindled noticeably after 1900.[11]

---

[9]Roscoe C. Martin, *The People's Party in Texas*, University of Texas, Bulletin 3308, Austin, 1933. See also Alwyn Barr, *Reconstruction to Reform: Texas Politics 1876–1906*, University of Texas Press, Austin, 1971.

[10]The first thirty years of the twentieth century are covered by Ralph W. Steen, "A Political History of Texas, 1900–1930," in Adams, *op cit.*, pp. 317–493. See also Richardson, *op. cit.*, chaps. 16 and 19.

[11]Also during this period the influence and support of the blacks diminished in the Republican party. With the establishment of the poll tax early in the century as a requirement for voting and the growth of white control within the party, by the 1920s black influence was practically nonexistent.

(1) Democratic Primary   One factor contributing to the domination of the Democratic party in Texas was the adoption of the direct primary by the Terrell Election Laws of 1903 and 1905. The laws were designed mainly for the Democrat party by making primaries mandatory for parties polling 100,000 or more votes for governor in the previous general election.[12] The Republicans were unable to reach this figure for several years. However, the Republicans could have held primaries during these years because the law was permissive, that is, it allowed parties polling between 10,000 and 100,000 votes to hold primaries if they wished. Only in 1942 did the Republicans draw fewer than 10,000 votes. Had the Republicans held primaries more often perhaps they would have been a stronger party. Republicans who were migrating to the state from other parts of the country as well as Republicans already in Texas would have had an opportunity at least to vote in their own primaries. But there was no place to go without them; and the idea became fixed in the minds of many voters that the Democratic primary was in fact the only election that mattered.

The general election merely ratified the choices made in the Democratic primary. Texans became accustomed to conducting politics within the shell of the Democratic party with the primary serving as the real election. This was unfortunate for several reasons. Participation in both primaries and general elections fell during the twentieth century, and part of the blame at least must be placed on the lack of party competition. Furthermore, candidates developed their own followings rather than having a party-based and supported organization. The one-party politics, in other words, failed to provide party responsibility and was a poor substitute indeed for a competitive party system. Finally, it is well to remember that the Democratic primary was a white primary from which blacks were excluded up to 1944.[13]

(2) Democratic Party Factionalism   Politics pursued within the Democratic party was based on factionalism. However, the factionalism differed from that in states such as Virginia, North Dakota, and Louisiana, where complete slates or tickets were offered by different factions at the primaries. Factions were identifiable, in other words, and supported candidates who represented their views. The candidates in Texas primaries, on the other hand, have had to stand on their own legs, setting up their own campaign organizations and adopting their individual platforms.

---

[12]O. Douglas Weeks, "The Texas Direct Primary System," *Southwestern Social Science Quarterly*, September, 1932. Also in Adams, *op. cit.*, pp. 531–557.

[13]The white primary was finally held unconstitutional in *Smith v. Allwright*, 321 U.S. 649 (1944). See Chapter 3.

Factions were fluid and loose and ordinarily concentrated on the race for governor. Nonetheless, there were factions of a more or less liberal or progressive stripe facing candidates of a more or less conservative nature. An analysis of governors nominated in Texas by the Democratic primary from 1906 to 1960 shows that most of the winners were middle of the road, which might be interpreted as conservative although not extremely so.[14] The factionalism, such as it was, was not racist in appeal as was true in many Southern states of the time, although it must be remembered that blacks were virtually excluded from Texas politics by the white primary.

Factionalism was influenced by issues in Texas. In the early part of this century, progressive ideas, such as those embodied in Woodrow Wilson's New Freedom, had their impact on Texas. Progressivism, a broad program of political, economic, and social reform of the middle class, swept over the whole country during the first twelve or fifteen years of the century. Alongside national leaders like Republican Theodore Roosevelt and Democrat Woodrow Wilson, Texas developed its own progressive leadership. Thomas M. Campbell, who was Democratic governor from 1907 to 1911, is regarded as the outstanding Texas progressive of the day. During his administration, an extensive number of progressive bills was enacted, including stronger regulation of trusts, corporations, and insurance companies, as well as a number of laws beneficial to labor and in furtherance of general welfare and political reform. Former Governor Hogg, who had supported legislation akin to progressivism when he was governor, endorsed Campbell and his progressive policies.

Following the progressivism of Governor Campbell, Texas entered a period of about twenty years dominated by "Fergusonism," so named because of the influence of James E. Ferguson, governor of Texas from 1915 to 1917, and his wife, Miriam A. Ferguson, governor from 1925 to 1927 and 1933 to 35. Ferguson waged a campaign aimed at the farmer in his quest for the governorship in 1914. After his victory, he shepherded through legislation helping the tenant farmer although it was later declared unconstitutional, and was credited with other progressive legislation. However, he was impeached and removed from office during his second term. He was convicted by the Texas Senate on ten counts, mainly charges of misusing public funds.[15] Removal from office in Texas carries an additional penalty of permanent ineligibility for holding public office in the state. Undaunted, "Farmer Jim" ran for governor in 1918, for President in 1920, and for U.S. Senator in 1922. He then got the bright idea

---

[14]Fred Gantt, Jr., *The Chief Executive in Texas: A Study in Gubernatorial Leadership*, pp. 326–327, University of Texas Press, Austin, 1964.
[15]Richardson, *op. cit.*, p. 293.

of having his wife run for office. The Fergusons campaigned on the slogan, "Two Governors for the Price of One," and won two nonconsecutive elections. Considerable opposition developed to the Fergusons over the years. One source of complaint was the liberal pardoning policy; some 2,000 pardons were granted in twenty months during the 1925–1927 administration of Mrs. "Ma" Ferguson. But despite high jinks of one sort or another the Fergusons to their credit were not racist and fought the Ku Klux Klan. They were also against prohibition, a very hot issue of the time, and during the 1933–1935 term cooperated with the New Deal. Mrs. Ferguson's second administration was followed by that of Governor James Allred (1935–1939), who is rated as the most liberal governor of Texas during this century.

After Fergusonism, another colorful figure appeared on the Texas political scene. Wilbert Lee "Pappy" O'Daniel served as governor from 1939 to 1941 and as U.S. Senator from 1941 to 1947. A flour salesman with a flair for showmanship, he launched his campaign for governor following an appeal for advice from listeners to his radio program on which he advertised "Hillbilly Flour." He ran on a platform including support of the Ten Commandments, abolition of the poll tax, more business and less Johnson grass. His accomplishments as governor and U.S. Senator were miniscule; his success at winning elections was a commentary on the weakness of the one-party system of the time.[16]

(3) The Republican Party   Between 1900 and the early 1920s, the Republican party practically dropped out of the picture in Texas. In 1923, R. B. Creager of Brownsville won the post of Republican National Committeeman for Texas and held it until his death in 1950. He was able through this position to rule the state party organization with an iron hand and to turn it largely into a machine for naming and controlling Texas delegations to Republican national conventions and for dispensing Federal patronage in Texas when the party held the presidency.

Democratic party factionalism caused the Republican party to act as a vehicle for Democrats dissatisfied with their party's candidates. Enemies of the Fergusons frequently voted for Republican party candidates for governor. Bitter antagonisms generated by the Ku Klux Klan were felt in the 1924 election. In 1928 the Democratic candidate for President, Alfred E. Smith, a Roman Catholic and "wet," prompted many Democrats to vote for the Republican Herbert Hoover, a Protestant and "dry"; and Hoover carried the state. The Republicans garnered enough votes in 1924, 1928, and 1932, to fall within the mandatory primary law. In 1945 the

---

[16]Key, *op. cit.*, pp. 265–271.

Republican organization finally persuaded the Texas legislature to increase the mandatory figure for primaries to 200,000 in hopes of relieving the party of the expense and bother of primaries. The new figure was not exceeded until 1952 when the Democratic candidate for governor, Allan Shivers, won the Republican as well as the Democratic party endorsement under a short-lived provision in the Election Code permitting cross-filing, which permits a candidate to be nominated by more than one party. Needless to say, this practice violates the concept of party responsibility.

The main lesson to be learned from the high Republican vote in selected elections during the first half of the twentieth century was that they were cast by errant Democrats who returned to the Democratic party after their cause for desertion had been removed. They were not true-blue Republicans. However, R. B. Creager did not want or expect lots of Republican votes. He maintained that the Republicans could not hope for more than a very occasional election victory when the Democrats gave up on their own candidates. The chief purpose of the Republican party, according to its leader, was to pray that the national party would poll a majority of electoral votes outside Texas, thus enabling the organization to dispense Federal jobs in Texas. This was the Republican attitude up to the 1950s.

RECENT DEVELOPMENTS

The Texas one-party system began to show signs of strain during the days of the Great Depression, strains which have since accelerated under the impact of numerous changes in Texas and in the nation as a whole. Industrialization, urbanization, general shifts in population, political progress of the blacks and Mexican Americans, the growth of the labor movement—these and other forces have influenced Texas party development. Also, Texas as a part of the South, has been affected by the many new developments that have come to this region.

Of particular importance to Texas party divisions has been the growth of government at all levels, but especially at the national level. The fact that the Democratic party, the traditional friend and protector of the South and the historic defender of states' rights and frontier individualism, should have been at the helm during Roosevelt's New Deal, Truman's Fair Deal, Kennedy's New Frontier, and Johnson's Great Society, generated great pressures on the Texas Democrats. Conservatives opposed many of the policies of the national government and some left the party permanently. Really, the wonder is that the party has not been split asunder. One reason why this has not been the case is that the conservatives, although dominant in Texas, have been growing more moderate in state policy and have cooperated in recent years with the national government toward achieving common goals.

Rebirth of the Republican Party

A key to the present and future of the party system in Texas is the rebirth of the Republicans, which is usually dated from 1952. During that presidential election year, General Dwight D. Eisenhower swept both Texas and the nation at large. Republicans poured into the Republican precinct conventions in record numbers that year in Texas. The Old Guard generally refused to accept the newcomers, claiming that many were really Democrats. Two sets of Republican delegates went to the national Republican convention; the one favoring Eisenhower was seated. Allan Shivers, Democratic governor of Texas, publicly headed a Democrats for Eisenhower group after the Democratic presidential candidate, Adlai Stevenson, refused to endorse Texas ownership of the tidelands.[17] The Republicans carried Texas in the 1956 presidential election as well as in 1952.

In 1953 the Republicans began to rebuild their party as an independent force rather than as a sometime vehicle for dissident Democrats, which had been the case during the Creager years. The first notable success was in 1956 when Bruce Alger was elected to Congress as a Representative from Dallas County. This was topped however, by the historic special election of 1961 in which John Tower, an unknown political science professor from Midwestern University in Wichita Falls, won the U.S. Senate seat vacated by Senator Lyndon Johnson who was elected to the vice presidency. (Johnson was on the 1960 general ballot as a candidate for both the U.S. senatorship and the vice presidency.) Tower was the first Republican elected to the U.S. Senate from Texas since Reconstruction. He defeated a conservative Democrat, William Blakley, who was opposed by many liberal Democrats. The turnout was small in the election, and liberals claimed Tower was elected because they had gone fishing. The same thing happened in 1966, when Tower was up for reelection. This time Tower's opponent was Waggoner Carr, former speaker of the Texas House of Representatives and attorney general. He too was a nonfavorite among the liberals, and again the turnout was light.

---

[17]The story of the Texas tidelands is a long and interesting one. The Texas tidelands consist of the submerged lands between the beaches along the Gulf Coast and three leagues from shore. Three leagues are equal to 10.36 land miles. The national government first contested Texas ownership in 1949. The discovery of oil on the lands was a factor. Congress, following a decision by the U.S. Supreme Court adverse to Texas, gave Texas title to the lands. For a history of the tidelands, see *Texas Almanac, 1972–73*, pp. 389–393, A. H. Belo Corporation, Dallas, 1972.

Tower won handily. However, in 1972 Tower won handsomely against a moderate Democrat, Barefoot Sanders, in the largest turnout in the history of Texas. Some 3,413,003 votes were cast. Tower won 54.6 percent of the two-party vote.

Generally speaking, the Republicans have done very well in the races for the highest political offices in Texas since the 1950s despite setbacks in 1964 and 1970. These include the elections for President, U.S. Senator, governor, and occasionally for lieutenant governor. In races for seats in the U.S. House of Representatives, the Republicans have not challenged all the Democrats, but have in recent years done fairly well in a limited number of races. The year 1972 was a very good year for Texas Republicans. The Republican candidate for governor, Henry Grover, barely lost to Democrat Dolph Briscoe, winning 48.4 percent of the two-party vote. Maurice Angly lost to Democrat Jesse James in the race for state treasurer in a close one; he received 48 percent of the two-party vote. Representation in the U.S. House of Representatives was increased from three to four seats; John Tower won his race for the U.S. Senate, as already mentioned. The Texas Legislature saw a record number, although still scanty, of Republicans with seventeen in the House and three in the Senate. Last, but hardly least, President Nixon swamped Democrat George McGovern for President, capturing 66 percent of the two-party vote and carrying all but eight Texas counties, including seventy-eight never before carried by a Republican in a presidential race.[18]

Where does the Republican party draw its strength in Texas?[19] Most votes come from the urban areas even though it is true that Nixon and Tower did well in rural counties in 1972. The cities have been the mainstay of the Republicans, and in setbacks suffered in 1964 and 1970 the rural areas voted overwhelmingly for the Democrats. Amarillo and Dallas are prime centers of Republican support; Houston and Lubbock are good; Fort Worth, Beaumont, Austin, El Paso, and Wichita Falls are fair. The urban vote can be attributed partly to good organization and dedicated individuals, but also to the influx of managerial, professional, and white-collar people who tend to be disproportionately Republican. Immigration from other states has been very important in this regard; but rural to urban flows within the state are also significant. Three geographical areas of Republican loyalty are of especial interest. The German-American counties around South Central Texas near San Antonio have

---

[18]The election figures were obtained from the secretary of state's office.

[19]The information about support of the Republicans is drawn largely from James R. Soukup, Harry Holloway, and Clifton McCleskey, *Party and Factional Division in Texas*, University of Texas Press, Austin, 1964; and Clifton McCleskey, *The Government and Politics of Texas*, 4th ed., chap. 4, Little, Brown and Company, Boston, 1972.

supported Republicans for years. Their support goes back to the Civil War when they opposed slavery and the Confederacy. However, changes are occurring in their allegiances. Most of the Panhandle counties are strongly Republican. This is probably because of the similarity of that area to the plains states where Republicanism and nonracial issues have predominated. A third area is Midland-Odessa. Relatively new, the oil-rich counties are populated with professional, managerial, and white-collar occupational groups, many associated with the oil industry. These groups tend to be Republican and conservative and are very influential in the area.

The Republicans still have a long way to go before becoming a regular second party in Texas. The weakest link in the chain is at the county, district, and precinct levels. But many factors favor Republicanism, including conservative Democratic disenchantment with the national Democrats, the changing economy, the efficient organization and the dedication of many Republicans, the conservative tradition of the state, and splits within the Texas Democratic party. A factor of considerable moment for the future is the political course mapped by former governor and former Secretary of the Treasury and of the Navy, John B. Connally. Connally switched to the Republican party in 1973 after heading Texas Democrats for Nixon in 1972 and serving in the Nixon Cabinet.

Liberal Democrats

V. O. Key, writing about Southern politics in the 1940s, declared that the Democrats of Texas had evolved a bifactionalism consisting of liberals and conservatives.[20] Controversies over the economy and ideology generated meaningful political divisions between the two factions. Today, it is commonplace to refer to the liberal and the conservative Democrats, although some would also like to add a third group, the moderates.

The New Deal and President Franklin D. Roosevelt proved to be too liberal for many conservative Democrats in the 1930s and 1940s.[21] A threatened split from the Democratic party by a group called the "Jeffersonian Democrats" failed to materialize in 1936, but in 1944 the "Texas Regulars" bolted the state Democratic party and placed their own candidates for President and Vice President on the general election ballot. Persons of similar persuasion joined the Dixiecrat or States Rights party in 1948, which also had its candidates for President and Vice President on the Texas election ballot. During these years of conservative bolts, the

---

[20]Key, *op. cit.*, pp. 254–271.

[21]For an account of factionalism in the 1930s and early 1940s, see Seth S. McKay, *Texas Politics, 1906–1944*, pp. 397–466, Texas Tech Press, Lubbock, 1955.

liberals were the loyalists. They roundly condemned the conservatives for deserting their own party. But in the 1950s and early 1960s it was the liberals who bolted from the conservative-dominated Democratic party state conventions. Groups such as the Democrats for Texas (DOT) were formed to carry on the cause of liberalism within the state.

The Democratic party primary was the scene of many a skirmish between liberal and conservative candidates. One highlight was the candidacy in the 1946 gubernatorial primary of liberal Homer P. Rainey who had been deposed as president of the University of Texas after a dispute with the Board of Regents. He was defeated by conservative Beauford Jester. Ralph Yarborough, leader of the liberals, was defeated in his quest for the governorship by conservative Allan Shivers in 1952 and 1954 and conservative Price Daniel, Sr., in 1956. Finally, however, in a historic victory for the liberal Democrats, he won a seat to the United States Senate in a special election called in 1957 to fill the vacancy created by the resignation of Price Daniel, Sr. Yarborough won a regular six-year term in 1958 and again in 1964. However, he was defeated in the 1970 and 1972 Democratic primaries. The U.S. Senatorship was the highest office and only statewide office held by a liberal Democrat up to 1972 except for Governor Allred's election in the 1930s. The similarity with the Republicans on this score is striking.

In the 1960 presidential election, the liberals supported the successful candidacy of John F. Kennedy for President and Lyndon B. Johnson for Vice President. In 1962, John Connally, then Secretary of the Navy in the Kennedy administration and long-time associate of Lyndon Johnson, decided to run for governor of Texas. He barely defeated Don Yarborough, the liberal who is no kin of Ralph, in the Democratic primary, but went on to win the election. The divisions within the Texas Democratic party were of concern to the Kennedy supporters when preparations were underway for the 1964 presidential campaign. To gain support in Texas and to attempt to get the warring factions together, President Kennedy made his fateful trip to Texas in November, 1963.[22]

The assassination of President Kennedy altered at least temporarily the course of Texas politics. It elevated a Texan to the Presidency who won liberal support for his domestic program but violent opposition to his Vietnam war policy.

The assassination contributed to John Connally's success in state politics. Wounded in the assassination, he received a great outpouring of

---

[22]Accounts differ as to the real reason for Kennedy's trip to Texas in 1963. The explanation for the trip most often given is that it was designed to patch up the feuding Texas Democratic party. See William Manchester, *The Death of a President*, p. 3, Harper & Row, New York, 1967. However, Governor Connally claimed it was to raise money for the campaign.

sympathy and proved unbeatable at the polls, winning handily his races for governor in 1964 and in 1966. Liberals were stymied in their campaigns for statewide office. However, in 1970 a moderate, Bob Armstrong, defeated a conservative, Jerry Sadler, the incumbent general land commissioner.

Despite the failure to win statewide offices, the liberals began to take on new life in the Texas Legislature. Aided by reapportionment, the Texas Senate began to change political complexion, and by 1971 was dominated by liberals and moderates. The Texas House of Representatives, however, remained relatively conservative until 1973.

Along with the changing complexion of the Texas Legislature, the liberals could also take some comfort in the changes in state policies. The trend was clearly in a moderate to liberal direction. Governor Connally in particular is credited with leadership in education and water resources, but Governor Price Daniel, Sr., and more recently, Governor Preston Smith promoted more liberal measures than had been anticipated. Governor Smith in his second term supported many liberal causes. The call for states' rights was submerged into new kinds of cooperation and less conflict with the national government under the Creative Federalism of President Johnson and the New Federalism of President Nixon.

The year 1972 turned out to be an unusual one for the liberals, and despite a mixed bag of election outcomes, it may be a turning point for them. The Sharpstown bank and insurance scandals mentioned in Chapter 1 shook the conservative leadership at the statehouse to its foundations. Irrespective of their guilt or innocence, all the top leaders, including the governor, the lieutenant governor, the speaker, the attorney general, and many of the Texas legislators as well were defeated in the Democratic primaries. Although liberals were not necessarily victorious, they made an impact. Ben Barnes, speaker of the House at the age of twenty-six, lieutenant governor at the age of thirty, and sometimes referred to as a potential presidential candidate, was defeated in the Democratic primary in his bid for the governorship. Liberal state representative Frances "Sissy" Farenthold of Corpus Christi received more votes than either Barnes or incumbent Governor Preston Smith. Smith won fewer votes (under 10 percent) than any incumbent governor in Texas history. Mrs. Farenthold won the right to oppose conservative Dolph Briscoe in the runoff which she lost. Liberals generally supported William P. Hobby of Houston, son of a former governor, for the lieutenant governorship against state Senator Wayne Connally, brother of John, in the runoff; Hobby won. Many liberals also supported John Hill against Crawford Martin for Attorney General. The speaker of the House, Gus Mutscher of Brenham, lost his House seat after resigning as speaker; his replacement,

Rayford Price of Palestine, also lost his race. The newly elected speaker of the 1973 legislature, Price Daniel, Jr., of Liberty, had the backing of liberals.

In the races for seats in the U.S. House of Representatives more gains were made for the liberals in 1972. State Senator Barbara Jordan of Houston, the first black woman in the Texas Senate, won her race for Congress. Charles Wilson, also a state senator of a liberal-moderate hue, won his race for the U.S. House. They joined a handful of liberals among the Texas delegation, including Bob Eckhardt of Houston and Henry B. Gonzales of San Antonio.

The 1972 Democratic party conventions were also of historic significance for liberals. For the first time they were given a share of delegates based on their relative strength at each level of the convention series. The ban on the unit rule was a great step forward from their standpoint. A liberal was elected vice chairman of the June Democratic state convention in place of the choice of the Democratic candidate for governor. The liberal was a black woman from Dallas, now state Representative Eddie Bernice Johnson. The September state Democratic convention elected two liberals to the enlarged national Democratic committee.

Where do liberal Democrats get their support?[23] Some rural counties in east and central Texas, a few in the Panhandle, and some in far west Texas have fairly consistently supported liberal Democrats in the primaries. Some of the support can be traced to the agrarian radicalism of the nineteenth century. The votes for liberals in the urban areas vary widely, but generally the liberals split the vote about equally with the conservatives in the primaries, at least in the twelve most urban counties. The organized labor movement has aided the liberals, and counties along the Gulf Coast where labor is strong tend to be liberal. These include Jefferson, Hardin, Galveston, and Harris counties and farther down the coast, Nueces County. El Paso and Presidio in far west Texas and Maverick County along the border are also good sources of support.

In addition to the support of organized labor and some of the farm groups, the liberal Democrats have friends among the blacks, college students, intellectuals, and some Mexican Americans. The percentage of blacks registering in Texas is higher than that of whites.[24] Their votes which are overwhelmingly liberal can be very significant. The Mexican-American vote is divided in loyalty. In the machine-dominated south Texas counties, the votes are conservative in some elections and liberal in others. In recent years some of the younger and more militant Mexican

---

[23]Soukup et al., *op. cit.*; McCleskey, *op. cit.*
[24]U.S. Bureau of the Census, *Statistical Abstract of the U.S.: 1972*, 93d ed., p. 374, U.S. Government Printing Office, Washington, D.C., 1972.

Americans are working in their own party, La Raza Unida, rather than for liberal Democrats. Others work with the liberals. The lowering of the voting age to eighteen was regarded as a boon for the liberals in Texas; but so far it is not clear that the vote of the young people is predominately liberal. However, a significant element of the college population supports liberal candidates. The group called the intellectuals is composed of a variety of persons, including journalists and university and college faculty. *The Texas Observer*, a fortnightly, is regarded as a voice of the liberals in Texas.

The liberal Democrats share in common with the Republicans the need to find more voters. It has been estimated that they can count on about one-third of the Texas electorate in state races.[25] New Texas election laws on single member districts, voter registration, residence requirements, and aid to illiterates ought to increase the votes for liberals. However, conservative Democrats, to whom we now turn, also receive votes from groups aided by these laws.

Conservative Democrats

It has been impossible to discuss Texas politics without constantly referring to the conservative Democrats who have controlled the state for many years. In harmony with the dominant individualistic and traditionalistic political culture of the state, the conservative Democrats have won a wide support diffused throughout the state. Since the 1940s, the conservative Democrats have held virtually all statewide offices, almost all the congressional delegation, most of the state legislature seats, and most of the district, county, and precinct offices as well.

Support for the conservative Democrats comes from both rural and urban areas.[26] It has been mentioned already that the liberals and the conservatives divide the votes in urban areas about equally. In the rural areas the conservatives do better than the liberals. Conservative candidates for governor, Preston Smith and Dolph Briscoe, for example, have outpolled the liberals there as well as the Republicans. Geographically, the conservative Democrats can count on some of the same areas as the Republicans—the Panhandle, the south plains area between the Panhandle and far west Texas, and counties around San Antonio. However, interestingly enough, the large but sparsely populated counties of far west Texas—Brewster, Presidio, Jeff Davis, Culberson, Reeves, and Pecos—are not among the top counties for the conservatives.

The 1972 election year was an unusual one for the conservatives as

[25]James E. Anderson, Richard W. Murray, and Edward L. Farley, *Texas Politics: An Introduction*, p. 85, Harper & Row, New York, 1973.
[26]Soukup et al., *op. cit.*, and McCleskey, *op. cit.*, chap. 4.

it was for the liberals and the Republicans. For one thing, there was no strong conservative Democratic leader in charge of the Democratic party. Democrats like John Connally were for Nixon in the presidential race; leaders like Barnes and Smith were lame ducks; and the Democratic nominee for governor, Dolph Briscoe, had not yet developed into a strong leader before the elections.

The conservative Democrats will probably find it difficult to maintain their supremacy for many more years, challenged as they are by the Republicans on one side and the liberal Democrats on the other. In addition, there are third parties to be reckoned with. Should the liberal Democrats ever gain control of the Democratic party machinery, it is likely that an exodus of conservatives to the Republican party will occur—more so than in the past. However, as long as the conservatives control the Democratic party machinery, there is no need to leave it.

Third Parties

Third parties have frequently played a major role in state politics. Examples abound and include the Progressives in Wisconsin, the Farmer Labor party in Minnesota, the Non-Partisan League in North Dakota, the Liberal and Conservative parties in New York, and the Populist party in Texas and in other states in the nineteenth century.

During the past thirty years the Texas ballot has contained candidates from the right or conservative fringes of the political spectrum. The Texas Regulars and the States' Rights party have been mentioned. In addition two parties, the Conservative and the Constitution, have had candidates, including such notables as General Douglas MacArthur. However, the most important conservative third party by far during these years has been the American Party. George Wallace was the candidate for President in 1968 and polled 584,369 votes or 19 percent of the total. He carried twenty-two counties, all but four being in East Texas, and in forty-six counties he ran second. Preliminary analysis suggests that Wallace drew about evenly from Humphrey, the Democratic candidate who carried the state, and Nixon, the Republican.[27] George Wallace waged his presidential campaign within the Democratic party in 1972. The American party fielded candidates, nonetheless; but without Wallace it did not do well nationwide and in Texas was not even on the ballot. The American party candidate for President, John G. Schmitz, received 6,039 votes in the write-in column.

On the left side of the political spectrum, Texas has seen candidates

[27]McCleskey, *op. cit.*, p. 116.

of several parties during the past forty years. Most recently, the Socialist Workers party has been successful in placing candidates for several statewide offices on the general election ballot. In 1972 the candidate receiving the most votes was Anne Springer who won 98,586 votes in the race for comptroller. Various splinter groups were formed to protest the Vietnam war. The New party formed after the 1968 Democratic convention held a national convention in 1972 and nominated Dr. Benjamin Spock for President. However, the party did not have candidates on the Texas ballot.

The third party of greatest interest in 1972 was La Raza Unida which had been functioning as a regional and local party since 1970. The party ran candidates for U.S. Senator, governor, lieutenant governor, and treasurer. Ramsey Muniz, the candidate for governor, polled 214,118 votes, enough to allow the party to hold a primary in 1974. The party has won a few offices in south Texas at the local level. It began in Crystal City and holds elective offices there, as we noted in Chapter 1.

CONCLUSIONS

Texas politics has often been the despair of those who attempt to make predictions. However, it is true that Texas politics is changing. The old one-party system as we have known it appears no longer capable of containing the numerous divisions and forces at work within the state. Just what will evolve no one can say for sure.

Chapter 5

The Texas Legislature: Organization and Powers

The Texas legislature is the first of the three great departments or branches of state government established by the Texas constitution,[1] and rightly so. It bears a special relationship to the people of Texas. It is their branch, so to speak, more so than the executive and the judiciary because the legislature consists of numerous representatives elected on a regular and frequent basis by the people from all sections of the state. It is also the major policy-making branch, deciding in the name of the people what laws shall be enacted. In an age when the executive branch has become the dominant branch all over the world, Texas is different. The legislature is reputedly the strongest of the three branches of Texas government and a powerful force to be reckoned with in state politics.

BICAMERALISM

The Texas legislature is composed of two houses, the House of Representatives and the Senate. Only Nebraska among the American states has a

[1]Section 1 of Article III of the Texas constitution reads as follows: "The Legislative power of this State shall be vested in a Senate and House of Representatives, which together shall be styled 'The Legislature of the State of Texas.'"

one-house, or unicameral, legislature. Unicameralism has, however, once again become a current reform topic as a result of reapportionment and the legislative modernization movement, both of which will be discussed later in this book. Unicamerialism is unlikely to be adopted soon in a state as conservative and as large as Texas. Also, the two houses are considerably different, and this may prove an obstacle. (It has been said that Texas has two unicameral legislatures!)

The House of Representatives is the larger of the two houses, consisting of 150 members, which is the maximum permitted by the Texas constitution. This makes it one of the largest in the nation, the median size being 100. The term of office of a House member is two years. A member must be twenty-one years of age, a qualified voter, a citizen of the state for two years, and for the last year a resident of the district from which he is elected.

The Senate is composed of thirty-one members who serve four-year terms. The terms are staggered to promote a more experienced body. The four-year term of one-half of the membership expires at one general election and the term of the other half at the next general election. (It may be recalled that general elections are held every two years.) However, the constitution directs that after each reapportionment, an entirely new Senate must be elected. Following such an election the cycle of staggered four-year terms then begins anew.

The qualifications for state senators are somewhat more stringent than for representatives. A senator must be twenty-six years old, a qualified voter, a citizen of the state for five years, and a citizen of the district for one year.

Constitutionally speaking, the House and the Senate are equal bodies. The Senate is, however, the more prestigious. Its smaller size allows for greater individuality and independence, and the longer terms of the members lead to greater experience. It is customary to speak of the House as the lower and the Senate as the upper chamber, although they are equal in that each body must approve in exactly the same language all bills, joint resolutions, and concurrent resolutions before they may be adopted. Nonetheless, each chamber has some powers denied the other. Revenue bills and impeachment proceedings must originate in the House whereas the Senate alone approves gubernatorial appointments and tries officials impeached by the House.

REPRESENTATION

Apportionment

The most important issue concerning state legislatures in recent years has been their system of representation or, more popularly, reapportionment.

A state legislature is composed of representatives elected by the people. On what basis shall the representatives be apportioned in order to be properly and fairly representative of the people? It may be recalled that the constitutional convention in Philadelphia nearly broke up over the issue of representation. The final result was a compromise by which a bicameral Congress was created with the members of the lower house apportioned on the basis of population and the members of the upper house on the basis of area with each state having equal representation.

The original constitutions of most of the states began with population as the basis of representation in both houses. In other words, representatives and senators each represented a given number of people rather than a county or some other geographical unit, such as a town. This was true of the Texas constitution of 1876 as well, except that senators represented qualified voters, a substitute for population, and no county was entitled to more than one senator.

The Texas constitution followed tradition by directing the legislature to reapportion itself after each Federal decennial census in order to take into account changes in population. This involved the practice of redistricting so that each district would contain equal numbers of people to be represented by the same number of representatives in the legislature. The one exception was that regardless of population no county could have more than one senator.

As the nation became urbanized (and it was not until 1920 that most Americans, for the first time, lived in urban places), state legislatures all over the nation grew reluctant to reapportion and redistrict after each census. The reason was primarily one of self-interest. Rural and small town legislators were fearful of losing their seats to the more densely populated areas. By the 1960s virtually all states, including Texas, were malapportioned—that is, legislators did not represent equal numbers of people. Malapportionment in Texas was compounded by an amendment adopted in 1936 which was deliberately designed to restrict the number of representatives from the urban areas. According to its terms, no county was allowed to have over seven representatives until its population exceeded 700,000. After that population point, it was allowed only one extra representative for each additional 100,000 people. Populous counties were denied equal representation in the legislature. For example, in 1960 Harris County (Houston) was assigned only twelve representatives, whereas on an equal population basis nineteen would have been required. It goes without saying that because of the constitutional restrictions, the Texas Senate was also malapportioned. Harris County with a population of 1,243,140 was allowed only one senator, the same as another district with only 157,454 people. The four most populous counties (Harris,

Dallas, Bexar, and Tarrant) had 35.7 percent of the state's population but only 12.9 percent of the senators.

For years there appeared to be no relief from malapportionment. The state legislatures would not act, and the courts followed the doctrine that the issue was a "political question," one not suitable for the courts. Then, the reapportionment revolution began. The U.S. Supreme Court in the famous case of *Baker v. Carr* held that apportionment of state legislatures was a justiciable issue.[2] It was ruled that malapportionment violated the equal protection of the laws clause of the Fourteenth Amendment to the U.S. Constitution by denying every citizen equal representation in state legislative bodies. By 1964 other reapportionment suits had been heard by the U.S. Supreme Court. The most important of these was *Reynolds v. Sims* in which it was ruled that both houses of a state legislature must be apportioned on the basis of population.[3] The "federal analogy" was specifically rejected—that is, the fact that the U.S. Senate was based on area (the state) did not mean that state senates could also be based on area (such as the county). The principle of equal representation was called "one man, one vote." The vote of every citizen was to count equally and to carry equal weight. Many other apportionment cases have been decided by the courts, and by no means are all the problems solved. One difficulty is that although it is reasonably simple to draw districts of equal population or substantially so, it is not easy to determine what is fair representation. For example, gerrymandering, or drawing districts to give an advantage to a particular party or faction, is possible with equally populated districts; in fact, it may be even easier than with unequal districts.[4]

The reapportionment revolution came to Texas in 1965. In a suit brought before a three-judge Federal district court sitting in Houston, the court declared unconstitutional the following three sections of the Texas constitution:[5]

1 The section restricting a county to one senator

[2]369 U.S. 186 (1962).

[3]377 U.S. 533 (1964).

[4]See Gordon E. Baker, "Redistricting in the Seventies: The Political Thicket Deepens," *National Civic Review*, pp. 277–285, June, 1972. The reason why it may be easier to gerrymander with equal districts than unequal is that a county or other geographical unit might be a natural political community in which the voters generally vote for candidates of the same party. When the criterion for redistricting is population only, then the county or other geographical unit may be split up and portions joined to other areas with no common interests to form a district equal in population to the others. The party or faction controlling the redistricting can break up the votes for the opposing faction or party by these splits. If area must be regarded in drawing up districts, it is less likely that natural political communities will be split for purposes of gerrymandering. At the same time, the districts might well be unequal in population if area or boundary lines must be preserved.

[5]*Kilgarlin v. Martin*, Civil Action No. 63 H 390, U.S. District Court, Southern District of Texas, Houston Division.

2   The section basing senatorial districts on qualified electors rather than population

3   The section limiting the number of representatives per county to seven until its population reached 800,000

A new reapportionment act was passed by the Texas legislature during the 1965 regular session, but it too was contested in the Federal courts. In a decision upheld by the U.S. Supreme Court, the new senatorial districts were accepted but the House districts were ordered reapportioned.[6] The House once again reapportioned in 1967.

The latest round of cases has followed the 1970 Federal census. The Texas legislature passed a new House redistricting law in 1971 in which gerrymandering was very much in evidence, reflecting the desire of the speaker to punish his opponents, called the "Dirty Thirty." The Texas supreme court in a suit challenging the law held that it violated the Texas constitution by unnecessarily disregarding county lines.[7]

The legislature failed during the regular session in 1971 to reapportion the Texas Senate. The task fell to the Legislative Redistricting Board. The board, which is composed of five state officials—the speaker, the lieutenant governor, the commissioner of the general land office, the attorney general, and the comptroller of public accounts—was created by a constitutional amendment approved by the voters in 1948. The board was established to provide a backstop in the event the legislature failed to redistrict. Inasmuch as the legislature had not redistricted since 1921, the need was obvious. However, the board had never been convened before 1971. Following the Texas supreme court decision invalidating the House districts, the board had been requested to redistrict the House as well. When it refused to do so, the Texas supreme court entered an order requiring it to redistrict the House.[8] The board thereupon redrew all the state legislative districts. The product was promptly challenged in four separate suits which were finally consolidated into one and heard by a special three-judge Federal court sitting in Austin.[9]

In addition to the argument that the House districts were unconstitutionally unequal in population, several other arguments were made by the plaintiffs. The most important was that the multimember House districts

---

[6]*Kilgarlin v. Hill*, 386 U.S. 120 (1967).

[7]*Smith v. Craddick*, 471 S.W. 2d 375 (1971). The Texas supreme court held that H.B. 783, the House districting law, violated Section 26 of Article III of the Texas constitution.

[8]*Mauzy v. Legislative Redistricting Board*, 471 S.W. 2d 570 (1971).

[9]The style of the case was *Register v. Bullock*. The four suits consolidated into one were as follows: *Curtis Graves et al. v. Ben Barnes, et al.*, Civil Action No. A-71-CA-142; *Diana Regester, et al. v. Bob Bullock, et al.*, Civil Action No. A-71-CA-143; *Johnny Mariott, et al. v. Preston Smith, et al.*, Civil Action No. A-71-CA-144; and *Van Henry Archer, Jr. v. Preston Smith, et al.*, Civil Action No. A-71-CA-145.

in the metropolitan areas invidiously discriminated against political and racial minorities. In Dallas County, for example, all eighteen of the representatives were elected from one multimember district. This meant, among other things, that each Dallas representative represented more people than any of the Texas congressional districts and a population larger than that of fifteen states. In addition, a place system was used, which has been fairly common in Texas. Each candidate had to run for one of the eighteen places. There was no residence requirement for any of the places; and as the court pointed out, all eighteen of the Dallas representatives could reside in the same apartment complex. The need to obtain a majority to win the place was also criticized for making it even harder for a minority to gain a voice in the Dallas delegation. Racial discrimination in the recruitment of Dallas County representatives was alleged. The charge was accepted by the court, which noted that historically racial discrimination had occurred in Dallas. Furthermore, the court agreed that there was an unconstitutional mixing of multimember with single-member districts in Texas. Harris County was the only large metropolitan county to be assigned single-member districts and gained an advantage over the other counties for that reason. For one thing, candidates for the House in Harris did not have to campaign over the entire county or contact so many people, making it less expensive to run there. The court also accepted the charge that multimember districting in Bexar County discriminated against Mexican Americans.

The final decision of the district court was that the House redistricting was unconstitutional whereas the Senate redistricting was constitutional. The court found the discrimination against blacks and Mexican Americans so blatant in Dallas and Bexar, respectively, that it ordered the immediate adoption of single member districts for those two counties. The legislature was ordered to redistrict the House by July, 1973. The U.S. Supreme Court denied a stay of the court's order pending appeal, and the new districts for Dallas and Bexar counties were drawn and residence requirements for candidates waived for the 1972 elections.

The U.S. Supreme Court ruled on the Texas legislative redistricting case in June, 1973.[10] It upheld the legislative districts drawn up by the Legislative Redistricting Board and reversed the decision of the lower Federal district court except for the requirement of single member districts for Bexar and Dallas counties. The nation's highest court was persuaded that the single member districts were a corrective measure for racial discrimination in the two counties. The decision of the U.S. Supreme Court was not unanticipated. The Court has been reasonably

[10] *White v. Regester*, 93 S.Ct. 2332 (1973).

strict when racial discrimination in the election process can be determined. At the same time, the Court adopted a more flexible stance toward state legislative redistricting early in 1973, permitting considerable population deviations among the districts.[11] The deviations of 9.9 percent in Texas were within its guidelines.

An important question to ask about reapportionment is what difference does it make? Although the final answer cannot be given until after a complete evaluation of performance before and after reapportionment, and even with the passage of time we may not be able to sort out all the different factors, it has already been apparent that reapportionment has had an impact. A large turnover of legislative personnel has occurred, with the average age somewhat lower, and urban areas, as would be expected, are better represented, although the suburban areas probably have the greatest advantage. In Texas there seems little question but that the complexion of both houses has changed. Nonetheless, it is not so clear that policy has changed very much. In fact, some observers have argued that the policy preferences of urban and rural legislators are not so different as anticipated and that increasing urban representation has not been very important in altering the output of the legislatures.[12] Nonetheless, it may be that the passage of some major legislation advocated by the Texas Urban Development Commission in 1970 reveals a more urban orientation on the part of the Texas legislature. For example, the legislature in 1971 established a State Department of Community Affairs and the Texas Advisory Commission on Intergovernmental Relations. Also, the state's first minimum wage law was passed in 1969 and mixed drinks were legalized in 1971.

Composition of the Legislature

Relevant to the Texas representation system is the composition of the Texas legislature—that is, who serves? Is the legislature really representative of the people? In the sense of being a microcosm of Texas the legislature is unrepresentative. Not all groups are represented in proportion to their numbers in the population at large. This has been particularly true of women, blacks, Mexican Americans, and Republicans. In the 1973 legislature, which represented a high point in representation of these groups, there were only six women, eight blacks, thirteen Mexican

---

[11]*Mahon v. Howell*, 410 U.S. 315 (1970).

[12]See, for example, Herbert Jacob, "The Consequences of Malapportionment: A Note of Caution," *Social Forces*, pp. 256–261, December, 1964; and Clarice McDonald Davis, "State Legislative Malapportionment and Roll-call Voting in Texas, 1961–1963," *Comment*, Institute of Public Affairs, University of Texas, Austin, 1962. However, some studies provide evidence of policy differences following reapportionment.

Americans, and twenty Republicans.[13] Also, young persons under thirty are underrepresented. Not a single senator in 1973 was under thirty; and only twenty-six representatives were, which amounted to 17 percent of the total House membership.

It is well known that attorneys are greatly overrepresented in the legislature in comparison with other occupational groups in the population. In 1973, about 71 percent of the senators were attorneys as were about 46 percent of the House members. Businessmen, farmers-ranchers, and teachers are some of the other occupational groups represented.

Members of the Texas legislature are more highly educated than the population at large. From two-thirds to three-quarters are college graduates. Insofar as religion is concerned, the legislators are overwhelmingly Protestant, with Methodists dominating in the Senate and Baptists in the House.

SESSIONS AND SALARIES

Texas is among a minority of states to retain regular biennial rather than annual sessions. Biennial sessions are a holdover from earlier times when lack of public business and an acute distrust of the legislature were key factors in reducing the time available to state legislatures. Most states are turning to annual sessions in an effort to cope with the demands of a complex, urban society in an era of rapid change.

The Texas constitution provides for biennial sessions not to exceed 140 days in length. Before 1960, there was no limit on the length of the legislative session, but the compensation, which was on a per diem basis, would cease after 120 days. The 140-day limit went into effect with the adoption in 1960 of an amendment allowing the legislature to set an annual salary not to exceed $4,800. In addition, the amendment provided for $12 per day for expenses up to 120 days of the regular session (a holdover from the 120-day limitation on pay) and mileage to and from the sessions not to exceed 10 cents a mile. The compensation schedule set forth in the Texas constitution is supplemented by legislative rules and statutes. For example, for the 1973 regular session, the House voted to allow each member $1,400 a month for staff salaries, $875 a month for office expenses, and $120 monthly for postage over and above other expenses. The senators voted themselves $5,000 a month for staff salaries and unlimited expense accounts. For the interim period between regular sessions, the House reduced the staff salary allowance to $1,200 monthly for each member, but it retained the other figures given above. The Senate

---

[13]Data about members of the legislature may be obtained from the Chief Clerk, Texas House of Representatives, and the Secretary, Texas Senate.

reduced the salary allowances to $2,800 monthly and retained the unlimited expense account. In addition, legislators are members of the state employee retirement system and come under social security.

In addition to the regular biennial session, which by law is convened on the second Tuesday in January of the odd years, the governor may call the legislature into special or called sessions not to exceed thirty days. There is no limit on the number of these special sessions, and one might very well follow another without a break. The governor also sets the agenda for the special sessions. Unless bills fall within the "governor's call," they may not be considered. It is common, however, to introduce them anyway in the hopes that the governor will amend his call to include them. In fact, bills not on the call have actually been passed. Also, it is possible to take some kinds of action not requested by the governor during a special session. An interesting example of this was the impeachment and trial of Governor James E. Ferguson in 1917 at a special session. Needless to say, the governor had not put his impeachment on the agenda. Approvals of executive appointments by the Senate also may take place without being on the agenda.

Another point of interest about Texas legislative sessions is the 1930 amendment which provided for a split session composed of three distinct periods. The first period of thirty days' duration was designed for the organization of the legislature, the introduction of all bills and resolutions, and the approval of the governor's appointments. During the second period, also of thirty days, the legislature was to work in committees studying proposed legislation. Then, during the final sixty days the bills were to be given floor consideration and passed or defeated. At any time during the entire session, the governor could submit and the legislature could consider and pass emergency measures.

Designed in the hopes of avoiding the last-minute rush, the procedure has never been followed. Availing itself of the provision that by a four-fifths vote the periods could be dispensed with, the legislature has always voted not to follow the procedures. Nonetheless, the split session amendment has had an effect. "Free introduction" of bills ceases after the first sixty days—that is, after sixty days special permission is needed to introduce them. Also, the Senate requires a four-fifths vote to consider a bill during the first sixty days, and this makes it impossible to pass controversial legislation early in the session.

As a final point we may note that the regular biennial sessions of the Texas legislature have been numbered consecutively since the state entered the Union. The legislature meeting in 1973 was the sixty-third in the history of Texas.

PRESIDING OFFICERS

Speaker

The speaker is the presiding officer of the Texas House of Representatives. He is formally elected by the House from among its own members every two years at the beginning of the regular session. A majority vote determines the outcome. Traditionally, the selection of the speaker has been a spirited affair. Toward the end of each session the candidates for the speakership of the next session will announce and try to get as many members pledged to them as possible. After the primaries, the candidates and their supporters will travel over the state to see new members in an attempt to get their support. The governor may use his influence, and the lobby, too, will play an important part. Thousands of dollars have been spent on campaigns. Except in rare instances, the outcome is settled long before the legislature meets for its regular session, and there is no contest on the floor. However, the selection of the speaker has been under attack of late, particularly as a result of the Sharpstown stock fraud affair, and some changes have been occurring. A departure from precedent occurred during the second called session of the 1971 Legislature when Rayford Price was elected to replace the speaker who had resigned. The vote was open to the public and was very close. As we shall see in Chapter 7, new laws were enacted in 1973 governing the campaign for the speakership although a bill to limit the speaker to one term failed.

The powers of the speaker may be briefly summarized as follows:

1 Exercising the usual powers of presiding officers in keeping order, putting questions to vote, etc.
2 Recognizing members who want to speak
3 Appointing the chairman and vice chairman of all committees; the entire membership of the Calendars, Rules, and House Administration Committees and half of the membership of the other standing committees; and all members of special (select) and conference committees
4 Referring all bills to committees
5 Interpreting the standing rules and ruling on points of order
6 Taking part in the debate if desired
7 Voting on all questions if desired

According to the House rules, the speaker may, if he wishes, designate another representative to be speaker pro tem. Otherwise, he simply turns the gavel over to any of his fellow representatives when he is not presiding.

The speaker is assisted by a parliamentarian whom he appoints.

Other house officers and employees work for the house as a whole and include the sergeant-at-arms and the several clerks—chief, calendar, journal, engrossing, and enrolling. Many a college student has served as an assistant sergeant-at-arms or in some other capacity during the sessions.

The speaker is paid the same salary as any member of the House, although he is given an apartment in the capitol building, the maintenance of which is also provided for by the State.

Lieutenant Governor

The lieutenant governor is the presiding officer of the Texas Senate. He is not a legislator, however. He is one of the seven executive officials listed in the Texas constitution in Article IV, to be discussed in Chapter 8. In sharp contrast to the Vice President of the United States, the lieutenant governor is the real presiding officer of the upper chamber. In fact, he is one of the most powerful men in Texas government and is sometimes regarded as more powerful than the governor.

Unlike the speaker, the lieutenant governor is selected in a statewide election. He runs his own campaign rather than joining the governor. In other words, the national practice of running the President and Vice President as a team is not observed in Texas. Senators may very well assist the candidate for the lieutenant governorship, and he may request their help. Candidates for lieutenant governor frequently are senators who have established ties with fellow senators prior to the race.

The powers of the lieutenant governor parallel those of the speaker with two exceptions:

1   The lieutenant governor cannot vote except to break a tie when the Senate is in official session.
2   The lieutenant governor possesses a greater appointment power, although this was not the case prior to the Sharpstown affair when both presiding officers held unlimited appointment powers. Their respective powers will be examined in more depth in the next chapter. Suffice it to say that the lieutenant governor appoints the chairmen and vice chairmen of all committees and all members.

The lieutenant governor is paid the same salary as a member of the legislature except when he is serving as governor. There is even less justification for this than there is for paying the speaker his low salary, inasmuch as it is quite clear that the lieutenant governor serves the entire state, which is his constituency rather than a single district. The speaker, as a member of the House, is elected from a district and not the entire state. The lieutenant governor, like the speaker, is entitled to the use of an apartment in the capitol, the maintenance of which is provided for by the State.

The senators elect from among their number a president pro tempore to serve as presiding officer in the absence of the lieutenant governor or whenever a vacancy exists in the office of lieutenant governor. The president pro tem is elected at the beginning of every session, both regular and called. The position is purely ceremonial, although should a vacancy occur in both the governorship and the lieutenant governorship, the president pro tem would become governor. By tradition, the governor and lieutenant governor always contrive to leave the state at the same time for one day during the term of a given president pro tem.[14] This enables him to be governor for a day. This is a unique occasion for the senator so honored. A special swearing-in ceremony is staged and a number of social events is arranged. Occasionally, attention is paid a project in which the president pro tem is particularly interested.

The lieutenant governor appoints a parliamentarian to serve during his term. As is true of the House, a number of other officers and employees also serve the Senate. The most important of these is the secretary of the Senate who supervises about 600 Senate employees. He is among the highest paid of all state officials, receiving in 1973 a salary of $30,000.

COMMITTEES

The Texas legislature, in common with other American legislative bodies, works through its committees. Woodrow Wilson years ago referred to Congress as committee government. This statement is applicable to Texas today. The Texas constitution requires all bills to be referred to committees, which is one indication of their importance. There are several kinds of committees. The standing committees are the regular or permanent committees. Special or select committees handle special assignments and are temporary. Joint committees consist of members of both houses. The conference committee is a special kind of joint committee. It is temporary, consists of ten members—five from each chamber—and its mission is to resolve differences between the houses on a bill passed by both. More information will be devoted to committees in Chapter 6.

[14]The governor or the lieutenant governor may not actually be out of the state although officially each is.

ASSISTANCE TO THE LEGISLATURE

To help the Texas legislature perform its many and complicated tasks several state agencies have been established for this purpose or are available. In addition private groups may be of assistance.

Texas Legislative Council

For years one of the greatest problems facing the Texas legislature was the lack of factual information concerning the problems with which it had to deal. To provide itself with a research arm the legislature, following the lead of other states, established the Texas Legislative Council in 1949.

The seventeen-member Council is composed of ten representatives appointed by the speaker and five senators appointed by the lieutenant governor. The lieutenant governor and the speaker serve as chairman and vice chairman, respectively. The Council in turn appoints an executive director who is in charge of research. The Council screens the numerous requests for research projects requested by the legislature. The staff, which is often supplemented by consultants, performs the research required to complete the projects.

The staff of the Council assists legislators in a variety of ways other than in conducting research projects. About 75 percent of the bills introduced by members are drafted by the staff; and legal and other advice is freely given year-round.

The Council has installed a computer system. Among other things, it tracks bills through the legislative process during the sessions. Also, Texas statutes have been put on magnetic tapes for storage and retrieval.

Legislative Budget Board

It would be difficult to overstate the importance of the Legislative Budget Board. Created in 1949 by statute, it prepares one of the two state budgets submitted to the legislature. The other budget is the one prepared by the governor. Both will be discussed in later chapters. The legislature not only favors the budget of the LBB, but it virtually ignores the governor's document.

The LBB is a ten-member statutory agency. The speaker, the chairmen of the House Revenue and Taxation Committee and the Appropriations Committee, and two other members of the House are members. On the Senate side, members are the lieutenant governor, the chairmen of the Finance Committee and the State Affairs Committee, and two other senators. The representatives and senators are appointed by the speaker and the lieutenant governor, respectively. In short, the LBB contains the most important members of the two houses.

The board appoints a budget director who is responsible for preparing the budget covering the state's expenditures for the ensuing two-year period, or in more recent years, occasionally for a one-year period. The budget, as well as the appropriation or spending bill to carry it out, is presented to the legislature soon after it meets in regular session (or in special session when there is a one-year budget).

In addition to the LBB, the state auditor's office and the comptroller of public accounts provide assistance in matters fiscal and budgetary. More information will be given about these officers in later chapters.

Legislative Reference Library

Of several library facilities in the capitol complex the most important for legislators is the Texas Legislative Reference Library, which is located in the capitol building itself. The oldest of the legislative service agencies, it provides legislators with legal references, bills, periodicals, and many other informational materials. It is open to the public as well. The library houses over 30,000 volumes relating to government, economics, politics, and law.

Note might be made too of the Texas State Library which administers the statewide library services and the State Law Library. Both are located on the capitol grounds.

Texas Research League

A private organization of long standing in Austin, the Texas Research League performs research activities upon request by the legislature and other branches of the state government as well as local governments. Financed by contributions from business and other private sources, the organization provides the service at no cost to the government. The league's fiscal studies for various legislative committees and commissions are among the best known.

Internship Programs and Presession Orientation

The legislature has been assisted in recent years by internship programs and presession orientations. A legislative internship program during the 1960s (from 1964 to 1969) enabled young graduates in law, political science, journalism, history, and similar fields to serve in the legislature in various capacities under supervision. The legislature and the Ford

Foundation contributed to the program. Interns served as committee clerks, performing bill analyses among other functions; as legislative aides in the governor's office; and so on. The Lyndon B. Johnson School of Public Affairs at The University of Texas at Austin currently maintains an internship program for its students, some of whom are assigned to the legislature.

The Texas Legislative Council and others associated with the legislature have held presession orientation sessions for new legislators for some time. In 1970, a more formal presession legislative conference to which experts were invited to make presentations was held for all legislators. It was sponsored by the League of Women Voters Education Fund and the Lyndon B. Johnson School of Public Affairs. The LBJ School has continued the conference under its conferences program.

PUBLIC INFORMATION ABOUT THE LEGISLATURE

Important in democratic government is the access of citizens to full, complete, and accurate information about the legislature. Until recently, the Texas legislature fell down badly in fulfilling this need. Each chamber is required by the Texas constitution to publish a journal of its proceedings. It is possible for the average citizen to receive a copy of each issue by requesting his legislator to put his name on the legislator's list for receiving copies. Each legislator is given a quota so that the number of citizens who can be served in this way is limited. The journals are available in many libraries across the state. They do not, however, contain more than the bare bones of legislative activities, including roll call votes, motions, captions of bills, and so on. The debates are not recorded. Texas has nothing comparable to the *Congressional Record.*

Beginning with the second called session of the 62nd legislature (1972) and continuing with the regular session of the 63rd legislature (1973–1974), records have been made for the first time of all the testimony given at committee hearings. Previously, motions and votes were about all that were recorded. The citizen had to read the newspaper or listen to the radio or watch television to give selected coverage of selected committees. At the present time the entire proceedings in a public hearing before a committee are recorded on tape. The tapes are available to the public for listening. Eventually they will be transcribed and placed in the Texas Legislative Reference Library.

The average citizen is dependent for virtually all his information about the Texas legislature from the news media. There are four major categories of news organizations that make up the capitol press corps. They are the wire services (Associated Press, United Press International), the largest daily newspapers in Texas, small local and weekly newspapers, and the electronic media—television and radio.

Representatives of the various organizations and services are housed in the state capitol building. A press table for their use is provided in each chamber. One is located on the floor of each house.

A new public service inaugurated by the 1973 legislature was the "hot line." Toll free calls may be made from anywhere in the state to a number in the capitol to find out the current status of any bill or resolution. The service is part of the electronic data processing system. Every bill and resolution is tracked through the legislative process.

There are also private services that for a fee will keep the citizen informed about the legislature during and between sessions. Lobbyists subscribe, usually as a matter of course, to these services. They receive daily digests of proceedings, bills introduced, news clippings from around the state, attorney general's opinions, court decisions, administrative regulations, notices of hearings, feature articles on Texas government, and so on. The private services cost more than the average citizen can usually afford and for that reason, if for no other, are not a substitute for public informational services.

LEGAL POWERS

Legislative Power

"The primary legislative power is that of enacting laws, and the most visible function of the legislature is to make public policy through drafting, considering, and passing bills and resolutions."[15]

The power to enact laws is a very important power in any modern society. In the Federal system the law of the states continues to be the nation's basic law despite the growth of the national government. Laws passed by the legislature affect citizens in innumerable and significant ways. In fact, it is difficult to do justice to the range and depth of legislation for which the Texas legislature is responsible. Chapter 11 reviews the major programs for which state money is spent—education, welfare, and highways are the big three. But this gives only an approximate idea of the breadth and importance of Texas laws.

It is strange that the legislature is not number one on the voter's hit parade since it is so important. Instead, most voters center their attention on the governor's race, if election statistics are our guide, rather than on contests for legislative seats. As a matter of fact, more interest may be

---

[15]Texas Legislative Council, *Texas Legislative Handbook*, p. 19, Austin, 1973. The handbook was prepared by Stanley K. Young.

generated in a race for county sheriff than in one for the legislature. Yet the platforms of the legislative candidates are sometimes more important than those of the gubernatorial candidates. The governor is powerless to carry out his legislative program without the cooperation of the legislature.

In addition to its legislative powers, important as they are, the Texas legislature also exercises nonlegislative powers. These will be reviewed briefly.

Constituent Power

A very important function of any state legislature is to take part in changing the state's constitution. Since there is no constitutional initiative in Texas, the only way that amendments to the state's fundamental law may be initiated is by legislative action. Calling a constitutional convention likewise involves the legislature. Or as was true of the amendment adopted in 1972, the legislature may itself sit as a convention. Subject to ratification by the people, then, the amendment and revision of the Texas constitution rest solely with the legislature. Another very important constituent power that should not be overlooked is the power to approve or reject amendments to the U.S. Constitution, once they have been submitted to the state legislatures by the Congress. If Congress chooses to submit the amendments to state conventions, the legislature also plays a role by providing for the election of delegates and other mechanics.

Administrative and Executive Power

Most of us do not realize that the legislature also has administrative powers. Gubernatorial appointees must be approved by the Senate. The legislature sets up administrative boards and commissions, defines their functions, appropriates the money for their support, and exercises general supervision and control over the entire administrative organization. The latter function is frequently called "legislative oversight." One of the state's two budgeting officers is a legislative agent. The executive and administrative officers may be called on for reports which they dare not, for political reasons, refuse to give. Through the state auditor, who is appointed by and is responsible to the legislature, there is a close check on all state expenditures. In the last analysis, officers of the executive branch may be impeached and removed by the legislature.

Investigative Power

One of the most important powers of the legislature, though not always used successfully, is that of investigation. Investigations may be conducted by either house or by both houses jointly. Each house usually has a general investigating committee, or a special committee may be appointed. Money is ordinarily made available to defray the expenses of the committee members and to provide the necessary clerks, stenographers, auditors, experts, etc. The attorney general and his staff may be asked for assistance. Any state agency or function may be investigated. The committees have the power to compel the production of books and documents necessary to the investigation, to compel the attendance and testimony of witnesses, and to administer oaths. False testimony given under oath is perjury. After the investigation is completed, the committee findings and recommendations, if any, are reported for the consideration and/or action of the legislature or the house concerned.

Electoral Power

The secretary of state delivers the returns of the election for the governor and lieutenant governor to the speaker of the House of Representatives on the first day after the organization of the legislature. A canvass of the returns is then made in the presence of both houses. Election is by plurality vote, but in case of a tie or contest, the legislature makes the decision. Although election returns for the other state constitutional executive officers are canvassed by the secretary of state, ties and contests in these elections are also settled by the legislature.

Judicial Power

It is common to classify some of the powers to which reference has been made as judicial or quasi-judicial because they resemble a court's power to hear and decide disputes. The power of the Texas House of Representatives to bring impeachment proceedings against officials and the power of the Senate to try them is judicial in nature. Impeachment is similar to indictment, and the Senate trial amounts to a trial with the Senate acting as a jury. Another judicial power is the power to order imprisonment for no more than forty-eight hours of persons who are judged guilty of disrespectful or disorderly conduct before the House or Senate.[16] This is similar to contempt of court proceedings. Legislators may also be judged by their peers for transgressions and punished by such means as public censure or expelled. Then, too, the legislature acts as the judge of the qualifications of its members when these are questioned. Judicial type powers to subpoena witnesses were mentioned in connection with investigatory powers.

[16]Texas constitution, Art. III, Sec. 15.

Congressional Redistricting: A Special Legislative Power

A special legislative power granted to the state legislatures by Congress is to draw up the districts from which members of the U.S. House of Representatives are elected. Congress assigns to each state the number of representatives to which it is entitled. Congress has varied as to the guidelines it provides in the drawing of the districts. Single-member districts are now required.

The Texas legislature had been derelict in redistricting the congressional as well as the state legislative districts prior to the reapportionment revolution. In fact, there had been no general redistricting law passed between 1933 and 1960. The Legislative Redistricting Board's jurisdiction does not extend to the congressional districts so there was no backstop in the Texas constitution. By the 1960s Texas had congressional districts with the largest population disparities of any in the nation. A decision by the U.S. Supreme Court in 1963 changed all this.[17] Although the case concerned Georgia and not Texas, the principle was set that congressional districts must be equal in population. The nation's highest court has recently distinguished between the degree of equality required of congressional as opposed to legislative districts. The former is to be more carefully scrutinized for equality than the latter.[18]

The Texas congressional districts were challenged in several suits in the 1960s and found unconstitutional. New districts had to be drawn to conform to the "one man–one vote" principle. The legislature in regular session in 1971 passed a new congressional districting act, using 1970 census data, and the act was promptly taken to court on the grounds of unconstitutional population disparity among the districts.[19] A three-judge Federal district court upheld the challenge and ordered the 1972 elections conducted under Plan C, one of three plans submitted by the plaintiffs. The U.S. Supreme Court granted a temporary stay, permitting the 1972 elections to be held under the 1971 law. Then, in a June, 1973 ruling, the high court decided that the 1971 law was unconstitutional but disapproved of Plan C.[20] The case was remanded to the lower Federal court for a decision as to what new plan of redistricting should be adopted to replace the 1971 law. In October, 1973, the lower court ordered the adoption of Plan B, which most closely tracked the 1971 law while at the same time satisfying constitutional standards of equality.

[17]*Wesberry v. Sanders*, 376 U.S. 1.
[18]*Mahon v. Howell, op. cit.*
[19]*Dan Weiser et al, v. Bob Bullock*, Civil Action No. CA-3-5202-D. For a discussion of the 1971 congressional redistricting law, see Wesley Chumlea, "Congressional Redistricting in Texas: Pattern for the 'Seventies,'" *Comment*, Institute of Public Affairs, University of Texas, Austin, November, 1971.
[20]*White v. Weiser*, 41 *U.S. Law Week* 4900 (1973).

Chapter 6

The Texas Legislature: Processes and Influences

To the casual visitor who views the Texas House of Representatives or the Senate from the gallery the legislative process may appear incomprehensible, absurd, or simply boring. The House may actually border on bedlam on occasion, and certainly has often lacked a sedateness people seem to expect. The Sharpstown stock fraud scandal, which cast a long shadow on the House, was apparently a sobering experience and seems to have encouraged a somewhat greater sense of dignity and decorum.

As a measure of the work performed, the glimpse from the gallery is very misleading. True, important action occurs on the floor of each chamber, but most of the actual legislative work takes place away from the chamber itself. The real work is often unseen and sometimes unsung. Endless committee meetings (noon, afternoon, and night), conferences with constituents who come to talk about legislation in which they are interested, interviews with administrative heads to satisfy job hunters, conducting a large correspondence, consultations with presiding officers and their staffs and other legislators, efforts to read all or part of the bills introduced, attending early morning delegation breakfasts or other meals with constituents or interest groups—here is where the real work lies. And toward the end of the regular session the pace gets very hectic indeed. There are many sleepless nights for the hardworking members of the legislature.

For the citizen who desires more understanding of the legislature it helps to look at the various stages through which proposed legislation must pass before becoming law. The legislative procedures are complex and detailed, but they can be mastered. Before reviewing the steps in detail, it is helpful to keep in mind that there are three major stages through which all bills must pass in each house:

1   Introduction
2   Committee consideration
3   Floor consideration

The fourth stage occurs after the bill has successfully survived the three stages in both houses. It is called:

4   Enrollment

PASSING A BILL

Introduction and First Reading

All proposals for laws, *i.e.*, "bills," in the Texas Legislature must be introduced by a member of the house in which the bill is introduced.[1] Unrestricted introduction of bills is allowed for the first sixty days. After that time, introduction of any bill except local bills, emergency appropriations, or emergency matters submitted by the governor is possible only by a suspension of the rules (which requires a four-fifths vote of those present) or by unanimous consent.

With the exception of proposals to raise revenue, which must originate in the House of Representatives, bills may originate in either house. In order to become laws, they must receive the affirmative action of both houses. For the purposes of this discussion, in which we shall follow the progress of a bill from its introduction until it becomes a law, we shall suppose that the bill originates in the House of Representatives.

Any member of the House of Representatives may introduce a bill by filing it in quadruplicate with the chief clerk, or a member may introduce it from the floor, although this is rarely done. If the bill proposes

---

[1]The Texas constitution speaks of bills when referring to proposed legislation. For example, in Section 30 of Article III, it is stated: "No law shall be passed, except by bill. . . ." However, the legislature also considers resolutions of various kinds and motions. These will be described later on in this chapter.

to alter an existing statute, the complete text of the old law must be given, additions underlined, and deletions enclosed in parentheses.[2] No bill, except a general appropriation bill, may contain more than one subject, which must be expressed in the title. The only actions taken upon introduction are that the chief clerk numbers the bill and the reading clerk reads it by caption to the House. The state constitution requires that for a bill to become a law it must be read on three separate days, but votes are taken only on the second and third readings. This requirement of three separate readings may be suspended in case of emergency, which must be stated in the bill in the form of an "emergency clause," by a four-fifths vote of those members present and voting. This reading of the bill by caption, or title, constitutes "first reading."

Reference to a Committee

The speaker then refers the bill to the proper committee. The House rules designate the types of bills by subject matter over which each committee has jurisdiction. In the 63rd legislature (1973–1974), there were twenty-one standing committees.[3] This was a considerable reduction from the forty-six committees of the preceding Texas House, which had given Texas the dubious distinction of having more House committees than any other lower house in the nation. However, the House also established twenty-three standing subcommittees, an action suggesting that the reduction of committees might be more apparent than real.[4] In Chapter 5 we noted that the speaker appoints all chairmen and vice chairmen of the standing committees and all members of three of the principal standing committees (Rules, Administration, and Calendars) and half of the members of the other committees. Members may select the committee on which they desire to serve, and seniority shall govern insofar as possible for half the membership of the standing committees other than the three mentioned. Seniority is defined as years of consecutive service in the

---

[2]In actual practice, this is done only with revisions of major laws.

[3]The twenty-one standing committees are as follows: Agriculture and Livestock, Appropriations, Business and Industry, Calendars, Criminal Jurisprudence, Education, Elections, Liquor Regulation, Natural Resources, Reapportionment, Revenue and Taxation, Rules, State Affairs, Transportation, Environmental Affairs, House Administration, Human Resources, Insurance, Intergovernmental Affairs, Judiciary, and Labor.

[4]The twenty-three standing subcommittees with their parent committee placed in parenthesis are as follows: Financial Institutions (Business and Industry); Industrial Development (Business and Industry); Consumer Protection (Business and Industry); Secondary Education (Education); Higher Education (Education); Vocational-Technical Training (Education); Pollution Control (Environmental Affairs); State Parks (Environmental Affairs); Wildlife Preservation (Environmental Affairs); Public Health (Human Resources); Mental Health and Mental Retardation (Human Resources); Public Welfare (Human Resources); Urban Affairs (Intergovernmental Relations); Local Government (Intergovernmental Relations); Texas-Mexico Relations (Intergovernmental Relations); Workmen's Compensation (Judiciary); Judicial Districts (Judiciary); Oil and Gas (Natural Resources); Water Conservation (Natural Resources); Executive Departments (State Affairs); State Institutions (State Affairs); Rail Transportation (Transportation); Motor Transportation (Transportation).

House. Each member of the House may select only one committee on the basis of seniority. The chairmen of the standing committees appoint members of the subcommittees falling within their jurisdiction.

As soon as the bill is referred to a committee, it is sent to the printer. The printed copy, called "first printing," includes the name of the committee to which the bill was referred and is then distributed to each member of the House.

Committee Consideration

Committee consideration of a bill is of tremendous importance. Since real deliberation is almost impossible on the floor of a legislative body, it is only in committee that a measure can be thoroughly studied. The standing committees hold regularly scheduled as well as called meetings throughout the session to consider the bills referred to them. Except for the Rules, Calendars, and House Administration Committees, no standing committee or subcommittee is allowed to meet while the House is in session without special permission by the House.

Before the bill is considered in committee, the committee staff will prepare a bill analysis which will be distributed to each committee member in advance of the meeting at which the bill will be considered.

No committee action or recommendation is valid unless taken at a formal meeting at which a majority of the members is present. Every committee meeting is open to the public, and public hearings for the purpose of getting citizen input are common. Advance notice of public hearings must be given to allow interested citizens time to make arrangements to come.

Much of the detailed work of the committees is done by special subcommittees appointed by the chairman of the standing committee. The establishment for the first time of standing subcommittees in 1973 indicates the importance of careful study by smaller groups than the full committees. There are at present two kinds of subcommittees—standing, which are described in the rules of the House, and more or less ad hoc subcommittees, which are appointed by the chairman to study a given bill not falling within the jurisdiction of the standing subcommittees. The House has long followed an "automatic subcommittee rule" whereby a bill is always referred to a subcommittee before action is taken by the full committee unless an exception is specifically made. Subcommittees report back to the parent committee following their study of a bill. Traditionally, some subcommittees have been created to kill bills. Some House members refer to them as the "deep freeze committees." Failure to report bills anywhere along the line means that they are dead for the session unless some special procedure is taken to force out the bills.

Committee Report

Committees do not report on all bills referred to them, and many bills are simply "pigeonholed." Provision is made, however, that, during the first seventy-six days of a regular session when a bill has been in committee for six days, the committee may be required to report, *i.e.*, discharged, by a two-thirds vote of the House. After the first seventy-six days, this may be done by a simple majority vote. The same provisions also apply to re-referring a bill to another committee.

Each committee report must include in summary a detailed analysis of the subject matter of the bill, specifically including (1) background information on the proposal, (2) what the bill proposes to do, (3) a section-by-section analysis of the content of the bill, and (4) a summary of the committee hearing.

Committee reports are advisory only and may take the form of a favorable report, an unfavorable report, a report of inability to agree, an amended bill, or a substitute measure. No minority report may be filed unless it has been signed by from two to four members of the committee (depending on the size of the committee) who were present when the vote was taken on the bill. If the report on the bill was unfavorable and a favorable minority report is not signed and filed with the calendar clerk within two days, the bill is dead.

Printing and Placing on the Calendar

After the committee has reported, printed copies, including any changes made in committee, of all favorably reported general bills are distributed to each member at least twenty-four hours before the bills are considered by the House, except during the last ten days of the session. Bills which receive an unfavorable majority report are not printed unless there is a favorable minority report and unless, within five days, permission to print is given by a majority of the House. In dealing with local bills, the committees may report favorably but with the recommendation that the bills not be printed. All other bills which receive a favorable committee report must be printed except on order of two-thirds of the House.

All favorably reported bills and those unfavorably reported but ordered printed by the House go immediately to the Committee on Calendars for assignment to one of eight calendars.[5] The purpose of a calendar is to determine the order in which bills shall be considered by the

---

[5]According to the House rules adopted in 1973 there are eight calendars, but one is concerned with motions of a memorial or congratulatory nature and does not really concern legislation. The seven important calendars are Emergency, Major State, Constitutional Amendments, General State, Local, Consent, and Resolutions.

House. The Calendars Committee is directed by the House rules to act promptly—seven days up to the last ten days of the session; and then it must act within seventy-two hours after referral. In the event the Calendars Committee fails to act within the time specified, it is in order for any member of the House to move that the bill be assigned to a specific calendar. The rules prior to the 1973 regular session required a two-thirds vote to sustain the motion during the first seventy-six days and only a majority during the remainder of the session. The rules of 1973 provided only for a simple majority throughout the session. After a bill or resolution has been assigned to a calendar, it retains its relative position until it reaches floor consideration although some exceptions can be made. When the bill has reached the top of the calendar to which it was assigned, it is then ready for floor discussion or "second reading."

Second Reading

All bills on their second reading are taken up in the order in which they appear on the calendar. However, every Monday (calendar Monday) the House may, by majority vote, take up a bill out of its regular order. Bills may also be taken up at any time regardless of their position on the calendar if they are made "special orders" by a two-thirds vote. Local and uncontested bills are considered at any time when ordered by a two-thirds vote of the House. Local bills, emergency measures submitted by the governor, and emergency appropriation bills have, in general, precedence over all other bills during the first sixty days of the session.

It is only on second reading, *i.e.*, when it is on its passage to engrossment, that the bill is given its first real consideration by the House. The bill is usually read by caption only, after which it is subject to debate and amendment. When the bill has been discussed and the amendments, if any, disposed of, the speaker puts (presents) the question of engrossment.[6]

[6]Both the House of Representatives and the Senate make occasional use of the legislative device known as the "Committee of the Whole," which is the entire membership or at least a quorum of either house sitting as a committee. It is ordered by a majority vote when it is desired to give further consideration to a bill on second reading or to enable all members to hear testimony on an investigation. The speaker does not preside but leaves the chair and selects someone else to serve as chairman. As far as they are applicable, the regular rules of procedure are followed. There is, however, considerably more freedom from parliamentary restrictions.

After the committee has finished its action on the bill, it then resolves itself back into a formal legislative body (with the speaker again presiding) and receives a report from the chairman of the Committee of the Whole. In other words, the formal legislative body officially receives a report of what it has just done as a committee. This report will consist of the official minutes of the committee, which are kept as though there had been a formal session. The bill then takes its place on the calendar, along with other bills on second reading, and is again subject to debate and amendment on the floor before a vote on passage and engrossment is taken, but the decisions of the committee are rarely, if ever, changed.

Engrossment

If a bill fails of passage to engrossment, it is dead unless a motion to reconsider it is made on the same or the following day by a member who voted on the prevailing side and the motion is passed by a majority vote. If the motion for engrossment carries, the bill is then sent to the engrossing clerk, where it is rewritten with all the amendments inserted exactly as passed. However, if the bill carries the emergency clause, the House may suspend the rules by a four-fifths vote and take up the bill on third reading and final passage immediately after passage to engrossment.

After the engrossing clerk has finished with the bill and the engrossed copy has been compared with the original and the amendments, the Committee on Engrossed Bills reports to the House that the bill has been correctly engrossed. The bill is then ready for its "third reading" and final passage.

Third Reading and Final Passage

The third reading is usually by caption only, and although discussion is in order, a two-thirds vote is required for amendment. After the bill has been read a third time, it is voted on for final passage. If it receives a simple majority vote, it is passed. If any changes have been made in the original bill during its progress toward final passage, it will be reprinted prior to its being sent to the Senate.

Action by the Senate

When received in the upper house, the bill follows substantially the same procedure as in the House of Representatives.[7] There are, however, a few major differences in the Senate rules:

1. The number of Senate committees is much less than in the House. During the third special session of the 62nd legislature (1972), new rules provided for a reduction to nine from the then existing twenty-seven standing committees.[8] There are also six standing subcommittees.[9] The

---

[7]Although it does not pertain to Senate consideration of House bills, it should be mentioned that the Senate, unlike the House, permitted the prefiling of bills prior to the convening of the 1973 regular session. The purpose of prefiling is to reduce the congestion that occurs during the early days of the session as hundreds of bills are drafted by legislative staff for introduction.

[8]The nine standing committees in the Senate are as follows: Administration, Economic Development, Intergovernmental Relations, Education, Finance, Jurisprudence, Human Resources, State Affairs, and Natural Resources.

[9]The standing subcommittees and their parent committee are as follows: Rules (Administration); Civil Matters (Jurisprudence); Criminal Matters (Jurisprudence); Nominations (State Affairs); Water (Natural Resources); and Agriculture (Natural Resources).

power of the lieutenant governor to make appointments to these committees was restricted during the third special session by a seniority system; but at the beginning of the 1973 regular session, seniority was virtually eliminated. The lieutenant governor appoints not only the chairman and vice chairman of each standing committee and subcommittee but also the membership of all standing committees and subcommittees. However, when making appointments to committees with ten or less members, three members must be senators who were members of the committee during the previous legislature; and four members of committees larger than ten must have so served.

2. A bill is printed only after the committee has reported on it, and then only if the report is favorable or on order of the Senate.

3. Calendars are very rarely followed. The usual way for a bill to be taken up on second reading is by motion, which requires approval of two-thirds of the senators, or during the first sixty days, four-fifths.

4. During the first sixty days a four-fifths vote is required to pass a bill. After that, only a simple majority is necessary.

Returning the Bill to the House

When the Senate passes or defeats a House bill, the secretary of the Senate so informs the House by message. If the measure has passed without amendments, it is sent to the enrolling and engrossing clerk of the House who then delivers a perfect copy to the speaker for signing. If, however, amendments have been added by the Senate, this fact is indicated in the secretary's message by the statement, "with accompanying Senate amendments." The bill is then subject to the following action by the House.

Action by the House on Bills with Senate Amendments

The amended bill is now printed and is considered privileged business. If it is agreed to by a majority of the House, the measure is passed. However, if the House does not accept the amended bill, a conference committee is usually requested. If the Senate does not agree to the request for a conference committee and insists that the House accept its amendments, the bill is dead unless the House or the Senate reconsiders and reverses its action which has caused the disagreement.

Sending the Bill to Conference

If the two houses do not agree on the bill, the usual course is to refer it to a conference committee. In the case of a bill introduced in the House, the initiative lies with that body which, by a simple majority vote, asks the

Senate for a conference. This action is reported to the Senate, and if agreed to by that body, again by a simple majority vote, the bill together with the amendments is sent to the committee.

All conference committees are composed of five members from each house and are appointed by the respective presiding officers. When the vote on the measure in the House has been close, two of its members on the committee are usually taken from those who voted on the losing side, *i.e.,* the minority, and three from the majority. When the vote has not been close, the minority is ordinarily given only one member. After the conference has been ordered but before the members of the committee have been selected, either house may instruct its members to follow a certain course of action as long as it is not in violation of the rules of that body concerning conference committees.

Action by the Conference Committee

The members of the conference committee from each house vote as a unit; therefore, a majority of the committee members from the House and a majority from the Senate must agree on the matter in dispute. Under rules approved by both houses only as recently as 1972 during a special session, the committee's action has been restricted to adjusting the differences between the House and Senate versions of the bill.[10] Before 1972 Texas had what was called a "free conference committee." The conference committee members were referred to as the "Ten Men Who Ruled Texas." These committeemen literally created new legislation, incorporating items not considered by either house and jettisoning provisions approved by both houses. The appropriations bill, which determines who gets what in Texas government, was handled in this manner; and it was not strange that a chorus of protest arose. Even the presiding officers were occasionally surprised to discover items in the appropriations law of which they were entirely unaware. The Sharpstown affair helped to clip the wings of the committee.

Report of the Conference Committee

After the committee has settled the question in disagreement between the two houses, the members report to their respective chambers. Their

[10]An idea of the limitations placed on the conference committees can be gained by the following excerpt from the Senate rules adopted by the Texas legislature in 1973: "Conference committees on appropriation bills, like other conference committees, shall limit their discussions and their actions solely to the matters in disagreement between the two houses." Price Daniel, Jr., speaker of the Texas House of Representatives of the 63rd Legislature, supported a bill, HB 5, which would have placed in the statutes the rules limitation on conference committees. It was killed in the Senate during the regular session. Once a bill is killed by either house, it cannot again be considered during the session, according to the Texas constitution.

HOW A HOUSE BILL IS PASSED

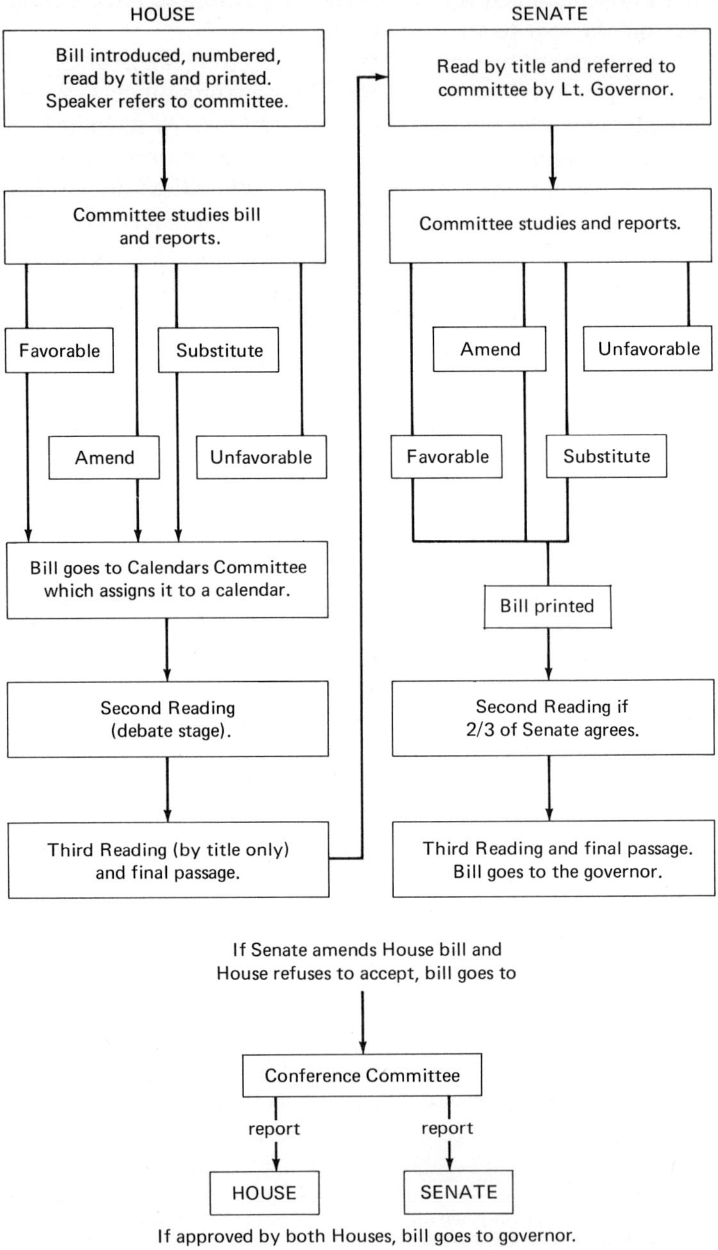

HOUSE
SENATE
Bill introduced, numbered, read by title and printed. Speaker refers to committee.
Read by title and referred to committee by Lt. Governor.
Committee studies bill and reports.
Committee studies and reports.
Favorable
Substitute
Amend
Unfavorable
Amend
Unfavorable
Favorable
Substitute
Bill goes to Calendars Committee which assigns it to a calendar.
Bill printed
Second Reading (debate stage).
Second Reading if 2/3 of Senate agrees.
Third Reading (by title only) and final passage.
Third Reading and final passage. Bill goes to the governor.
If Senate amends House bill and House refuses to accept, bill goes to
Conference Committee
report
report
HOUSE
SENATE
If approved by both Houses, bill goes to governor.

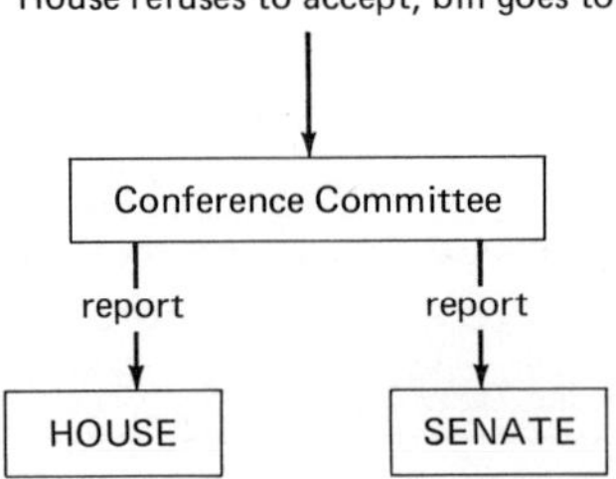

report may not be amended and must be accepted or rejected in full. If for any reason the report is not acceptable to either house, it may by mutual agreement send the bill back to the same committee for further consideration, or in the case of a House bill like the one we are considering, the House may request a new conference of the Senate. When no agreement can be reached by the committee itself, or if its report is not accepted by either house, the bill is dead.

Enrollment

When the report of the conference committee is agreed to by both houses, the bill is sent to the enrolling and engrossing clerk of the House for copying in its official, final form. After enrollment, the bill is then sent to the House Committee on Rules, and if the bill is found correctly enrolled, this fact is so reported to the House.

Signing by the Presiding Officers

The reading clerk of the House then reads the enrolled bill by caption, after which it is signed by the chief clerk and the speaker. Then the bill is sent to the Senate, where it is likewise read by title and signed by both the president and the secretary of the Senate.

Action by the Governor

After the bill has been signed by the presiding officers of both houses, it is sent by messenger to the governor for his action. If he signs the bill, or if he simply does nothing, it becomes a law; but if he vetoes it, a two-thirds majority of each house is necessary to override the veto and put the bill on the statute books.

When Bills Go into Effect as Laws

No bills passed by the legislature, except general appropriation acts, go into effect until ninety days after the adjournment of the session, except in case of an emergency, which must be stated in the preamble or in the body of the act and receive a record vote of two-thirds of those elected to each house. Such an emergency bill becomes effective as soon as it is signed by the governor or is filed without a veto with the secretary of state.

Ways in Which a Bill May Be Killed

A bill which has originated in the House of Representatives may be defeated at several different stages in its passage through the legislature:

1 The committee may fail to report the bill, and no action is taken by the House to keep it alive.

2 The bill may receive an unfavorable committee report with no minority report, in which case it does not go on a calendar for House consideration.

3 The House may refuse to consider the bill even though a minority report has been made.

4 The bill may never be reached on the calendar.

5 It may be tabled.

6 It may be postponed indefinitely.

7 It may be amended by striking out the enacting clause.

8 It may fail to pass to engrossment.

9 It may fail on third reading and final passage.

10 It may be defeated in the Senate by any of the above methods.

11 If the bill is amended by the Senate, the House may refuse to concur in the Senate amendments.

12 If a conference committee is appointed, it may not be able to come to an agreement on the differences between the two houses.

13 Either house (or both) may refuse to adopt the conference committee report.

14 Either house (or both) may fail to pass a vetoed bill by the required two-thirds majority.

Adoption of Resolutions

There are three types of resolutions: simple, concurrent, and joint. *Simple resolutions* require the action of only one house. They are voted upon only once, usually upon introduction, without having been referred to a committee. No action by the governor is necessary. They are used for such purposes as authorizing the creation of special committees, expressing the opinion of the body, adopting the rules, inviting distinguished speakers to address the legislature, memorializing a person, recalling a bill from the other chamber, authorizing expenditures from the contingent expense fund, determining the number and salaries of the employees, or dealing with anything affecting only that particular house.

Concurrent resolutions, which are practically the equivalent of joint resolutions in the national Congress, require affirmative action by a majority of both houses.[11] Most are not referred to a committee and are

---

[11]The legislature makes occasional use of concurrent resolutions to state its interpretation of a law or to give its opinion to an administrative body concerning the administration of a law. Although such resolutions have no real legal standing, they are not completely without influence.

usually voted on only once. Unless providing for *sine die* adjournment, they must be sent to the governor for his action and may be vetoed by him. They are primarily used to adopt the joint rules of the two houses, state the legislature's interpretation of laws, give permission to sue the state, memorialize a person, or request Congress to follow a certain line of action. They are not laws (as legislation may not be accomplished by resolution) and have no standing in the courts but are sometimes used to accomplish the same purpose as laws, as, for example, giving permission for an individual to sue the state.

Joint resolutions also require affirmative action by both houses, but action by the governor is not necessary. They are mainly used to propose an amendment to the state constitution, although they may also be used to recommend the calling of a state constitutional convention and to ratify a proposed amendment to the United States Constitution.

The procedure on joint resolutions is the same as for bills except where a proposal is being made to amend the state constitution. When this is the case, a two-thirds majority of those elected to each house is required for passage. In the House of Representatives such proposals are not given the usual three readings if the resolution receives the required two-thirds majority on the second reading. If it receives only a simple majority on the second reading, it is nevertheless passed to engrossment, and subsequent proceedings are the same as for the passage of a bill. It must, however, receive a two-thirds vote on third reading and final passage. Failure to get this majority at the final stage kills the proposed amendment, and it may not be brought up again unless a motion to reconsider is adopted or the rules are suspended by a two-thirds vote.

The Senate, acting under its own rules, requires that joint resolutions proposing constitutional amendments be given three separate readings on three separate days. A two-thirds majority is, of course, necessary for final passage.[12]

LEGISLATIVE INFLUENCES

A recital of the steps through which proposed legislation passes leaves out the interesting and intense drama that often develops and omits the immense and numerous pressures under which the legislature operates. After all, the procedures are not ends in themselves. They are used to accomplish goals. People differ, sometimes violently, over what government should and should not do. Politics has sometimes been defined as conflict over goals. It is important to know, then, *who* influences the

---

[12]This discussion of legislative procedure has been adapted from Dick Smith, *How Bills Become Laws in Texas*, 4th ed., Lyndon B. Johnson School of Public Affairs, University of Texas, Austin, 1973.

legislature and by *what methods* the legislature can be influenced to support or oppose policy goals.

General Public

In a democracy one would expect public opinion to be the biggest influence on the legislature insofar as determining what laws are passed is concerned. It is an influence but not in the manner often assumed. The voice of the general public or broad masses of people is generally not directly felt by the legislature. As we have already seen in Chapter 5, legislative races tend to be neglected by the voters. The public is also prone to neglect the legislature while it is in session. Polls in Texas have indicated that few people interviewed can remember what the legislature has done, either good or bad.[13] Occasionally, however, an issue arouses widespread concern—liquor by the drink, the sales tax, the Sharpstown scandal—and pressure is felt. For example, a proposed sales tax on food during the second called session of the 61st legislature (1970) brought on an outcry not soon to be forgotten. In the House gallery mothers and children carried placards reading, "Tax on Food—the Legislative Retirement Act," "Tax Beer, not Beans," and many others. But this is not typical. For the most part, when we deal with public pressures on the legislature, we are dealing with special interest groups who represent only segments of the mass public.

The Lobby

In contrast to the general indifference of the general public to the legislature is the keen interest of special publics. Individuals and groups seeking to influence the legislature (as well as other governmental branches and levels) constitute the *lobby.*

Contrary to the impression of some citizens, perhaps most, there is nothing sinister about the lobby per se. Any attempt to influence legislation—whether it be by the governor, the private citizen, the Texas State Teachers Association, the AFL-CIO, the League of Women Voters, the Texas Manufacturers Association, or the Baptist Convention, to give only a few examples—is lobbying. There is nothing wrong with frank, open, and honest lobbying. In fact, it is highly desirable and is really an exercise of the constitutional right of petition and free speech. Just as

---

[13]"The Texas Poll," *The Dallas Morning News*, Oct. 12, 1969. The Beldon poll asked respondents what they liked or disliked about the actions taken by the Texas legislature. Only about three in ten could think of anything they liked and only about five in ten anything disliked. For an article on how Illinois citizens feel about their legislature, see Charles W. Dunn and Samuel K. Gove, "Legislative Reform Vacuum: The Illinois Case," *National Civic Review*, pp. 441–446, October, 1972.

"every dog has his day in court," so every group or individual has a perfect right to press his views on the legislature as long as he does so within the confines of the law.

The Texas lobby differs, however, from the lobby in other states in certain respects. Although business groups are more numerous than any other kind of lobby group in all states in which studies have been made, they are regarded as more powerful in Texas.[14] Many business corporations, trade associations, and other business entities maintain year-round offices in Austin, which makes it easier to influence the legislature. The Texas lobby may also differ from that in other states by being more numerous. As we shall see, Texas law requires lobbyists to register. As many as 5,000 lobbyists have registered, many more than in other states with registration laws. In general, Texas has been classified as a strong pressure-group state and it would be anticipated that lobbying would play an important role in legislative processes and outcomes.[15] Although business dominates among lobby groups in Texas, there are many other kinds of lobbyists in Texas. During the regular session of the 63rd legislature (1973) several new lobbyists appeared on the scene. One was Common Cause, the Texas affiliate of the national organization founded by John Gardner in 1970. The purpose is to be a people's lobby, to represent general, broad interests not represented by the self-interested special-interest groups. Another new group was the Texas Women's Political Caucus, which was organized to encourage women to enter the political arena and to promote the interests of women by political means. Still another was NORML, an acronym standing for National Organization to Reform Marijuana Laws. Consumers and students each organized lobbies. Ecology groups continued their efforts from previous sessions. No doubt more groups will be organized as new interests develop.

Lobbyists employ a variety of methods to reach their goals. These will be reviewed briefly.

Influencing Nominations From the viewpoint of special-interest groups, the most successful method of lobbying is to influence the nomination in the primaries of those state officials who are in a position to

[14]See Bryan D. Jones, "Why the Texas Legislature Is the Way It Is," in Richard H. Kraemer and Philip W. Barnes, *Texas: Readings in Politics, Government, and Public Policy*, pp. 136–137, Chandler Publishing Company, San Francisco, 1971. When asked to identify the most powerful interests represented by lobbyists at the capitol, Texas legislators cited business interest more often than any other kind of interest. When compared with selected states where similar surveys had been taken, the references to business groups in Texas were greater: 64 percent in contrast to 28 percent in California and 42 percent in Ohio, the two states in the lowest and highest range. Groups representing education, particularly the Texas State Teachers Association, were identified by 14 percent of the representatives and 24 percent of the senators as powerful.

[15]Belle Zeller (ed.), *American State Legislatures*, pp. 190–191, Thomas Y. Crowell Company, New York, 1954. All the states are ranked according to their pressure-group strength on the basis of judgments expressed by experts in the states.

determine legislative policy, *e.g.*, the governor, lieutenant governor, and members of the legislature. Interested individuals, groups, and organizations are extremely active in races for the governorship and lieutenant-governorship and to a lesser extent in legislative races. Not only is the governor's legislative influence important to them but also his appointing power, as he can put "safe" men on the various state boards. The interest in the lieutenant governor with his immense power as the Senate's presiding officer needs no explanation here. Since the administration of a law is as important as the law itself, lobbyists and the groups they represent are also interested in influencing contests for other state offices. It is obvious that better control is to be had, not only of the legislature but of the administrative organization as well, by helping put the right men in key positions originally rather than attempting to influence them after election.

Groups with large memberships, like the American Legion, the Texas State Teachers Association, labor unions, etc., are in an especially favorable position. The candidates need votes to be elected. The organization has votes, often a large number. It may also have a particular legislative program. It is only natural, then, that prospective candidates will, to say the least, lend an attentive ear to the proposal of a well-organized pressure group with a large membership. If an agreement is reached, the candidate is endorsed by the group, and word is passed to the rank and file that "So-and-so" is their candidate. Large corporations may suggest to their employees that a certain candidate is a fine man who deserves support. Even church groups sometimes engage in this sort of indirect lobbying.

Then there are campaign expenses. It costs money to run for office—large sums of money for important statewide offices—and these expenses are increasing all the time. Huge sums are required for the necessary legitimate expenses for campaign headquarters, television programs, radio broadcasts, plane transportation for the candidates, newspaper advertising, billboard posters, campaign literature, etc. A candidate without funds simply cannot compete. In most instances, at least where statewide offices are concerned, he must either have funds from outside sources or give up all chances of obtaining the office.

Lobbyists and pressure groups, therefore, furnish campaign funds to candidates who share their views or will do their bidding (of course it is better to get a man who leans your way in the first place). In recent years, some persons interested in promoting certain social, political, and economic ideas have, instead of contributing directly to a particular legislative candidate, contributed to a central clearinghouse for campaign funds. The money is then used in those areas where it will do the most good.

Legislative candidates in rural areas, where campaign expenditures need not be so great, have been especially singled out for help in financing their campaigns. After all, a legislative vote from one area is just as good as one from another. If the legislator who has received assistance does not "deliver" once he is in office, he is marked for defeat at the next primary or election. In case interested individuals or groups have not contributed to the campaign of a successful candidate, then campaign debts still outstanding can be paid.

Too much emphasis cannot be given to the importance of assistance in financing campaigns. Some observers believe that this is the most effective method of influencing legislation. Many officials, both in the executive branch and in the legislature, enter office with political obligations due their financial supporters. Some members of the legislature could, in all propriety, be addressed by the presiding officers as "the gentlemen from this or that corporation or organization" rather than by the usual form of "the gentlemen from this or that county." If favorable legislators sit in the legislative body itself, the lobbyist in Austin can relax and assume the role of a benevolent onlooker, for he knows that his suggestions will be followed and his bills introduced and pushed. All the lobbyist has to do is to furnish information and instruction to the legislator and see that the instructions are carried out.

Retainers' Fees An especially common and possibly as effective method of exerting influence in the legislature is the payment of retainers' fees to the lawyer-legislators. There are many lawyers in the legislature. It is the business of a lawyer to represent the interests of his client. Many corporations, therefore, make a practice of putting legislative members of the legal profession, especially if they are committee chairmen, on their legal staffs. Then when a bill comes up involving the industry or business concerned, their representative is already sitting in the legislature, ready to care for the interests of his clients. Under these conditions, is the legislator a representative of his constituents or of his employer? Sometimes these retainers' fees are paid only temporarily, but on occasion they are a more or less permanent arrangement. The practice of putting legislators on the payrolls of corporations and pressure groups is legal, provided the legislators' actions do not violate ethics laws.

Favors to the Legislators All sorts of favors are extended by lobbyists to the legislators, their families, and friends. Passes to theaters and other places of amusement; guest privileges at private clubs; jobs to relatives and close friends; gifts of candy, fruit, liquor, etc.; opportunities to buy at wholesale; inside information on lucrative business deals;

buying or leasing property at below market price—these and many other favors are calculated to keep the legislator in a friendly frame of mind.

Aid in Bill Drafting   Although the Legislative Council and the Legislative Reference Library provide help to the legislators in drawing up bills, this service is often performed by lobbyists. Since the lobbyist is very likely to be a lawyer, preferably one with legislative experience, some of them have become expert bill draftsmen. By doing such favors for members of the legislature, the lobbyist creates an obligation that can be repaid with a favorable vote.

Influencing Appointments to Committees   The committees to a large extent determine the work of the legislature. If a pressure group can influence the presiding officers who, as already noted, have considerable power to name committee members, it can ordinarily influence the makeup of committees and thus the legislative product. This is one reason why special-interest groups are vitally interested in races for the lieutenant-governorship and in the selection of the speaker and why they contribute money to the campaigns for these offices. The races can be very expensive. For example, it has been estimated by a knowledgeable official[16] that the speakership contest in 1961 cost each side about $150,000, although races with little or no opposition are much less expensive. But in any case, much of the cost is defrayed by groups and individuals who are interested in exerting influence in the legislature.

Appearing before Committees   If the lobbyist does not already control a committee, he may work on the members after the committee assignments have been made. Public hearings offer an opportunity for the lobbyist to state his views. He may present a written brief as well as an oral argument, but most lobbyists realize that there is little opportunity to go into the merits and demerits of a bill before committees. For this reason, lobbyists make daily contacts with the committee members all during the session. If a bill is in conference committee, special efforts will be exerted. Since there are only two votes in a conference committee, *i.e.,* the members of each house vote as a unit, it is necessary to control only a majority of the members from one house to block the passage of unfavorable legislation.

Social Lobby   All lobbyists entertain. Several organizations keep suites in Austin for hungry and thirsty legislators who are welcome to come by for a sandwich or a drink or just to visit with friends. Others

[16]Ben Barnes, then speaker, as quoted in *The Dallas Morning News*, Jan. 29, 1967.

have breakfast tables at the hotels where legislators can stop by and have breakfast with their lobbyist host. Still others have weekly buffets. Members of the legislature are often taken on short vacations to the seashore, to horse races, or on hunting and fishing trips. Most of the entertaining is not on an elaborate scale and consists of taking legislators to luncheon and dinner, providing a comfortable and congenial place to relax, and always having good liquor available.

Entertaining is not for the purpose of buying a legislator's vote but of establishing a friendly relationship between legislator and lobbyist. As one legislator put it, "They sorta kill you with kindness." All things being equal, legislators will be more receptive to suggestions made by friends, especially if the matter is of no great importance to the member's constituents. Probably a majority of bills are matters of indifference to most legislators, so why not vote with one's friends? As long as the legislator does not flout some serious local desire, he is ordinarily in little danger of not being reelected, no matter how he votes. It is likely that his constituents do not know how he votes on most questions and probably would not care if they did, as long as he attends to the local interests of the district.

Letters and Telegrams　One of the favorite methods of attempting to influence legislation, particularly by groups with large memberships, is to overwhelm the legislator with telegrams and letters from his constituents advocating a particular line of action. In this way it is hoped that an appearance of widespread public interest in the measure can be created. When the communications are largely identical, showing clearly that they have been "inspired," the average legislator will pay little heed to them. On the other hand, an original letter from a constituent will ordinarily be given close attention. Unfortunately, few private citizens are sufficiently interested to take the time to write their representative or senator.

Encouraging Attendance of Voters at Committee Hearings
Another method used by lobbyists for large membership groups is having as many of their members as possible appear before committees when a particular bill is given a public hearing. If enough people attend these hearings, the legislator may be inclined to believe that there is widespread public demand for the bill—or at least that a large enough group approves it to make it politically unwise to oppose or ignore their wishes.

Home District Lobbying　It is the business of a good lobbyist to know as much as possible about legislators, personally and politically. He probably knows who the legislator's friends and supporters are back home and who has influence with them. With this type of information, a lobbyist can generate strong political pressure on the legislators from the "right" people in their home districts. It may all be done quite indirectly. Let us say the lobbyist and his associates have influence with a person or organization who can influence a person who has influence with a major supporter of the legislator. In this roundabout way, pressure is brought on the legislator, who, remembering campaign favors of the past and considering those he expects to receive in the future, "sees the light" but never realizes where the pressure really came from.

Community or "Grass Roots" Lobbying   Within recent years various kinds of organizations with large financial resources have concentrated their efforts on propaganda in the belief that in the long run the best way to influence legislation is through influencing public opinion, so that the people will elect favorable legislators and other state officials. After election, the officer will be faced with a public opinion favorable to the group's program. If a legislator really represents his constituents, he will thus be in favor of what the pressure group wants. If the "right" sort of public opinion can be created, much has already been accomplished toward controlling the elections and the legislature as well. Practically every channel of public information is used: the press, radio, television, lecture platform, schools, pamphlets, etc. The use of so-called grass roots lobbying as a means of influencing legislative and administrative action is constantly growing.

Favorable Aspects of Lobbying

The average lobbyist attempts to develop a personal relationship with as many legislators as possible so that when he presents his client's views he will be looked upon as a reliable and dependable friend rather than the representative of some interest or pressure group. Rarely will the established lobbyist try to pressure a legislator he knows to be opposed to his client's views, and rarely will he ask a member directly to vote for or against a bill. The preferred technique of most lobbyists is simply the establishment of feelings of friendship, respect, and confidence on the part of the legislators. Nearly every member of the legislature is on good terms with one or more lobbyists, and well he might be, for the lobby serves several very desirable purposes.

1 Enables the Voter to Help Direct Legislation   Unless a voter belongs to an organization which maintains a lobby at the state capitol, almost his only chance to help direct lawmaking is at the polls, when he selects the governor, lieutenant governor, and members of the legislature.

If his industry, labor union, professional organization, or interest group has a lobbyist at the legislature, the voter's influence is then continuous rather than just at election time. His lobbyist can let the legislators know what at least a part of the public wants.

2 Furnishes Much Valuable Information to the Legislators. Lobbyists are usually among the best informed people around the legislature. Large organizations may even have a private research staff to analyze bills and their effect on the concern's interests. Some lobbyists have established excellent reputations for giving accurate and detailed data to the legislature which could be obtained in no other way. Who better than the lobbyist should know how a particular bill will affect his client?

3 Keeps Constituents Informed Most citizens have no idea how their legislators vote on particular questions. Since the information is rarely carried in the press and few voters read the House and Senate journals, it is up to the lobbyist to keep the members of his group informed concerning the votes of their representative and senator. Unless one subscribes to an expensive private legislative service, the lobby is almost the only source for information of this type.

4 Gives Representation to Economic Groups It is at least a debatable question whether representation should take into account only numbers or should also include economic and other interests. The regulation and balancing of the various and often conflicting economic and class interests are among the principal tasks of modern legislatures. Lobbies and pressure groups may be considered at least a type of economic representation. If all groups were equally represented (and just how would you weigh economic representation?), there might be no objection to lobbying, but as it is, the groups with the largest financial resources are usually the best represented. But are not business, trade, or professional groups (the oil industry, labor, and the Texas Medical Association, for example) justified in maintaining lobbies to protect themselves and to advance their interests? Probably so, as long as the general welfare of the state is not jeopardized and as long as the methods used are legitimate. Lobbying activities should, however, be regulated. This question will be considered in the next chapter.

The Governor

Texas governors have frequently been leaders in legislation, although their influence with the Texas legislature has depended a great deal upon their concept of their legislative role and their personal attributes. It is not too much to say that governors tend to be judged by their legislative performance regardless of their preferences in this regard. After all, they are elected more on the basis of their policy promises than on any other, and policy necessarily involves legislation.

Constitutional Powers   The governor is granted several constitutional powers which are legislative in nature. Quite clearly, the framers of the Texas constitution anticipated at least some gubernatorial influence to be exerted on legislation.

1 Veto   The power to veto legislation is probably the most important of the legislative powers given to the governor by the constitution. As stated by one authority, "In practice, the veto power probably has been the most valuable means of gubernatorial control of public policy."[17] This is suggested by the fact that no vote has been overridden since 1941. The legislature has been unable or unwilling to muster the necessary two-thirds vote. The veto is, however, a negative resource, but by skillful use of it the governor may turn it into a positive force to shape legislation. Governors have done this by threatening to veto a bill unless it is changed. The bill often is changed to meet the governor's objections. The governor may also use his power to veto as a bargaining device.

Let us say that a legislator has a favorite bill he does not want vetoed, so he asks the governor for a conference concerning it. The chief executive might ask the legislator how he stands upon some favorite "administration measure." A politically wise legislator would think twice before saying he opposed the governor's measure.

2 Special Sessions   In special sessions of the legislature, laws are supposed to be passed only upon those subjects submitted by the governor. By submitting one topic at a time, the governor centers the spotlight of publicity on that issue and may be able to force an unwilling legislature to consider a new question or a part of his program which failed or was ignored at the regular session. It also puts him in a good trading position with the members of the legislature, for he can promise to submit "pet" topics of individual legislators if they will support his measure. For these reasons, special sessions of the legislature have been very effective and have played a vital part in determining public policy.

3 Messages   Gubernatorial messages may or may not have much influence with the legislature. If the governor is personally popular with

---

[17]Fred Gantt, Jr., *The Chief Executive in Texas*, p. 178, University of Texas Press, Austin, 1964. Quoted by permission. Gantt's book is an excellent treatment of the influence of the Texas governor on legislation. Much of the material in this section is taken from this source, and the authors wish to express their indebtedness.

the legislators or they approve the general outlines of his program, they may be inclined to support his policies as outlined in the message; otherwise much of his program may be ignored. Yet the legislature seems to expect the governor to outline his program to them, even if they reject it. Too frequent use of messages, however, may antagonize the legislators, since they resent what they consider unwarranted gubernatorial interference. By and large, messages are the least effective means the governor has to influence legislation. Their effectiveness seems to depend largely on whether public opinion is ready to accept the governor's ideas.

4 Appointments The governor has considerable appointing power in his own right and can sometimes influence friendly department heads to take his suggestions concerning appointments in their departments. All members of the legislature are interested in these jobs, for all have many constituents who desire to be on the state payroll or to be members of the numerous state boards. The member consequently seeks help from the governor, who thus has another opportunity to solicit support for his legislative program. Political appointments definitely strengthen the governor's position with the legislature.

Every member of the legislature is conscious of the governor's influence, and some of them will vote for a measure having the governor's support in order to win executive approval of bills or to secure appointment of friends and constituents to office. But all governors have, at one time or another, clashed with the legislature and had parts of their programs turned down. Yet on the whole, the governor's legislative influence, as exercised through his legal powers, is an important factor in legislation.

Other Sources of Power and Other Methods   In addition to the constitutional powers of a legislative nature, the governor can draw on other resources for the purpose of influencing the legislature and can employ a variety of methods, usually of an informal nature. Overall, he has one unique resource of immeasurable significance in all his endeavors: he alone *is* the governor, and when he asks for support, his authoritative position lends considerable weight to the request.

1 Influencing Legislative Presiding Officers The governor is virtually forced to exercise whatever powers he can muster, constitutional or otherwise, to influence the lieutenant governor and the speaker. As we shall see in the next section, their powers over legislation are considerable; and to carry out a legislative program their cooperation, willy-nilly, must be secured. In fact, the governor's relationship with them can spell defeat or victory for his program. The governor has his work cut out for him in dealing with the legislative leaders. The lieutenant governor is elected statewide in his own campaign and can assume a correspondingly independent posture on legislation. The speaker is selected by House members. Although some governors have influenced the selection of the speaker, they do so at some risk inasmuch as the members tend to resent outside influence.[18]

2 Lobbying and Working the Lobby The governor lobbies just as others do who wish to influence the legislature. He normally relies on members of his staff for day-to-day liaison with the legislators. They line up witnesses to testify at committee hearings or to pressure certain legislators; they talk to legislators in various contexts and times; and so on. Many people are unaware that the governor and his aides also "work the lobby." That is, they request the help of the lobbyists to persuade legislators to support the governor. In his dealings with the legislators the governor employs bargaining methods such as those already mentioned under the discussion of the veto. He may offer to assist blocs or factions in return for their support of his legislation. In his relations with legislators, the governor will also resort to many of the methods lobbyists use to establish good personal relations. He calls informal conferences; invites members to breakfast, lunch, or dinner; holds receptions and other social affairs. These seemingly little things can be quite important and successful. As one authority has said, "without exception, governors, staff members, and legislators say they consider a conference to be one of the most successful and frequently used techniques in the legislative process."[19]

3 Appeals to the People and Creation of Citizen Committees
The governor can also use his position to go over the heads of the legislature and appeal directly to the people by means of the press, radio and television. The governor's press secretary, one of the most important members of his staff, can be of great help in presenting the governor and his program in a favorable light. If the governor can gain wide public support for a program, the legislature is likely to go along with it also. Governors have used this device of appealing to the public rather sparingly and with varying success. There can be, however, no doubt but that on occasion it has played a significant role in building support for the governor's program.

Mention should also be made of citizen committees. The governor can kill several birds with one stone by appointing groups of citizens to a special study committee. Important research into a problem can be undertaken and interest generated; the governor can postpone action on a

---

[18]For examples of this, see *ibid.*, pp. 238–242.
[19]*Ibid.*, p. 245. Quoted by permission.

problem until a more timely occasion by insisting on a study; the citizens can act as conveyor belts to and from the public, bringing in information and also developing favorable public opinion on the question at issue; and so on. Citizen committees have been used very successfully by all recent governors.

Final Observations   In the last analysis, the adoption of the governor's program may result not so much from the governor's powers and methods just described as from the fact that he and leading members of the legislature are often from the same faction of the Democratic party, hold the same political, social, and economic views, and represent essentially the same economic interests. Thus, their ideas on important state questions more or less coincide. Even so, some of the state's most popular governors have failed in getting major portions of their legislative programs adopted.

One reason for this failure on the part of the governor is that he and the legislature represent different constituencies. The legislators are elected from the various sections of the state and, until quite recently, were predominately from the rural areas and small towns and represented their ideas. The governor, elected from the entire state, of necessity has to give more emphasis to a statewide program and more weight to the ideas of urban regions, for there is where most of the votes are. This inevitably leads to conflict. With the reapportionment of the legislature, this situation should gradually change, but even so, there will be conflict, for the individual legislators are more interested in the things that affect their particular districts than in those concerning the state as a whole.

Also, although the governor runs on a platform, it is his own, not that of a party. Since no legislator runs on the governor's platform, legislators feel no moral obligation to support the governor's measures. It may be that, in the absence of a well-developed two-party system with strong cohesion in each party, almost all governors will have some difficulty getting their legislative programs adopted.

Leadership within the Legislature

It is relevant in a discussion of legislative influences to consider the wielders of power within the legislature itself. Critics of the Texas legislature have complained, as will be examined in the next chapter, that the leadership has become too powerful vis-à-vis the average member. Insofar as the presiding officers are concerned, they do possess an awesome array of powers with which to control the legislative process and output. Three of their powers will be reviewed briefly here.

1 Appointing Committees Needless to say, whoever can control committees has a great deal of power in the legislature. Traditionally, the speaker and the lieutenant governor have held virtually a monopoly on the appointment of committees and their chairmen. This has changed somewhat. But a study of committee chairmen appointed to the most important House committees in 1959 and from 1963 to 1969 showed that the speaker appointed only House members from his own faction.[20] These persons were expected to vote down the line for the speaker.

The method of selection of the speaker should also be considered in connection with committee assignments. During the time Representative Gus Mutscher of Brenham was speaker (1969–1972), a pledge system was used to force members into line. At the beginning of the session the speaker would collect signed pledge cards by which the member promised to support him for another term for speaker. If a member refused, he was unable to get a committee assignment of his choosing and also generally was unable to get his bills favorably considered. On the other hand, a member who collected pledge cards for the speaker could exchange his support for a powerful position, such as chairman of the House Appropriations Committee.[21] This situation was entirely different in the 1973 legislature as we shall see in the next chapter; and new legislation forbids these practices.

2 Referring Bills The power of the presiding officers to refer bills to committees can also help determine the fate of legislation. Some bills can be referred to one of several committees because the subject matter overlaps the jurisdiction of the committees as laid out in the rules. The presiding officer can then choose the committee most likely to support or kill the bill, depending on his plans for the legislation. It has been customary for certain committees to be favored by the presiding officers because they will act predictably on the side of the officers. In the House, for example, a committee has been designated as the "speaker's committee." Sometimes it has been the State Affairs Committee, one of the most powerful in the House. In the 1973 legislature it was said to be the Rules Committee. Occasionally a bill is re-referred from one committee to another in order to get the action desired.

3 Control of the Agenda Another very important factor in the influence of the presiding officers is their control over the agenda. The

<hr>

[20]Melvin Hairell, "The Politics of Committee Assignments in the Texas House of Representatives," unpublished M.A. thesis, University of Texas at Austin, 1971. Cited in Clifton McCleskey, *The Government and Politics of Texas*, 4th ed., pp. 139–140, Little, Brown and Company, Boston, 1972.

[21]Sam Kinch, Jr., and Ben Procter, *Texas under a Cloud*, pp. 98–99, Jenkins Publishing Company, Austin and New York, 1972. The pledge card system did not originate with Mutscher. It had been used by other speakers and was a method for gaining a first term as well as a second term for the speaker.

lieutenant governor is especially strong here. It will be remembered that the Senate rarely follows the calendar and that bills are usually taken up only on motion, which requires a two-thirds vote (or a four-fifths vote during the first forty-five days when little legislation would be taken up anyway). Since the lieutenant governor has the power of recognition, he can refuse to recognize a senator for the purpose of making a motion to take up a bill. Thus the lieutenant governor can effectively prevent something to which he is opposed from being considered on the floor. It also puts him in a good bargaining position, since he can swap recognition for support of measures he wants passed and discipline those who oppose him by refusing recognition. Furthermore, since it takes a two-thirds vote (twenty-one of the thirty-one senators) to approve the motion, with eleven senators on his side (and surely a lieutenant governor would have that many supporters in the Senate), he can kill any bill he wants to, even if, for political or other reasons, he recognizes the senator to make the motion to "make a run with his bill." It is much easier to exert control at this stage of the procedure when a two-thirds vote is required than on the floor of the Senate, where only a simple majority (one-half plus one) is necessary to pass the bill.[22] For all practical purposes, then, the lieutenant governor not only controls the agenda of the Senate but can often defeat any bill to which he is opposed.

The speaker is in a little different position with respect to control of the agenda. The House has tended to follow its many calendars; but, even so, the speaker in the past has frequently "laid out a bill" for floor discussion at his discretion. Some speakers have been accused of dictating the order of legislation—at least the important bills—and indeed, it would be difficult to cite any bill from 1963 to 1972 that passed the House against the wishes of the speaker. Before 1972 the speaker could control the order of business by appointment of close political allies to the Rules Committee. The Rules Committee, which had the power to make the calendars, simply gave priority to bills desired by the speaker and placed bills not desired at the bottom of the calendar in question. This assured an early or delayed consideration or no consideration at all as desired. In 1972 new House rules were adopted, and the House was supposed to follow the calendar order set by the Calendars Committee. However, the entire membership of the committee as well as of the Rules Committee was appointed by the speaker so that he can receive favorable consideration at the very least. Nonetheless, it appears that the House had greater control of its agenda in the 1973 legislature than in previous sessions.

---

[22]One result of this is that bills are rarely killed on the Senate floor. The big hurdle is the two-thirds vote to get the bill on the floor in the first place. If this is done, the bill will ordinarily be passed, though it may be amended.

Party and Constituency Influences

In two-party states an influence upon legislation would be the party organization within each house of the legislature. These states have party leaders and caucuses and other groups, somewhat patterned after the congressional party organization. In Texas, a one-party state, the legislature has not organized along party lines, although in the 1971 legislature the Republicans in the House organized a caucus. Factions within the Democratic party are not well organized, although some informal meetings of like-minded legislators occur.[23] Generally speaking, one can say that the factions are fluid, forming and reforming over given issues.

A body of literature has been written on the subject of the influence of constituency or district upon the voting behavior of members of Congress. Unfortunately, there has been little written on the influence of constituency upon the behavior of members of the Texas legislature.[24] We can only surmise that it has been a factor, as at least many legislators claim that their first obligation is to vote their district.

---

[23]Jones, *op. cit.*, pp. 131–133.
[24]For a brief discussion of constituency pressures, see *ibid.*, pp. 137–138.

Chapter 7

Texas Legislative Improvements

A nationwide movement to modernize state legislatures occurred in the 1960s, sparked in large part by the reapportionment revolution. It may be recalled from Chapter 2 that the current movement to revise state constitutions also owes a great deal to reapportionment. Important in explaining the progress toward legislative improvements has been a rebirth of citizen interest in their state legislatures. Citizen groups have been formed in many states. One such group, the Texas Assembly, met in 1967 to study and to make recommendations concerning the Texas legislature.[1] Various indicators suggest that the efforts to change legislatures have borne fruit. In 1966, for example, only twenty state legislatures held annual sessions whereas by 1973 thirty-seven did so. Also, in 1966 the average biennial salary of legislators was $9,933, but in

---

[1] A Texas Assembly meeting in 1970 to study "The State and the Urban Crisis" also recommended legislative modernization.

1972 it was \$15,798.[2] A reduction in the number of committees, better physical facilities including office space, larger and more professional staffs, and better communication with the public are other changes which have taken place in many states.[3] In Texas we have seen a reduction in the number of committees and some other reforms, but much remains to be accomplished. The need for improving the Texas legislature will occupy our attention in this chapter.

A highlight of recent modernization movements of relevance to the Texas legislature was the publication in 1971 of a pioneer study of all the state legislatures by the Citizens Conference on State Legislatures (CCSL), a nonprofit, nonpartisan, and private group.[4] Relying upon a body of massive data never before gathered, the study consisted of an analysis of the structures and procedures of all fifty legislatures, individually and collectively. Each state legislature was ranked according to the degree to which it was adjudged functional, accountable, informed, independent, and representative. The first letter of each of these five criteria were combined to form the acronym F.A.I.I.R. The scores of each state on all five criteria of the F.A.I.I.R. system were combined to obtain an overall ranking. California was ranked first in the nation, Alabama was last, and Texas was thirty-eighth. Texas was forty-fifth on functional, thirty-sixth on accountable, forty-third on informed, forty-fifth on independent, and seventeenth on representative. The rankings are based partly on judgment and should not be regarded as "scientific," although the findings are of great value and interest. They suggest that the Texas legislature has a long way to go before it ranks with the best states.

Concern for improvements in the Texas legislature has resulted in several studies. Among these was a report by a "Committee of 100," appointed by the speaker in 1970 to study and to make recommendations for improving the House of Representatives. The Senate in the same year authorized the Eagleton Institute of Politics at Rutgers University to study the Senate interim committee system, and a report was completed. But the real impetus for reform has come only recently, from the reactions to the Sharpstown stock fraud case of 1971.

The first public knowledge of the scandal occurred on the eve of the inauguration of Governor Preston Smith and Lieutenant Governor Ben

---

[2]Citizens Conference on State Legislatures, *Research Memorandum, No. 16*, Kansas City, Mo., December, 1972.

[3]See *The Book of the States*, 1972–73, pp. 47–58, Council of State Governments, Iron Works Pike, Lexington, Ky., 1972. Earlier editions of the biennial publication also contain information about legislative modernization. See also the Council of State Governments quadennial edition of *American State Legislatures: Their Structures and Procedures*.

[4]The CCSL was organized in 1965 and is headquartered in Kansas City, Mo. The popular version of their landmark study is readily available in paperback. See The Citizens Conference on State Legislature (written by John Burns), *The Sometime Governments*, Bantam Books, Inc., New York, 1971.

Barnes in January, 1971, shortly after the Texas legislature had convened for its regular biennial session.[5] The U.S. Securities and Exchange Commission, an agency charged with enforcing Federal securities laws, filed a civil complaint in Federal district court in Dallas against twenty-eight defendants, including Frank Sharp of Houston, former Texas speaker and attorney general, Waggoner Carr, and former state insurance commissioner, John Osorio. The complaint charged the defendants with selling unregistered securities and with deceiving the public. The S.E.C. asked for a temporary injunction to stop the illegal activities. This was issued and eventually made permanent against most of the defendants. No state political figures were defendants in the suit, but the complaint also alleged that Frank Sharp and his associates had attempted to get state legislation passed by providing loans to state officials with which to purchase stock, the price of which was then manipulated to assure a profit. It was this charge that eventually linked leaders of the Texas House of Representatives and the governor and his close friend, Dr. Elmer Baum, who was chairman of the Democratic State Executive Committee and a member of the State Banking Board, to Sharp.

The central figure in the scandal was Frank Sharp, a banker and real estate developer, best known for Sharpstown in Houston, a subdivision he named after himself. He also controlled the Sharpstown state bank, other state banks, and several insurance companies. The whole story is not known, but perhaps $30 million was involved in various dubious financial transactions. For one thing, Sharp was accused of obtaining $6 million, a sum never recovered, from the Jesuit Fathers who owned and operated the Strake Preparatory School for Boys in Houston. Sharp was found guilty on two minor counts in Federal district court in Houston, was fined $5,000, and given a three-year probated sentence. In return, he was expected to tell all he knew before appropriate forums. He was granted immunity from prosecution for what he might say from both the Federal and the state governments.

As the story unfolded, it appeared that Sharp wanted very much to have the Texas legislature pass new state banking legislation. The deposits in his Sharpstown State Bank were insured by the Federal Deposit Insurance Corporation which was questioning the loans made by the bank to Sharp enterprises and, in general, was keeping close tabs on his operations. Sharp stated in testimony before a House general investigating committee that he wanted to get the F.D.I.C. off his tail. The proposed legislation would do this by setting up state-chartered corpora-

[5]There are many sources of information about the Sharpstown stock fraud scandal. The best is Sam Kinch, Jr., and Ben Proctor, *Texas under a Cloud*, Jenkins Publishing Co., Pemberton Press, Austin and New York, 1972.

tions with authority to insure deposits in state banks, or so Sharp thought. The lawyer who drew up the legislation claimed that it would have supplemented Federal insurance rather than supplanted it by providing for insurance above the Federal maximum, which at that time was $15,000 per account, to $100,000.

At any rate, Sharp discussed the legislation with the speaker and others. Legislation was introduced containing the concept during the regular session of the legislature in 1969, but it was not acted upon. Then, in the summer of 1969 Sharp testified that he met the speaker in Houston. They exchanged problems. The speaker needed money and Sharp wanted the banking legislation. A tacit agreement was reached, according to Sharp. Shortly thereafter Sharp arranged for loans to be made to the speaker, the speaker pro tem, two top aides to the speaker, the speaker's father, the chairman of the House Appropriations Committee, the governor, and Dr. Baum. The loans were used to purchase stock in National Banker's Life Insurance Company whose president was John Osorio and which was controlled by Sharp. The stock served as collateral for the loans; hence no money was risked by the politicos involved. The price of the NBL stock was then manipulated by Sharp's associates. The S.E.C. charged that they "made a market." Many of the individuals named above sold the stock at a profit to the Jesuit Fathers for a price above even the inflated market price. The exact amount of profits made on the deal varied with the source. One estimate is $359,150.50 for all the persons who bought the stock.[6] However, the speaker lost money by later transactions.

Meanwhile, the legislation desired by Sharp began to move. On August 26, Governor Smith called the second special session of 1969. The bank deposit insurance bills desired by Sharp were introduced by the speaker pro tem on September 5. Then on the eighth, the governor submitted to the legislature the subject of additional bank deposit insurance protection, allowing the bills to be considered. (The governor sets the agenda of special sessions, as we have seen in Chapter 6.) The bills were passed in the House on the same day and on the next by the Senate. However, the governor vetoed the bill after considerable pressure from the banking commissioner and several bankers, including former Texas Governor Allan Shivers.

For their part in the passage of the legislation, the speaker, the speaker pro tem, and the speaker's principal aide were indicted by the Travis County Grand Jury for bribery and ultimately convicted in 1972,

---

[6]Bernard D. Nossiter, "Texas Bonanza: SEC Lawsuit Says Governor, Politicians Were Enriched," *The Washington Post*, Feb. 21, 1971, in Eugene W. Jones, Joe E. Ericson, Lyle C. Brown, and Robert S. Trotter, Jr., *Practicing Texas Politics*, pp. 420–427, Houghton Mifflin Company, Boston, 1971.

after trial in Abilene in state district court. The case was appealed, but the final outcome was not known at the date of writing.

The scandal hovered over the speaker and his team during the entire regular session of the 1971 legislature. The "Dirty Thirty," a small group of Republican and Liberal Democrats, reminded him of the scandal by one means or another during the entire session.[7] The news media also kept the issue alive. Nonetheless, the speaker was able to control the House without difficulty until he was indicted and convicted. He resigned at the time of the second special session in March, 1972. It was during this session that some of the legislative reforms to which reference has been made in the preceding chapters occurred. One result of the scandal was that the demand for legislative reforms grew to a crescendo. The scandal greatly influenced the outcome of the primaries and the general elections of 1972. The top state leadership was turned out of office—the speaker, the speaker pro tem, the governor, the lieutenant governor who was seeking the governorship, and the attorney general. In addition a very high turnover occurred in the legislature. There were seventy-seven new faces in the House and fifteen in the Senate. Not since 1953 had there been so many new representatives. Reform became the key theme of the 1973 legislature. The more important of the reform issues will be considered next.

ETHICS AND LOBBYING

Ethics Legislation

The Texas constitution contains thirteen provisions defining, providing for punishment of, or prohibiting one way or another dishonest behavior by public officials.[8] Unfortunately, honesty in government is not easily resolved by constitutional limitations. The legislature has attempted to regulate behavior by statute as well. But many problems remain unresolved; and some people question both the desirability and the feasibility of securing good government by means of "legislating morality."

In 1957 the Texas legislature passed ethics legislation in response to

[7]The group got its name from a vote on House Concurrent Resolution 87, called the Farenthold Resolution. On March 15, 1971, during the regular session of the 62nd legislature Representative Frances ("Sissy") Farenthold of Corpus Christi moved the consideration of the resolution which proposed a joint committee to investigate the Sharpstown affair as it concerned public officials. The speaker refused to recognize Mrs. Farenthold for the purpose of introducing the resolution. The ruling was appealed and the motion to appeal was seconded. On the vote that followed, 118 representatives sustained the ruling of the chair, but 30 opposed it; hence, the name "Dirty Thirty." The actual number of representatives opposing the speaker on various votes during the session varied somewhat from this figure, but the name stuck.

[8]George D. Braden, *Citizens' Guide to the Texas Constitution*, p. 68, Texas Advisory Commission on Intergovernmental Relations (prepared by the Institute for Urban Studies, University of Houston), Austin, 1972.

scandals of that period involving insurance companies, naturopaths, legislators, and state executive officials. The law established a legislative code of ethics, one of only a few in the nation at the time. By its provisions no legislator or other state official or employee was permitted to have any interest or engage in any business or profession which was in substantial conflict with the proper discharge of his public duties. Specifically, the act prohibited employment, gifts, favors, or services that might reasonably tend to influence public official and employees. And so on. But there was no provision for enforcement, although expulsion, removal from office, or discharge constituted penalties for noncompliance.

All efforts to strengthen the ethics law failed until the Sharpstown affair. Suddenly, in 1971, ethics bills became very popular with legislators. An ethics bill designed to strengthen the law had been introduced in six previous sessions of the legislature. Now it was reintroduced, and the sponsor acquired over 100 cosponsors. Before the regular session was over in 1971, two new ethics measures were passed. The first was a constitutional amendment in which regulation of ethics by an Ethics Commission was combined with the removal of the constitutional provision on legislative salaries, which would then be recommended by the new commission. The voters may have believed that the new amendment was a sneaky way of getting a salary increase. At any rate, they rejected the amendment at a special election in May of 1971. The second of the ethics measures was passed virtually at the stroke of midnight on the last day of the session and was a compromise following heated debate in both houses. The new law would have made some significant improvements in the old ethics law, but it was ruled unconstitutional by the Texas attorney general on numerous grounds, including vagueness.

The legislature convened in 1973 in an atmosphere heavy with concern about ethics legislation. The newly elected speaker, Price Daniel, Jr., who had campaigned on a reform platform, made ethics legislation the first of nine bills in a reform package. Both the governor and the lieutenant governor pledged support for some kind of ethics legislation. The lieutenant governor called a citizens conference on ethics in government in March, 1973, and its report recommended many reforms.

Passing an effective law on ethics is not easy. One of the difficult problems is to define adequately conflict of interest and to provide guidelines for conduct where none may exist. It must be remembered that the opportunities for conflicts of interest have increased with the times. Government spends much more money than ever before tend affects many more citizens than ever before. Also, public officials have become more affluent, investing their money in stock or having other financial holdings in concerns conceivably affected by government action.[9] Also, some kinds of conflicts of interest are difficult if not impossible to avoid. Legislators are also taxpayers, parents, gainfully employed in some occupation, seekers of recreation, and so on, and legislation which they consider and vote on will affect them as well as the general public.

Despite the difficulties, the Texas legislature at the regular session in 1973 enacted new ethics legislation. The speaker's bill, House Bill No. 1, was passed after amendment and protracted controversy. It repealed the 1957 law although incorporating a few provisions from it, including some standards of conduct.

The 1973 law is based on the general principle that public office is a public trust, and no legislator or other public officer or employee should use his office for personal gain. The philosophy is summed up in Section 1 of the new law, which reads in part as follows:

> It is the policy of the State of Texas that no state officer or state employee shall have any interest, financial or otherwise, direct or indirect, or engage in any business transaction or professional activity or incur any obligation of any nature which is in substantial conflict with the proper discharge of his duties in the public interest.

It is fairly easy to state the general principle of the public interest taking precedence over private interest, but it is harder to determine how best to define and to regulate conflicts between private and public interest. One of the most important principles for accomplishing these purposes is public disclosure of financial and other interests by public officials and employees. The 1973 law requires the filing of financial statements by elected officers, salaried appointed officers, appointed officers of major state agencies, and executive heads of state agencies, all of whom are defined in the law. The statements, which are to be filed in April every year with the secretary of state, are to contain financial activities not only of the public officer or employee but also of his spouse and dependent children. The content of the statement includes a list of professional and occupational income and real estate bought and sold (with gain or loss). It also includes debt, consisting of notes over $1,000 owed to others; gifts over $250 except from close relatives; and a list of corporations controlled and of memberships on corporate boards of directors. Actual dollar amounts need not be listed. Instead categories are used, such as under $1,000; $1,000–5,000; $5,000 or more.

Appointed officers not required to file financial statements must

---

[9]Marver H. Bernstein, "Ethics in Government: The Problem in Perspective," *National Civic Review*, pp. 341–347, July, 1972.

disclose their interest, provided it is substantial as defined by the law, in businesses regulated by government agencies.

Another principle of ethics legislation related to disclosure is disqualification. That is, a legislator or other public official should refrain from voting or taking official action on matters in which he has a direct personal or financial interest. The Texas constitution contains such a provision for legislators.[10] The 1973 ethics law extends the constitutional language to elected or appointed members of boards or commissions having policy direction over a state agency. These officers are required to disclose any personal or private interest in any measure or proposal or decision pending before the agency, and then, they are to refrain from voting.

Methods for enforcing ethics legislation are also subjects of considerable controversy. During the 1973 regular session of the legislature, the proposal for an independent Ethics Commission to serve as a watchdog and to enforce the provisions of the ethics and other bills was defeated. Instead, the secretary of state was assigned the task of receiving financial statements and various administrative tasks related thereto. For example, he was charged with conducting a continual survey to see whether persons required to file statements have done so.

The 1973 law also provides penalties and means of enforcing them for violations of the various sections. Most violations are misdemeanors and may be prosecuted in Travis County or other county as stated in the Code of Criminal Procedure. These include violating the section entitled "Prohibited Acts" which ban representation before state agencies by legislators for compensation except in certain circumstances, such as an adversary proceeding. An interesting new method of enforcement concerns the members of boards and commissions who fail to disclose their personal interest, if any, in matters before them. They are subject to removal from office by a court trial, provided they are not subject to the impeachment provisions of the Texas constitution.

Lobby Regulation

Interrelated with ethics legislation is the regulation of lobbying. Ethics legislation is, however, directed more at the conduct of legislators and other public officials whereas lobby control is generally concerned with the actions of outsiders who seek to influence the government. Nonetheless, the behavior of both outsiders and governmental officials and employees is involved in both kinds of legislation.

---

[10]Section 10 of Article III.

For all practical purposes Texas had no legislation regulating lobbying until 1957.[11] The legislature, prodded by the scandals of that year which we have mentioned, enacted the Lobby Registration Act of 1957, also known as the Lobby Control Act. Highlights of the act included the following:

Registration   All persons, whether for compensation or not, who attempted by direct communication to influence legislation for someone else had to register, as did persons working for themselves if they spent in excess of $50 during a session for direct communication. The registrant had to give his own name, address, occupation, and the same information about the person or organization for whom he was acting, plus a brief description of the legislation in which he was interested.

Reporting Expenditures   Each registrant had to make monthly reports during the legislative session giving the total amount spent (including entertainment expenses) for direct communication during the preceding month.

Administration   The chief clerk of the House of Representatives prepared the forms for registration and kept the records, which were open for public inspection.

Prohibited Practices   The following practices were forbidden:

1   Giving or receiving contingent fees (compensation contingent upon the passage or defeat of legislation)
2   Appearance of unauthorized persons on the floor of either house unless invited
3   Preparing or using false, counterfeit, forged, or fictitious communications

Penalties   Persons who willfully or knowingly violated any provisions of the act could be fined not more than $5,000 and/or imprisoned for not more than two years.

The 1957 law was criticized on many counts. It was pointed out that only natural persons had to register as lobbyists, excluding corporations or other associations. Only expenses incurred in arguing for

[11]The Lobby Control Act of 1907 was an early attempt at regulation. It outlawed all attempts to influence legislation "by means other than appeal to reason," and persons found guilty could be imprisoned. *Vernon's Texas Statutes*, 1948, Penal Code, arts. 179–183. Needless to say, it is unenforceable. For more information about lobby regulation, see James R. Soukup, "Lobby Regulation in Texas," *Comment*, Institute of Public Affairs, University of Texas, Austin, May, 1958.

and against legislation had to be reported; also only total expenditures were required, with no breakdown concerning the person on whom the expenditure was made or its purpose. Furthermore, reports of expenses were to be filed only during the legislative session. There was no provision for a special enforcing agency.

The spirit of reform of the 1973 legislature also brought forth proposals to strengthen the Lobby Control Act. House Bill No. 2, the second bill of the speaker's reform passage, provided for significant change. After being amended, it was finally passed. It repealed the 1957 law.

The new law has answered some of the criticisms of the 1957 attempt to regulate lobbying. It defines "persons" in such a way that corporations, associations, partnership, clubs, and other organizations are included as well as natural persons. Lobbying is still defined in terms of "direct communication," but executive and legislative employees, legislators-elect, and candidates for the legislature are included among those who are contacted for lobbying purposes.

Three categories of persons who engage in "direct communication" are required to register: (1) a person who spends more than $200 in a calendar quarter, exclusive of certain personal expenses, such as travel and lodging; (2) a person who receives compensation for lobbying on behalf of others; and (3) a person who lobbies as part of his regular employment, regardless of whether he is paid for lobbying.

The new law has two exceptions from registration for those who contact government officials on legislative matters. They are persons associated with the media for purposes of conveying information and persons invited to appear to testify.

Persons who are required to register as lobbyists must, with some qualifications, report more frequently and must prepare more extensive reports than under the 1957 law. Reports are required monthly during the session and quarterly during the year. Expenditures must be broken down into categories, including postage and telegraph, publication and advertising, travel and fees, entertainment, gifts, loans, and political contributions. Also, information about the organization for whom the person lobbies must be included. "The number of members of the group and a full description of the methods by which the registrant develops and makes decisions about positions on policy" are required. In addition to the lobbyist's full name and address and similar kinds of information, he must also include "the full name and address of each person who made a contribution or paid a membership fee in excess of $500 during the preceding twelve-month period" to him or to the person who pays him.

Much stricter provisions for enforcement have been written into the

1973 law. Violation of all but one section is a misdemeanor. The lone exception, which carries a felony penalty, is violation of the section prohibiting the payment of a lobbyist contingent upon the passage or defeat of proposed legislation. A new penalty is the requirement that the state must be paid three times the compensation received by the lobbyist should he fail to report the money he has received for lobbying as required. The provisions of the act are to be enforced by the attorney general or any county or district attorney. The district court in Travis County may issue an injunction upon application by any citizen of the state. Statements that must be filed under the law are given to the secretary of state.

Another new law enacted by the 1973 legislature to which reference has already been made in Chapter 3 is House Bill No. 4 which regulates campaign contributions and expenditures. The lobby, as we have already mentioned, is interested in the races for the legislature. Regulation of campaign financing also is a kind of lobby control law and should be mentioned here although we will not repeat the information contained in the earlier chapter.

SALARIES AND SESSIONS

Legislative salaries and sessions are very much related to the question of ethics and lobbying. Texas has a part-time legislature whose members receive salaries smaller than that received by their secretaries. The public, then, has no claim to the entire time of a legislator, and the low pay positively invites conflicts of interest. Legislators must have sources of income other than that which the state provides and must devote a good share of their time to their own, private pursuits. This simply cannot be the best way of assuring close attention to the public business in the public interest. Furthermore, real problems of recruitment to the legislature occur. Qualified citizens who cannot leave their employment for part of the year and who need a living wage are excluded from service. No doubt the relatively high turnover in membership which is characteristic of the Texas House in particular can be ascribed in part to the low pay and part-time work. The turnover leads in turn to lack of an experienced legislature.

The Citizens Conference on State Legislatures has recommended that Texas pay its legislators $15,000 a year. By way of comparison, members of Congress who serve full time are paid $42,500 annually. Some authorities recommend a salary as high as $22,000 for the Texas lawmakers. Nonetheless, the voters have repeatedly turned down efforts to raise the $4800 ceiling set in 1960. Substantial increases in the salaries of the presiding officers have also met with defeat. The 1973 legislature once again submitted an amendment to the voters to raise their salaries. Appearing on the November, 1973, ballot, the proposal would increase the salary to not greater than $15,000 a year. The amendment also would set up annual sessions to which we now turn.

Thirty-seven state legislatures in 1973 operated on an annual basis. Texas continues to follow the biennial system. Yet, the volume of business is large. In 1973 2,746 bills and 97 joint resolutions were introduced in the regular session of 140 days; of these, 688 bills passed and 9 joint resolutions. This excludes a thousand or more simple and concurrent resolutions. The biennial state budget has climbed to well over $9 billion. What private business would limit its board of directors to only a few months every two years to manage a $9 billion operation? The Texas legislature has been unable to perform well under these restrictions. On occasion, as many as half of the bills enacted into law have been passed during the very last week of the session when no one can be sure of what is going on. Many bills have had to be killed by the governor's veto after the session has adjourned because of inadequacies borne in haste.

It is quite clear that 140 days every two years is not enough time to consummate the business of the state. Statistics covering the forty-year period from 1931 to 1971 show that on the average the Texas legislature is in session 176 days every two years, which is considerably more than the constitutionally prescribed 140.[12] Special sessions almost always have to be called.

The Citizens Conference on State Legislatures has proposed not only that the Texas legislature hold annual sessions of unrestricted length but also be able to call itself into special session, if needed. It is argued that the independence of the legislature will be increased by enabling it to handle its own session time without having to rely on the governor or being constrained by the present constitutional provisions.

COMMITTEES AND STAFFS

The Texas legislature has already adopted some reforms in committee selection and performance. The changes have assured greater experience in committee membership and greater member choice in selection of committees. Also, the number of committees on which a legislator may serve has been reduced in both houses. This should give him more time.

---

[12]Clifton McCleskey, *The Government and Politics of Texas*, 4th ed., p. 131, Little, Brown and Company, Boston, 1972.

But most important of all, the conference committee has been limited to resolving differences on bills passed by both houses. Yet, there are some other changes that have been recommended.

One of these is the greater use of joint committees. These committees would help to cut down the work of both houses by avoiding the duplication of committee hearings on the same legislation and other procedures. A unicameral legislature is the ultimate solution to the problem of duplication, the conference committee, and many other problems; but it is not a viable solution for the near future, as we have already indicated. It is encouraging to note that in 1972 the House Appropriations and the Senate Finance Committee held joint hearings on the budget. Perhaps more joint committee proceedings will occur in the future.

Interim committees have posed other problems. In the past there have been numerous committees authorized to study problems between sessions; many were never appointed; some were criticized for failure to contribute anything very productive. Interim committees are a stopgap for continuous sessions and leave a lot to be desired. The standing committees are now authorized to continue between sessions; and this is an improvement, but not a permanent solution to the need for legislative attention to state problems.

Staffing continues to be in need of improvement even though the legislature in 1973 authorized more money and had more staff; but the degree of professionalism required in modern times has yet to be reached. Unless each committee develops an expertise to match that of the interest groups and executive branch, the legislature will operate at a disadvantage.[13] Today's problems are too complex for amateurs.

PROCEDURES

The procedures by which the Texas legislature operates have been criticized on numerous grounds, probably best summed up by the general comment that both democracy and efficiency are lacking to the degree desired. In Chapter 6 the powers of the leadership over legislation were examined. The changes made by the House, in particular in 1972 and 1973, may be the answer to some of the charges of dictatorial controls of the flow of legislation. The important appropriation bill, for example, required seven days of debate in the House during which time over 300 amend-

---

[13]See The Citizens Conference on State Legislatures (written by Felton West and Henry Holcomb), *The Houston Post,* *"Recipe for Reform,"* *An Investigative Series on the Texas Legislature,* Kansas City, Mo., 1972; and Tom Johnson, "Legislative Committees Lack Adequate Staffs," *Dallas Morning News,* Oct. 31, 1971.

ments were offered.[14] This was quite a change from the "quickie" consideration given in prior years when the bill was passed in an hour or so with few or no amendments.

One of the most common criticisms of Senate procedure is that the calendars are rarely followed. The usual way to get a bill on the floor is by a motion, which requires a two-thirds vote to be approved. Is it not strange that a bill that could pass by majority vote once it is considered can be defeated by the high majority required to put it on the agenda? The two-thirds vote also facilitates the lieutenant governor's powers over the flow of legislation.

Another criticism concerns the end of the session rush. Of course, unrestricted annual sessions would remove the need for the extremely hurried last weeks of the 140-day session; but it is human nature to procrastinate, and rushes do occur in annual session states. What is needed is a procedure for governing the flow of legislation. The Citizens Conference on State Legislatures suggests a series of deadlines and presession activities. However, the split session device, which contains deadlines, has not really worked in Texas. Of course, it has never been tried.

Another shortcoming of legislative procedure in Texas, according to critics, one that also bears some substantive content, concerns the consideration of local and special bills. Approximately half of all bills introduced in the legislature are special or local in nature.

Much valuable time is wasted by the passage of local and special laws, many of which are not properly the province of the legislature anyway. In an effort to prevent the legislature from dealing individually with matters relating to persons and property which should be covered by general legislation and to keep down legislative interference in matters of purely local concern, the state constitution severely restricts the use of special legislation. Furthermore, it states that whenever a general law can be made applicable, no special law is to be passed. Authorization is given, however, for legislative enactment of game and fish laws. Despite these constitutional restrictions, hundreds of local and special laws are introduced in each regular session. They may affect only a handful of people but must go through the same processes as all other bills.

The evasion of the constitutional prohibition is accomplished as follows: It will be recalled that, where a general law can be made applicable, no local or special law shall be enacted. The legislature has interpreted this to mean that, if a general bill can be made applicable to a

<hr>

[14]For an interesting description of the House marathon debate, see "Seven Days in April," *The Texas Observer*, pp. 3–5, May 11, 1973.

single locality, it is perfectly constitutional. For years now it has been customary to pass a local bill under the guise of a general law by having the bill read so that it would apply to "all cities (or counties or school districts) in Texas having a population between [this and that number], according to the last preceding federal census." By careful use of population figures these "bracket laws," as they are called, can be made applicable to only one county or city. The constitutional prohibition against local laws is thus circumvented.[15] As a result, all sorts of local bills are introduced and passed as general laws because they are, on their face, "statewide" in application.

Occasionally a governor will refuse to sign measures which apply to only one locality, but most become law without question. Many of these measures are drafted back home by the interested parties. The legislator introduces them as an accommodation, in many instances not even knowing their contents or implications. Some of them deal with issues of considerable importance, while others are trivial. Yet the time and energy of the legislature are consumed by them.

Another type of special legislation deals with monetary claims against the state. Since the state cannot be sued without its consent, the usual way of collecting claims against it is by means of a special law appropriating money to the person concerned. Some of these bills are investigated closely, but many are passed with little or no consideration. Nearly every member will have one or more such bills which he feels he must introduce for a constituent. Whether given careful study or passed as a courtesy to the sponsor, this type of legislation takes time which could well be used for more important matters.

PRESIDING OFFICERS: POWERS, ELECTION, TENURE

Speaker

One of the most important results of the Sharpstown stock fraud affair was to focus attention on the office of the speaker and to generate proposals to reform it. Price Daniel, Jr., the reform-minded speaker of the 1973 legislature, pledged his support for a statute limiting the speaker to

---

[15]An example of an elaborate type of bracket law is given in the following: *"Be it enacted by the Legislature of the State of Texas:* Section 1. This Act shall apply in all independent school districts, whether created under the General Laws or by Special Act of the Legislature and having a board of seven (7) trustees and where the greatest geographic portion of all such independent school districts are situated within the boundaries of a city having a population in excess of two thousand, six hundred and twenty (2,620), as shown by the last preceding Federal Census and where heretofore, four (4) trustees were elected for two (2) year terms on the first Saturday in May in even-numbered years and three (3) trustees were elected for two (2) year terms in odd-numbered years."

one term as one solution to the problem of high-handed leadership in the House under some of the previous speakers. The House and Senate passed the bill, but the attorney general ruled it unconstitutional and it was dropped. Nonetheless, steps may be taken to limit speakers to one term. This would revive a tradition. Historically, very few speakers have served more than one term. However, during the past forty years five speakers served two consecutive terms—in other words, for half of that period. Speaker Gus Mutscher, until his involvement in the Sharpstown case, appeared headed for an unprecedented third term. In view of the clamor for a one-term speaker it is instructive to note that the Citizens Conference on State Legislatures does not favor limiting the terms of the presiding officers. It favors the competing principle of experience and continuity of leadership. The citizens group also contends that one-term speakers weaken the legislature vis-à-vis the executive branch. It is probably best not to overreact to a given historical event but to consider what on balance would give the House democratic, yet effective, leadership.

We have already mentioned how the speaker's powers to appoint committees were curbed to a degree by the House in 1972 and 1973. The speaker continues to hold extensive powers, however, as a review of the list in Chapter 5 will show. But these powers may be wielded in a more democratic manner if the speaker's term of office is limited and the method of his selection changed.

The 1973 legislature passed two bills regulating the campaigns for speaker. Legislation regulating campaign financing has applied to the election of public officials and has not fitted the selection of the speaker who is elected by members of the House. The new laws attempt to fill the void. House Bill No. 8 strictly regulates campaign contributions and expenditures in the speaker's race. Candidates must file with the secretary of state at periodic intervals complete statements of contributions, loans, and expenditures. For example, each expenditure over ten dollars must be accounted for, including the purpose and the name and address of the persons receiving the money. In addition the purposes for which money may be expended are strictly limited. Further, no corporation, labor union or other organization can make any contribution at all; and individuals, other than the candidate, are limited to $100. Failure to file the statements is a misdemeanor as are other violations of the law. Conspiracy to circumvent the act is also a misdemeanor.

The other law, House Bill No. 9, regulating the speaker's race is very unusual. It prohibits what is described as "legislative bribery." It, in effect, makes unlawful political bargaining that involves threats or promises of various kinds. Examples are promises of appointments to committee chairmanships and to other positions or favorable consideration of legislation and threats to not appoint and to not support legislation. Specifically allowed, however, is contacting or communicating with representatives on the substantive issues of legislation. Legislative bribery is a felony.

Lieutenant Governor

Efforts were made by the 1971 and 1973 legislatures to curtail the lieutenant governor's appointment powers, but they were only partly successful. Other changes in the office have been suggested from time to time.

The Citizens Conference on State Legislatures has recommended that the lieutenant governor be stripped of his great legislative powers and be replaced by the president pro tempore, who is elected by the Senate from its members. This would give the Senate its own leadership and make it more independent of the executive branch. This could be done by changing Senate rules. The lieutenant governor, it has also been recommended, should run with the governor as a team and carry on the latter's program should something happen to him to cause a vacancy in the office. If the lieutenant governor should run with the governor, the Senate probably would not want him as the strong presiding officer that he is now.

COMMUNICATIONS

One final subject pertaining to legislative improvements will be mentioned. This concerns the free flow of information between the public and the legislature. Various improvements in this regard have been made in recent years and will not be repeated here. But it is of interest that two of Speaker Daniel's reform bills concerned information, and both were enacted into law. House Bill No. 3 was an amendment to the 1967 open meetings law. The amended version clarified the meaning of meeting by government bodies, required a three-day advance public notice of meetings, allowed tape recordings by citizens, and generally broadened the application of the earlier law. The legislature was, for example, brought within the law's provisions for the first time. The second law, House Bill No. 6, concerned public access to public records and was called by Common Cause "one of the best of its kind in the country."[16] It set a policy that the citizen has a right to inspect government records during

---

[16]*Common Cause Texas Newsletter*, p. 4, June 12, 1973.

normal office hours and to have them reproduced at a reasonable cost, the fee to be set by the Board of Control. If denied access to records other than those excluded, such as personnel files, student records at state-supported institutions, all court records, and so on, the law provided that the citizen could seek aid from the attorney general's office, and the attorney general or the citizen is authorized to seek a writ of mandamus to compel the public official or body to make information available. Willful destruction of records is a misdemeanor.

Another issue, which was national in scope at the time of the 1973 legislature's regular session, was the question whether newsmen should be protected against court action requiring them to divulge their sources of information. Bills for this purpose were introduced and considered in the legislature but failed to pass. They directly bear on the problem of informing the public about legislative and related activities, although they are broader in scope than bills concerning the legislature.

CONCLUSIONS

The Citizens Conference on State Legislatures has declared that the most important decision-making bodies in the entire American political system are the state legislatures.[17] Unless these bodies are strengthened, the entire system will suffer. As Federal revenue sharing becomes a reality and the Federal government closes down programs, the wisdom of this remark becomes all the more apparent. The states will be required to take on more responsibilities. The Texas legislature should be strengthened so that it may play its role in a democratic and efficient manner.

[17]Citizens Conference on State Legislatures, *Sometime Governments*, p. xi.

Chapter 8

The Texas Governor

The most prominent and visible state official in Texas is the governor. He is the official representative of Texas in its relations with the other states and with the United States government. He symbolizes the state for its citizens. Elected statewide rather than from districts, he represents a different constituency and has a different perspective in many respects from the legislature. In a sense, only the governor can speak for the state as a whole.

The governorship is created by Article IV of the Texas constitution, which establishes the executive branch of the state government. Unlike the U.S. Constitution, the executive article does not vest the executive powers of the state in one official but, instead, distributes them among several. For this reason, Texas has what is called a plural executive. The governor is designated the chief executive and is considered first among equals. A comparison of the provisions in the U.S. and the Texas constitutions vesting executive authority illustrates very well the differing concepts of the executive branch. Section 1 of Article II of the U.S. Constitution reads as follows:

The executive powers shall be vested in the President of the United States.

Section 1 of Article IV of the Texas constitution reads:

> The Executive Department of the State shall consist of a Governor, who shall be the Chief Executive Officer of the State, a Lieutenant Governor, Secretary of State, Comptroller of Public Accounts, Treasurer, Commissioner of the General Land Office, and Attorney General.

The American states have generally created weaker governors than the framers of the U.S. Constitution intended for the chief executive of the United States. But the trend has been to increase the powers of the governor. The most populous, urban and industrialized states, called the megastates in Chapter 1 of this text, have relatively strong governors. Texas has remained outside the mainstream of this development in most respects and still retains what is usually described as a "weak governorship." As an indication of this, we may look at an index of the relative position of all fifty state governors as measured by four criteria—tenure potential (term of office and number of terms allowed), veto power, appointment power, and budget power. In 1971 Texas ranked fiftieth or last on the index.[1] Since then, Texas has gained a couple of points by providing for a four-year gubernatorial term that will begin in 1974. But it is rather surprising that Texas, one of the megastates, should not have the "strong governor model." However, a word of caution is in order. Not everything can be measured by an index of formal powers. Some Texans question whether the governor is really "weak." They point to Governors John B. Connally, Allan Shivers, and others who managed to make significant accomplishments while in office. The index is not sensitive enough to measure all the political, personal, and other factors of significance. Also, it does not measure the power of the governor in relation to other groups in the state. Although a state governor may rank low on the index, he may be a strong figure relative to others in the state. Nonetheless, it remains true that structurally, or whatever we want to call it, the Texas governor is weaker than the governors of the other megastates and is a prime target of constitutional revisionists and other proponents of executive reforms. Reformers agree with Governor Shivers who described the Texas governorship as something of a "paper tiger."[2]

---

[1]Joseph A. Schlesinger, "The Politics of the Executive," in Herbert Jacob and Kenneth N. Vines (eds.)., *Politics in the American States*, 2d ed., p. 232, Little, Brown and Company, Boston, 1971.

[2]Allan Shivers, "The Governor's Office in Retrospect," in Fred Gantt, Jr., Irving O. Dawson, and Luther G. Hagard, Jr. (eds.), *Governing Texas*, 2d ed., p. 321, Thomas Y. Crowell Company, New York, 1970.

THE ABC'S OF THE OFFICE

Selection

The Texas governor is selected by direct popular vote. A plurality is sufficient to elect, although a majority is required for nomination in the primaries. The governor is normally inaugurated on the third Tuesday in January following the November general election.[3] The inaugural ceremony is traditionally held outdoors on the capitol steps. The chief justice of the Texas supreme court administers the oath of office to the governor, who then gives a brief address. The lieutenant governor is sworn in at the same time and place and also delivers an address. On the eve of the inauguration and on inauguration day, a variety of festivities and events take place—inaugural balls, prayer breakfasts, parades, and the like. The ceremonies are dwarfed by the inauguration of the President but are similar in purpose and pageantry. They represent a peaceful transfer of political power accompanied by the symbolism of legitimacy. Following the completion of his term of office, the governor's portrait will be hung alongside those of his predecessors in the capitol rotunda.

Term of Office

From 1876 to 1972 the Texas governor served a two-year term with no constitutional limitation on the number of terms he could have. By tradition, Texas governors were limited to two terms until Governor Allan Shivers broke the two-term barrier in 1954 with an unprecedented third term. Since Shivers served out the unexpired term of Governor Beauford Jester, who died in office, he has served as governor longer than any other person in Texas. Governor Price Daniel, Sr., and John B. Connally also served three terms, but to date no governor has served four terms. Governor Daniel failed in his bid for a fourth term.

The issue of a two-year versus a four-year term for the Texas governor was a hot one for a number of years. By 1972, forty-two states had granted their governors the longer term. Finally, in 1972, Texas joined the parade. The voters approved a constitutional amendment that provided for the four-year term to begin in 1974 for the governor and other executive officials listed in Section 1 of Article IV of the Texas constitution. No restrictions were placed on the number of terms a governor may serve. As constitutional revision proceeds in Texas, the governor's tenure will be reevaluated. Although it is unlikely that a two-year term will be

[3]Section 4 of Article IV of the Texas constitution provides that the "Governor shall be installed on the first Tuesday after the organization of the Legislature, or as soon thereafter as practicable."

restored, it is less unlikely that the number of terms will remain unrestricted. Seventeen states in 1972 restricted tenure to two consecutive terms, and eight states denied the governor a second consecutive term.[4]

The choice of 1974 as the year in which the new four-year terms will begin is worthy of comment. As mentioned in Chapter 3, some states have tried to separate the state elections from the elections for President and Vice President. Texas will join these states in 1974. The election of the governor and other high executive officials will always be during the off year and never during the presidential year. This is potentially of considerable political significance and bears close watching. For one thing, the total number of votes is considerably less in the off year. The composition as well as the size of the electorate for the governor may be affected.

Compensation

The governor's salary, which was set by the 1876 constitution at $4,000 yearly, was raised to $12,000 by an amendment in 1936. In 1954 another constitutional amendment allowed the legislature to determine the governor's salary, thereby avoiding a multitude of future amendments. The salary was set at $25,000 in 1955 and has been increased several times since then. In 1969 the Texas governor received $55,000, the highest salary of any governor in the nation. The governor of New York has since leapfrogged over the Texas chief executive with his $85,000 a year salary, but Texas was second highest with $63,000 at the date of writing.[5]

The many obligations of the governorship require a rather large outlay of funds. As ceremonial head of the state, the governor must of necessity live in a rather expensive manner, entertaining frequently and well. To help defray his expenses, the state furnishes the governor with housing, the governor's mansion (which is a tourist attraction as well), with servants to run it and an expense account. The governor also is given the use of an official limousine and an airplane. During Preston Smith's administration, the plane's nose was adorned with a polka dot bow tie, the governor's personal symbol.

Qualifications and Limitations

The constitutional qualifications for the office of governor specify only age, residence and citizenship. The governor must be at least thirty years

---

[4]*The Book of the States: 1972–73*, p. 151, Council of State Governments, Iron Works Pike, Lexington, Ky., 1972.

[5]*Ibid.*, p. 156. The $63,000 figure is from the 1973 appropriation act.

old, a citizen of the United States, and a resident of the state for five years immediately preceding his election.[6] In addition to these qualifications, he may not hold any other office—civil, military, or corporate—during the term for which he is elected, nor may he practice any profession, although he may serve as an ex officio member of state boards. It will be noted that the chief executive does not have to be a qualified voter; and Texas has had one governor, W. Lee O'Daniel, who, through failure to pay the poll tax, was not a voter at the time of his first election. While the legislature is in session, the chief executive must live where the sessions are being held and at all other times at the capitol unless legally required or authorized to live elsewhere.

A bare recital of the legal qualifications for the governorship tells us nothing about other attributes necessary or desirable in the chief executive. Professor Fred Gantt, in his picture of the "composite" Texas governor, indicates that the governor has been typically a native Texan born of socially acceptable parents of modest means.[7] He has come from a medium-sized city or small town in central or east Texas, has had some governmental experience, usually at the state level, and has been a lawyer. He has been forty-eight years old, married, and the father of several children. He has belonged to many organizations, including a leading Protestant denomination, usually Methodist or Baptist, and the Masons.

From Gantt's composite, it is clear that the recruitment and election process has added qualifications for the office not set by the Texas constitution. A screening has occurred, eliminating blacks, Mexican Americans, women (except for Mrs. Ferguson), persons of minority religious denominations, and so on. This may be the subject of criticism or regarded as simply a reflection of the dominant groups and attitudes in Texas.

In order to win election, the governor must be politically acceptable to the voters and must normally obtain the backing of a significant number of powerful groups or interests in the state. Governor Preston Smith was somewhat unusual in winning his race in 1968 without the support of many established interests and also by moving up the ladder from the position of lieutenant governor. Although other lieutenant governors have become governor, they usually became the chief executive upon the death of the governor and then were subsequently elected to the office.

---

[6]Although there is no specific religious qualification, the Bill of Rights of the state constitution states that no one shall "be excluded from holding office on account of his religious sentiments, provided he acknowledges the existence of a Supreme Being" (Art. 1, Sec. 4). This provision is probably unconstitutional, as the United States Supreme Court declared a similar requirement in the Maryland constitution invalid in 1961 in *Torcaso v. Watkins*, 367 U.S. 488.

[7]Fred Gantt, Jr., *The Chief Executive in Texas*, pp. 69–70, University of Texas Press, Austin, 1964.

Governors after Annexation

Feb.	19, 1846–Dec. 21, 1847	J. Pinckney Henderson
May	19, 1846–Nov. —, 1846	A. C. Horton[a]
Dec.	21, 1847–Dec. 21, 1849	George T. Wood
Dec.	21, 1849–Nov. 23, 1853	P. Hansborough Bell
Nov.	23, 1853–Dec. 21, 1853	J. W. Henderson[b]
Dec.	21, 1853–Dec. 21, 1857	Elisha M. Pease
Dec.	21, 1857–Dec. 21, 1859	Hardin R. Runnels
Dec.	21, 1859–Mar. 16, 1861	Sam Houston[c]
Mar.	16, 1861–Nov. 7, 1861	Edward Clark
Nov.	7, 1861–Nov. 5, 1863	Francis R. Lubbock
Nov.	5, 1863–June 17, 1865	Pendleton Murrah[d]
July	21, 1865–Aug. 9, 1866	Andrew J. Hamilton (provisional)
Aug.	9, 1866–Aug. 8, 1867	James W. Throckmorton[e]
Aug.	8, 1867–Sept. 30, 1869	Elisha M. Pease
Jan.	8, 1870–Jan. 15, 1874	Edmund J. Davis[f]
Jan.	15, 1874–Dec. 1, 1876	Richard Coke[g]
Dec.	1, 1876–Jan. 21, 1879	Richard B. Hubbard
Jan.	21, 1879–Jan. 16, 1883	Oran M. Roberts
Jan.	16, 1883–Jan. 18, 1887	John Ireland

[a]Lieutenant Governor Horton served as governor while Governor Henderson was away commanding troops in the war with Mexico.

[b]Lieutenant Governor Henderson became governor when Governor Bell resigned to take his seat in Congress to which he had been elected.

[c]Houston refused to take the oath of allegiance to the Confederacy and was deposed. He was succeeded by Lieutenant Governor Edward Clark.

[d]Murrah's administration was terminated by the fall of the Confederacy.

[e]Throckmorton was removed by the military. Pease, provisional governor who succeeded him, resigned Sept. 30, 1869.

[f]Davis was appointed provisional governor after he had been elected governor.

[g]Coke resigned to enter the United States Senate and was succeeded by Lieutenant Governor Hubbard.

Succession

The constitution states that in case the governor dies, resigns, is removed from office, is unable to serve, or is out of the state, the lieutenant governor exercises the powers of governor. We have already discussed the lieutenant governor in his role as presiding officer of the Texas Senate. As noted before, he is also an executive officer; and when acting as chief executive, is paid on the same basis as the governor.

By legislative enactment, in case the lieutenant governor vacates his office for any of the reasons given in connection with the governor, the president pro tempore of the Senate is next in line of succession, followed by the speaker of the House of Representatives, the attorney general, and the chief justices of each of the fourteen courts of civil appeals in the numerical order of the districts.

Governors after Annexation *(cont.)*

Jan. 18, 1887–Jan. 20, 1891	Lawrence Sullivan Ross
Jan. 20, 1891–Jan. 15, 1895	James S. Hogg
Jan. 15, 1895–Jan. 17, 1899	Charles A. Culberson
Jan. 17, 1899–Jan. 20, 1903	Joseph D. Sayers
Jan. 20, 1903–Jan. 15, 1907	S. W. T. Lanham
Jan. 15, 1907–Jan. 19, 1911	Thomas M. Campbell
Jan. 19, 1911–Jan. 19, 1915	Oscar Branch Colquitt
Jan. 19, 1915–Aug. 25, 1917	James E. Ferguson[h]
Aug. 25, 1917–Jan. 18, 1921	William P. Hobby
Jan. 18, 1921–Jan. 20, 1925	Pat M. Neff
Jan. 20, 1925–Jan. 17, 1927	Miriam A. Ferguson
Jan. 17, 1927–Jan. 20, 1931	Dan Moody
Jan. 20, 1931–Jan. 17, 1933	Ross S. Sterling
Jan. 17, 1933–Jan. 15, 1935	Miriam A. Ferguson
Jan. 15, 1935–Jan. 17, 1939	James V. Allred
Jan. 17, 1939–Aug. 4, 1941	W. Lee O'Daniel[i]
Aug. 8, 1941–Jan. 21, 1947	Coke R. Stevenson
Jan. 21, 1947–July 11, 1949	Beauford H. Jester[j]
July 11, 1949–Jan. 15, 1957	Allan Shivers
Jan. 15, 1957–Jan. 15, 1963	Price Daniel
Jan. 15, 1963–Jan. 21, 1969	John B. Connally
Jan. 21, 1969–Jan. 16, 1973	Preston Smith
Jan. 16, 1973–	Dolph Briscoe

[h]Governor Ferguson was removed by impeachment and was succeeded by Lieutenant Governor Hobby.

[i]Lieutenant Governor Stevenson became governor when Governor O'Daniel resigned to enter the United States Senate.

[j]Lieutenant Governor Shivers succeeded to the governorship upon the death of Governor Jester.

Source: Adapted from Rupert Norval Richardson, *Texas, the Lone Star State*, pp. 553–554, Prentice-Hall, Englewood Cliffs, N.J., 1943.

The constitution made no provision for succession should the governor-elect die after election but before taking office. To remedy this situation and to prevent a possible dispute over the succession to the governorship or a possible vacancy in the office, a constitutional amendment ratified in 1948 provides that, if the governor-elect should die, the lieutenant governor-elect will act as governor until after the next general election. In case the governor-elect should become disabled or fail to qualify, then the lieutenant governor will act as governor until a person has qualified for the office of governor or until the next general election. To clarify further the succession to the governorship, the legislature, acting under the authority of the amendment, has provided that if both the governor-elect and the lieutenant governor-elect die or become permanently disabled, the speaker of the House and the president pro tempore of the Senate shall call a joint session of the House of Representatives and the Senate to elect a governor and lieutenant governor for a regular constitutional term, which is now four years.

Removal

Removal is by process of impeachment, although no causes are given in the constitution. The charges are brought by simple majority vote of the House of Representatives, with trial in the Senate. After the House votes the articles of impeachment, the governor is suspended from office while the trial is in progress. A two-thirds vote of the senators present is necessary to convict. The punishment is removal from office and prohibition from holding any other state office. Impeachment and conviction do not, however, bar the offender from being elected to a Federal office.

The Texas statutes have a provision whereby the House of Representatives may be convened for purposes of impeachment by the speaker upon petition of fifty members or by a majority of the membership. If articles of impeachment are voted and the Senate is not in session, either the governor or the lieutenant governor may convene the upper house to conduct the trial. If no meeting has been called within fifteen days after voting the articles of impeachment, the president pro tempore of the Senate may call that body into session. In the event that he fails to act after five more days, the Senate may be convened by a petition bearing the signatures of a majority of the members. This procedure has never been used. In fact, only one state executive official has been impeached—Governor James E. Ferguson, in 1917.

The charges against the governor, and his subsequent conviction and removal from office, resulted from charges of misuse of state funds and the governor's political attack on The University of Texas and its governing board. Some years after the trial the legislature attempted, through an "Amnesty Act," to remove the disabilities (prohibition from holding any other state office) stemming from the impeachment conviction, but it was later repealed by the legislature and still later declared unconstitutional by the attorney general and the Texas supreme court.[8]

Impeachment is quite clearly an extraordinary method of removing the governor from office and one available only to the legislature when it is in session. Another procedure for removal, one not dependent on the legislature, is the recall. In the eleven or so states with the recall, the voters may remove an executive official before his term is up. The procedure involves the initiation of a petition signed by either a specified

[8]28 S.W. (2d) 526.

number or a percentage of voters requesting removal. This is then submitted to the voters for approval or rejection. The recall has been rarely used. In fact, only one governor (Governor Frazier of North Dakota in 1921) has ever been recalled. Proposed constitutional amendments providing for the recall have been introduced in the Texas legislature and considered during constitutional revision deliberations in 1973 and 1974. With the initiation of a four-year term for governor and other high state executive officials, the recall takes on added significance as a weapon for voters if they choose to get rid of officials engaged in illegal or outrageous conduct. The two-year term was so short that it was possible, if desired, to replace a governor or other official relatively frequently by the normal election route.

THE POWERS OF THE OFFICE

The powers of the Texas governor may be classified into formal, that is, those given by law; and informal, that is, those derived from other sources although they may stem indirectly from the legal powers. It is customary to group the formal powers of the governor into three principal categories: the executive, the legislative, and the judicial powers.

Executive Powers

Since the Texas constitution designates the governor as the chief executive, one would expect him to possess a battery of awesome powers over the executive branch, enabling him to carry out his constitutional duties. This is not, however, the case. Although the constitution directs the governor to take care that the laws are faithfully executed, the constitution and statutes fail to give him powers commensurate with his responsibilities. Nonetheless, he possesses a variety of executive powers to which we now turn.

Appointment The appointment power enables the executive to hire the people who execute the laws, an essential means by which he may control administration. In Texas, a governor who was reelected under the two-year term system prior to 1974, had the authority to appoint people to fill approximately 1,000 positions, mainly in the executive branch.[9] Insofar as individual officers are concerned, the governor appoints only one of the constitutionally enumerated seven in Section 1 of Article

---

[9]"Functions and Organization of the Office of Governor of Texas," *Report to Governor-Elect Preston Smith*, p. 4, Texas Research League, Austin, December, 1968.

IV—the secretary of state, a position that is elective in most states. He also appoints three statutory department heads—the adjutant general, the commissioner of labor statistics, and the executive director of the Department of Community Affairs—as well as the Director of the Office of State-Federal Relations and about nine other state officials of lesser stature. As for boards and commissions, the governor appoints all the members of some, only one member of others, a minority greater than one of still others, and a majority of others. He appoints the Texas representatives on numerous interstate compact boards. He appoints some local boards and officials, such as pilot boards and branch pilots at various ports, and the governing boards of the river authorities. He is allowed, of course, to appoint members of his own office staff, which will be discussed more fully later in this chapter. It should also be mentioned that the governor himself serves on eight boards in an ex officio capacity, that is, by virtue of his office. Although the Senate usually approves the appointments, there have been significant exceptions. For example, Governor Preston Smith was forced to withdraw a few nominees and others were rejected outright.

The governor fills vacancies in all state and district offices in the executive and judicial branches of the government, but the appointees serve only until the next general election. He also fills vacancies in the United States Senate until an election can be held. He cannot fill vacancies in the state legislature or in the Texas delegation to the national House of Representatives, but calls special elections to fill them.

The appointing power is not, however, without its limitations:

1. All appointments require confirmation of two-thirds of the senators present, which is a rather high majority compared with the simple majority needed to confirm presidential appointments.

If the governor makes a recess appointment, *i.e.,* if the Senate is not in session when the appointment is made, the appointee's name must be presented to that body during the first ten days of the next session, either regular or special. The Senate may not, however, call itself into extraordinary session to pass on the governor's recess appointments. If the nominee is rejected by the Senate, the governor must present another. If the Senate refuses to approve an appointee during the session, the governor may not reappoint the same person to that office after adjournment. He may, however, appoint someone else, whose name will then be presented to the next session.

There is a fairly strong tradition of "senatorial courtesy" which serves as a further limitation on the governor. If the senator from the appointee's district objects to the appointment strongly enough, other senators tend to join with him to prevent confirmation. It is difficult for the outsider to know just how this system of senatorial courtesy works; however, it is generally understood that a senator can virtually block any gubernatorial appointee from the senator's own district if he wants to. For this reason, governors usually consult the senator concerned before announcing an appointment to the press.

2. The appointment power does not extend to the heads of five major state departments and two boards, all of whom are elected and thus independent of the governor.

3. The members of boards and commissions serve for overlapping terms, usually of six years, with one third of the members appointed every two years. Unless there are deaths or resignations, the governor cannot appoint a majority of the members until the second of his two-year terms. The situation will be different under the new four-year term system.

4. The boards and commissions appoint the executive director who is in charge of the actual administration of the functions entrusted to them; he is not appointed by the governor, in other words.

5. Some offices require technical qualifications or some other kind of attribute which limit the pool of appointees from which the governor must choose. For example, two members of the State Commission for the Blind must be blind. Still other offices must be apportioned among different economic or professional groups or geographical sections of the state.

6. The governor must make certain appointments from lists submitted to him by other governmental agencies or by private organizations.

Despite these limitations, the appointing power is probably the governor's most important executive power. Since, as we shall see, many of the state's most important activities are controlled by boards and commissions, the governor had been able to exercise a measure of authority in administration by appointing a majority of the members after two or four years in office.

Removal   The power of removal of appointees or the right to fire them is another power essential to control over the execution of the laws. The Texas governor, unlike the President, has no inherent power of removal of executive officials. In fact, it has been claimed that he has virtually no removal power at all.[10]

The Texas constitution is at the root of the problem. There is a strong presumption, supported by considerable authority, that state

---

[10]Clifton McCleskey, *The Government and Politics of Texas*, 4th ed., p. 196, Little, Brown and Company, Boston, 1972.

officers may be removed only by some kind of judicial proceeding, which is specified in the constitution or in the statutes.[11] The key language in this regard is found in Section 7 of Article XV, which states that the legislature shall provide "for the trial and removal of all officers of this state, the modes for which have not been provided in this Constitution." A glance at the "modes" provided for in the constitution shows that impeachment and address are mentioned and some additional methods for judges. Impeachment followed by trial is a legislative proceeding, as we have already said in Chapter 5 when describing the judicial powers of the legislature. Address consists of a request by two-thirds of the legislature to the governor that he remove certain officials. Both impeachment and address apply only to certain officials, not to all.[12] The methods applicable only to removal of judges other than address and impeachment do not involve action by the governor. (See Chapter 10 for more details.) Another constitutional method of removal is by *quo warranto* proceedings, a legal procedure by which the legal right of a person to hold office is determined by the courts. Apparently, the attorney general, who is elected independently of the governor, must initiate these proceedings. Other methods involve a trial of some sort, as indicated by the language quoted above from the Texas constitution. So there we have it: the governor is without the power to remove officers.

However, there are ways of getting around the constitution and vesting some removal powers in the governor and other executive officials. First, the constitutional language refers only to "officers" and not to "employees." Hence, by classifying a position as that of an employee, it is possible to avoid the restrictions on removal from office. Second, the legislature has established offices with no set term, allowing the appointee to serve only at the pleasure of the governor or other executive official.[13] As a result of these two ploys, the governor has some removal powers. His immediate aides, for example, are employees and may be hired and fired as he desires. Certain other appointees serve at his pleasure. One example is the Director of the Department of Community Affairs.

[11]Two principal cases are *Dorenfeld v. State*, 73 S.W. (2d) 83, and *Knox v. Johnson*, 141 S.W. (2d) 698.

[12]For a table showing what officials are governed by what removal provision in the Texas constitution, see George D. Braden, *Citizens' Guide to the Texas Constitution*, pp. 46–47, Texas Advisory Commission on Intergovernmental Relations, Prepared by the Institute for Urban Studies, University of Houston, Austin, 1972.

[13]The Texas legislature has passed legislation specifically designed to permit firing of superintendents of state hospitals. They have been designated as employees, take no constitutional oath of office, and serve at the pleasure of the board under which they serve. See McCleskey, *op. cit.*, p. 198, fn. 22.

Fiscal In modern times, the budget is the key to the control of policy and administration. Using a classic definition of politics, the budget determines who gets what, when and how. In terms of administration or execution of the laws, budgetary control is crucial to the chief executive. As we shall see, the Texas governor lacks the requisite powers to control the budget and herein lies probably the basic weakness of his office today.[14] (The budget will be discussed at greater length in Chapters 9 and 11.)

The governor is required by the Texas constitution to submit estimates of revenues to the legislature at the beginning of every regular session. By statute he is designated as chief budget officer of the state and is authorized to present a budget containing estimates of expenditure needs of the executive agencies for the coming fiscal period, which is two years in Texas. The governor has been provided with staff assistance for this purpose. His principal aide is the budget director, formally called the Director of Operations Analysis. However, in 1949 the legislature established the Legislative Budget Board which prepares a budget also; and the legislature uses the LBB estimates as the basis for consideration of the budget during the legislative session, virtually ignoring the governor's budget except when some policy issue is pressed by him. Texas is one of only two states with a dual budgetary system. Forty-four states have executive budgets only.

Following the adoption of the budget by the legislature, it must be executed or carried out. The governor has little authority over budget execution. He lacks the assistance of an office comparable to the U.S. Office of Management and Budget, formerly the Bureau of the Budget. He also lacks the President's power to impound funds, to transfer funds from one agency to another, to regulate the rate at which agencies may spend funds, and other components of supervision. The legislature has, however, granted the governor some powers. To select one of several provisions at random by way of example, the written approval of the governor is required before funds appropriated to the Texas Alcoholic Beverage Commission may be spent on rentals.[15] Although never secure in his role in budget execution, three Attorney General Opinions written in 1972 placed the governor in a very tenuous position.[16] One denied the governor the power to transfer appropriated funds from one state agency

---

[14]For an extended discussion, see "Better Budgeting and Money Management for Texas," *A Report to Governor Preston Smith and the Texas Legislature*, Texas Research League, Austin, February, 1971.

[15]*Ibid.*, p. A-3. The report contains an appendix in which are listed numerous provisions from the 1970–1971 biennium appropriation act which gives some budget execution authority to the governor.

[16]Att. Gen. Op. M-1141 (1972); Att. Gen. Op. M-1191 (1972); Att. Gen. Op. M-1199 (1972).

to another; another said the governor could not withhold approval of funds even though circumstances had changed from the time they were appropriated by the legislature; and the third held that the governor may not transfer funds from one item of appropriation to another within an agency. The exact status of the governor's power is unsettled.

Planning   The governor was designated the chief planning officer of the state by statute in 1967, and a Division of Planning Coordination was established in his office. Earlier in 1965, a state planning program got underway by temporary legislation that expired in 1967. The new planning role of the governor has increased his capacity to direct the administration of Texas laws. For one thing, the governor has been able to obtain information about the operation of state agencies not available heretofore. He has also been able to bring about some needed coordination among state agencies whose functions overlap and to assist in getting them to work toward common goals. He has also been able to provide guidance in the more orderly development of the state's urban and rural areas by his control of state programs assisting financially and otherwise voluntary regional planning organizations, often called Councils of Governments or COGs.

Planning is probably an esoteric subject to the average citizen, but it carries great potential for the people of Texas. Speaking very generally, planning is designed to enable the people to control their destiny by determining what their objectives and goals are and how they may best reach them. Planning involves research into the available human and physical resources of the community, region, or state; projections into the future; coordination of functional plans for transportation, water development, recreation, and so on; and much more.

Planning was brought home to many Texans by the Goals for Texas program, which was initiated in 1969 by the Office of the Governor. Phase one involved an inventory of basic goals and objectives of the principal state agencies. Phase two was directed at the people who were invited to express their ideas about the future growth of Texas. Coordinated by the regional Councils of Governments, about 7,000 people participated.[17]

Reports and Ordinances   Planning is one resource by which the governor may direct the work of Texas agencies, but it carries little

[17]See Office of the Governor, Division of Planning Coordination, *Goals for Texas, Phase One*, Austin, September, 1969; and *Goals for Texas, Phase Two*, Austin, September, 1970.

enforcement power. This is true also of his constitutional authority to require reports, including financial, from all administrative agencies.[18] He may also inspect at any time the books, accounts, vouchers, and public funds of the agencies.

As the chief executive of the state, the governor may issue proclamations and decrees, although his power in this regard is in no way comparable to the power of the President to issue executive orders. The Texas legislature tends to pass laws in great detail instead of in broad, general terms with the details to be filled in by executive order. Most of the governor's decrees and proclamations deal with relatively unimportant matters, such as declaring "Cleanup Week" or "Better Gardens Week" or calling attention to some topic that sponsors wish to associate with the prestige of the governor's office. Consequently, the governor's proclamations usually do not have the force of law and are relatively meaningless hortatory declarations. One exception was the executive order establishing the Texas Urban Development Commission in 1970. The importance of the commission will be examined in later chapters.

Head of State   As noted at the beginning of this chapter, the governor is the head of the state of Texas. From this position flow several executive functions. The Texas constitution expressly makes him the official channel of communications between Texas and the Federal government and the other states in the Union. To help him in his contacts with the Federal government, the legislature created the Division of State-Federal Relations. Formerly a division in the governor's office, it was made a separate statutory agency in 1971. The director, a gubernatorial appointee who serves at the pleasure of the governor, has offices in Washington. He keeps state officials informed of Federal programs affecting Texas and advises Federal agencies of state policies and points of view. In general, he serves as the governor's liaison man between the state and the national government and is authorized to act for local governments in their dealings with Federal agencies. When one considers the many Federal financial assistance programs and guidelines with which the states must abide in order to participate in the various programs, the importance of the governor and the state in having a "contact man" on the Washington scene is evident.

In his relations with other states, the governor may grant or refuse

----

[18]The Texas constitution provides in Section 24 of Article IV that executive officers shall report to the governor semiannually on funds received and disbursed, and that the governor may require from them "information in writing . . . upon any subject relating to the duties, conditions, management, and expenses of their respective offices and institutions."

requests from other state governors for extradition of fugitives from justice. All requests from Texas for extradition are made in his name. He is the Texas representative on the Interstate Oil Compact and a member of the board of the Southern Regional Education Compact.

Military and Law-Enforcement Powers

The Texas constitution designates the governor the commander-in-chief of the Texas military forces except when they are in the service of the United States. Although the Federal government bears the responsibility for defending the nation and the states are forbidden except with congressional consent to maintain armies and navies, the states may establish militias. Today the Texas state militia is composed of the National and the State Guards. The Texas National Guard is composed of the Army National Guard and the Air National Guard. It and the State Guard are directed by the adjutant general who is appointed by the governor and subject to his orders as the governor's agent. As commander-in-chief, the governor may call out the militia and assume command of the Department of Public Safety (which includes the famed Texas Rangers, at present an eighty-eight–man force, and the Highway Patrol) in times of disaster, riot, invasion, insurrection or raids by hostile Indian tribes. He may also declare martial law in any area where the militia is needed to assist the civil authorities in maintaining law and order.

The governor's power in the traditional field of law enforcement or criminal justice is quite limited. Texas follows the traditional pattern among the states of a decentralized police and prosecutory system. Law enforcement rests essentially with local and district officials—city police, county sheriffs, county attorneys, and district attorneys. At the state level, the governor has some emergency authority over the Department of Public Safety, but that is about it. One new development was the establishment of the Texas Criminal Justice Council in response to the Federal Omnibus Crime Control and Safe Streets Act of 1968. The Council, which is located in the governor's office, has responsibility for the development of a state plan for criminal justice and for administering Federal Law Enforcement Assistance Grants. It works closely with regional planning organizations and local governments.

Legislative Powers

The governor's legislative powers, both formal and informal, were discussed in Chapter 6. For the reader's convenience, the formal legislative powers will be reviewed here and developed more fully.

Special Sessions The governor may call the legislature into special session at any time for any reason but must state the purpose in his proclamation asking the legislators to return for the extraordinary meeting. Unlike the President of the United States, he may not call either house alone into special session. There is no limit to the number of sessions a governor may call, but each one is limited to thirty days. He could, if he wished, keep the legislature meeting constantly.

In special sessions the legislature may pass laws only upon matters submitted to it by the governor, but it may perform other functions, such as impeachment and passing on gubernatorial appointments. In controlling the subjects for legislation, the governor may sometimes exert a rather wide influence. He does not introduce a bill as such but simply gives the legislature the topic. He may, of course, have a "spokesman" introduce a bill which he and his advisors have drawn up.

Despite the governor's theoretical control of the subject matter of legislation at special sessions, the custom has developed that legislation on other topics may be passed unless some member of the house in which the bill is being considered raises a point of order which is sustained by the presiding officer. If such bills are passed and the governor either signs them or files them without his signature with the secretary of state, that action is sufficient to validate them.

Message The governor may give messages to the legislature at any time, either in person or in writing. The constitution requires him to give an opening message to the legislature and one on his retirement from office. He may also deliver or send special messages from time to time during his term. In addition, the governor may submit emergency matters to the legislature during the regular session, and he is required to give the legislature an estimate of the money required from taxation and account for all public monies received and disbursed by him. All gubernatorial messages are printed in the House and Senate journals. The legislative program of the governor is usually embodied in his opening message or in special messages in which he submits "emergency" matters for legislative consideration. Such messages usualy are not so effective here as they are in two-party states, and certainly they are not heeded to the extent of the President's message when his party is in control of Congress.

Veto Every bill which passes both houses of the legislature must be sent to the governor for his approval or veto. If he signs the bill, it is filed with the secretary of state. If he vetoes it, the bill, along with the veto message, is sent back to the house where it originated. The veto message is then read and printed in the journal of that house. The vetoed bill may be considered at once, postponed to a later date, or referred to a committee. If repassed in each house by a two-thirds vote of all members present, the veto is overridden and the bill becomes a law.

If the governor receives the bill while the legislature is still in session, he has ten days, exclusive of Sundays, in which to consider it. If the bill gets to him during the last ten days of the session or after adjournment, he has twenty days, including Sundays, after the adjournment of the session in which to act upon it. A veto here is absolute, since the legislature has no chance to reconsider. No matter when the bill is received, if the governor does not sign it, it becomes a law. This varies from procedure in the national government. There, if the bill gets to the President during the last ten days of the session or after adjournment, it is dead without the President's signature (the pocket veto). The use of the veto gives the governor considerable power. Even though he may be unsuccessful in getting his program passed by the legislature, he can usually prevent bills of which he disapproves from becoming law, although most governors use the veto sparingly.

In itemized appropriation bills, the governor has a power which the President of the United States does not have in that he may strike out particular items without vetoing the entire bill. He may not, however, reduce items but must veto the specific item in its entirety. Since the major appropriation bills (many parts of which are itemized) are ordinarily passed in the closing days of the session, the use of the item veto allows the governor to have at least some voice in the financial affairs of the state.

Judicial Powers

Pardon and Reprieve Until the adoption of a constitutional amendment in 1936, the governor had an unlimited pardoning power, but as a result of this amendment, he is now rather severely limited. He may revoke a parole or a conditional pardon and grant one thirty-day reprieve in a capital case at his own discretion. Other acts of clemency can be granted only upon the recommendation of the Board of Pardons and Paroles.[19] The governor can take no action, except in the instances noted

[19]Among the acts of clemency which may be granted by the governor upon the recommendation of the Board of Pardons and Paroles are the following: reprieve and stay of execution (postponing the carrying out of the death penalty); full pardon (legally "wiping out" the offense and conviction therefor); commutation of sentence (reducing the sentence); conditional pardon (serving the rest of the sentence outside the penitentiary but under supervision); reprieve (postponing the carrying out of the penalty); emergency reprieve (granting a furlough because of illness or death in an inmate's family or because of need for medical treatment not available in the prison system); release from reporting (releasing the

above, until the board has officially brought the matter to his consideration. He is not required to grant clemency if it is recommended by the
board but may not do so without its recommendation.

There can be no pardon for impeachment, but in cases of treason the
governor may, with the advice and consent of the legislature, grant
reprieves, commutations of punishment, and pardons.

Political and Other Informal Powers

To complete the discussion of the powers of the Texas governor we must
turn from the three categories of formal powers to the informal, chief
among which are his political powers. The political powers were described in Chapters 3 and 4 and need not be reviewed in detail. But it is
well to remember that since Reconstruction, the governor has been the
leader of the state Democratic party. He has normally controlled the
Democratic State Executive Committee, the Democratic state convention, the Texas delegation to the national Democratic party convention,
and so on.

Other informal powers of the governor are somewhat nebulous; but
if the governor defines his role as a state leader, he may use his authority
as governor and his personal and political resources to mobilize support
to attain his goals. Governor John B. Connally, for example, is recognized
for his contributions to water development and to education.[20] The
governor has access to the media, he may create study committees, he
may make personal appearances, and he may resort to all manner of
methods to focus attention on a given problem and to move the state in
the desired direction.

THE GOVERNOR'S OFFICE

Much has been written about the Executive Office of the President in
which agency are grouped the advisers and aides closest to the President.
The Texas governor also has an executive office, called the Governor's
Office, which has been created to assist him in the performance of his
duties. There is little doubt that the governor needs assistance in modern

---

parolee from the necessity of reporting to his parole supervisor). Gubernatorial clemency may also take
the form of remission of fine, restoration of driver's license or the right to apply for one, restoration of
hunting rights, and remission of bond forfeiture.

[20]For an excellent discussion of Governor Connally's role in water development, see Glenn H.
Ivy, "Gubernatorial Leadership: Statewide Water Supply Development in Texas," in Richard H.
Kraemer and Phillip W. Barnes, *Texas: Readings in Politics, Government, and Public Policy,* pp. 196–209,
Chandler Publishing Company, San Francisco, 1971.

times. Four assistants were all the help he needed in 1918, but this is no longer true. The office has grown to sizable proportions, employing over 240 people in 1972.

The governor's responsibilities are obviously dwarfed by those of the President, but nonetheless, he too is a tremendously busy man. A glimpse of his work is given by the following excerpt from a study of the organization of Texas state government:

> Any recitation of formal powers and duties fails to convey an adequate picture of the activity that characterizes the Governor's office—activity that is routine in part and yet crowded with the unusual in the variety of problems and situations presented.
>
> Contacts with the many State agencies and institutions—receiving their reports, counseling with them on means of advancing the public interest in their respective fields, attempting to co-ordinate some of their activities through interagency committees and other devices—all make heavy demands upon the time and energies of the Governor or his staff.
>
> Investigation and planning for the development of the State and its resources and the general well-being of the people call for frequent and extended conferences with department heads, members of the Legislature, officials of local government, civic associations, and individual citizens.[21]

The governor's work had accelerated to such an extent by the late 1960s that Governor-elect Preston Smith in 1968 requested the Texas Research League to undertake a study of the governor's office and to make recommendations for its reorganization.[22] Most of the suggestions of the league were carried out in a reorganization of the office. Additional changes were made during the four years Smith served as governor.

Speaking very generally, the Governor's Office in 1972 was divided into two major components. One was headed by the executive assistant to the governor, an aide who has traditionally been closest to the governor. He should be distinguished from the governor's administrative assistants. The other component was headed by the Assistant for Program Development. Informally, the part of the office headed by the executive assistant was called the "political" side and the part headed by the Assistant for Program Development was the "program" side.

Under the executive assistant were grouped the following personnel and offices: Legal Counsel, Staff Services Officer, Administrative Assistant for Appointments, Accounting Division, Public Information Office and Press Secretary, and the Human Relations Committee. Among the

---

[21]Texas Legislative Council, *Manual of Texas State Government*, p. 3, Austin, 1953.
[22]"Functions and Organization of the Office of Governor of Texas," *op. cit.*

best known of this group was the press secretary who, as one might guess, was the public relations arm of the office.

Under the Assistant for Program Development were: the Division of Operations Analysis (budget), the Division of Planning Coordination, the Office of Comprehensive Health Planning, the Office of Criminal Justice Planning, the Office of Informational Services, and the Committee on Aging.

The Governor's Office under Preston Smith's administration was highly regarded. The quality of the personnel appointed to fill the various positions was unusually good. The turnover was less than customary following the Connally administration. The reorganization no doubt helped also. Perhaps the main thing was that the Governor's Office had become institutionalized, providing for continuity of personnel and programs.

Each governor must mold the office to his own needs and desires; therefore, there will always be some changes when a new governor takes office. This was the case when Dolph Briscoe succeeded Preston Smith. However, the basic structure below the top assistants remained much as it was under Preston Smith although observers noted a certain proliferation of offices and personnel under Briscoe.

IMPROVING THE GOVERNORSHIP

As observed at the beginning of this chapter, the Texas governorship is a prime target of constitutional revisionists and other reformers. It is easy to point out the reasons why the office is described as "weak." Among the more important are the following: (1) the plural executive created by the Texas constitution, which leaves the governor without power over other high executives except for the secretary of state; (2) the numerous constitutional and statutory limitations as well as senatorial courtesy upon the appointment power; (3) the lack of removal powers; (4) the lack of adequate budgetary powers; (5) the general lack of power to direct the administration by issuing orders and enforcing requests for reports and the lack of power in law enforcement; (6) the short two-year term from 1876 to 1972.

The trend among the American states has clearly been in the direction of strengthening the governor. The "strong governor model" with a cabinet system has been supported by reformers and is advocated for Texas. Most states have a cabinet system although they do not necessarily have all the components of the "strong governor model." In the next chapter we shall discuss the model and its application to Texas.

One final point needs to be stressed in talking about improving the governorship. This is the proposal to provide assistance to the governor-elect so that the transition from the old to the new administration will be a smooth one. The new governor is not sworn into office until after the legislature has been in session for usually one week and the budgets have already been submitted. He must submit his own budget immediately and in order to provide leadership, learn quickly how to work with the legislature and the administration as well as the other actors on the political scene. The assignment is unrealistic. The governor needs help immediately after election to learn the ropes. Both Governor Preston Smith and Governor John Connally recommended assistance to the governor-elect for the reasons given. To date no action has been taken on the matter.

Chapter 9

The Texas Administration

Administration as a function of government may be defined as the carrying out of policies or laws enacted by the legislature. The organization established for this purpose is commonly referred to as the bureaucracy. Administration as function and organization has been described as follows:

> When the government constructs a mile of highway, there is an example of administration. When the government sets up and operates a university, a hospital, or any other institution, there is an example of administration. When the government, through its agents, enforces a pure-food law, or a code of fair competition, there are other examples of administration. In a word, all the departments, offices, and agencies of government that are concerned with actually doing the things that the state has declared shall be done are engaged in administration.[1]

[1]Kirk H. Porter, *State Administration*, p. 4, Appleton-Century-Crofts, Inc., New York, 1938.

In modern times, the role of the administrative agencies as initiators of policies as well as policy interpreters and executors has been stressed.

We would expect the Texas governor, who is the chief executive entrusted with the responsibility for seeing that the laws are faithfully executed, to be the director or manager of the Texas administration or bureaucracy. But this is not true for reasons given in the last chapter. We also took note of the differences between the Texas and U.S. constitutions insofar as the vesting of executive functions in the governor and the President respectively was concerned. The differences extend also to the organization and functions of the administration.[2]

The U.S. Constitution says virtually nothing about the agencies and officers, other than the President himself, who actually administer Federal laws. Except for minor references to department heads, the departments are not mentioned and the regulatory and other independent agencies are not even indirectly referred to. In short, the huge administrative structure of the national government is a product of statutes enacted by Congress with some minor exceptions accounted for mainly by executive orders. The President has been given authority by Congress to reorganize the administration, subject to certain conditions, such as a Congressional veto and a prohibition against abolition or creation of statutory agencies. The U.S. Constitution is about as flexible as it is possible to get on the subject of the administration. This enables administrative changes to be made as times dictate without the necessity for constitutional amendment. However, politics and tradition may operate as barriers to administrative change.

The Texas constitution has much more to say about the administration than the U.S. Constitution and is, correspondingly, much less flexible a document in that regard. The Texas constitution sets the outer limits for the Texas administration in several respects. Among the more important are the following:

1. It creates a plural executive. As we observed in the last chapter, the governor is only one of seven executive officials listed in the constitution. Five of the seven are elected and are accountable for their actions directly to the people rather than to the governor. The duties of the seven officials are spelled out to some extent in the constitution.

2. The constitutional provision on separation of powers (Article II)

---

[2]The junior author of this textbook participated in a graduate seminar devoted to the study of the Texas administration at the Lyndon B. Johnson School of Public Affairs at the University of Texas in the spring of 1973. Some of the data and ideas used in this chapter are derived from the seminar and the report prepared by the students. The authors wish to acknowledge their debt to them. For more information about the seminar, see *The Constitution of Texas and the Administrative Structure of the State, A Report Prepared by the Seminar on Constitutional Revision,* Lyndon B. Johnson School of Public Affairs, University of Texas at Austin, 1973.

has been the basis for Texas Attorney General Opinions that seriously restrict the powers of both the Texas legislature and the governor to execute the budget, that is, to supervise the spending policies of the administrative agencies.

3. The constitution at the present time either establishes directly or indirectly seventeen boards and commissions and, in some instances, spells out their duties as well.

4. The constitution establishes a number of funds the specific management of which is sometimes also regulated. These will be discussed in Chapter 11.

The constitutional limits are supplemented by statutory law enacted by the Texas legislature. As a matter of fact, most of the Texas law dealing with the administration is statutory rather than constitutional. Subject to constitutional restrictions and specifications, the legislature determines the structure of the administration, its functions, and appropriates the money to carry out its activities. The Texas legislature, more so than in other states, is the ultimate master of the administration through its control of the purse, its power to criticize and correct by investigation, and, although used only once, the power to remove by impeachment. The legislature often attempts to control minute details of administration, not only through regular statutes but also through "riders" on appropriation bills, specifying exactly how the money is to be spent. In the day-by-day conduct of its affairs, however, the administration enjoys considerable autonomy, encouraged by the absence of control over budgetary execution by either the legislature or the governor, by the weakness of the governor's authority in general, and by the disintegrated or fragmented type of administration, all of which we shall discuss in this chapter.

GROWTH OF ADMINISTRATION

The administrative branch of state government was originally very small and of little importance, for the state had few functions, therefore few laws to be administered. But with the growing complexity of the social and economic system and the acceptance of the philosophy of the service state, the administrative branch of state government has grown by leaps and bounds. In fact, one of the amazing developments of this century has been the prodigious growth of the administrative function in all the states. Each time the body politic, acting through its legislature, decides to undertake a new function, there must be a corresponding expansion of the administration. A single statute may result in the appearance overnight of a mushroomlike growth of administrative agencies, bureaus, and personnel.

In terms of intergovernmental relations, the growth of the Texas administration has been caused in part by the partial or complete transfer of local functions to the state, as has been true of public education, highway construction, and public welfare. It has also been caused in part by the national government, particularly by the Federal grant-in-aid programs mentioned in Chapter 1. The national government has encouraged the states to expand old and to take on new functions by offering Federal money and assistance. Examples include the "701" program under which the states assist local governments with comprehensive planning and the comprehensive state planning programs; water development; and law enforcement planning and improvement. Some of the growth may be traced to interstate cooperation. As problems have exceeded the control of any one state, the states have cooperated to resolve them in many instances. Texas belongs to seventeen organizations created by interstate compact. Some of the most important are the Interstate Oil Compact, the Education Commission of the States, and the Southern Regional Education Board.

The growth of state administration is often overlooked by the citizen because the national government is such a giant. But it is a fact that in certain respects the states have grown faster than the U.S. government. The number of state employees, for example, is greater than the number of Federal civilian employees. In 1971, the number was 2,741,000 for the Federal government; 2,832,000 for the states; and 7,612,000 for the local governments.[3] In Texas there were 140,000 state employees, 403,000 local employees, and about 160,000 Federal employees. More significant is the fact that the number of Federal civilian employees has remained more or less the same for almost thirty years whereas the number of state-local employees has about tripled.[4]

An explanation of the far greater number of state-local government employees than Federal employees is that the states and their local governments have retained the major responsibility for administering domestic programs in the United States. The national government has such heavy global tasks that it has left many of the domestic chores to the subnational units of government. The states and local governments finance about two-thirds of domestic expenditures. Contrary to popular impression, it is also true that most of the money spent by state and their

---

[3]U.S. Bureau of the Census, *Statistical Abstract of the United States, 1972,* 93d ed., p. 431, U.S. Government Printing Office, Washington, D.C., 1972. The figure given is for all employees. The number of full-time equivalent employees is less, but no figure for the national government is given, preventing a comparison.

[4]Arthur A. MacMahon, *Administering Federalism in a Democracy*, p. 107, Oxford University Press, London, 1972.

local governments is generated by themselves rather than coming from the national government.

In Texas, the expansion in both state expenditures and agencies has been considerable in recent years. In 1940, total state expenditures a year were only $165,717,000; in 1950, they were over $527,000,000; in 1960, over $1,184,384,000; in 1970, $3,648,508,000; and the latest figures indicate that over $4,800,000,000 will be spent in 1974. As for the number of state executive agencies, in 1931 there were 99; in 1944, 122; in 1959, 145; in 1968, about 160; and in 1972, about 200.[5]

STRUCTURE OF ADMINISTRATION

Generally

Overall, the organization of the Texas administration is characterized by fragmentation, an almost infinite variety, and a heavy reliance on boards and commissions. The fragmentation is apparent in the very large number of agencies and officials, most of whom are not directly accountable to the governor for their actions. The infinite variety of agencies is evidenced in part by looking at their nomenclature: boards, departments, officers, commissions, councils, foundations, services, committees, and associations. The most common name applied is board or commission; and in fact, Texas does vest in boards and commissions the lion's share of responsibility for administering activities affecting the citizens of Texas.

Except for the top executive officials, such as the governor and lieutenant governor, there is no consistent pattern to be observed in the exclusion or inclusion of agencies in the Texas constitution. Constitutional and statutory agencies and officers share many of the same properties expressed in terms of amounts budgeted for them, whether they are elective or appointive, and their relative importance. Nor is there uniformity in administrative control. Some are administered solely by one official and others by a commission or board, regardless of the purpose or importance of the agency.

No attempt will be made here to discuss all the state administrative agencies. Instead, we will look at the principal units of administration and

[5]It is impossible to reach consensus on what to count in order to determine the number of state agencies in Texas. This is why there are variations in the number given in various sources. The figure 200 was based on the number of executive officials and agencies listed in the *Guide to Texas State Agencies*, 4th ed., Bureau of Government Research, Lyndon B. Johnson School of Public Affairs, University of Texas at Austin, 1972. A 1972 report by the Texas Research League suggests that the 77 operating agencies that receive money from the appropriation act are the most significant. However, the report excluded state-supported colleges and universities and grouped together some agencies. See Office of the Governor, Division of Planning Coordination, *Quality Texas Government—People Make a Difference*, A Report Prepared by the Texas Research League, p. 1, Austin, 1972.

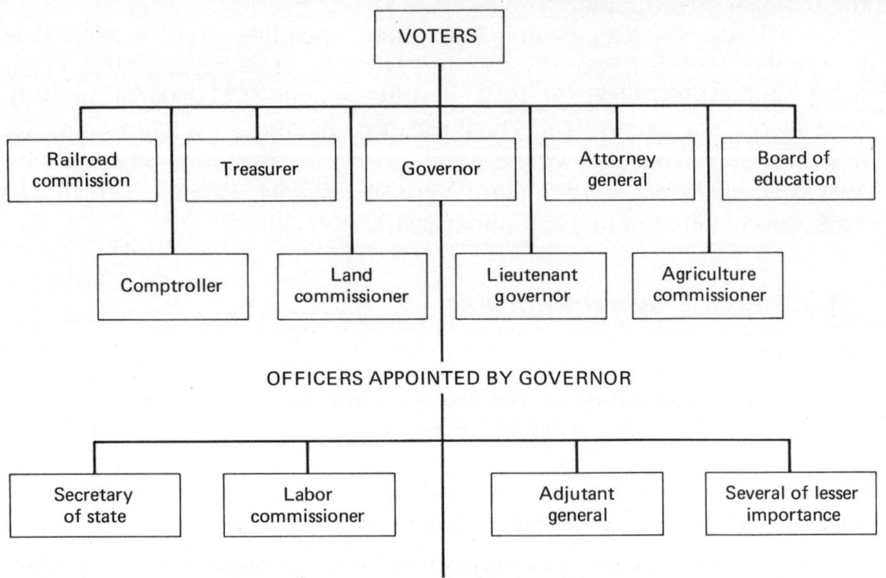

principal managerial functions associated with good administration, and then proceed to an evaluation of the Texas administration.

Major State Officials Other than the Governor

The administration of the national government is dominated by the eleven great departments—State, Defense, Treasury, etc.—each headed by an official, usually called a secretary, appointed by and removable at the pleasure of the President. The heads of the departments, together with whomever the President chooses to invite, make up the Cabinet to advise the President. In Texas the governor appoints thirteen statutory officers and one constitutional officer, but only the secretary of state (the constitutional officer) and a handful of the others head major agencies. As we have seen, his power of removal is virtually nonexistent. Departments in Texas or their equivalent are headed by elective officials or by boards or commissions for the most part. In fact, the number of single-headed agencies, whether appointed by the governor or headed by an elective officer, is small. Needless to say, there is no cabinet in Texas. We shall briefly examine the major state officials other than the governor in the next section. Unless otherwise indicated, all the officials serve four-year terms.

Lieutenant Governor   Known for his legislative role and powers, which are considerable, the lieutenant governor is a constitutionally created executive official elected statewide. Aside from serving as a spare tire for the governorship, his executive officials are minimal.[6] It is ironic that the budgetary powers exercised by the lieutenant governor in his legislative capacity are normally regarded as executive powers. The importance of the office of lieutenant governor in Texas, prompting some observers to say it is the most important one of all, stems from the legislative rather than the executive side of the office.

There is a trend toward electing the governor and the lieutenant governor as a team. In 1972 fifteen states provided for the joint ticket.[7] It is very likely that the executive side of the lieutenant governorship would increase and the legislative side decrease in importance should Texas adopt it. The rationale for the change is that in the event something happened to the governor, the governor's programs would be continued by the lieutenant governor.

Secretary of State   The secretary of state, the only appointive state executive officer provided for in the constitution, is a gubernatorial appointee. He exercises a variety of constitutional and statutory duties that almost defy classification.

As the chief election officer of the state, he certifies to the county clerk a list of the candidates who have been nominated for state and district office so that the clerk can put their names on the general election ballot. He receives, tabulates, and certifies returns for state and district elections.

Among his "secretarial" duties are the keeping of the great seal of the state and attesting the governor's signature on all commissions to office and gubernatorial proclamations, serving as custodian of official state records, keeping the original laws of the legislature, and authenticating the publication of laws. He also arranges for the publication of proposed constitutional amendments.

He has many duties with regard to corporations. Texas corporations, with the exception of banks and insurance companies, receive their charters from him, and those incorporated in other states must receive permits from him before doing business in Texas. The Uniform Commercial Code is also administered by the secretary of state.

---

[6]He appoints four members of the twelve members of the Texas Council on Marine-Related Affairs, one of six members of the Governor's Committee on Interstate Cooperation, and is the first vice-chairman of the Texas Commission on Interstate Cooperation.

[7]*The Book of the States, 1972–73*, p. 146, Council of State Governments, Iron Works Pike, Lexington, Ky., 1972.

Among his miscellaneous duties are the registration of labor-union organizers operating in the state and the appointment of notaries public and public weighers. In addition, he conducts extradition hearings for the governor.

From a political standpoint, the secretary of state is known as the "governor's man." The secretary's political ties to the governor have led to proposals for an elective office. A related reason is to make independent of the governor the administration of election laws. Joint resolutions have been introduced in the Texas legislature to change the secretary of state to an elective officer but to no avail.

Attorney General   The attorney general is another of the executive officials enumerated in the Texas constitution. He is the chief law officer of the state.

His constitutional and statutory duties fill hundreds of pages of the statutes. He and his staff (the attorney general appoints about 116 assistant attorneys general) represent the state in all cases before the supreme court and courts of civil appeals in which the state is a party, and they advise district and county attorneys in all actions in their courts where the state is an interested party.

He is the legal adviser to the governor and all other state officials, agencies, and institutions. This advice is given in writing in the form of an opinion. Although these opinions are not binding either on those who ask for them or on the courts, they are usually followed and are of considerable influence in the courts in the event that a case involving the question arises.

The department often assists legislators in preparing bills and gives opinions concerning the constitutionality of proposed legislation if asked to do so by legislative committees. Prosecutions for violations of the antitrust laws of the state are started by the attorney general. In addition, he investigates and prosecutes election frauds in any election involving two or more counties.

Commissioner of the General Land Office   The general land office is administered by the commissioner, one of the seven constitutional executives. The commissioner has responsibilities in connection with the millions of acres of state public lands. For many years Texas was unique among the states because only Texas had public lands upon her admission to the Union and was allowed to keep them. Then, in 1958, Alaska, upon statehood, was given the right to select some 102.5 million acres of United States land area as a potential tax base. Some other states have land administration officials, but their duties do not include the administration of state public lands as is the case in Texas.

Among his duties, the commissioner of the general land office supervises the leasing of the state's 22.5 million mineral acres. These include the famous tidelands, which extend from the beaches to three leagues, or 10.36 miles, and from which the public school fund is enriched from the many oil and gas leases. The commissioner also administers the Veterans Land Program, which was initiated in 1949 to reward veterans of World War II by facilitating their purchase of land for farming. A new office under the administration of the commissioner is the Environmental Division. We may also note that the commissioner is an ex officio member of the Legislative Redistricting Board, which we discussed in an earlier chapter.

Commissioner of Agriculture The commissioner of agriculture is one of the few statutory heads of departments in the Texas administration and the only elective one. The office was established by statute in 1907. The commissioner administers the Department of Agriculture which is composed of five divisions and services, all having to do in some manner with laws relating to agriculture, horticulture, and kindred industries.

One of the department's major duties is to enforce the laws regarding the control of plant pests. It also enforces various acts concerning commercial marketing of citrus fruit, eggs, and various vegetables. It has considerable authority over growers of seeds and plants, requiring them to meet certain standards. It checks insecticide residue on food crops. The market news service operated by the department provides daily quotations for Texas agricultural products. The department also enforces the laws regarding weights and measures. This includes testing the accuracy of scales, pumps, meters, and the like.

All in all, the Agriculture Department plays an important role in regulating, promoting, and providing service for one of the state's largest industries.

Comptroller of Public Accounts and the Treasurer These two officials are the "money men" of Texas.[8] Both are state constitutional and elective officials. Their financial duties will be discussed at greater length in Chapter 11, but their importance in the administration requires some attention to them in this chapter.

---

[8]An interesting résumé of the responsibilities of the two officials is contained in the *Texas Government Newsletter*, Charles Deaton, February 19, 1973. Students may note that all Texas warrants are signed by the treasurer and the comptroller.

The comptroller is the state's chief tax officer and accountant. No less than twenty constitutional provisions concern his duties in addition to numerous statutes. Among his assignments, he certifies estimates of state revenues before every legislative session and also certifies estimates of revenues under the pay-as-you-go amendment to be discussed in Chapter 11. A nonfiscal duty is his service as a member of the Legislative Redistricting Board. He is also an ex officio member of five statutory boards. Officers similar to the comptroller in the other states are usually appointed rather than elected.

The treasurer is the custodian of the state funds. His constitutional duties are few. By statute he is a member of several boards, the two most important of which are the State Banking Board, which charters state banks, and the State Depository Board, which determines where state money shall be deposited in banks around the state. The treasurer is a constitutionally elected officer in forty states.

Adjutant General   The adjutant general, who is appointed by the governor with the consent of the Senate and is the governor's agent in military affairs, is a statutory official whose position was created in 1905 although its origins go back to 1836. The office carries a two-year term. The adjutant general heads the adjutant general's department, which has responsibilities for administration of the state-federal program pertaining to the Texas Army and Air National Guard and the Texas State Guard. The National Guard is now primarily a responsibility of the Federal government which defrays most of the expense of equipment and training. Nonetheless, the adjutant general's department has numerous duties concerned with such matters as procuring property; providing buildings, equipment, and sites; supervision and control of the transportation of troops; preservation of records; and so on.

Director of the Department of Community Affairs   The executive director of the Department of Community Affairs, which was established by statute in 1971, is appointed by the governor and serves at his pleasure. The newly created position is significant for several reasons. From the standpoint of administrative structure, it is one of the few single-headed statutory agencies, and it is also under the control of the governor. The provision that the director of the agency shall serve at the pleasure of the governor is intended to allow the governor to fire him if he chooses. The new agency is also important because it further institutionalizes the obligation of the state to assist local governments, a problem to be considered more fully in later chapters.

The Department of Community Affairs was formerly the Division of

State-Local Affairs in the Governor's Office. It operates through six divisions: Community Services, Comprehensive Planning Assistance, Special Programs, Housing, and the Texas Office of Economic Opportunity.

Commissioner of Labor Statistics   Another statutory head of a department appointed by the governor is the commissioner of labor statistics, who heads the Department of Labor and Standards, formerly called the Bureau of Labor Statistics. The commissioner is appointed by the governor for a two-year term. The principal responsibilities of the department involve the enforcement of the industrial relations laws.

Director of Federal-State Relations   A statutory officer appointed by the governor for an indeterminate term, the Director of Federal-State Relations, is another important official. His duties were reviewed in Chapter 8.

Boards and Commissions

The vast majority of administrative agencies in Texas are multiheaded agencies headed by a board or commission rather than by an official. The total number of boards and commissions is very impressive and indicative of their general importance in the scheme of things. There are about 131 statutory boards and commissions in the Texas state administration. Eleven boards and commissions are created by the Texas constitution and six more are mentioned or indirectly based on the state's fundamental law. Some of these are also provided for by statute. Not all the agencies are significant. Perhaps about seventy-seven operating agencies bear the brunt of the administration of the state, with thirty-three being most important. It is impossible to list all the important boards and commissions, but a few references will be proof positive that they are integral and basic to Texas administration.

At the top of most lists of important state agencies would be the Texas Railroad Commission, which will be discussed in a later chapter. This is an agency of concern to the entire world because of its regulation of the oil industry. It has other duties as well. In the field of banking and finance, important agencies are the Banking Board, the Finance Commission, the State Securities Board, and the Insurance Board. In welfare and health the key agencies are the State Department of Public Welfare, the State Department of Health, and the Department of Mental Health and Retardation. In education, the State Board of Education plays a dominant role in public education; and the Coordinating Board, Texas College and

University System, as well as the Boards of Regents of the various state institutions of higher learning, administer the system of higher education. In the field of law enforcement or criminal justice, there are the Department of Public Safety which is headed by a board, the Board of Pardons and Paroles, and the State Prison Board. In natural resources, we have the Texas Parks and Wildlife Department which is headed by a board, the Water Development Board, the Water Quality Board, the Water Rights Commission, and the Air Control Board. This list hardly exhausts the number of key boards and commissions whose activities affect the lives of the citizens of Texas in countless ways.

The structural aspects of the board and commission system in Texas are bewildering and account for a great deal of the administrative variety about which we have commented. However, if there is a typical board, it consists of three citizens appointed by the governor with Senate consent for six-year staggered terms. The citizens serve part-time without pay except for expenses and a per diem. They are in charge of the agency, but they appoint an executive director who actually supervises and administers it on a day-by-day basis.

Texas makes considerable use of ex officio boards which are composed of officers who hold other positions. Of the approximately 900 members of the statutory boards and commissions, 160 are ex officio. Thirty-seven boards are wholly or partially ex officio. In addition there are several ex officio constitutionally created boards such as the Legislative Redistricting Board. Ex officio boards were first created to facilitate administration. The members were normally in Austin because of their official position, and a special trip was unnecessary. Also, it was thought that the members might bring special perspectives and talents to the business of the board.

Another special kind of board is the licensing or examining board. Texas has thirty-one of these. An example is the State Board of Morticians.

Boards and commissions may be very desirable for certain kinds of administrative functions, such as performing in a quasi-legislative or quasi-judicial capacity. At the national level, the independent regulatory agencies, such as the Interstate Commerce Commission and the Federal Communications Commission, have been designed to be independent because their functions have been to make policy and to decide cases within an administrative context. The Texas Railroad Commission would be a Texas version of such a commission. However, in Texas the boards and commissions are also used to administer what are called executive functions rather than quasi-judicial or quasi-legislative. Boards and commissions may also be desirable to provide advice. We will return to this question a little later on in this chapter.

CRITICISMS OF THE TEXAS ADMINISTRATION

The Texas administration has long been the target of critics for a host of reasons.

Fragmentation and Lack of Sound Organizational Principles

A recurring criticism is that the Texas administration is too fragmented, too uncoordinated, and too duplicative. In short, it lacks good, sound organizational structure. Contributing to the disorganization has been unplanned and uncoordinated growth. Each succeeding legislature has added on new offices, boards, commissions, or whatever, with little or no thought about how they fit into the existing pattern. In many instances, it would be more logical to consolidate and reorganize some of the older agencies so that they could administer the new function, but that would require overturning part of the administrative machinery already in existence. The legislature has frequently followed the line of least resistance, leaving existing structure alone and setting up an entirely new agency to carry out the added activity. Of course, this is not always true. In recent years a few efforts have been made to reorganize or to regroup agencies. For example, for many years the "701" program of planning grants to local governments was administered by the State Department of Public Health; but in 1969, the program was transferred to the Division of Planning Coordination in the governor's office.

Lack of Control by the Governor

Another criticism of long standing is that the governor lacks the controls he needs if he is to be the director or manager of the state administration. Instead, power is diffused and decentralized. For this reason, the Texas administration has been called a headless system, where responsibility for what goes wrong is hard to pinpoint. The governor, who is supposed to be the chief administrator, simply does not have the power to supervise and direct the vast administrative organization that has been built up. The factors accounting for his lack of control have been reviewed in Chapter 8 and need not be reviewed at length again. By way of summary, let us say that the governor is hampered by: (1) the long ballot creating the plural executive and the election of boards, allowing many officials and board members to act independently of the governor; (2) the numerous statutory and constitutional restrictions on the appointment powers in addition to the long ballot; (3) the lack of removal power; (4) the board and commission system; (5) the lack of adequate budgetary and personnel powers; and (6) general lack of power to order compliance with requests for information and to enforce the laws.

Injudicious and Excessive Use of Boards and Commissions

As we have seen, a dominant characteristic of the Texas administration is the large number of independent boards and commissions with responsibility for administration. The pros and cons of the board and commission system are numerous and heated. On their behalf, it is argued that they are more democratic than single-headed agencies appointed by the governor. They encourage citizen participation and input into the administration. They permit a great variety of viewpoints to be expressed. They promote continuity in decision making by the long and staggered terms. They provide a measure of insulation from politics for the executive director and the agency and add checks and balances to the administration, guarding against a strong governor.

Against the boards and commissions, it is argued that they fragment the administration so that no one knows who is doing what to whom and no one is really responsible for what goes on. They are more easily manipulated by interest groups. They can more readily be used to serve private rather than public interests than a system of unifunctional departments under the governor's control. At least the governor is visible; the people know who he is and what he is doing. They can vote him in and out of office; but they cannot really get at a system of numerous, independent boards. Some boards are elective, it is true; but generally speaking, the turnout is poorer in comparison with the governor's race. The people are not as interested in or knowledgeable about elections for board members.

In addition to the arguments about boards and commissions in general, other arguments are made about certain kinds of boards. The ex officio board is criticized on several grounds. It is argued that the members, particularly the governor and attorney general, already have too many duties to begin with without adding more by service on ex officio boards. The result is that the officials give too little attention to the work of the ex officio boards while at the same time their regular work tends to get shortchanged. Furthermore, the duties of the officer may be unrelated to the duties of the ex officio board. For example, the attorney general serves on the State Building Commission. Finally, it is argued that ex officio members are independent of one another on the board and may be like three men riding the same horse, trying to lead it in different directions.

Another category of board subject to criticism is the licensing board. The members come from the occupation or profession to be regulated. This assures some competency on their part, but at the same time the board members may be acting more in the private interest of the occupation or profession than in the larger public interest. They may even use the board as a vehicle for keeping down competition within their particular trade or profession.

Critics of boards and commissions generally concede their desirability for certain purposes. We have mentioned the quasi-legislative and quasi-judicial agencies. A plural membership to allow different points of view to be represented and voiced and a measure of insulation from normal political processes are regarded as desirable in their case. However, in Texas the boards and commissions are used for normal executive functions. They are not quasi-courts or quasi-legislatures. Execution of the laws, not deliberation and debate or judicial consultations, is the function they perform.

Weaknesses in the Budgetary System

As we said in Chapter 8, Texas has an unusual budget system. Two major criticisms of budget administration are: (1) duplication in the preparation of the budget and (2) lack of supervision over the execution of the budget.[9]

Unnecessary Duplication   It is argued that the legislature and the governor unnecessarily duplicate the work of preparing the budget under the dual budgetary system. The result is that neither the governor's budget office nor the Legislative Budget Board commands resources necessary for the best possible results. Each staff is spread too thinly. By joining forces, it would be possible to develop a larger and more competent staff.

Lack of Supervision over Spending   The greatest shortcoming of the Texas budget system, according to critics, is the absence of supervi-

---

[9]For a critique of the budget system, see *Better Budgeting and Money Management for Texas, A Report to Governor Preston Smith and the Texas Legislature*, Texas Research League, Austin, February, 1971.

sion over the spending of funds by state agencies after they have been appropriated by the legislature. In Chapter 8 we took note of the Attorney General Opinions that ruled unconstitutional gubernatorial controls. The Attorney General has also held unconstitutional supervision by the legislature and a proposed commission composed of both the legislature and the governor.[10] Each agency is an island unto itself insofar as actual spending of the money is concerned. Agencies are encouraged to spend all the money appropriated even though it may not be necessary because circumstances have changed during the course of the two-year budgetary period. On the other hand, other agencies may be starved for funds because changing conditions require additional expenditures. And so on. Under the present headless system, it is impossible to provide budgetary leadership necessary to attain state goals with the greatest economy and efficiency.

Lack of Sound Personnel Administration

Personnel administration in Texas is decentralized, which should not be surprising in view of what has already been said about the nature of Texas administration.[11] The legislature sets personnel policies in the general appropriations act every two years (or oftener when annual bills are adopted) and other statutes, but nowhere is there a central administration agency for determining, administering, or evaluating personnel policies. In fact, it is not an exaggeration to say that there are no state employees in Texas. There are only employees of the Highway Department, the Welfare Department, the Texas Railroad Commission, and so on.

Absence of Information   One of the glaring shortcomings of the present personnel system is the absence of information about it. This is not to say that no studies have been made, but essential data about employees and employment practices are not regularly collected by any central agency. One result is that we really do not know what the quality of our state employees is.

No Central Hiring Agency   A disadvantage of the decentralized system is that there is no one central hiring agency to which a prospective employee or employer may go. Quite literally, a college student or other person seeking a job in Texas state government must go to each separate agency for information except for the few serviced by the Merit System

---

[10]Att. Gen. Op. 0-4609 (1942); Att. Gen. Op. V-1254 (1951); Att. Gen. Op. M-824 (1971).

[11]Most of the information about the Texas personnel system in the text is from the report, *Quality Texas Government—People Make a Difference, op. cit.*

Council to be described below. Employers also find it difficult to know what applicants are available for job vacancies or openings.

Inadequate Wage and Salary System   In 1961, the legislature passed the Position Classification Act. Under the supervision of a classification officer employed by the auditor, more than 1,300 full-time positions in the major state agencies have been classified into twenty-one pay groups or grades, each having a minimum of eight salary steps. However, the practice has been to classify most employees in the first two steps, which are at the lowest end of the pay scale, of each grade. Also, instead of rewarding employees for good work by merit raises, the legislature has passed across-the-board raises for everyone.

Texas ranks below other states in pay scales for its employees.[12] The legislature has, however, for the past ten years or so given raises which, in percentage terms, have exceeded the rate of inflation.

We should also take note of the fact that Texas state employees receive fringe benefits. They are members of the State Employees Retirement System, which was set up in 1947 and has constitutional status. The employee pays 6 percent of his regular salary into the retirement fund. The state contributes a like amount. The accumulated sums are then used for payment to the employee upon retirement. In addition to normal pensions, disability payments are available to employees who have worked for the state for ten years. Also, state employees participate in a group insurance program. However, each agency has its own rules so that benefits and contributions vary considerably.

Lack of a Merit System   The Texas personnel system is also distinguished, if that is the proper word, by the absence of the merit system (except for a few agencies) for recruitment and promotion of employees. Texas operates under a kind of spoils system. Supporting a successful candidate for one of the elective administrative offices or the legislature is a good way of getting a job; or short of that, being a friend or ally of supporters. However, Texas has been spared the wholesale firings and hirings after each election, associated with the spoils system. The fact that the Democrats have for years controlled all the state administrative positions has been a stabilizing factor. Also, Texas has many outstanding employees who are retained because of their abilities and service to the state.

---

[12]*Ibid.*, p. 50. The monthly pay for the average full-time state employee in Texas in 1970 was $554, whereas in all the states it was $643.

Eleven agencies have the merit system mainly because it is required as a condition for receiving Federal grants-in-aid for programs they administer. The agencies are serviced by the Merit System Council, which is composed of three members appointed by the Texas Employment Commission for six-year overlapping terms. The agency administers examinations to prospective employees of the agencies employing its services, and appointments are made from the highest three scorers on the examinations. Among the important agencies using the council's services are the Texas Employment Commission, the State Department of Health, the State Department of Public Welfare, and the Department of Mental Health and Retardation.

Discrimination in State Employment A new awareness of the problems of minorities has drawn attention to the status of these groups in state employment. Also, several Federal and state laws prohibit discrimination in state employment on the basis of race, color, religion, sex, or national origin.[13] A 1972 study indicates that the proportion of blacks and Mexican Americans in state employment is less than their percentage of the total population although it is greater than their percentage of the general labor force.[14] Some 81 percent of the employees were Anglo, 8 percent black, and 10 percent Mexican American. The blacks and Mexican Americans were also employed primarily in lower paying jobs. As for women, they almost equal men in the percentage of state jobs held (48 percent), but again, as with the two minorities, their salaries are lower.

Lack of an Ombudsman

A criticism of the Texas administration of more recent vintage than most of the others is the absence of an ombudsman, although bills have been introduced in the legislature to establish the office. The ombudsman derives its name from a Swedish official who is the prototype for modern versions of the office. An ombudsman is an office independent of the executive and legislative branches established for the purpose of receiving and investigating complaints made by citizens against the administration. In this day and age when the bureaucracy is so large and performs so

[13]Among the most important Federal laws are the Equal Pay Act of 1963, which prohibits sex discrimination; the Age Discrimination Act of 1967, protecting persons between forty and sixty-five years of age; Executive Order 11246, which prohibits discrimination without regard to race, color, religion, sex, or national origin; and the Equal Employment Act of 1972, which extends Title VII of the Civil Rights Act of 1964 to state and local governments. *Ibid.*, p. 17. Section 3a of the Texas Bill of Rights prohibits discrimination on account of sex, race, color, creed, or national origin; and general statutes (Art. 6252-16) forbid agencies to employ or discharge a person on the basis of the same factors.

[14]*Ibid.*, pp. 94–103.

many functions, the citizen is more helpless than before to petition for redress of grievances. At the same time the opportunities for unjust treatment have multiplied. The more conventional avenues of redress are often out of reach for the average citizen for reasons of cost, such as court cases, or ignorance or simple cumbersomeness. Several states, including Hawaii, Nebraska, Iowa, and Oregon, have experimented with a version of the ombudsman. At the University of Texas at Austin a student ombudsman has been appointed to handle student complaints. As one writer on the subject has observed, the ombudsman has clearly arrived.[15]

ADMINISTRATIVE REORGANIZATION

Strong Executive Model with Cabinet

Many of the criticisms of the Texas administration examined in the preceding pages would be answered by the adoption of a strong governorship and cabinet system. However, there are objections to the plan, and these will be reviewed together with the arguments for it.

Components of the Model The strong governor model addresses itself to virtually all the criticisms made of the governor as an administrator.

1. It would require the reorganization of the administration into unifunctional single-headed departments of approximately twenty in number. The governor would appoint and remove the department heads.

2. It would eliminate the long ballot. Only the governor and the

[15]Bernard Frank, "The Ombudsman Concept Is Expanding in the United States," *National Civic Review*, p. 235, May, 1972.

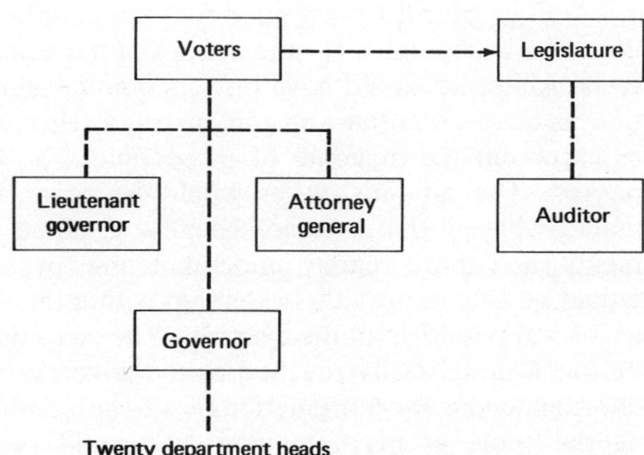

lieutenant governor and, perhaps, the attorney general would be elected. All the other elective officials and boards would be appointed or eliminated. The governor and lieutenant governor would run as a team, much like the President and Vice President today.

3. The heads of the departments would meet with the governor in a cabinet to assist him with the management of the administration.

4. The governor would be in charge of budget preparation and execution. The legislature would adopt the budget and appoint the auditor to check on the legality of expenditures made by the administration. (The auditor is discussed in Chapter 11.) Adequate staff assistance would be necessary, and it might be provided for in a Department of Administration.

5. A Department of Administration, in which the management functions could be grouped, is an optional component of the strong executive model. Pioneered by the state of Minnesota, the department is under the control of a manager appointed by the governor. Budgeting, personnel, and purchasing functions would be assigned to the department. The governor would then be provided with the managerial tools he needs to manage the administration.

6. The planning function would be placed in the governor's office or in a Department of Administration.

7. The governor would be given power to reorganize the administration, subject to a legislative veto and such other conditions as the legislature chooses to impose.

An Evaluation   The strong executive concept has been incorporated in the Model Constitution prepared by the National Municipal League and endorsed by many other groups, such as the National Governor's Conference.

On its behalf, it is argued that the people would be able to hold the governor accountable for the actions of the administration for which he is responsible; he would have powers commensurate with his responsibilities as chief executive and administrator. He would be in a position, then, to carry out the mandate of the people. The buck could no longer be passed. The administration would be organized on a rational basis, manageable by the governor because grouped into a few major departments, and more readily understandable by the people. The governor would be able to provide leadership within the administration, by serving as a focal point for all the agencies. The goals desired by the people could be much more easily reached as the governor would be in a position to coordinate the far-flung activities of the administration. With the managerial tools at his command, he would be equipped to direct the administration in a more efficient, economical, and democratic manner.

Against strengthening the governor it is argued that the strong governor model has many drawbacks and would not really do what its supporters claim it would. The present system provides protection against a weak governor, which is what is really needed. A strong governor can persuade and cajole to get the administration to work toward his goals; he can surmount the fragmented system. A weak governor in charge of an integrated administration would be a disaster. The whole administration would suffer from lack of leadership.

Another argument is that we do not elect a governor for his administrative skills. He is elected for his political and policy prowess. If the administration is dependent upon him to the extent proposed by the strong executive model, it could well become a political machine.

A related argument is that no governor could possibly handle all the complexities of an administrative system. As mentioned, he is not elected for his administrative skills and is unlikely to be a top-rate administrator in any event. The more responsibilities he has as an administrator, the less well he can cope with them. Too much responsibility can mean inability to cope with any. It is just as well to keep some of the administration independent or at least capable of continuing regardless of who the governor happens to be. A criticism of the U.S. President is that he has been given too much authority; no human being can possibly handle well all this authority, and the nation suffers for it.

A rather traditional argument against the strong governor model is that it is too dangerous insofar as the people's liberties are concerned. We need checks and balances. True, there are other checks and balances in the system—the legislature, the courts, the voters, and so forth—but nonetheless, there is a line that should not be crossed.

One final argument concerns the long ballot. It is contended that having several elective officials is desirable. They offer an opportunity for leadership to be developed and for opposing factions or parties to have a say in government, which is particularly desirable in a largely one-party state like Texas. However, we might comment that very few holders of the elective executive offices other than lieutenant governor have gone on to higher posts. One exception is the attorney general.

The Party System   One final consideration should not be overlooked when addressing ourselves to the strong executive model. The Texas administration has so far operated under a largely one-party system. A reorganization of the administration and a strong governor should be examined in the light of what happens if Texas becomes a two-party system. Proponents of the strong model argue that a two-party system is all the more reason for having a strong governor. The governor will be able to carry out the mandate of the people under such a system.

Opponents of the strong model argue that the two-party system would result in too much instability and lack of continuity. If a merit system is incorporated into the organization, there would be protection against wholesale changes after an election. At the same time, however, the merit system would make it difficult for the new governor to carry out his program. The career personnel who would administer it would be in a position to obstruct his goals. This, by the way, is a common criticism of the Federal administration where the merit system is applied to over 90 percent of the civilian positions.

Other Reorganization Proposals

It is not necessary, of course, to adopt the entire strong executive model package in order to bring about changes in the Texas administration. Also, some proposals for change, such as adoption of the ombudsman or improving wage and salary scales, are not directly related to the model. Furthermore, it may be that less sweeping recommendations based on historical traditions may have a better chance of passage. One of these is the proposal by the Texas Research League to set up a state budget commission.[16]

The commission would be composed of the present personnel of the Legislative Budget Board, which was described in Chapter 5, with the governor as chairman. "The present executive and legislative budget staffs would be combined under a Director appointed by the Governor for a two year term with the consent of the other Commission members."[17] The commission would prepare and execute the budget. The staff would assist with the preparation, adoption, and execution of the budget. The principal advantage of the proposal is that it would not require a radical change from the present system and would retain the participation of the legislature in budget preparation. One principal disadvantage to date is that attorney general rulings have held it unconstitutional.

Toward Implementation of Reorganization Proposals

Reorganization proposals have been pressed upon the American people for about sixty years. Illinois in 1917 was the first state to reduce the number of state agencies and to reorganize on a more rational basis. Since then, "37 States have reorganized substantially, and one-third of those actions have taken place in the past five years [1965–1970]."[18]

[16]*Better Budgeting and Money Management for Texas, op. cit.*
[17]*Ibid.*, p. 17.
[18]*The Book of the States, op. cit.*, p. 141. See also George A. Bell, "States Make Progress with Reorganization Plans," *National Civic Review*, pp. 115–119, 137, March, 1972.

Texas has made less progress toward reorganization than most states. With constitutional revision underway at the date of writing, the prospects for a change in the constitutional outer limits of administration appear more promising than ever.

But numerous words of caution are necessary. There is a built-in resistance to reorganization. Many officers and employees are fearful of change. Furthermore, various interest groups which have working relationships with administrative agencies do not wish to see them disturbed. Private citizens with special interests in a particular agency often oppose any attempt to change it saying, in effect, "I'm all for economy and efficiency in government, but don't touch the X department." Until a majority of the voters become convinced that a thorough administrative reorganization will make it easier for the state to have a really efficient and responsible government, special interest groups will make it difficult for the legislature to withstand the political pressure to leave things as they are. Also, the tradition of a weak governor in Texas, at least insofar as his formal powers are concerned, is a barrier to adoption of a strong executive model.

Finally, we should not place too much faith in the mere fact of reorganization, should it come about. It takes willing and capable people to make it work. The boxes on an organization chart may be moved around on paper, but the real interpersonal relationships are not so easily shifted about. To date, we know too little about the actual consequences of administrative reorganization upon the functioning of the state government.

Chapter 10

The Texas Judiciary

The Texas judiciary or court system is the third great department of government established by the Texas constitution. The judicial branch of government has the function of administering the rule of law in society. It is a basic assumption of our political organization that all citizens, regardless of their social or economic status, are equal before the bar of justice. Not only are all citizens equal, so are the state and its servants. For this reason our government is rightly regarded as a government of laws and not of men.

Our judicial system exists, in part, to settle disputes between persons and to punish criminals. It serves the further purpose of protecting and maintaining the civil rights of citizens, particularly of the minority groups, against infringement by the state or any individual. Accordingly, the Texas judiciary has the important function of interpreting and enforcing the state Bill of Rights. In addition to enforcing state statutes, the Texas courts are to some extent called upon to interpret and apply Federal laws and even, in certain instances, the Federal Constitution. Insofar as they are called upon to make such interpretation, they are required to correlate the state with the Federal structure.

As in all the other states except Louisiana, Texas courts apply the basic rules of procedure of the common law, the principles of which are incorporated into the statutes. Yet, because of our Spanish and Mexican heritage, there exists a submerged, though significant, strain of civil-law principles, particularly in the areas of mineral and land law, riparian rights, and community property.

COURT STRUCTURE

The Texas court structure is much more elaborate and complex than the Federal judiciary. The differences are apparent from examining the key provisions of the U.S. and Texas constitutions. Section 1 of Article III of the U.S. Constitution reads in part as follows:

> The judicial Power of the United States shall be vested in one supreme Court, and in such inferior Courts as Congress may from time to time ordain and establish.

In contrast the comparable provision from Section 1 of Article V of the Texas constitution reads:

> The judicial power of this state shall be vested in one Supreme Court, in Courts of Civil Appeals, in a Court of Criminal Appeals, in District Courts, in County Courts, in Commissioners Courts, in Justices of the Peace, and in such other courts as may be established by law.

In fact, one of the courts listed in the Texas judicial article is not even a court. This is the commissioner's court. Found in every county, it is composed of the county judge and one commissioner from each of four commissioners precincts within the county. It is the county board, an administrative and quasi-legislative body, which serves as the head of the county government.[1]

It is helpful in understanding Texas court structure to think of the courts as forming a pyramid of five tiers. At the lowest level are two courts, the justice of the peace and the municipal court, both of which are trial courts with original and limited jurisdiction. Jurisdiction is the right to hear and determine cases. The next tier is composed of county courts,

---

[1]The designation of the county board as a court is a relic from early American history when administrative offices were frequently vested with judicial powers and judicial offices, administrative powers. Texas is the only state in which the county board is still called a court.

which are trial courts with limited, original, and some appellate jurisdiction. The third level consists of the district courts or general trial courts, with original and some appellate jurisdiction. They hear and try felonies or serious crimes as well as many other cases. The fourth tier is composed of intermediate appellate courts which hear only cases on appeal with minor technical exceptions. And finally, at the very top of the pyramid, are two courts, the supreme court and the court of criminal appeals. Both are appellate courts of last resort.

Justice of the Peace Courts

The justice of the peace court has jurisdiction over minor civil and criminal cases. The commissioners courts divide each county into not less than four or more than eight justice of the peace precincts, with a justice court in each, except that, in precincts where there is a city of 8,000 or more inhabitants, there are two justices. All justices of the peace are elected for four-year terms. Justices of the peace need not be lawyers. However, unless they are lawyers or have served more than two terms, they are required by statute to take within one year after assuming office forty clock hours of legal training in a state-supported college or university. After the first year, they are required to take twenty hours of training annually. The Judicial Qualifications Commission, which will be described later in the chapter, has the power to take punitive action if they do not fulfill the training requirement.

Justices of the peace courts have jurisdiction in criminal matters where punishment is by fine alone and the fine does not exceed $200, but they cannot impose jail sentences except for contempt of court, in which case the imprisonment cannot exceed one day. A person who has been fined by a justice of the peace court may serve out his fine in jail (at the rate of $3 a day) but he must serve a minimum of ten days.

Justice courts may try civil cases where the amount involved is $200 or less, provided exclusive jurisdiction has not been given to county or district courts.

As in all other trial courts of the state, a person charged with a misdemeanor—an offense not punishable by death or imprisonment in the penitentiary—is entitled to a jury trial if he requests it. In civil cases, a jury is used if either party to the case requests it and pays a jury fee of $3. In both instances, the jury has only six members. Appeals may be taken to the county court in civil cases where the judgment is for more than $20 and in certain other cases expressly provided by the laws of the state.

The justice of the peace is also designated as a magistrate; *i.e.,* he may conduct an investigation or preliminary hearing of any person charged with a criminal offense[2] to determine whether there is sufficient evidence to hold the accused person in jail for indictment by the grand jury or the filing of an "information" by the prosecuting attorney. In addition he serves as coroner, in that he holds inquests when death occurs in prison, when a person is killed in the absence of witnesses, when a corpse is found, or when the circumstances surrounding a death indicate that unlawful means were used. The four most populous counties are required by law to appoint medical examiners to serve as coroners in place of the justices of the peace. The commissioners court makes the appointment.

Every justice of the peace is automatically the judge of the small claims court, which has concurrent jurisdiction with the justice of the peace court in all actions for the recovery of money where the amount in dispute does not exceed $150, or if wage or salary is involved, does not exceed $200. A $3 filing fee, a jury fee of $3 (if either party asks for a jury), and a fee of $2 for citation are the only fees which the court may charge. The hearings are informal, and lawyers are not necessary, as no formal pleadings are required. Unless a jury has been requested, a judge renders the judgment. A dissatisfied party may appeal to the county court if the amount in controversy exceeds $20.

Municipal Courts

In 1899, the legislature provided for the establishment of a corporation court in each incorporated municipality in the state. In 1969, the name of the court was changed to municipal court by statute, and in 1971 the name of the judge was correspondingly changed from recorder to municipal judge.[3] In some cities incorporated under general law, the mayor is ex officio municipal judge. In home rule or special charter cities, the judge is selected in accordance with the provisions of the charter. Only nine municipalities in 1973 were authorized to have more than one municipal court or judge.

The municipal court has original and exclusive jurisdiction within the territorial limits of the city in all criminal cases arising under municipal ordinances (predominantly traffic cases). It also has concurrent jurisdiction with the justice of the peace courts in regard to other criminal cases arising within the city where the punishment is by fine only and where the maximum of such fines does not exceed $200. Appeals are

---

[2]County Commissioners and judges of all Texas courts, except civil appeals judges, are also designated as magistrates.

[3]*Vernons Civil Statutes*, Art. 1194A (1969); Art. 1196 (1971).

taken to county court. (It is very common to appeal convictions of driving while intoxicated to the county court.) The municipal courts have no civil and no final jurisdiction.

County Courts

Each county has a county court presided over by a county judge, who is elected every four years. This court has original jurisdiction—the trial of cases in the first instance—in all cases of misdemeanors where exclusive original jurisdiction is not given to the justice of the peace courts and where the fine imposed exceeds $200. In civil cases, it has exclusive original jurisdiction where the amount involved is over $200 and not in excess of $500. In controversies involving over $500 and not over $1,000, these courts have concurrent original jurisdiction with the district court. As we have seen, certain cases may be appealed to the county court from the justice and municipal courts. Appeals are taken from the county court to the court of civil appeals or to the court of criminal appeals.

The county court has general probate jurisdiction in that it probates wills, appoints guardians of minors and persons of unsound mind, and exercises similar powers. In these matters appeals go to the district court. Mentally ill persons are committed to mental hospitals by the county court.

In most of the more populous counties of the state, where the dockets of the county courts are crowded, the legislature has set up one or more special county courts, which are to be distinguished from the "constitutional" county courts. The regular county judge, who is also the principal administrator of county business affairs, is relieved of all or part of his judicial duties so he can spend more time on county affairs. There are fifty-six of these courts, which are called, variously, county courts at law, county probate courts, county civil courts at law, county criminal courts, and county criminal courts of appeal. The jurisdiction of the special county courts differs from that of the "constitutional" county courts. Civil jurisdiction extends to $5,000 and in at least one county to $10,000.

There are no specific qualifications for the county judge other than that he must be "well informed in the law." For all practical purposes this is meaningless, and studies have shown that about half of the regular county judges are not licensed attorneys.

District Courts

The district court is the chief trial court of the state. The number of these courts and the regions served by each are determined by the legislature.

There are over 200 separate district courts, each serving one or more counties. Sessions of the court must be held at least twice a year at the county seat of each county in the district. In counties of large population, there may be several district courts. Most of the courts exercise both civil and criminal jurisdiction, but in almost all the larger metropolitan areas, they exercise one or the other jurisdiction exclusively. Those with exclusive criminal jurisdiction are known as criminal district courts.

The district courts have original jurisdiction over felonies, divorce, misdemeanors involving official misconduct, suits for damages and slander, controversies over land titles, contested elections, and certain other matters. Their original jurisdiction is concurrent with that of the "constitutional" county courts in cases where the amounts in controversy exceed $500 but not $1,000. Above $1,000 their jurisdiction is exclusive except for concurrent jurisdiction with the special courts as determined by the legislature. They have appellate jurisdiction in probate matters originally handled in the county courts. All cases tried in the district court may be appealed to higher state courts.

Each district court is presided over by a district judge, who is elected for a term of four years. He must be at least twenty-five years old, a resident of Texas, a resident of the district for two years immediately preceding his election, and must have four years' experience as a lawyer or a judge.

Trial by a twelve-man jury can be had in all cases in the district court, although in civil cases the request must be made by one party to the suit, who is required to pay a small jury fee.

Courts of Civil Appeals

A peculiar feature of the Texas judicial system is that above the district courts there are two branches of courts, one for civil and one for criminal cases, entirely independent of each other. On the civil side, between the trial courts and the supreme court, the state is divided into thirteen supreme judicial districts, in each of which there is a court of civil appeals consisting of a chief justice and two associate justices elected for six-year terms.[4] They must have the same qualifications as members of the supreme court.

These courts have no original jurisdiction except to issue certain writs. Their appellate jurisdiction extends to all civil cases over which the district courts have original or appellate jurisdiction. It also extends to those cases in which the county courts have original jurisdiction and

---

[4]These courts are located at Austin, Fort Worth, San Antonio, Dallas, Texarkana, Amarillo, El Paso, Beaumont, Waco, Eastland, Tyler, Corpus Christi, and Houston. Since Houston is in two districts, there are two courts there.

those where the county courts have appellate jurisdiction if the amounts in dispute exceed $100. The judgments of these courts are final in all matters of fact and on certain matters of law.

Supreme Court

The highest civil court in the state is the supreme court, which consists of a chief justice and eight associate justices. They are elected for six-year overlapping terms.

The judges must be at least thirty-five years old, citizens of the United States and residents of the state, and have been practicing lawyers or both judges of a court of record and lawyers for at least ten years.

In general, the supreme court has final appellate jurisdiction over questions of law involving disagreements of judges of any court of civil appeals upon a material question of law or where a court of civil appeals holds differently from another court of civil appeals or the supreme court on the same question of law or where the constitutionality of a legislative act is involved. Furthermore, it has appellate jurisdiction over cases involving the state's revenues, cases to which the Railroad Commission is a party, and in any case involving errors of substantive law by a court of civil appeals. Also, the court has original jurisdiction to issue writs and to conduct proceedings for removal of judges.

Court of Criminal Appeals

For criminal cases, the highest court in the state is the court of criminal appeals, which has appellate jurisdiction in all criminal cases except those appealed from a justice or corporation court to a county court where the fine imposed by the county court shall not exceed $100. All decisions of the court of criminal appeals are final. The court consists of five judges, elected for six-year overlapping terms. There are also two permanent commissioners and two rotating commissioners to assist the court. This provides in practice for a nine-member panel.

Court Officers

The constable is the executive officer of the justice of the peace court, while the sheriff and his deputies serve as executive officers of the district and county courts. These officers not only arrest offenders and take charge of the prisoners but also produce them in court, serve citations, keep order in the court, carry out court orders, and have charge of the jury.

All courts except the justice court also have clerks who keep the records and collect fees. The appellate courts appoint their own clerks, while the clerks of the county and district courts are elected for four-year terms. In counties of less than 8,000 population the clerk of the county court serves as ex officio district clerk. All courts with criminal jurisdiction have prosecuting attorneys. The one for the court of criminal appeals is called the state prosecuting attorney. He is appointed by the court for a term of two years. When a criminal case is appealed to the court of criminal appeals, it is not handled by the original prosecutor but by the state prosecuting attorney, who acts for the state. The county and district attorneys, who serve as prosecutors in the county and district courts, are elected and serve for four years. The county attorney also serves as prosecutor in the justice of the peace court.

The supreme court and the court of criminal appeals have reporters who prepare the decisions of the courts for publication. The district courts have shorthand reporters to make transcripts of the trials.

THE JURY SYSTEM

The Grand Jury

The grand jury consists of twelve persons chosen by the district judge from a list of sixteen prepared by the jury commissioners for each term of the district court.[5] Their function is not to try cases but to investigate offenses and bring indictments. An indictment is a written statement of the grand jury formally accusing a person of a crime when there is sufficient evidence to warrant it. A vote of nine is sufficient to bring an indictment. No person may be tried on a felony charge unless indicted by a grand jury. Those accused of a misdemeanor may also be brought to trial by another procedure. Upon sworn testimony of a creditable person charging someone with a criminal offense—"a complaint"—the district or county attorney may bring the person to trial on what is known as an "information," which is based on the complaint. The purpose of this procedure is to avoid the necessity of impaneling a grand jury in order to bring a person to trial in minor cases.

The Petit (Trial) Jury

Under the laws of Texas anyone brought into court for any reason may demand a jury trial. This does not, of course, apply to the three highest

---

[5]At each term of the district court the district judge appoints from three to five persons to serve as jury commissioners. They make lists of prospective grand jurors. In a county with more than one district court, the statute which created the court designates the district judge who will be responsible for selecting the jury commissioners.

Table 6 The Texas Judicial System (Constitutional Courts)

Court	Personnel					Jurisdiction			
	Term	Qualifications	Salary	Removal by *	Original	Appellate	Concurrent	Exclusive	Final
Justice of the Peace	4 years	Qualified voter of the state	Salary set by county	District Court, for cause, with jury trial	Criminal: Misdemeanors not exceeding $200, no confinement Civil: Cases not exceeding $200	None	With County Court: Criminal: All misdemeanors to $200 Civil: $20–$200	Civil: Up to $20	Civil: Cases not exceeding $20
Small Claims Court (J.P.—ex officio)					Civil: Not exceeding $150, or $200 in wages	None	With J.P. Court	None	Civil: Cases not exceeding $20
"Constitutional" County Court	4 years	Person "well informed in the law of the state"	Salary set by county	District Court, for cause, with jury trial	Criminal: All misdemeanors Civil: $200–$1,000 Probate: All cases Juvenile: All cases	From J.P. Court: Criminal: All cases Civil: $20–$200 (all trials *de novo*)	With J.P. Court Criminal: All misdemeanors to $200 Civil: $20–$200 With District Court: Civil: $500–$1,000 Juvenile: All cases	Criminal: All misdemeanors over $200/jail Civil: $200–$500	Criminal: Cases not exceeding $100 Civil: $20–$100

District Court	4 years	25 years of age; resident of district for 2 years; lawyer or judge for 4 years	Set by law	Impeachment; Supreme Court for cause	Criminal: All felonies Civil: All cases over $500 Juvenile: All cases	From County Court: Probate: All cases	With County Court: Civil: $500–$1,000 Juvenile: All cases	Criminal: All felonies Civil: All cases over $1,000	Probate: All cases
Court of Criminal Appeals	6 years over-lapping	35 years of age; lawyer or judge and lawyer for 10 years	Set by law	Impeachment; address, Supreme Court for cause	None	From County and District Courts: Criminal: All cases over $100	None	None	Criminal: All cases over $100
Court of Civil Appeals	6 years over-lapping	35 years of age; lawyer or judge and lawyer for 10 years	Set by law	Impeachment; address, Supreme Court for cause	None	From County and District Courts: Civil: All cases over $100	With Supreme Court: Civil: All cases over $100 (exceptional)	None	Civil: All cases over $100, as to fact
Supreme Court	6 years over-lapping	35 years of age; lawyer or judge and lawyer for 10 years.	Set by law	Impeachment; address, Supreme Court for cause	None	From Court of Civil Appeals: Civil* From County and District Courts: Civil (exceptional)	With Court of Civil Appeals Civil: All cases over $100 (exceptional)	None	Civil: All cases over $100 which reach the Court

*All judges are subject to removal by action initiated and/or consummated by the Texas Judicial Qualifications Commission.

†Cases in which the Court of Civil Appeals disagrees on a material question of law; cases in which the Court of Civil Appeals holds contrary to a decision of another Court of Civil Appeals or of the Supreme Court; cases involving the construction or validity of an act of the legislature; cases involving the revenues of the state; cases involving an error of substantive law committed by a Court of Civil Appeals; cases to which the Railroad Commission is a party.

LINES OF APPEAL

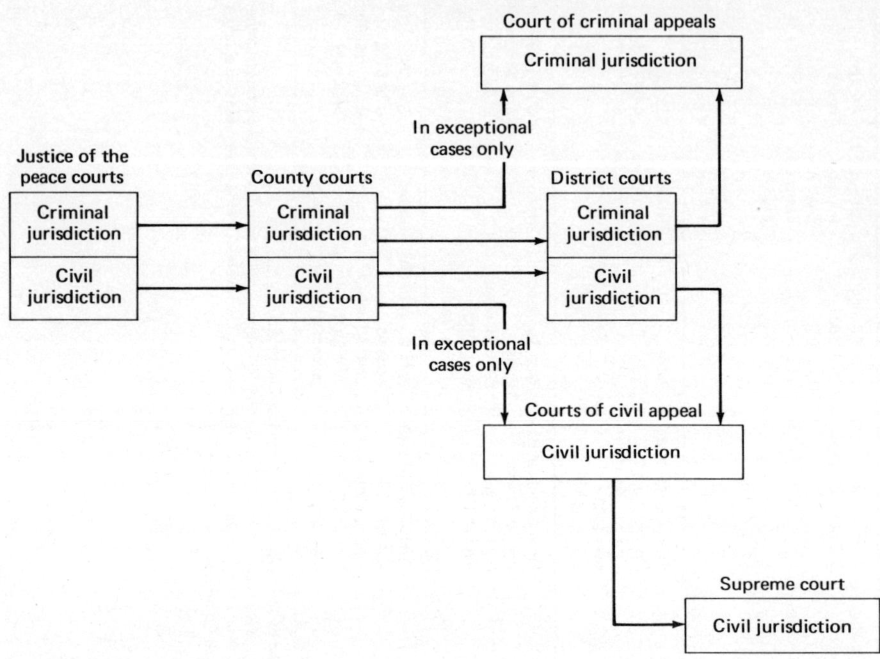

appeal courts (the court of civil appeals, the court of criminal appeals, and the supreme court), where all decisions are made by the bench of judges. The jury in the justice of the peace and county courts consists of six, but the district court uses a jury of twelve. Matters of both law and fact are determined by the jury in the justice of the peace and county courts, but in the district court the jury determines only questions of fact, the law being determined by the court. Unanimity is required for a decision in all criminal cases; but in civil cases the consent of only five of six jurors in the justice of the peace and county courts and ten in the district court are needed for a decision. If a jury cannot reach a verdict, it is discharged, a new jury is impaneled, and a new trial is called. In a criminal case if the jury's verdict is against the defendant, the judge may, before pronouncing the sentence, disregard the verdict and order a new trial if he thinks the jury has not done substantial justice. In civil cases the judge may instruct the jury to find for either party if he thinks the law, as applied to the developed facts, is clearly in favor of that party. This is known as the instructed verdict.

All jurors are determined by lot through the use of a jury wheel. The names of all potential jurors in the county are placed on cards, and these are then placed in a hollow wheel. As the wheel is turned by a handle, the slips of paper on which the names are written fall out through a slit in the rim. From the names thus selected, the jurors are summoned for court duty when the need arises.

Qualifications for Jurors

Qualifications for both grand and petit jurors are the same. Women were not allowed to serve on juries until after the adoption of a constitutional amendment in 1954 which requires them to do so. A juror must be a citizen of the state and county and qualified to vote in the county, at least eighteen years old, be of sound mind, of good moral character, able to read and write, and not have been convicted of a felony or be under indictment of theft or any felony. In addition, one must not have served as a juror in the district court for six days during the preceding six months or for six days in the county court during the preceding three months or have acted as a jury commissioner within the preceding twelve months.[6]

There are only four groups automatically exempted from jury service: (1) all persons of sixty-five years of age or older; (2) all women who have legal custody of a child or children under ten years of age; (3) all students in public or private secondary schools; and (4) students enrolled in colleges and universities. The judge may excuse others from service.

JUDICIAL SELECTION AND TENURE

Selection

Texas is one of approximately thirty-two states to provide for the popular election of most judges.[7] Texas uses the partisan rather than the nonpartisan system so that candidates are nominated by party primary or convention and run in the general election on a party ticket.

The election method of selecting Texas judges must be considered in conjunction with the method for filling judicial vacancies. The governor with Senate consent fills by appointment all vacancies in district and appellate judgeships. The county commissioners court fills those in county courts and justices of the peace.

Since Texas has a tradition of long tenure for district and appellate

---

[6]Illiteracy and recent jury service do not disqualify one from jury service if there are not enough jurors otherwise available.

[7]*The Book of the States, 1972-73*, pp. 130–132, Council of State Governments, Iron Works Pike, Lexington, Ky., 1972. Some of the thirty-two states also provide for the merit system or Missouri plan for selection of some judges. Few states employ the same method for every judge in the system.

judges, most vacancies in these offices are caused by death or resignation, thus allowing the governor to fill them by appointment. Because of the tradition of reelection of higher court and district judges, a majority of those on the bench at any one time originally received their positions by gubernatorial appointment. This means that Texas has an appointive-elective selection system rather than simply an elective one.

What criteria, other than ability, does the governor use in appointing judges? A study of judicial selection in Texas by Professors Henderson and Sinclair[8] shows that the most important factor (25.9 percent) is friendship with the governor, followed by activity in affairs of the state bar (22.4 percent), friendship with a senator (10.3 percent), and miscellaneous factors, including political or civic activity and support of lawyers (21.3 percent). Assuming that the governor thinks the prospective appointee qualified, the determining influences will be personal, political, and bar ties, all of which overlap. Personal ties will probably be the most important, and politics is personal in Texas. Since Texas state government is still dominated by one party, the governor will be relatively free from party pressures. What all of this seems to mean is that the governor appoints his friends or friends of friends.

Yet the governor is not completely free in his choices. The appointment must be cleared with the senator concerned, although senatorial courtesy is not very strong in filling judicial vacancies. Also, the appointee must face the voters at the next general election, and no governor wants his appointees defeated at the polls. The governor, therefore, will not knowingly make an appointment which will run counter to strong local feelings on the part of the bar or political groups. All in all, appointing judges to fill vacancies is one of the main aspects of the governor's appointing power. Since well over 50 percent of the district and appellate judges originally reached the bench by way of gubernatorial appointment, the governor largely determines the type of higher judiciary the state has.

Removal of Judges

There are three traditional methods of removing judges: by impeachment, by address, and by a higher court. Texas uses all three to some extent. District and appellate judges are removable by the impeachment process and by the governor on address of two-thirds of the legislature. District judges may also be removed by the supreme court upon proceedings

---

[8]Bancroft C. Henderson and T. C. Sinclair, *Judicial Selection in Texas: An Exploratory Study*, Public Affairs Research Center, University of Houston, Houston, 1964.

started by ten or more practicing lawyers in the district. County judges and justices of the peace are removable by district courts for stated causes, but only upon written charges and after a jury trial. Although these procedures might be used to remove an obviously dishonest judge, it would be difficult if not impossible to use them against a judge whose conduct is merely unethical or one who is mentally or physically incapacitated. Even though these problems rarely arise, they do come up occasionally and reflect adversely on the entire court system. In an attempt to solve the problem, the 1967 Texas Legislature, acting under authority of a constitutional amendment adopted in 1965, provided a new method for removing district and appellate judges. A 1970 constitutional amendment authorized the legislature to extend the removal to all judges, and the legislature has done so.

Under the system, a judicial qualifications commission[9] investigates complaints and may hold hearings regarding misconduct and disability of judges. The commission may censure a judge; make him retire if disabled; and if there has been judicial misconduct, issue a public or private reprimand or recommend removal to the Texas supreme court, which makes the final decision. To protect the judges and the public, due process is observed in all the proceedings.

Retirement Plan for Judges

There is a retirement system for district and appellate judges financed jointly by the state and the judges, who have 5 percent of their salaries withheld by the comptroller. After ten years of service, one year of which must be immediately preceding, a judge may retire at sixty-five. Annuities ordinarily cannot exceed 50 percent of the last salary received; but to encourage retirement of elderly judges, it is increased by 10 percent if the retirement is by the age of seventy. At the age of seventy-five, retirement is mandatory. A retired judge may not practice law before the courts of the state and still be eligible for the annuity payments, but he may, with his own consent, be recalled to active judicial duty by the chief justice of the supreme court or the presiding judge of the administrative district in which case he will not receive retirement pay but full judicial salary.

County judges, justices of the peace, and municipal judges are not members of the state's judicial retirement system and are dependent on the retirement system, if any, of their particular political subdivision.

[9]The Texas Judicial Qualifications Commission is composed of nine members: two justices of the courts of civil appeals and two district judges appointed by the supreme court, two members of the state bar appointed by the directors of the bar, and three citizens appointed by the governor. All appointments require senatorial confirmation and are for six-year overlapping terms.

JUDICIAL ADMINISTRATION

Administrative Judicial Districts

In an attempt to expedite business in the district courts, the legislature has divided the state into nine administrative judicial districts. The governor designates one district judge in each administrative district as the presiding judge, who calls an annual conference, and such special conferences as may be necessary, of all the district judges in his administrative district. Each district judge must report to the conference on the disposition of cases and the number of cases pending in his court. If too much business has accumulated in one court, the presiding judge may assign any judge, or a retired judge who consents, in his administrative district to assist in clearing the dockets. If none of his judges is available, he may call on the presiding judge of another administrative district to furnish judges to help dispose of the litigation. A district judge may also temporarily be assigned to another court if the regular district judge is absent, disabled, or disqualified.

The chief justice of the supreme court calls annual, and may call special, meetings of the presiding judges of the administrative judicial districts. At these meetings uniformity of judicial administration and the condition of the dockets of all district courts in the state are studied. If the chief justice finds the dockets of the courts in one administrative district crowded, he may assign, on a temporary basis, judges from other districts to those needing assistance.

The transfer of judges by the presiding judges of the administrative judicial districts and by the chief justice of the supreme court is a small first step toward a more unified court system. Another step in this direction is the authority of the supreme court to order cases transferred from one court of civil appeals to another.

Texas Civil Judicial Council

In 1929 the legislature created an Advisory Civil Judicial Council to make a continuous study of the organization, procedure, and operation of the civil courts and to suggest methods of simplifying procedure, expediting business, and improving the administration of justice in general. The council is composed of both ex officio and appointive members, so that the bench, bar, and laymen are well represented. Serving ex officio are the chief justice of the supreme court, two justices of the courts of civil appeals designated by the governor, two presiding justices of the administrative judicial districts also designated by the governor, and the chairmen and immediate past chairmen of the civil judicial committees of the

House and the Senate. The appointed members are seven lawyers and two laymen, one of whom must be a journalist, all appointed for six-year terms by the governor, who must, however, select two of the lawyer members from a list made by the state bar. The members serve without pay. Reports of the council carry considerable influence and have been instrumental in increasing the size of the supreme court from three to nine and in changing the power of making rules of civil procedure and practice from the legislature to the supreme court.

Rule-Making Power of the Supreme Court

The constitution of 1876 allowed the supreme court to make rules of procedure for the courts, but in actual practice they were made by the legislature. In 1891, the constitution was changed to conform with this practice, in that the court was allowed to "establish rules of procedure not inconsistent with the laws of the state."[10] Over the years, considerable dissatisfaction with this arrangement developed, and since 1941, the supreme court, by legislative enactment, has been vested with full rule-making power in civil practice and procedure. After promulgation by the supreme court, the rules are effective unless disapproved by the legislature. Rules of criminal procedure, insofar as they are not stated in the constitution, are still made by the legislature.

The State Bar

In 1939, the legislature provided for the creation of the state bar, composed of all the practicing attorneys of the state. Members of the bar are considered state officials and constitute an administrative agency of the judicial department of the state. Under authority given by the statute, the supreme court has promulgated rules concerning the conduct, discipline, and disbarment of members of the bar. All such regulations, however, must be submitted to the membership for approval. A grievance committee in each congressional district may institute proceedings in a district court to reprimand or disbar any practicing attorney in the district for unethical, fraudulent, or dishonest conduct.

The general executive agency of the state bar is the board of directors composed of the officers of the bar and not more than thirty additional members elected by the members of the bar. The president is elected annually.

The bar has been quite active in studying proposals to improve the

[10]The Constitution of the State of Texas, Art. V, Sec. 25.

administration of justice in Texas. Annual meetings of the state bar are often used as sounding boards by proponents of particular reforms, such as appointment of judges, a new state constitution, etc., thus helping to inform the public on these issues.

CRITICISMS OF THE TEXAS COURT SYSTEM

The original judiciary article of the constitution of 1876 was one of the most unsatisfactory in the entire document. A complete revision was adopted in 1891, but since then no major changes have been made in court organization or administration, with the result that Texas has one of the more antiquated judicial systems.

Fragmentation and Complexity

The Texas court system is excessively fragmented and complex. In 1973 there were approximately 2,468 courts and 2,508 judges.[11] Texas has more judges than Great Britain. As we have seen, there are five levels of courts and many different kinds at a given level. Below the district court level, for example, there are nine different kinds of courts.[12] The jurisdiction of courts overlap. From the standpoint of administration, each trial judge is independent, and the system has been described as composed of independent fiefdoms.

Supreme Courts Texas is only one of two states to have two supreme courts. This has caused problems. The court of criminal appeals has been swamped with cases, and each judge has a higher case load than any other in the system or any other appellate court in the nation.[13] The supreme court, by being limited to civil jurisdiction, cannot assist the other court. Then, there is the question of the wisdom of forcing the courts of last resort to specialize as either civil or criminal.

Intermediate Appellate Courts As we have seen, Texas has no intermediate appellate courts between the trial courts and the court of criminal appeals. The courts of civil appeals, as the name indicates, handle only civil cases. This is another reason for the heavy case load

---

[11]The totals are based on statistics contained in *Forty-fourth Annual Report*, Texas Civil Judicial Council, Austin, 1973.

[12]They are as follows: county courts, county courts at law, county civil courts at law, county courts for criminal cases, county criminal courts, county courts for criminal appeals, county probate courts, municipal courts, and justice of the peace courts. Although paid by the county, the juvenile courts and domestic relations courts are district courts of special jurisdiction.

[13]*Forty-fourth Annual Report, op. cit.,* p. iii.

carried by the court of criminal appeals. There is no buffer between it and the trial courts below.

District Courts   One of several criticisms of the district courts is that they are unbalanced in terms of case load. Never in the history of Texas has there been a real judicial redistricting act which has drawn the districts to conform to the principle of equalizing the dockets. This means that in practice some judges are extremely busy with a crowded docket whereas in other districts there is little to do. This is a very serious problem with criminal cases in the large cities. In an effort to keep up with the growing case load, each legislature creates new district courts; but the problem never seems to get resolved by this method. Another criticism is that the district judges in the larger metropolitan counties are too specialized. A district judge may serve as a domestic relations judge, for example, and be unable to decide other cases even if he has ample time to do so. In addition, each judge heads a court, and lack of coordination for such purposes as management may well occur.

County Courts   Texas is one of only a handful of states to retain the county judge in a dual capacity—as head of the county's administrative board, the county commissioners court in Texas, and as a judge of a county court. The problem in Texas is compounded by the fact that the county judge is not required to be an attorney. It is true that judges of county courts-at-law must be attorneys, but these courts have been established in only twenty-nine counties. We have already commented upon the various kinds of county courts, which adds to the complexity of the system, and creates the same kind of specialization that is true of the district courts. Another criticism is that the county courts are swamped with cases from the lowest courts from which there is an almost unlimited right of appeal, and that the cases are tried *de novo*—that is, the trial is repeated all over again in the county court.

Justices of the Peace and Municipal Courts   About 90 percent of all cases are tried in the two lowest courts, many of them being traffic cases. It is in these courts that the citizen sees the judicial system in action. Unfortunately, the system is not at its best at this level.

Many people, both lawyers and laymen, are dissatisfied with the justice of the peace court. Since no legal background is required for the office, justices are chosen from all walks of life. There have been old-age pensioners, housewives, mechanics, farmers, writers, barbers, and representatives of many other callings, but few lawyers elected to the office.

Justices sometimes hold court in their living rooms, places of business, or even their yards. In one reported instance a complaint was tried in a beer tavern. The charge was "drunkenness in a public place."[14]

Justices in many counties formerly were paid from fees collected in court cases rather than by a fixed salary. A constitutional amendment adopted in 1972 has ended this practice. Yet, "making the office pay" by collecting fines from guilty pleas may be continued indirectly in those counties where the commissioners courts base the salary of the justices of the peace on the amount of fees collected during a prior year.

Justices of the peace are not courts of record. This is one reason why appeals from the JP court are handled by a new trial in the county courts. (This is true of municipal courts as well except for the Wichita Falls municipal court. The county court now has a record to review, and the number of appeals from the municipal court has been reduced to practically zero.) Another reason for requiring trials *de novo* from the JP court has been to assure that the parties get a fair trial. This is a reflection on the quality of justice in the lowest courts.

Selection and Tenure of Judges

Many students of the Texas judicial system believe that one of the most serious defects is the election of judges. Some cogent criticisms of the elective system, made by Robert W. Calvert, former chief justice of the Texas supreme court,[15] are as follows:

1. It tends to reward the lawyer who is a good politician, yet there is little or no relation between political and judicial ability.

2. It discourages the candidacy of the legal scholar who does not like politics or has no flair for it.

3. It requires the expenditure of large sums of money, usually beyond the candidate's personal means. This requires campaign contributions from sources which eventually could prove embarrassing to both the judge and the donor.

4. It takes the time of the incumbent judge which should be devoted to his judicial duties.

5. Because of the desire of an incumbent judge for reelection, decisions of many close questions are likely to be politically oriented.

6. Election is by an apathetic and poorly informed electorate. On the average, there are about 240,000 fewer votes cast in races for the

---

[14]See Robert M. Hays, "Fee System: J.P.'s Justice Breeds Contempt for Law," *The Dallas Morning News*, June 1, 1960.

[15]Robert W. Calvert, "Selection of Appellate Judges," *Texas Bar Journal*, February, 1963.

supreme court than for the governorship. Of those who do vote, many "vote blind," depending on familiarity with names, proximity of residence, place on the ballot, and other much immaterial things.

Yet despite the elective system, Texas judges have, on the whole, been of a rather high quality, especially in the appellate courts. One probable reason for this is that the state really does not have a true elective system but an appointive-elective one[16] in that, as we have seen, over 50 percent of higher court judges first receive their positions through gubernatorial appointment and are subsequently elected. But the general quality of the judiciary could be improved if all judges were appointed.

IMPROVING THE ADMINISTRATION OF JUSTICE

Since early in this century, large segments of the bar, press, and public have discussed proposals to remedy some of the defects of the judicial system. One of the more comprehensive proposals has come from the Chief Justice's Task Force for Court Improvement, which originated in the judicial section of the Texas state bar in 1970.[17] The plan calls for a complete rewriting of the judiciary article of the constitution and would set up a unified court system and provide a new method of selecting judges. The number of words in Article V would be reduced by 80 percent. The proposals were submitted to the 1973 legislature during the regular session but were not passed. Most of the proposals have also been submitted to the Texas Constitutional Revision Commission and the legislature-convention of 1974.

Reform of Court Organization

The Chief Justice's Task Force has followed proposals made by earlier bar groups and others in Texas in its plan for reorganization of the Texas courts; and yet, there are some differences as well.[18] In general, the Task Force would greatly simplify the court structure. At the top, there would be only one court of last resort. The court of criminal appeals and the supreme court would merge. The size of the court would eventually reach

---

[16]See Henderson and Sinclair, *op. cit.*

[17]For a brief history of the Task Force and a discussion of their proposals, see "Proposed Revision Article V, Texas Constitution," *Texas Bar Journal*, pp. 1001–1018, Nov. 22, 1972. See also *Justice at the Crossroads: Court Improvement for Texas*, Chief Justice's Task Force for Court Improvement, Austin, 1972. A somewhat different plan of court reform has been proposed by the House Judiciary Committee of the Texas legislature. Consult *Streamlining the Texas Judiciary: Continuity with Change*, A Report of the Texas Judiciary Based on a Four-Year Study by the House Judiciary Committee, Austin, December, 1972.

[18]The discussion that follows is based on the draft of Article V published by the Task Force on December 15, 1972.

nine after the incumbent members vacated their positions by retirement or for other reasons. The court would be called the supreme court and would have final appellate jurisdiction in both civil and criminal cases.

The courts of civil appeals would become courts of appeals with jurisdiction over criminal cases as well as civil. The number of courts and judges and the court's jurisdiction would be determined by the legislature.

The legislature would be empowered to divide the state into districts or to authorize a state agency to do so. There would be only one trial court in each court as determined by the legislature. The district courts would be courts of general jurisdiction. Judges could specialize but not the court itself.

The legislature would also be authorized to create county courts. No county could have more than one county court, but one county court could serve more than one county. The number of judges and other court personnel would be set by the legislature. County judges would no longer serve as the presiding officers of the county commissioners courts. The commissioners courts would be renamed commissions, and their head would be called the president. Incumbent county judges could determine whether to continue to serve on the county commissioners or on the county court, provided they were attorneys. Incumbent nonlawyer county judges would be relieved of their judicial duties.

The justices of the peace and municipal courts would be abolished and their judicial duties undertaken by the county court. Nonjudicial duties could be performed by magistrates, who would not have to be attorneys. They would be appointed as determined by the legislature.

All the courts would be courts of record and all judges would be attorneys. No judge would be permitted to practice law on the side. The legislature would determine the jurisdiction of all courts.

Reforms in Administration

Administration of the judicial system would be centralized under the Task Force proposals. The chief justice of the supreme court, called the chief justice of Texas, would be at the head of the system. The supreme court would be authorized to make rules of procedure for the courts subject to legislative approval. A judicial council would formulate rules of administration, subject to supreme court approval.[19] Pursuant to the rules of

---

[19]The members of the judicial council would be the chief justice as chairman; two judges of the courts of appeals, three trial judges, and one district clerk, each appointed by the supreme court of Texas; four members of the state bar appointed by its board of directors; and two members of each house of the legislature appointed as provided by each house.

administration, the chief justice would be empowered to transfer cases from one appellate court to another and to assign judges as needed to any court in the system. The supreme court would be authorized to transfer cases from one level to another.[20] To assist the chief justice, the Task Force contemplated that the legislature would establish a court administrator who would be kind of a business manager. Regional court administrators were also envisaged. Should the chief justice be unable to perform his duties, the supreme court would be able to designate a temporary replacement from among its members.

Judicial Selection and Tenure

All judges in Texas would be selected for six-year terms by nonpartisan elections unless the voters opted for a merit system for appellate judges. The merit system of judicial selection would be contained in a separate constitutional amendment submitted at the same time as the amendment revising Article V. Approval of the separate amendment would also enable the legislature to extend the merit plan to all judges.

Under the merit plan, a nominating commission composed of eleven members, including the chief justice of Texas as presiding officer,[21] would submit to the governor a list of three names of qualified attorneys from whom the governor would choose in making an appointment to fill a vacancy in a judgeship. If the governor failed to make the appointment within sixty days after receiving the list, the chief justice would do so. The appointee would then be subject to approval or rejection by the electorate at the next general election.[22] His name would be placed on the ballot without any party designation or any other candidate. Assuming he is approved, he would be subject to the same kind of election every sixth year thereafter. Ballots used by the merit system are normally in the following style: "Shall (Judge or Justice or Chief Justice) _____________ of the (Supreme Court or Court of Appeals or District Court or other court) be retained in office? Yes____ No____."

The present Judicial Qualifications Commission and its duties would be retained under the Task Force proposals as would the retirement systems.

[20]This provision was patterned after a California law permitting the supreme court to call up a case from a lower court, such as a redistricting case, to facilitate its disposition; or to send back a case to a lower court for more information before the supreme court made its final decision.

[21]The other members would include two citizens of the state licensed to practice law who would be appointed by the board of directors of the state bar; six citizens not licensed to practice law, two of whom would be appointed by the governor, the lieutenant governor, and the speaker of the House; and one judge of a court of appeals and one district judge appointed by the supreme court.

[22]To enable the appointee to serve on a trial basis during a reasonable period, the general election at which he would be voted upon must occur at least ten months after his appointment.

Financing

The state would be responsible for absorbing the costs of the judicial system. Fees collected by the courts would, however, be remitted to the state to help defray the costs. Salaries of judges would be set by the legislature.

Jury System

The Chief Justice's Task Force in making recommendations did not address itself to the jury system, but it too has been severely criticized. Many feel that the use of the jury in complicated civil cases is unwise and that it would be better to restrict its use to criminal cases of a serious nature. The average juror knows nothing about a technical question in, let us say, corporation law; yet, he is asked to pass on all kinds of topics upon which only an expert should be expected to rule. Even in criminal cases the jury system does not always work satisfactorily. One of the main reasons for this is the dislike of jury duty by many of the better qualified citizens with the result that all too often persons totally unfit for this duty are the only ones who will serve. Judges habitually call for a list of potential jurors several times as large as the number desired. In at least one instance nearly half of those called either failed to report at all or else were excused by the judge before attorneys even questioned them. Through indifference, the citizens of the state seem to be slowly killing the jury system.[23]

PENAL CODE REVISION

A development of considerable import for the Texas judiciary and Texas law was the passage by the Texas legislature in 1973 of the first revision of the Texas penal code in 117 years. Widely acclaimed as landmark legislation, the revised code was the result of several pressures but probably none so important as the realization that substantive criminal law in Texas had been sadly neglected far too long. Public alarm at rising crime rates also helped draw attention to the need for reform.

After five years of study, a special committee of the Texas state bar presented a proposed revised penal code to the 1971 legislature, but it was not passed.[24] However, after changes in several provisions and sep-

---

[23]It is interesting that in England, the home of the common law and the jury system, the use of the grand jury has all but been abandoned and the use of the trial jury severely curtailed.

[24]For a discussion of the 1971 version of the code, see Page Keeton and Seth Searcy III, "A New Penal Code for Texas," *Texas Bar Journal*, pp. 980–990, Dec. 22, 1970.

arate submission to the legislature of the most controversial subjects, the legislature in 1973 did adopt, after amendments, the bar's proposals.

General Principles of Penal Law

The purpose of the penal code is to define conduct deemed harmful to society and to assess punishment for it. The revised penal code for the first time articulates and codifies the general principles underlying the code. Among these are culpability, criminal responsibility, and defenses to prosecution.

Culpability   An essential component of a crime is the mental state of the individual at the time of the act. For example, did he intend to kill another human being? Was the death an unavoidable accident? Did he know what he was doing? The legal term for these mental states is *mens rea* or "guilty mind." The penal code employs an alternative term, "culpability" (from which the word "culprit" is derived), or blameworthiness. The revised code for the first time carefully and rationally defines four mental states (from highest to lowest insofar as degree of criminal responsibility is concerned), one of which must be present for a crime to be committed. These are: (1) intentional; (2) knowing; (3) reckless; and (4) criminal negligence. Intentional, according to the code, refers to having "a conscious objective or desire to engage in the conduct or cause the result." Knowing means that the individual was aware that his conduct would almost certainly cause the result. Reckless is being "aware of but consciously disregarding a substantial and unjustifiable risk that the circumstances exist or the result will occur." Criminal negligence, the most controversial of the four, means that the individual ought to be aware of a substantive and unjustifiable risk but engages in behavior that grossly deviates from what a reasonable person would do.

Criminal Responsibility, including Corporate Criminal Responsibility   The revised penal code throws out the old common-law distinctions that assigned degree of responsibility for a crime on the basis of whether one was a principal, accomplice, or accessory. At present, responsibility is more simply determined on the basis of whether the individual participated in the crime or was responsible for the participation of some other person in it.

The code also for the first time incorporates the principle of corporate criminal responsibility. The special bar committee working on the penal code project stated that it was only a historical accident that

Texas had not observed the concept earlier.[25] Also, Texas was the only state not to hold corporations criminally liable for illegal acts.

Defenses The revised penal code collects general defenses to criminal responsibility in one chapter. Defenses excuse one from prosecution for conduct that would otherwise be a crime. The best known of these is probably insanity.[26] The revised code tosses out the famed "McNaughten Rule" under which a defendant is insane only if he cannot distinguish the difference between right and wrong. The language substituted is as follows:

> It is an affirmative defense to prosecution that, at the time of the conduct charged, the actor, as a result of mental disease or defect, either did not know that his conduct was wrong or was incapable of conforming his conduct to the requirements of the law he allegedly violated.

Punishments

An outstanding accomplishment of the 1973 revision of the penal code was to rationalize and codify punishments in place of the bewildering variety and combination of possible sentences under the old code. Concomitantly, the code attempted to make the punishment fit the crime and avoid irrationalities and contradictions. For example, under the old code stealing six bushels of oranges was punishable by up to ten years in the penitentiary whereas stealing a truckload of watermelons cost the guilty party a maximum $100 fine.

The revised code groups all misdemeanors into three classes—A, B, C—graded according to the severity of the punishment. Within each class there is margin for discretion in sentencing the guilty party. The three misdemeanor classes are as follows:

> Class A misdemeanor: fine up to $2,000 and/or confinement in jail up to one year;
> Class B misdemeanor: fine up to $1,000 and/or confinement in jail up to one year;
> Class C misdemeanor: fine not to exceed $200 and no jail term.

The code also groups noncapital felony offenses into three classes. With the reinstatement of the death penalty by a separate statute to be

---

[25] *Ibid.*, p. 985.

[26] In addition to the insanity defense, the code lists mistake of fact, intoxication, duress, entrapment, and age affecting criminal responsibility.

discussed later in this chapter, there are four felony grades, which are as follows:

Capital: death;
First degree felony: five to ninety-nine years in the state penitentiary or life imprisonment;
Second degree felony: two to twenty years in the penitentiary and in addition a fine up to $10,000 may be imposed;
Third degree felony: two to ten years in prison and in addition a fine up to $5,000 may be imposed.

Repeater offenders are assessed heavier penalties than first offenders. For example, if a person has had a prior felony conviction on his record and is found guilty of a new felony, his punishment will be set one degree higher than normally assigned for the offense. Third-time felony repeaters are automatically given life imprisonment.

The penalties apply, of course, to specific offenses to which we turn next.

Offenses

One shortcoming of the old 1856 penal code was the excessive number of offenses all concerned with the same act, for example, theft. The new code codifies offenses by drastically reducing their number and by organizing them into appropriate categories.

Offenses against the Person   The revised code groups crimes against the person in one title and greatly clarifies the definitions pertaining to them. Criminal homicide is, for example, defined in straightforward fashion as "intentionally, knowingly, recklessly, or with criminal negligence" (terms already defined) causing the death of an individual. The various kinds of homicide are classified as murder, capital murder (added by the death penalty statute), voluntary manslaughter, and criminally negligent homicide. The sexual offenses have been redefined as well as grouped together. Heterosexual relations between consenting adults in private are no longer classified as crimes. Homosexual relations remain crimes. Other offenses against the person are kidnapping and assaultive offenses.

Offenses against Property   Another title of the code collects offenses against property. A major improvement over the old code was the consolidation of some fifty theft offenses into one. The old common-law crimes such as theft by false pretext, conversion by a bailee, shoplifting, embezzlement, and swindling with worthless check, all of which caused endless difficulties in the courts, have been superseded by the one offense called theft. The punishments are applied in a rational manner: the lesser the value of the item stolen, the lesser the penalty. For example, stealing an item worth less than $5 is a Class C misdemeanor whereas one between $20 and $200 is a Class A misdemeanor. Also, inflation has been recognized. No longer is it a felony to steal articles worth more than $50; the line separating a misdemeanor from a felony has been raised to $250.

The legislature added to the state bar's provisions on theft and made separate offenses with separate punishments for the stealing of livestock or parts thereof.

Other offenses against property include arson, robbery, burglary, and criminal trespass.

Other Offenses   Other offenses grouped into titles in the revised penal code are inchoate offenses, offenses against the family, offenses against public administration, offenses against public order and decency, and offenses against public health, safety, and morals. Space precludes examining each of them. Suffice it to say that under inchoate offenses the code for the first time incorporates the concept of criminal conspiracy. Elements of criminal conspiracy include intention to commit a felony; agreement with one or more persons that they engage in conduct that would constitute the offense; and an overt act performed in pursuance of the agreement. An agreement may be inferred from acts of the parties.

Multiple Prosecutions

Although a matter of criminal procedure rather than substantive crime, the revised penal code carries a new section not in the state bar committee's version. For the first time it allows a defendant to be prosecuted in a single criminal action for all offenses arising out of the same criminal episode with sentences to run concurrently. Formerly, the defendant had to be tried separately on each offense committed. However, if he so elects, the defendant may be prosecuted on each offense separately with the sentences to run consecutively.

Death Penalty Statute

The state bar's proposals for a revised penal code excluded the issue of capital punishment. One reason for this was that the U.S. Supreme Court in 1972 had ruled unconstitutional the Texas statute imposing the death penalty.[27] It was also a controversial issue deemed desirable to separate from the code.

The Texas legislature joined at least thirteen other states in 1973 when it reinstated the death penalty following the court decision.[28] The reason why action was taken in the face of the adverse ruling was that the high court was very closely divided on the issue, voting 5 to 4 against the death penalty. Also, each of the nine justices wrote a separate opinion. And only two of the five-member majority ruled that the death penalty was per se unconstitutional as cruel and unusual punishment in violation of the due process clause of the Fourteenth Amendment. The other three based their opinion on the fact that the penalty had been erratically administered. In other words, as one justice said, the few individuals singled out for the death penalty among the many who committed capital crimes were in reality picked at random and not according to due process. Chief Justice Warren Burger in a dissenting opinion suggested that the states might meet constitutional standards by making the death sentence mandatory for given crimes and defining specifically the conditions under which either the judge or jury could impose the death penalty.

The new Texas law, which amends the penal code, enumerates five categories of murder for which the death penalty may be imposed. They are:

1 "murder for hire, whether the defendant is the killer or employer";

2 "murder of peace officers or firemen who are carrying on their lawful duties";

3 "murder by an inmate of a penal institution employee";

4 "murder while escaping from a penal institution, regardless of whether the victim was an employee there"; and

5 "murder while also committing burglary, robbery, kidnapping, arson or forcible rape."[29]

The life or death of the defendant lies with the jury. After the jury determines that he is guilty of murder, it then must decide whether to ask for his life. In order to impose the death sanction, all members of the jury must answer yes to three questions:

1 Was the defendant's conduct that caused the death of the deceased deliberately committed and "with the reasonable expectation that the death of the deceased or another would result";

---

[27] *Branch v. Texas,* 92 S. Ct. 2726 (1972).

[28] "13 States Restore Death Penalty," *State Government News,* pp. 2–4, May, 1973.

[29] The summary language is taken from "Streamlined Penal Code Could Be Most Lasting," by Art Wiese, *The Houston Post,* June 10, 1973.

2 Was "there a probability that the defendant would commit criminal acts of violence that would constitute a continuing threat to society"; and

3 If raised by the evidence, was the defendant's conduct in killing the deceased, "unreasonable in response to the provocation, if any, of the deceased"?[30]

If ten or more of the members of the jury answer no to any of the three questions or issues, the defendant is automatically given a life term.

The statute also provides for the automatic review of the judgment of conviction and sentence to death by the court of criminal appeals within sixty to ninety days.

Regulation of Illicit Drugs

Another issue too controversial for the state bar's proposed penal code was the problem of control of illicit drugs. The 1973 legislature enacted a new law, the Controlled Substances Act, which made significant changes in the drug laws.[31] Briefly, it sets out a new schedule of drugs with corresponding penalties for both delivery and possession within each category. The hard drugs—heroin, morphine, cocaine, and the like—carry the harshest penalties: five to ninety-nine years in the penitentiary for delivery and two to twenty years and a $10,000 fine for possession. The law reduces the penalty for possession of marijuana from a felony to a misdemeanor if the amount is four or less ounces. Marijuana is no longer classified as a narcotic. However, various offenses involving marijuana remain felonies. The Department of Community Affairs was directed to undertake further drug research, work out educational programs, and act as a clearinghouse for Federal funds. The Health Commissioner was given authority to alter the schedule of drugs; and the Director of the Department of Public Safety was authorized to regulate the registration of drugs by manufacturers and distributors.[32]

CONCLUSIONS

Renewed efforts in the 1970s to bring about judicial reform and the success with penal code revision are indicators of the movement toward modernization of Texas state government to which reference was made in Chapter 1.

---

[30]The language is from the penal code, H. B. 200, 63rd Legislature, Regular Session, 1973.

[31]H. B. 447, 63rd Legislature, Regular Session, 1973.

[32]For a summary of the new law, see "New Drug Law," *The Texas Observer*, pp. 8–9, June 15, 1973.

With this chapter, we conclude our study of the basic constitutional framework and state political and governmental institutions as well as progress toward their modernization. We turn next to what state government does—state policies and programs and how they are funded. In the language of systems analysis, we will be essentially concerned with the outputs of the Texas state political system.

Chapter 11

The State's Finances

Texas state government costs more than 4.8 billion dollars a year, and its expenditures continue to grow steadily. In 1973, Governor Dolph Briscoe signed into law the largest two-year state spending bill in history, providing for 9.7 billion dollars for the 1974–1975 fiscal period. This represented about a billion dollars more than the two one-year budgets adopted during the preceding biennium. It also represented a 900 percent increase from the 1 billion dollar two-year budget of 1950–1951.

Texas is not unique among the states with respect to rising state expenditures. From 1950 to 1970 expenditures of the states grew from 15 billion dollars to 85 billion dollars, approximately a six-fold increase.[1] The increases have been caused by many factors.[2] Inflation has taken its toll

---

[1] U.S. Bureau of the Census, *Statistical Abstract of the United States: 1972*, 93d ed., p. 421, U.S. Government Printing Office, Washington, D.C., 1972. The figure includes intergovernmental transfers, mainly Federal assistance. This is true also of the Texas figures given in the text.

[2] Charles L. Schultze, Edward R. Fried, Alice M. Rivlin, and Nancy H. Teeters, *Setting National Priorities: The 1972 Budget*, pp. 138–139, The Brookings Institution, Washington, D.C., 1971.

since much of the state budget is dependent upon goods and salaries, both of which are affected by rising price levels. Also important are long-term factors, such as population increases, urbanization, and affluence, all of which increase demands for governmental services of one kind or another.

EXPENDITURES

Expenditures for the 1972 budget year are listed according to major functions of state government in Table 7.

From the table it is apparent that the "Big Three" expenditures are public education, public welfare, and highways, which together account for almost 85 percent of the total. This has been true for many years although the public welfare program overtook highways for second place in 1971.

Education

The largest expenditure by far is for public education, which includes both the public schools (elementary and secondary) and higher education. About 65 percent of the total outlay is for the public schools and 35 percent is for higher education. The costs of higher education have been increasing greatly since the mid-1960s, and the ratio of higher to public schools has correspondingly grown. In 1966 it was 20:80. Nonetheless, the lion's share of the education budget still goes to finance the public schools.

Table 7   Net Disbursements, State of Texas, Fiscal Year Ended August 31, 1972

Function	Amount* (in millions of dollars)	Percentage of total
Public education	$1,807.8	47.7
Public welfare	758.5	20.0
Highways	606.5	16.0
Eleemosynary and correctional	178.2	4.7
Other costs	439.7	11.6
Total	$3,790.7	100.0

*The dollar amounts are approximate and have been rounded so that they do not quite add up to the total expenditure figure of $3,790,834,698.

Source: Based on the *Annual Report of the Comptroller of Public Accounts, State of Texas 1972*, Part 1A, pp. 3, 7, Austin, 1972.

The great bulk of the state's expenditures for the public schools is in support of the Minimum Foundation Program, enacted in 1949 and since amended, to underwrite financially certain minimum or basic standards in the public schools. The program will be examined at length in Chapter 12. The program has resulted in a higher than average amount of state aid for the support of public schools when compared with other states. In 1971, the proportion of Federal, state, and local expenditures for the schools was as follows:[3]

Federal	11.28 percent
State	47.81 percent
Local	40.91 percent

It will be noted that the state's share, 48 percent, was the greatest of all. This contrasts sharply with the national average, which in 1970 was about 40 percent:[4]

Federal	6.6 percent
State	40.7 percent
Local	52.7 percent

Expenditures for public education are virtually certain to continue to climb. Even though the number of public school children has stabilized and begun to drop slightly in the 1970s, there are built-in cost increases, including a ten-year teacher salary schedule with automatic raises required by law. In addition, the possibility of a basic change in school financing loomed large at the time of writing (1973). The prospects are good that the already substantial state share of public school financing will increase. The problem will be examined in the next chapter.

The expenditures for higher education have been growing at a prodigious rate. Appropriations for the 1965–1967 biennium were increased about 36 percent over those for the preceding two-year period. More recently, the rate of growth was 21 percent (between 1969–1971 to 1971–1973). The larger expenditure figures for higher education reflect efforts to elevate Texas colleges and universities to a position of national eminence. They also reflect political pressures to supply higher education to all populous communities in the state (and some not so populous) and higher costs of educating the growing college student population.

---

[3]*47th Biennial Report, Years of Transition, 1970–72,* Texas Education Agency, p. 22, Austin, 1972. Estimates were given for 1972 in the report and actual expenditures for 1971.

[4]Robert D. Reischauer and Robert W. Hartman, *Reforming School Finance,* p. 5, The Brookings Institution, Washington, D.C., 1973.

Public Welfare

Public welfare programs climbed to second place among Texas expenditures in 1971. About 20 cents of every state budget dollar goes for these programs. The steep rise in costs began in 1966 as a result of numerous factors. Insofar as Texas is concerned the most important was the response to new Federal laws and court decisions which required not only higher payments to persons on welfare and more medical assistance but also an expansion of the welfare rolls.

From Table 8 it can be determined that the most expensive of the state public assistance programs is medical assistance for which 337 million dollars was spent in 1972. However, as was true of all the programs, the Federal government paid most of the cost. The state share of medical assistance was 35 percent, the highest of all the categories. Overall, the state contributed 30 percent to the public assistance programs.

In 1974, as we shall see in Chapter 13, the Federal government assumed the financial and administrative responsibility for three of the public assistance programs: Old Age Assistance, Aid to the Blind, and Aid to the Permanently and Totally Disabled. Nonetheless, the public welfare costs absorbed by the state are expected to increase. A principal reason is that medical assistance for the needy will become more expensive.

Table 8   Net Fund Expenditure for Public Assistance by Source of Funds and Program for Fiscal Year Ended August 31, 1972

Program	Total	Source Federal	Source State	Percent from state
Total	$655.2†	$456.2	$198.9	30
Old Age Assistance	136.5	101.5	34.9	26
Aid to Families with Dependent Children	156.3	117.1	39.2	25
Aid to the Blind	3.3	2.4	.9	29
Aid to the Permanently and Totally Disabled	19.4	14.4	5.0	26
Medical Assistance	337.3	218.9	118.4	35
Work Incentive Program	1.4	1.0	.3	23

*The figures have been rounded.

†This figure includes two Federal assistance programs for which no state funds are provided. They are Cuban Refugee Assistance and Aid to U.S. Citizens Returned from Foreign Countries.

Source: Annual Report, Texas State Department of Public Welfare, p. 51, Austin, 1972.

Another reason is that the Federal government has sharply reduced its support of the social services program, to be examined in Chapter 13.

Highways

For many years, the highway program was second only to public education among state expenditures. In third place in 1972, some 16 cents of every state dollar went for highways. About 240 million or one-third of this money came from the Federal government. Everyone is familiar with the Interstate Highways, which is financed with 90 percent of Federal funds and 10 percent state. Federal-state financing of other highway programs is more evenly matched. A new program for the 1970s is highway beautification for which the state's share will be 26.5 million dollars spread over a five-year period.

As has been true of the other major items in the Texas state budget, highway expenditures are also scheduled for increases. Inflation has hit highway construction and maintenance particularly hard, and transportation planning indicates a continued demand for more and better highways in the future. This will be discussed in greater detail in Chapter 14.

Eleemosynary and Correctional Facilities

State institutions for the ill and needy and correctional institutions have taken the same proportion of the state dollar for a number of years, around $4\frac{1}{2}$ percent. The state funds provide for state homes for dependent and neglected children (a children's home has been maintained since 1887), hospitals for persons afflicted with mental illness and tuberculosis, state schools for the mentally retarded, the state prison system, the Texas Youth Council and the schools it operates for juvenile delinquents.

Other Functions

The expenditure category "other" in Table 8 includes a multitude of different items. In order of cost the most expensive item consists of grants to political subdivisions; the next, conservation, health, and sanitation; the third, interest on the debt; and the fourth, law enforcement. The amounts involved range from 84 million dollars on the local grants to 45 million dollars for law enforcement. The fifth item consists of parks, monuments, and museums (26 million dollars); and the sixth, regulation of business and industry (21 million dollars).

Executive and administrative costs, which include support of the offices of the governor and the attorney general and of the Board of Control, have usually run about 1 percent in the past. In 1972, the figure was 1.2 percent of the total budget dollar. The judiciary and the legislature each cost the state under 1 percent of the total expenditures. Thus, the expense of maintaining the three branches of government is a very small component of the total state budget dollar. The programs they administer cost the money.

REVENUE AND TAXATION

The increasing cost of state government has necessitated a corresponding growth in the state's revenues. For many years, the primary sources were the property tax and a few licenses and fees. Later, severance taxes on natural resources, notably crude oil and natural gas, supplied a major portion of the state's income. In recent years, the system has become increasingly diversified and complex as new levies have been imposed to meet the heavy revenue requirements. Supplementary to the tax structure has been the development of a massive program of Federal financial assistance.

The major components of the current revenue structure are shown in Table 9. As indicated in the table, taxes and licenses produced about 64 percent of the total revenue in 1972. It might be expected that taxes would pay for all of governmental services; but as we see in the table, there are other sources. Nationally, there has been a trend toward relying more and more on nontax revenues, including lotteries, user services for parks, higher tuition for colleges, and so on. (Lotteries are constitutionally forbidden in Texas.)

Table 9   State Revenue Receipts in Texas, Fiscal Year Ended August 31, 1972

Source	Amount* (in billions of dollars)	Percentage of total
Taxes and licenses	2.574	64.2
Federal aid and other grants and donations	1.163	29.0
Other	.272	6.8
Total	4.009	100.0

*The amounts are approximate and have been rounded so that the total may not equal the actual figure of $4,008,561,298.

Source: Based on data from the *Annual Report of the Comptroller of Public Accounts, State of Texas, 1972*, Part 1A, pp. 3–5, Austin, 1972.

Included with taxes in Table 9 were fees for the principal licenses issued primarily for regulatory purposes, such as motor vehicle licenses and driver licenses, but which are also significant as revenue producers. In some instances the line between a tax and a license is a fine one.

Financial aid from the Federal government in the form of grants in 1972 accounted for virtually all of the 1.2 billion dollars given in the table. The remaining funds, amounting to only 6.8 percent, come from a variety of sources, including rents and royalties on minerals; interest; sales of sand, shell, gravel, and real estate; and collections from pay patients in state hospitals and special schools.

Texas Tax History

It is important to realize that the tax structure is constantly changing because of new developments in the state's economy and the constant demand to increase existing services and provide new ones. Development of the state's tax system is most readily reviewed in three broad periods: (1) the period preceding 1930; (2) the period from 1930 to 1960; and (3) the period from 1960 to the present.

From its early days well into the twentieth century, the state government financed itself essentially by the property tax, the poll tax, and a few occupation taxes. The property tax accounted for about three-fourths of the state's revenue at the time of World War I and for about one-third of the total tax revenue as recently as 1932. (By way of contrast, the property tax produced only 1.5 percent of the state's revenue in 1972, and a constitutional amendment providing for the gradual phasing out of the state ad valorem tax except for one program was passed in 1968.) During the first thirty years of this century, six taxes were enacted which, in due time, provided a major share of the state's revenue. These were: (1) the severance tax on crude-oil production (1905); (2) the corporation franchise tax (enacted in 1893, with a major revision in 1907); (3) the inheritance tax (1909); (4) registration fees for motor vehicles (1917); (5) the gasoline tax (1923); and (6) the severance tax on sulphur production (1923).

As recently as fiscal 1959, these six taxes, with substantially increased rates and changes in base, produced 63 percent of the state's tax income. Collectively, they produced about one-third of the state's total tax revenue in 1966, even after adoption of the broad-based sales tax. These and the state property tax were an important part of the legacy of the pre-1930 era.

Beginning in 1930, Texas faced several years of financial crisis. For fourteen consecutive years, the state's expenditures exceeded its income.

Studies were made of the broad-based sales and income taxes adopted in other states, but Texas chose to increase rates on existing taxes and to enact selective new taxes; however, revenues from the state property tax dropped from 25 million dollars in 1930 to 15 million dollars in 1939 because of reductions in assessed valuations and the adoption of the $3,000 residence homestead exemption.[5]

A major omnibus tax bill passed in 1941 constituted the chief tax development in the 1940s. Primarily, it was designed to finance state-Federal social-security programs initiated in the 1930s and to alleviate treasury deficits. This law imposed several new taxes and, as well, raised the rates of some existing ones. The revenue produced from these sources and the growth of the state's economy during World War II stabilized finances through the 1940s. In 1947 and 1948, voters approved constitutional amendments which lowered the maximum state property tax rate from 77 to 42 cents per $100 assessed valuation. In brief, it may be said that the state's tax structure during the 1940s was based primarily on the taxation of natural resources and selective sales taxes.

The tax policy of the 1950s was quite similar to that of the previous period in that it still rested on selective sales taxes and taxes on natural gas and oil. Tax problems continued to recur with almost every legislative session, and it was apparent that temporary and piecemeal solutions would not continue to meet the state's needs indefinitely. This realization brought about a formal attempt to solve the tax problem on a more long-range basis. Between 1957 and 1961, several tax study groups reviewed the situation and concluded that Texas was faced with chronic insufficiency of funds rather than a one-time financial crisis. After considering a number of tax measures, the 1961 legislature adopted a 2 percent retail sales tax with exemptions provided for groceries, feed, seed, fertilizer, farm machinery, drugs, and other specified items. The adoption of this broad-based tax marked a major change in Texas tax policy and provided promise of meeting future revenue needs of the state with a growth tax which would produce additional revenue as the economy grew.

Tax history since the adoption of the 2 percent retail sales tax in 1961 has been primarily one of gradually increasing the rate and expanding the coverage or base. By 1973 the sales tax rate was 4 percent and only a few kinds of transactions were exempt, most notably those involving food (but not restaurant meals); prescription drugs; and farm feed, seed,

---

[5]The first $3,000 valuation of a homestead is automatically exempted from state ad valorem taxation. In 1972, the voters approved a constitutional amendment permitting local governments to exempt from local property taxes *not less than* $3,000 of homesteads owned by persons sixty-five years of age or older.

fertilizer, machinery, and equipment. In addition other taxes had been raised. A semimajor tax bill passed in 1971 raised taxes on cigarettes to 18½ cents a pack (the third highest tax in the nation as of January 1, 1973), and on liquor and beer. The legalization of sales of mixed drinks in 1971 permitted a new liquor tax to be levied. The franchise tax on business was also increased that year.

Urged on by the governor, the Texas legislature refrained from passing a new tax bill in 1973. However, the Texas Research League and other groups have predicted that new taxes will be inevitable in the near future.[6] To date Texas has avoided both the personal income tax and the corporate income or profits tax.

One other historical development should be mentioned. The state government has been gradually phasing out the state property tax. In 1968 the voters approved a constitutional amendment that required the abolition of the tax after 1978 except for a 10-cent levy to support bonds for college buildings.

The Revenue Pattern

The sources of Texas state revenues for fiscal year 1972 are shown in the figure on page 235.

Sales Taxes The sales tax yields the most revenue in Texas as it does for the fifty states collectively. Prior to 1961 Texas had only a selective sales tax which was levied on such items as playing cards, gasoline, cigarettes, and automobiles. In 1961, as we have noted, the broad-based sales tax was introduced and applied to most transactions. Legally, the 1961 tax was called the "Limited, Sales, Excise, and Use Tax"; but the number of exemptions from the tax are not great enough to warrant the word "limited" and the term "general sales tax" has prevailed.

As the comptroller's chart indicates, over 20 cents of the revenue dollar come from the general sales tax. When we add the cigarette tax, the highway motor fuel tax, the auto sales tax, and the alcoholic beverage tax, sales taxes as a group account for over 40 percent of the revenue dollar and two-thirds of the tax dollar (exclusive of licenses).

Gross Receipts and Production Taxes Gross receipts and production taxes (primarily on oil and natural gas), which have comprised as

---

[6] *TRL Bulletin on Texas State Finance*, p. 1, Texas Research League, June 4, 1973. The headline read: "No New State Taxes This Year But 1975 Outlook Bleak."

SOURCE OF THE STATE REVENUE DOLLAR IN TEXAS — 1972

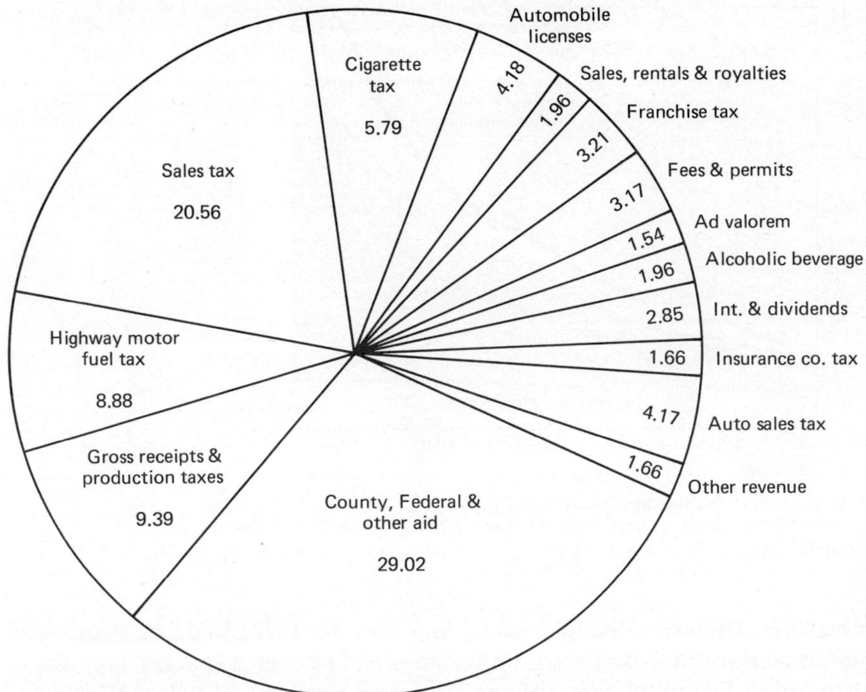

Source: *Annual Report of the Comptroller of Public Accounts, State of Texas, 1972*, Part 1A, p. 5.

much as 22 percent of the state's income, have declined in relative importance and account for only 9 cents of the income dollar.

Federal Aid The largest single source of revenue for Texas state government is Federal aid. (The county and other aid grouped with Federal aid is negligible.) Although Federal assistance is not new, its growth and increased fiscal significance are comparatively recent, as stated in Chapter 1. The steep increase from 1964 to 1973 in Federal financial aid to the states and local governments is very apparent from the chart on page 236.

Historically, grants for the construction of highways were for many years the most important segment of Federal aid. The expansion of grant-in-aid activity for public welfare has been so rapid since the mid-1930s, however, that grants for this purpose have exceeded those for highways ever since except for a brief period from 1958 to 1966 when the

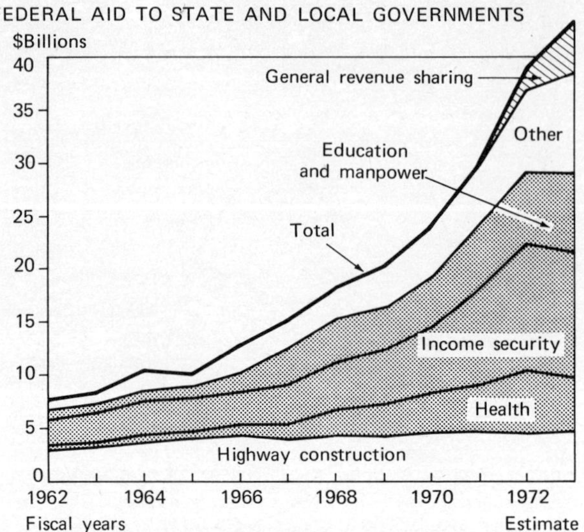

Source: Office of Management and Budget, *Special Analysis of the United States Government, Fiscal Year 1973*, p. 239, U.S. Government Printing Office, Washington, D.C., 1972.

Interstate Highway System was launched. In 1972, Federal grants for public welfare in Texas were three times as large as grants for highways, accounting for 15.26 cents of the Texas state revenue dollar. Highways were next with 5.99 cents; public education was third with 4.76; and public health was fourth with 0.45 cents. All others totaled 2.24 cents of the dollar. Federal grants for public schools increased significantly after the enactment of the Elementary and Secondary Education Act of 1965, which for the first time provided Federal aid on a broad rather than very limited scale.

The most significant new development in Federal financial aid is general revenue sharing, which was provided for in the State and Local Fiscal Assistance Act of 1972, mentioned in Chapter 1. A total of 30.1 billion dollars has been obligated for the program over the calendar years 1972 through 1976. Although not signed into law until October, 1972, the first payments were made retroactive to January 1, 1972, and the first checks were mailed late in 1972. The money received by Texas was not recorded for the 1972 fiscal year budget inasmuch as the year ended on August 31.

Under general revenue sharing, Texas is expected to receive approximately 1.3 billion dollars over the five-year period. For 1972, Texas received 246.6 million dollars of which 82.1 million dollars were retained by the state and 164 million dollars were distributed to local governments. The 1972 law provided that the states were to receive one-third of the funds and the local governments two-thirds. The Texas state government will receive about 315.1 million dollars over the five-year period.

As we said in Chapter 1, the purpose of general revenue sharing is to allow more flexibility in state and local spending of Federal funds. No program strings have been attached to the state funds, and the money may be spent for any public purpose. Local governments must spend their share on any or all of seven broadly defined "priority areas"—public safety, environmental protection, public transportation, health and recreation, social service programs for the poor and aged, financial administration, and libraries. Also, they may spend any amount for capital expenditures.

Although there are few program strings, there are many restrictions attached to the funds. These include a prohibition against using revenue sharing funds to match Federal funds for other Federal grant-in-aid programs; against using the funds to discriminate on the grounds of race, color, national origin, or sex; and against reducing the amount of state financial aid already given to local governments. Also, several Federal regulations governing wage rates on projects financed by the money must be observed. Furthermore, reports describing the purposes of the expenditures and various accounting and auditing regulations must be prepared. A special fund must be established in which to deposit the money.

The states are automatically entitled to money from general revenue sharing without application or matching grants, in contrast to Federal aid programs in the past although they too have been moving in this direction. The amount which each state receives is determined by one of two formulas; the one yielding the most revenue for the state is employed. Both formulas utilize three factors—population, tax effort, and inverse relative income (to measure poverty). In addition one of the formulas takes into account whether the state has the personal income tax and its proportion of urbanized population. In general, need, population, and tax effort are the main criteria.

Within the state, the local governments receive their two-thirds share on the basis of criteria similar to those used for distribution among the states. However, the state may adopt an alternative local distribution system. Only general-purpose local governments are eligible for the funds.

Late in 1972, Governor Preston Smith appointed a Texas Revenue Sharing Council, composed of state and local officials, to plan for the administration of the new funds. The Texas Advisory Commission on Intergovernmental Relations provides staff assistance to the council. The

1973 legislature set up a special fund for the deposit of the money from the general revenue sharing program. It is called the "Federal Revenue Sharing Trust Fund."

Other Revenue Receipts   Taxes, licenses, and Federal grants-in-aid provided for 95 percent of the total revenue receipts in 1972. The remainder came from a variety of sources, including land sales, rentals, and royalties (primarily oil and gas royalties from the state's lands), interest and dividends (including interest on state deposits and securities held by the state such as those in the Permanent University Fund), and fees and permits.

INDEBTEDNESS

In addition to raising money for the financing of regular operating expenses, it is often necessary for governments to borrow money for large capital outlays and emergency situations. The State of Texas is no exception, having resorted to the issuance of bonds on several occasions throughout its history. In recent years, the outstanding bond indebtedness of the state has increased appreciably and reflects expanded progress for which the state and its institutions have assumed responsibility.

In common with a handful of states, Texas has a stringent constitutional limitation on the creation of debt. The provision states:

> No debt shall be created by or on behalf of the State except to supply casual deficiencies of revenue, repel invasion, suppress insurrection, defend the State in war, or pay existing debt; and the debt created to supply deficiencies in revenue shall never exceed in the aggregate at any one time two hundred thousand dollars.[7]

In effect, this provision prohibits the issuing of state full faith and credit or general obligation bonds without a constitutional amendment. Several constitutional amendments have been submitted to authorize specific bond issues. The first of these, in 1933, permitted the issuance of 20 million dollars in bonds to match Federal funds for financing unemployment relief. The next came in 1946, when the voters authorized issuance of 25 million dollars of Veterans' Land Bonds. Proceeds of the issue were used to purchase land for resale to veterans of World War II. The maximum bond issue authorized under this program was subsequently increased to 100 million dollars in 1951, to 200 million dollars in 1956, to 350 million dollars in 1963, and to 400 million dollars in 1967. An

---

[7]Constitution of the State of Texas, Art. III, Sec. 49.

amendment submitted at the November, 1973, special election would increase the authorization to 500 million dollars.

Constitutional amendments permitting the issuance of bonds have been concerned with higher education. In 1947, the state's colleges and universities, with the exception of The University of Texas and Texas A & M University, were authorized to issue ten-year bonds for building purposes. These bonds were secured by the pledge of a 5-cent property tax levied for this purpose. At the same election, The University of Texas and Texas A & M University were authorized to issue a total of 15 million dollars in bonds for buildings and other permanent improvements, payable from income from the Permanent University Fund. Both of these bond authorization provisions were subsequently amended and enlarged in 1956, and a 1965 constitutional amendment provided additional funds and borrowing authority for institutions of higher education. The state property tax for such purposes was increased from 5 to 10 cents on the $100 assessed valuation, raising the maximum from 42 to 47 cents. The twenty-year life of the former program of financing construction at state colleges and universities was extended indefinitely. Also approved in 1965 was a constitutional amendment which authorized the issuance of 85 million dollars in bonds for a college student loan program. This was increased in 1968 to 200 million dollars.

A debt amendment to the constitution in 1957 authorized issuance of up to 200 million dollars in bonds to finance local water-development and conservation projects. Proceeds of bond issues under this authority were used to purchase bonds of local governmental entities which were issued for water projects but which could not be sold in the regular bond markets. An amendment approved in 1966 permits the Texas Water Development Board to issue an additional 200 million dollars in bonds for water-development purposes, bringing the total amount of state debt authorized for water-development purposes to 400 million dollars. Then in 1971 the voters approved the issuance of water development bonds for water quality control. The new total is 500 million dollars. The issuance of 75 million dollars in bonds to finance state park development was approved by the voters in 1967.

In 1972, the voters permitted an increase in constitutionally set interest rates to a weighted average of 6 percent. Prior to this time, most of the authorized bond issues also carried a specific interest rate, which frequently was lower than the going rate and bonds could not at times be sold.

Texas state agencies also issue so-called revenue bonds which are secured by income produced by a project or facility. Such revenue bonds have been issued without a constitutional amendment. The courts have not included them within the definition of debt. In 1973, revenue bonds constituted 76 percent of the debt held by state institutions of higher learning. A good example of the kind of obligation involved is the tuition bond, which The University of Texas at Austin and Texas Tech University were allowed to issue for construction purposes in 1971.

The total debt of the state government in 1970 was over one billion dollars.[8] The figure includes all debt, not just the general obligation bonds issued under authority of constitutional amendments.

FISCAL ORGANIZATION AND ADMINISTRATION

In the Texas state government, no single agency or department is charged with administration of fiscal affairs. Instead, the handling of financial matters is divided among several different and completely independent agencies. This disintegrated organization results from the fact that most of the fiscal agencies were initially given independent status by constitutional and statutory provisions. The plan has been carried intact through the years so that today it is little different from the original constitutional blueprint for handling the state's money.

The six major state agencies which have responsibility in financial administration are the office of the Comptroller of Public Accounts, Treasury Department, Board of Control, Executive Budget Officer, Legislative Budget Board, and the office of the State Auditor. In addition, there are several boards and departments whose work is wholly or partly financial in nature but whose significance is secondary to those already mentioned. These include the State Tax Board, the Board to Calculate the Ad Valorem Tax Rate, the Board of County and District Bond Indebtedness, and the Coordinating Board.

In the following pages, the functions and duties of the major agencies involved in state financial operations and administration will be examined.

Comptroller of Public Accounts

The office of comptroller of public accounts is by far the largest fiscal office and one of the most vital in the state's entire administrative network.

The basic duties of the comptroller's office fall under two broad

[8]*Texas Municipal Reports, MAC Special Report No. 84: The Public Debt in Texas*, Municipal Advisory Council of Texas, Austin, August 23, 1971. This report is unique. It is the only complete report of all public debt in Texas. The grand total of all state and local government debt in 1970 was 6,918,907,000 dollars. By 1973, state debt had increased to 1.6 billion dollars.

headings: tax administration and accounting. Through the years, several other important duties have been assigned to the comptroller.

Tax Administration   The administration of various state taxes has become an increasingly important function, while accounting and fiscal-control activities have been diminished somewhat in importance. The more important taxes for which the comptroller's office has responsibility are a number of severance taxes, the chain-store tax, certain occupation taxes, the admissions tax, the motor fuel tax, the franchise tax, the inheritance tax, and the retail sales tax. The office is responsible for assessing these taxes, devising forms and procedures, receiving collections, and enforcing legal provisions applicable to each tax. In relation to these taxes, the comptroller is the state agent who deals directly with the persons or firms paying them.

In other cases, the comptroller does not deal directly with the particular taxpayer but supervises the county tax assessor-collector who performs the actual work. Under the present system of state property taxation, the comptroller is required to supervise 254 county assessors, who are, in fact, agents of the state government in performing this particular function. Other taxes assessed and collected locally, but supervised by the comptroller, are the motor vehicle retail sales and use tax and various occupation taxes.

Since 1967, the comptroller has been charged with the responsibility of collecting the municipal sales tax which in 1972 was levied in over 600 cities and towns. The proceeds are remitted after the comptroller deducts a collection fee.

Accounting   The comptroller is the principal accounting officer of the state and, in theory at least, the fiscal control officer. He is required to maintain a double-entry system of bookkeeping, with the ledgers and accounts necessary for showing the state's revenue collections and expenditures. The statutes specify in detail certain of the accounts which are to be kept so that, in effect, the comptroller does not have complete administrative freedom in this task. The accounts are segregated into different funds which are nothing more than separate entries composed of certain resources which must be used for the financing of specified activities. Thus, there are the General Revenue Fund, the State Highway Fund, the Available School Fund, and more than 200 other special funds, each having its own separate receipts from taxes and other sources which can be disbursed only for functions designated by law to be financed from that particular fund and no other. Most funds are not created by the constitution, but those that are contribute to inflexibility in financial decision making.

The principal accounting tasks of the department are preparation of warrants[9]—checks—for the payment of state obligations, preparation of deposit warrants covering receipts from the various revenue sources, and recording of information from such documents into books of account. The accounts are set up on a cash, rather than an accrual, basis. This means that receipts are taken into account only when actually received in the form of cash rather than at the time actually earned and that expenditures are accounted for only when paid rather than when incurred. Responsibility for preauditing a major part of the state's expenditures rests in the comptroller's office but is quite limited in its application. In fact, the office has no cognizance of a claim until it is presented; then it is checked only to see that an appropriation exists for its payment and that the expenditure is in accord with statutory requirements. There is no examination concerning the propriety of the obligation before it is incurred.

The state's primary financial reports and statements are prepared in the comptroller's office, but they are few in number and limited in content. Only statements of operation, covering the receipts and disbursements of one or more funds for a given period, are prepared. Balance sheets, as this term is generally understood, are not used in the state's accounting system except for those prepared by the state auditor during his postaudits and those prepared by the accounting staffs of individual state agencies. The principal financial reports issued by the comptroller are the three-volume annual report at the close of each fiscal year and brief monthly reports analyzing revenues and expenditures. The annual report is the main source of data on the state's financial operations and is rather widely distributed.

Other Functions   The comptroller has numerous other miscellaneous duties. He is required to certify the rate of state property taxation to county tax assessors-collectors each year so they can apply it to assessed valuations of property in their particular jurisdictions. The rate is set each summer by the Board to Calculate the Ad Valorem Tax Rate.[10] The comptroller is required to register all bonds issued by the state and by local units of government in Texas and to approve all contracts between counties and private attorneys for the collection of delinquent taxes. Mileage tables upon which the travel expense reimbursements of legislators and state employees are computed are maintained in the comptroller's office. He also acts as custodian for important legal papers owned by the state, such as deeds to land and contracts, and maintains a complete

---

[9]Generally speaking, warrants are handled as though they were checks, but they are not considered negotiable instruments in the same sense as a check.

[10]This board is composed of the governor, the comptroller, and the treasurer.

inventory of all physical property belonging to state agencies and institutions.

One of the comptroller's most important duties was added by a constitutional amendment in 1942. Before an appropriation bill can be sent to the governor for his consideration, the comptroller must certify that there will be sufficient revenue to cover the total amount appropriated. If he finds that the amount exceeds the cash and his estimate of income in the fund or funds from which the appropriation is made, the bill is dead unless the legislature, by a four-fifths vote of the total membership of each house, declares an emergency and an imperative public necessity and passes the bill again or the legislature provides the necessary additional revenue.[11] In actual operation, this gives the comptroller a large degree of control over the fate of legislative appropriation bills. A possible limitation on the comptroller's influence in this regard was initiated in 1959, when the legislature created a Committee on State Revenue Estimates, composed of the governor, the auditor, and the director of the Legislative Budget Board, to review the comptroller's estimates. Up to the present, it would appear that this committee has neither circumscribed nor diminished the comptroller's power.

State Treasurer

The office of state treasurer, like that of the comptroller, is one of the oldest in Texas state government. As might be expected, the principal functions of the treasurer's office are the receipt, custody, and disbursement of state funds. The department obtains receipts on deposit requests from the comptroller's department. Funds thus obtained are kept in the custody of the treasurer or in depository banks and are disbursed only in compliance with appropriation acts of the legislature and upon warrants drawn by the comptroller of public accounts. All warrants covering disbursements of funds from the state treasury are generally prepared with preprinted signatures of the treasurer and comptroller and must, with minor exceptions, be presented for payment within two years after the close of the fiscal year in which they were issued. The treasurer keeps a register of all warrants issued, as well as a deposit register. He must maintain a daily cash balance record and close his accounts annually on August 31, the end of the state's fiscal year. He is required to make an annual report to the governor on the financial condition of the treasury and such other reports as the governor may request. Reports summarizing transactions in state funds are issued monthly.

---

[11]For an earlier discussion of this duty, see Dick Smith, "New Financial Procedure in Texas," *State Government,* May, 1947.

State funds in the custody of the treasurer are kept in demand and time-deposit accounts in banks selected by the State Depository Board. This board, composed of the treasurer, the banking commissioner, and an appointee of the governor, selects depositories for state funds. For many years, virtually all the state's cash was deposited in demand accounts in Texas banks and earned little interest. After repeated suggestions by the state auditor, more funds are now placed in time-deposit accounts in which they receive a considerably higher rate of interest. The Treasury Department also has custody of all personal property, such as money, stocks, bonds, and other securities, which has escheated to the state, plus the proceeds from the sale of real property the state has acquired by escheat. It also provides safekeeping for cash and securities entrusted to the treasurer under statutory requirements applying to insurance companies.

Aside from its function in the receipt, custody, and disbursement of state monies, an important part of the department's work is the sale of liquor and cigarette tax stamps to wholesalers. The treasurer may serve as ex officio treasurer and fiscal agent for any unit of local government in the state so that local indebtedness in any form may be made payable at the treasurer's office. If such an arrangement is entered into, the state receives a commission based on the principal paid at the treasurer's office. All the fees thus collected are appropriated by the legislature to a maintenance, equipment, and contingent expense account in the treasury department.

Board of Control

The Board of Control is the central purchasing and building management agency for the state government. This board is composed of three members appointed by the governor with the advice and consent of the Senate for overlapping terms of six years. Membership on the board is part-time, but a full-time executive director selected by the board exercises, under its guidance, all functions assigned by law to the Board of Control.

The most important function of the board is purchasing. Purchases by any agency of state government must be made through the Board of Control or under its supervision. The three categories into which purchases are classified are contract; open-market; and emergency: spot and local. Contract purchases are those which suppliers contract in advance to sell to the state at a stipulated price. Contracts are entered into on the basis of competitive bidding. In addition to price, the board considers such factors as financial and performance ability of the builder to repair stocks, adaptability, and use of the commodities. Contracts are usually for one fiscal year, although the board has authority to contract for items on more or less than an annual basis if this proves economical.

Noncontract purchases are sometimes necessary because of the impossibility of predicting all items which will be needed by an agency during a six- or twelve-month period. The board has statutory authority to purchase noncontract items in the open market on the basis of competitive bids. Such purchases require more time and result in more delay than contract purchases. In an emergency situation, the agency needing the supplies or services usually telephones, or otherwise contacts, the Board of Control so that as many bidders as possible can be notified. The lowest and best bid is accepted, and the purchase is usually made from a closely located vendor. If the need for the article is so pressing that the requisitioning agency cannot lose the time required to contact the board, it may purchase in the open market on its own initiative, although this practice is discouraged and is kept to a minimum.

Spot purchases are those not exceeding $100 which may be made by an agency without prior board approval. Similarly, local purchases are authorized by the board when perishable commodities are required.

The board is also responsible for the transfer and/or sale of surplus properties, including improvements to be removed from right-of-way properties acquired by the Highway Department. It has the duty to supervise, control, and manage buildings, grounds, and utilities owned or used by the state, except for those under the jurisdiction of institutions of higher education and the Department of Mental Health and Mental Retardation. Handling leases and rentals for state agency occupancy in every city where state offices are maintained and supervising and maintaining the state cemetery in Austin are also among the board's responsibilities.

The Budget Agencies

A budget is defined as a plan of financial operation for a given period of time. It shows what the state's agencies propose to spend during the period covered and how these expenditures are to be financed. As we have already explained in earlier chapters, Texas unlike most states has two budgets, one prepared by the Legislative Budget Board and the other by the governor's Division of Operations Analysis. In addition, the Coordinating Board, Texas College and University System, has budget functions relating to the state-supported and state-aided institutions of higher education.

The Texas state government fiscal year begins on September 1 and ends on August 31 of the following year. Texas is one of only three states not to conform to the Federal fiscal year (July 1–June 30). A bill to change to the Federal year was vetoed in 1973. The budgetary period is normally for two years; but in 1968–1969 and 1972–1973, annual budgets were adopted.

The task of preparing the budget for a two-year period begins in each even-numbered year. The budget agencies spend several months planning the broad outlines of the document and carrying out special research assignments which may have been directed by the last legislature. Attention is then devoted to preparation of forms and instructions which operating agencies will use in submitting their budget requests. The Executive Budget Office and the Legislative Budget Board work together so that one set of coordinated instructions is sent to each operating agency. For several months following release of the forms, budget examiners work with personnel in the agencies and assist them in the preparation of departmental requests. Departmental estimates are then submitted to the two budget agencies for analysis by their respective staffs. Joint hearings for all agencies are then held by the two budget offices to clarify details and obtain additional information which may be helpful in evaluating financial needs. When the hearings are concluded, the budget agencies compile their respective estimates into separate documents for submission to the legislature.[12]

Thus, the legislature is faced with two sets of recommendations for all state expenditures. To date, the legislative budget, reflecting a desire to hold costs to a minimum, has made lower spending recommendations than the governor's budget. Recommendations for completely new programs involving additional cost have appeared more often in the governor's budget.

In recent years, numerous improvements in the state's overall budgetary process have been made. One of the most significant is the inclusion of all expenditures, including Federal funds and those from other sources, in the budget documents presented to the legislature. This has made it possible to get a complete picture of the state's spending and its revenue requirements. Another improvement is that budgetary expenditures have been enacted into law in the form of a single appropriations bill, making for more balanced consideration of spending requirements of the various operating agencies. The legislative budget initiated the use of program costs, as well as character and object costs, work-load statistics, and material descriptive of the agencies to which appropriations are made. The executive budget has, in recent years, also incorporated this type of information, making the budget more intelligible to both legislators and laymen as well as making it more valuable as a management

---

[12]Vernon A. McGee, "A Legislative Approach to State Budgeting," *State Government,* Vol. 26, pp. 200–204, August, 1953.

tool. Line itemization of specific salaries and other types of expenses has been reduced, and the budget is more flexible and allows more administrative discretion than in the past.

The 1973 legislature adopted two new budgetary laws that promise additional budgetary improvement. One required that "fiscal notes" be attached to committee reports on bills and resolutions, exclusive of appropriation bills. The notes, or "price tagging," are designed to enable the legislature to estimate what proposed legislation will cost the state in the future—the next five years, by the terms of the new law. The Legislative Budget Board is given the responsibility for making the estimates. During the 1973 regular session the House experimented with price tagging, and found it very useful in avoiding blind spending.

The second law requires the Legislative Budget Board to make a "performance report" to the legislature on the first day of each regular session. The report is to contain information about the operational efficiency and program performance of agencies receiving an appropriation in the most recent general appropriation act. Unit-cost measurement, work-load efficiency data, and program output standards are to be developed by the LBB for this purpose. The general idea behind performance or program budgeting is to find out what the state's expenditures are really accomplishing for the people of the state and whether alternatives would be more economical and more effective.

Despite the improvements in the budget system, much remains to be accomplished. We have already commented in Chapters 8 and 9 about the problems of duplication in budget preparation and about the need for budget execution authority.

The State Auditor

The state auditor is appointed by the Legislative Audit Committee,[13] with confirmation by the Senate, for a two-year period. He may be removed at any time by the committee without a hearing. The auditor appoints other personnel.

The principal duty of the state auditor is to audit all financial records and transactions of state agencies after the transactions have occurred and to check on their legality. Much of his work relates to the adequacy of internal controls in the agencies under examination. It may be said that this audit is a check by the legislative branch of state government on the integrity and efficiency of the executive branch. To promote a uniform system of accounts, he has authority to require changes in the accounting

---

[13]The six-member committee is composed of the speaker of the House, who serves as chairman, the chairmen of the House Committees on Appropriations and Revenue and Taxation, the lieutenant governor, and the chairmen of the Senate Committees on Finance and State Affairs.

or records system of any state agency. He has access to all state records, books, accounts, and reports and may demand assistance from state officials and employees. The auditor also has the difficult assignment of examining the activities of each state agency to determine the quality of service being rendered and to determine if there is duplication of effort among agencies.

Upon the conclusion of each examination, he makes a written report to the head of the agency concerned, with recommendations for the correction of any deficiencies and suggestions for improvement. Copies are sent to the governor, the lieutenant governor, the speaker of the House of Representatives, and all members of the legislature. The auditor also submits an annual summary report to the governor.

Another duty of the state auditor is that of administering the Position Classification Act of 1961. The office recommends to the Division of Operations Analysis and the Legislative Budget Board the salary ranges for classified positions and any changes in classification.

The automatic data-processing systems division in the auditor's office formulates plans for the development and management of such systems in state agencies. The director of the division carries on this work with the assistance of programming analysts.

Other Fiscal Agencies

A number of other state administrative organizations are concerned with work which is wholly or partially financial in nature. Most of them are composed of state department heads serving ex officio. They meet only at designated times to carry out the duties imposed upon them by law, usually a single function.

The part-time boards, their designations generally indicating their fiscal duties, are the following: Board to Calculate the Ad Valorem Tax Rate, State Tax Board (Intangible Tax Board), State Depository Board, Board of County and District Road Indebtedness, and the Board to Approve Contracts for Fuel and Public Printing.

Full-time agencies performing fiscal functions are the State Highway Department, which supervises the registration of motor vehicles and collects the license fees, and the Alcoholic Beverage Commission, which assesses and collects the alcoholic beverage excise tax.

FISCAL REORGANIZATION AND REFORM

Despite the fact that the state's system of financial organization and administration has been the target of criticism for decades, genuine improvements have been made. An excellent postaudit is now performed by an agent of the legislature. These audit reports have certified the state's financial transactions and the fiscal integrity of state personnel, as well as suggesting and fostering many procedural and managerial improvements of lasting value. The comptroller's system of inventory and property control enables the state to know what it owns and where its properties are located. Mechanized accounting operations are being used increasingly by the comptroller's office, the Board of Control, and other larger agencies. The comptroller uses electronic data processing for his accounting records, warrant writing, and much tax work. Orderly development and proper management of automatic data-processing systems in state agencies is promoted by a specialist in this field in the office of the state auditor. The purchasing operation in the Board of Control has been completely reorganized to save additional money on purchases and to expedite procurement. Both legislative and executive budget documents now contain estimates of all state expenditures, and all appropriations are included in one bill.

At the same time, it must be recognized that these steps are only a beginning and that real fiscal reform is yet to come. The various spending agencies are relatively independent of the central fiscal offices, and the governor has only limited control over either. The bulk of all money handled by state officials is deposited in the state treasury and thus comes under the fiscal control and management of the legislature through the appropriations process, but a number of funds are still outside the state treasury. In most cases, these are deposited in banks and expended by the collection agency without legislative review. Elective department heads and the use of boards for certain fiscal functions are, to some critics, basic impediments to the establishment of a topflight financial system.[14]

Central Finance Department

The trend in American states for many years has been toward integration of the principal financial functions into a single department responsible to the governor. This trend is based on the theory that financial activities constitute the basic tools of management and that the use and control of them are properly a prerogative and responsibility of the chief executive. Along with this trend has come increased interest in fiscal activities on the part of a number of state legislatures. In many states, there is enough

[14]The presence of so many plural agencies in this particular field of administration is evidence that the state has failed to distinguish properly between (1) policy-making, quasi-legislative, and judicial functions, and (2) purely administrative functions. For the former, boards may be desirable; for the latter, experience has shown single administrators to be more effective.

concern with the budget process to justify the appointment of staff members who give full time to fiscal analysis. In Texas, this function is performed by the Legislative Budget Board staff. In addition, a number of interim legislative committees, some with citizen members, have studied various aspects of state finances in recent years. The whole budget process is neither solely executive nor solely legislative, but is a cooperative process in which both branches of state government are involved.

Department of Taxation

A central department of financial administration, if installed in Texas, might absorb the functions of the Board of Control, the treasury department, the executive budget staff, and the fiscal operations of the comptroller's office. It would not, however, take over any tax-administration functions which are presently scattered among the several agencies but centered principally in the comptroller's office. These functions are best handled by a single Department of Revenue or Taxation directed by an appointed administrator. This agency should be the one central organization for administration and supervision of the state's taxes. In addition to administering specific taxes, the agency should also conduct continuous research in state and local taxation and assist local governments in the exercise of their taxing powers.

It must be emphasized that much of the reorganization suggested here could not be achieved without amending or revising the state constitution. Especially is this true of appointing key officials who are now elective. At the same time, considerable progress could be made by the legislature on its own volition even under present constitutional restrictions. In fact, proposals to create a separate revenue department to handle tax functions have been introduced in recent legislatures, but they have not received serious consideration.

Financial Practices and Procedures

A number of improvements in financial practices and procedures would also make for more effective state financial administration. Among these is increased emphasis on program budgeting, where activities and programs are designated objects of expenditure, rather than specific items such as salaries, supplies, and equipment. The present excessive earmarking of revenues for specific purposes might be reduced or curtailed so that expenditure patterns could be made more flexible and responsive to established need.

Revenue-estimating functions should reside in the budget preparation agencies, and detailed explanations of the various estimates should be included in the budget documents. Finally, execution of the budget should be through a system of quarterly allotments, with agencies required to get quarterly approval on all expenditures. This would help to ensure that funds appropriated would last until the end of each fiscal year and that expenditures would be tailored to available revenues if the latter fell below original estimates.

As state government grows and becomes more complex, it may be that the legislature will need additional time for budget consideration or that there will be need to reassess the state's financial situation more frequently. Most states now have annual legislative sessions, thus limiting appropriation bills to a one-year period. A few of these states limit the sessions in alternate years exclusively to budget consideration and appropriations. The one-year appropriation bill for the 1968, 1969, 1972, and 1973 fiscal years gave this idea a trial run in Texas.

Closely related to the operating budget of the state is the need for a long-range capital budget. This would cover a five- or seven-year period and project capital needs of all state agencies, priorities of accomplishment, and methods of financing. Such a capital budget not only is a vehicle for orderly development of permanent improvement projects, such as land acquisition, building construction, and public-works installations but also relates these needs to the state's available resources at all times. Moreover, it would facilitate timely and accurate computation of capital improvement costs which must be provided in each operating budget.

Accounting procedures could be improved through greater centralization into the single financial agency proposed earlier and through the achievement of more uniformity in systems and terminology. Many hold that all expenditures should be accounted for on an accrual basis,[15] in which all costs are recorded in the accounts when incurred, regardless of when paid. Budgetary accounting might be employed so that periodic statements comparing estimated versus actual operations could be prepared for the governor and the legislature. Finally, improvements should be made in the annual financial reports which are prepared from the central accounting records. There should be a balance sheet for each separate fund, as well as one showing the overall financial condition of state government at the close of each fiscal year.

---

[15]It should be recognized that there are those who hold that the cash basis is the better method of accounting for state funds.

Chapter 12

Public Education

In the United States, public education is primarily a state-local governmental responsibility. This is clearly evident from the budget figures reviewed in the last chapter. In Texas, public education is also the most expensive of the programs financed by the state, costing over twice as much as any other.

HISTORY

Expenditures are a reflection of a commitment by the people of Texas to public education, a commitment that reaches far back into Texas history. In fact, one of the grievances that led to revolution from Mexico was the Mexican government's neglect of popular education. Following the revolution, the constitution of the Texas Republic (1836) supported public education in principle; and in 1839, the Third Congress of the Republic set aside part of the public domain for both the public schools and higher education.[1]

Public Schools

The first Texas state constitution (1845) provided for the establishment of a system of free schools and for an ad valorem tax for their support. On January 1, 1853, a legislative act establishing a uniform state-school system was passed. In 1854, the Permanent School Fund for the public schools was created by statute. Lands previously set aside for the schools and an investment trust constituted the body or corpus of the fund. The idea behind the fund was to provide non-tax revenue on a continuing basis and to allow Texas school children to share the revenue "from diminishing, irreplaceable natural resources."[2] The corpus of the fund was not to be spent, only the income.

The Civil War and Reconstruction interrupted the normal development of public education in Texas. It was not until 1875, when the present Texas constitution was drafted, that the modern framework for public education was created. The framework included carry-over provisions from earlier laws and had to be amended, but it was, nonetheless, the basis of the current system.

The constitution of 1876 in Article VII, the education article, commands the state legislature to provide for "an efficient system of free public schools" and establishes a Permanent School Fund and an Available School Fund for partial financing of the system. The Permanent School Fund provisions reaffirm the dedication of lands, funds, and other property set apart for the public schools prior to 1875. The Available Fund consists of the income from the Permanent School Fund and proceeds from taxes dedicated for the schools.[3] The constitution requires that the money in the Available School Fund be annually distributed on a per capita or per pupil basis.

The 1876 constitution reflected the attitudes of the day and required separate public schools for blacks and whites. It was not until after 1954 that Texas embarked on a desegregation policy. This was the direct result

---

[1]Congress set aside 50 leagues (221,400 acres) for the support of two universities, one for the eastern half of the state and the other for the western half. Congress designated 3 leagues of land (4,428 acres) for schools in each county. In 1840, this was increased to 4 leagues. However, no public educational institutions were created during the life of the Republic.

[2]*Statement Relating to Constitutional Provisions for the State Permanent School Fund*, Presentation to the Texas Constitutional Revision Commission, May 12, 1973.

[3]Section 3 of Article VII requires part of the proceeds from the poll tax, the occupation tax, and the state property tax to go to the public schools. If the yield from the taxes and the income from the Permanent School Fund are insufficient, then general funds may be used.

of the famous U.S. Supreme Court decision in *Brown v. Board of Education* in which public school segregation by race was held unconstitutional. The problem of desegregation in the public schools has not been entirely resolved although nowhere in the state today is a dual system required by law. In 1969, the Texas voters approved a constitutional amendment deleting the requirement for separate public schools for blacks and whites.

Higher Education

The history of public-supported higher education has somewhat paralleled that of public education. In 1858, a bill establishing "The University of Texas" was passed, and a Permanent University Fund was created for its support. The fund, like the Permanent School Fund, consisted of public lands set aside in 1839. It also included $100,000 in U.S. government bonds and "railroad lands" (one of every ten sections of public lands granted to railroads). The corpus of the fund was not to be spent, only the income.

The Civil War and Reconstruction dealt higher education a hard blow. The University of Texas was not established as planned, and many of the University lands were sold or otherwise disposed of. However, the 1866 constitution provided for a Permanent University Fund, and the 1876 constitution supported higher education.

The 1876 constitution commands the legislature to establish a university of the first class to be styled, "The University of Texas." In addition, the constitution designates Texas A & M College as a branch of the University. (This may be news to A & M students.) The constitution set up the Permanent University Fund for the support of the University of Texas and its branches. Set apart for the fund were "one million acres of the unappropriated public domain of the state" and declared to be included in the fund were "all lands, and other property (theretofore) set apart and appropriated" for the university, together with the proceeds from sales of the land and property.[4] The income from the fund, which is known as the Available Fund (which should be carefully distinguished from the Public School's Available Fund), is "subject to appropriation by the legislature" for the "maintenance, support and direction of a university of the first class."[5]

The constitution also provided for higher education for blacks by authorizing the establishment of a "college or branch university for

---

[4]*Statement to the Texas Constitutional Revision Commission* by A. G. McNeese, Jr., Chairman, Board of Regents, The University of Texas System, Austin, Texas, June 29, 1973.
[5]Texas constitution, Sections 10 and 11 of Article VII.

colored youths."[6] The first colleges for blacks in Texas were established with private funds from Northerners.[7] Alta Vista Agricultural College, near Hempstead, was the first state-supported Negro college in Texas and was a sister school of Texas A & M College. It failed for lack of students, but it was reestablished in 1879 as Prairie View Normal School to train teachers. It is now known as Prairie View A & M University. Until 1947, Prairie View was the only state-supported institution of higher learning open to black students. In a move to forestall the admission by court order of blacks to The University of Texas Law School at Austin, Texas State University for Negroes, now called Texas Southern University, was established in 1947 in Houston.[8] However, by the 1950s, all state institutions of higher education in Texas were legally required to accept students of all races; and that is the situation today. The two predominantly black universities remain a part of the state higher education system.

The history of public education in Texas is a varied and interesting one, but we will not be able to review it further.[9] We turn next to the present-day system of public education in Texas.

PUBLIC SCHOOL SYSTEM

Texas has one of the largest public school systems in the United States (the third largest in 1972). In 1972, about 2.8 million pupils were enrolled. This is 1 million more than in 1950 and 600,000 more than in 1960. However, enrollment has been stabilizing in the 1970s, is expected to drop slightly and then to increase again in the 1980s. The total cost of the system is over 2 billion dollars a year.

State Administration of Public Schools

The management or administration of the huge public school enterprise in Texas is divided between the state and local governments. Although the

---

[6]Texas constitution, Section 14 of Article VII. This provision is still in the constitution.

[7]The first black private college in Texas was Wiley College, founded in Marshall in 1873. It was followed by Tillotson College at Austin in 1881. During the same year, Paul Quinn College at Waco and Bishop College at Marshall were opened. Bishop College was subsequently moved to Dallas.

[8]The legal history of black admission to hitherto all-white state colleges and universities in Texas began in 1946 when Heman Marion Sweatt, a Houston Negro, was denied admission to the University of Texas Law School solely on the grounds of race. Basing its decision on a 1939 Missouri case, the state legislature built a separate college in Houston to provide law training for blacks in Texas, which was hitherto lacking. Sweatt persisted in his efforts to enter the University of Texas and finally succeeded. The case was decided by the U.S. Supreme Court in *Sweatt v. Painter*, 339 U.S. 629 (1950).

[9]For early histories of education in Texas, see Frederick Eby, *The Development of Education in Texas*, Macmillan, New York, 1925; and J. J. Lane, *The History of Education in Texas*, U.S. Bureau of Education, Washington, 1903.

public schools have been regarded as local institutions, the state has always played the dominant legal role. The local school district, the principal local governing unit, is legally a creature of the state, and may be created, altered, or abolished as determined by the Texas constitution and statutes.

Texas Education Agency The state organization created to administer the state responsibility for the public schools has been modified in response to changing demands. The present organization was established in 1949 by the Gilmer-Aikin School laws, which are a major landmark in the history of public school education in Texas.[10] Some changes have occurred since 1949, but the basic structure remains.

The principal state agency entrusted with the responsibility for administration of the public schools is the Texas (or Central) Education Agency. It consists of either three or four units, depending upon whether the State Board of Education, which doubles as the State Board of Vocational Education, is counted once or twice.

1 State Board of Education   The State Board of Education is the policymaking arm of the TEA. It is composed of one member elected from each of the congressional districts. At present the board has twenty-four members.[11]

As the policymaking arm of the TEA, the state board has extensive powers over the state's public schools. Among its principal duties are the following:[12]

1   Preparation and presentation to the Legislative Budget Board and the governor of the proposed budgets for operating the Minimum Foundation Program of Education and other programs for which it has responsibility

2   Appointment of the commissioner of education with Senate consent

3   Approval of textbooks

4   Hearing of appeals from decisions of the commissioner of education

5   Management of the Permanent School Fund investments

[10]The laws were named after the chairmen of the Texas House and Senate committees which drew up the legislation. Senator A. M. Aikin of Paris was still serving in the legislature in the 1970s.

[11]The original State Board of Education provided for in the constitution of 1866 was composed of the governor, the comptroller, and the secretary of state. In 1928, a constitutional amendment reconstituted the board as a body of nine members appointed by the governor with the concurrence of the Senate for overlapping terms of six years. The state board remained a nine-member group until 1949 when it was changed to a twenty-one member body with one member being elected for a six-year term from each congressional district as constituted in 1949. The Texas constitution leaves to the legislature the question of whether the board shall be appointive or elective.

[12]*Biennial Report, Years of Transition 1970–72*, Texas Education Agency, p. 6, Austin, 1972.

6 Adoption of policies and standards affecting the public schools

7 Preparation and submission of reports on public education to the governor and the legislature

The board also serves as the Board for Vocational Education. Since the enactment of the Vocational-Technical Act of 1969 by the legislature, increasing emphasis has been placed upon vocational education in Texas. The state Board of Education's duties in this area have correspondingly increased. Among other responsibilities, it advises the Texas State Technical Institute with its four branch campuses at Waco, Harlingen, Sweetwater, and Amarillo.

2 State Commissioner of Education   The state commissioner of education, appointed for a term of four years by the State Board of Education with Senate concurrence, is the chief executive officer of the Texas Education Agency.[13] As such, he has the responsibility for "promoting efficiency and improvement in the public school system of the state."[14] He serves as executive secretary to the board, supplying them with information as needed. He has been empowered to prescribe rules and regulations necessary for implementing the duties vested in him by the board and the legislature. His executive responsibilities extend to the State Department of Education.

3 State Department of Education   The third component of the Texas Education Agency is the State Department of Education. It consists of the professional, technical, and clerical staff appointed and organized to perform the duties of the TEA as determined by state law, the State Board of Education, and the State commissioner of education. The members and agencies of the department are under the immediate direction and supervision of the commissioner of education and his deputy. The commissioner has powers of appointment and may delegate both ministerial and executive powers to his subordinates in the department as he sees fit.

Regional Centers   We should also take note of the twenty Regional Education Service Centers set up by the State Board of Education in 1965. Their purpose is "to provide educational services to the school districts and to coordinate educational planning in the region."[15] Originally designed to provide a variety of supplemental services concerned with audiovisual libraries, their scope has been expanded since then to

[13]Prior to the Gilmer-Aiken School Laws of 1949, the title of the position had always been state superintendent of public instruction. Although originally appointive, the office was elective from 1884 to 1949 and continues to be so in twenty states. *The Book of the States, 1972–73*, The Council of State Governments, p. 310, Iron Works Pike, Lexington, Ky., 1972.

[14]*Biennial Report, op. cit.*, p. 6.

[15]Texas Education Code, Section 11.33.

TEXAS EDUCATION AGENCY

Source: Texas Education Agency, 1973.

encompass a variety of services, including computerized class scheduling. The centers are managed by separate boards of directors and have been described as representing "an intervening level between the State Department of Education and local school districts."[16]

Basic State Laws

The state of Texas enacts the basic laws pertaining to the public schools. These were substantially recodified by the Texas Education Code of 1969.

Compulsory Attendance   Though considered one of the essentials of a satisfactory public education program, compulsory attendance was slow in coming to Texas. It was not until 1915 that the legislature adopted a law requiring children between eight and fourteen to attend school, and even then enforcement was poor and exceptions to the law were many.

The compulsory minimum attendance is now 165 days and the age limits are seven to seventeen. Exempted are several categories of children, including those whose body or mental condition renders attendance inadvisable, children who are blind, and children attending vocational-technical education schools.

Free Textbooks   In November, 1918, a constitutional amendment was passed for the adoption of free textbooks and dedicated a portion of the state property tax for their purchase. Currently, the State Board of Education sets aside a portion of the Available Fund and uses proceeds from the sale of disused books for this purpose.

A textbook committee of fifteen members, appointed by the State Board of Education upon the recommendation of the commissioner of education, examines and recommends adoptions of books for the public schools. Each of the members must be an experienced and active educator engaged in teaching in the public schools of the state, and at least a majority of them must be classroom teachers. No person connected with a textbook publishing concern may be appointed to the committee, nor is the author or associate author of any textbook published by a publishing house eligible for membership.

It should be emphasized that the powers of the Textbook Committee pertain to recommendations only. Its recommendations are made to the commissioner who, in turn, submits his recommendations to the State

---

[16]*The Challenge and the Chance*, Report of the Governor's Committee on Public School Education, p. 18, Austin, 1968.

Board of Education. Both the commissioner and the board may remove books from the committee's recommended list of adoptions, but no titles may be added to the list by them. Likewise, neither the commissioner nor the board may reduce a recommended multiple adoption to a single adoption.

Interested groups and individuals appear before the Textbook Committee to voice objection to or approval of given books. For example, fundamentalists oppose the teachings of evolution, groups opposed to world government object to inclusion of the United Nations, and, more recently, women liberationists have complained of the portrayal of woman's role in society.

Teacher Certification, Compensation, and Tenure The most essential part of any school system is a corps of well prepared teachers. No one may teach in the Texas public schools, except upon an emergency basis, who has not been certified. The certification code adopted by the legislature provides for two classes of certificates: provisional and professional. Each type is permanent, with the provisional based on completion of an undergraduate teacher certification program and the professional upon completion of at least thirty hours beyond the baccalaureate degree. All certificates are issued by the TEA.

To obtain good teachers, good salaries must be provided. Realizing this, the legislature in 1969 adopted a precedent-setting ten-year minimum teacher salary schedule with built-in automatic raises.[17] Called "the best state-guaranteed salary schedule in the nation," the plan was "indexed" on a beginning salary of $600 per month for a teacher with a B.A. degree and no experience. Eighteen pay grades were established and other salaries were set in percentage relationship to the $600 base. A 5 percent increment was provided for each year of experience up to ten years. The minimum salary paid to a new teacher with a B.A. degree at the time the plan went into effect in 1970–1971 was $6,000 for ten months. In ten years time the teacher would be assured of an annual salary of $11,040, an increase of 84 percent. The increase would include two extra automatic 10 percent raises ($60 a month in 1974, $66 in 1978). The average salary paid on the basis of this schedule in 1970–1971 was $7,968; it will be $10,820 in 1980–1981. However, it should be emphasized that the salary figures are those provided by the Minimum Foundation Program, to be discussed later, and do not include the supplements by the local school districts. Actual salaries are higher than the figures given. Two-thirds of

---

[17]The information about the salary schedule is from *Texas Public School Finance: Fewer Students, More Money*, Texas Research League, pp. 19–24, Austin, April, 1973.

the teachers and other school personnel earned at least $500 above the minimum schedule in 1971–1972.

Public school teachers are required to belong to the teacher retirement system, which has constitutional status. The retirement act provides for full benefits, based on standard annuity, at age sixty-five with ten or more years of service and at age sixty with twenty or more years of service. Reduced benefits based on a percent of standard annuity are provided at any age with thirty or more years of service, at age fifty-five with twenty or more years, and at fifty-five with fifteen through nineteen years of service. Those covered by the system pay a percentage of their full salary into the retirement fund. The accumulated contribution, plus interest, are matched by the state. The amount of each benefit depends upon the amount contributed and the age upon retirement. Teachers and employees in fully state-supported colleges and universities are also in the system. Retirement credits of the teacher retirement system, the state employee retirement system, and the judicial retirement system are transferable.[18]

Several factors have tended to improve the status of teachers. One of these, an optional teacher tenure bill, was passed by the legislature in 1967. If the plan is adopted by the local school district, all teachers will be hired under a "probationary contract" for a fixed term, not to exceed three years, but this may be extended for one more year. After the probationary period is completed, a "continuous contract" must be made or the employment terminated. The provision is not applicable to those who were (as of September, 1967) already on a permanent contract basis as defined by their school district. Once a teacher is hired under a "continuing contract," he can be dismissed only for a cause or because of the necessity of reducing staff. A teacher may, however, be returned to probationary status for up to three years. Teachers may contest the actions of their board of trustees and have the right of appeal to the commissioner of education and subsequently to the State Board of Education. A further provision adopted in 1967 authorizes boards of trustees to establish procedures for consulting directly with teachers, rather than through administrators, on educational policy and conditions of employment.

Another safeguard for the teacher is that before any teaching certificate—without which he cannot teach—may be canceled by the commissioner of education, the person affected must be notified and must be given the opportunity to be heard. If the teacher is not satisfied, he

---

[18]Teachers and employees of the fully state-supported colleges and universities are also under the Federal OASDHI program (social security). Social security coverage is optional for the public schools.

may appeal further to the State Board of Education and finally to the courts.

Quarter System   The legislature has enacted a law requiring the public schools to operate on the basis of a quarter system rather than the traditional nine to ten months with a summer vacation. The 1973 legislature changed the mandatory date for the new system to the 1974–1975 school year from the originally set 1973–1974 period. Schools are required to offer 180 days of instruction for students and 10 days of in-service education for teachers during any three of the four calendar quarters of the year. Prior to 1974–1975 the system was optional.

State-supported Kindergarten   A part of the Minimum Foundation Program, to which we will turn shortly, the inauguration of state-supported kindergarten is deserving of special mention. The program was initiated in 1970–1971 for only the disadvantaged and educationally handicapped children, such as the non-English speaking, who were five years and five months old. The original plan adopted by the legislature envisioned full implementation of kindergarten to all five year olds in 1977, but the legislature in 1973 changed the date to the 1973–1974 school year. However, funding was a problem in 1973. The school districts received state aid sufficient to support a full day program for all five year olds for half the school year or, alternatively, one-half day programs for the entire year.

Local Public School Administration

The basic local unit of government for public schools is the school district. The county also performs public school functions, but the traditional county organization based on the county school superintendent and the county school trustees has greatly decreased in importance in Texas.

School Districts   The most important single fact about school districts in modern times is the steady diminution in their numbers. In Texas thirty odd years ago (1940–1941) there were over 6,400 districts; twenty years later (1950–1951) there were 2,505; ten years later (1960–1961), 1,187; and in 1973 there were 1,149.[19] The most important reason for their decline in number is that public schools are too expensive for a small community to maintain, and current laws require local tax contribu-

---

[19]*Texas Almanac 1972–73*, p. 560, A. H. Belo Corporation, Dallas, 1972. The 1,149 figure is from the Texas Research League.

tions. Hence, districts consolidate with others and go out of existence as independent entities or are annexed or simply cease.

The two basic kinds of school districts are the independent and the common school district. Independent school districts account for well over 1,000 of the 1,149 districts.

1 Independent School Districts These districts were recognized as far back as the 1876 constitution which reaffirmed the then common practice of municipal control of schools and provided that the legislature might constitute any city or town as an independent school district. Today, the more common practice is for the independent school district to be a unit separate and apart from the municipality and one not necessarily coterminous with the city's geographical boundaries.

The policymaking body of the independent school district is the board of trustees, usually composed of seven members. The trustees are elected in a nonpartisan election held the first Saturday in April in most districts. The school board exercises a variety of important functions. The board decides upon the number and location of schools within the district. It lets contracts for building new schools and provides for the maintenance of the old. It hires and fires teachers, decides on curriculum, and selects textbooks within the guidelines of state law and the TEA. The board adopts the school budget. One of the most important duties is to set the ad valorem tax rate subject to the statutory limit of \$1.50 on each \$100 valuation and to service voter-approved bonds.

The school board appoints the school superintendent who is the manager of the public school system for the district. In the large metropolitan areas he is highly paid (some are within the \$50,000 range) in recognition of his enormous responsibilities.

2 Common School Districts The common school districts outnumbered the independent school districts as recently as 1953–1954. Their decrease is directly related to the rapid urbanization of Texas inasmuch as they are administrative units for essentially rural and county schools.

There are several kinds of common school districts described in the Texas Education Code.[20] The ordinary district is governed by a board of three school trustees elected for staggered three-year terms. The board has a few of the same duties as its counterpart in the independent school district, such as building and maintaining schools. But, unlike its counterpart, the common school district board does not set its tax rate. The county commissioners court determines the rate, which is the same for the county and state ad valorem tax. Also, the common school district

---

[20]These include the rural high school, the common line, and the consolidated school districts. In addition, the legislature has provided for some new kinds of districts that are neither fish nor fowl. They seem to be special districts for educational purposes. They include rehabilitation districts for handicapped persons, the county industrial training school district, and the countywide vocational school district.

board does not appoint the school superintendent; and in fact, the board is under the general supervisory authority of the county superintendent, who even approves teacher contracts.

County Responsibilities The public schools of the state are regulated and serviced to some extent by county government. About 100 counties have county school superintendents and county school trustees in whom are vested duties of some importance. In addition, the county commissioners court administers the county permanent school fund in the approximately 200 counties still retaining it from the days when public lands were set aside for education in each county.

In most counties the county superintendent is elected, although in counties having over 350,000 population he is appointed by the county school trustees. In either case the term of office is four years. The county judge serves as ex officio county superintendent in counties without the office except where the legislature has provided for the transference of the duties to the superintendents of the independent school districts.

The county superintendent has authority to apportion the income arising from the county available fund to the common and independent school districts in the county, to transfer pupils from one common school district to another, to keep records of all teacher certificates held by persons teaching, and to approve teacher contracts in the common schools. He has authority over independent school districts with less than 150 scholastics and approves reports to the TEA of independent districts with less than 500 students.

The county school superintendent is the secretary of the five-member county board of trustees. The board has authority over the common school districts and may classify the schools of the county, determine the boundaries of school districts, set up a school transportation system, and hear and pass on appeals from decisions of the county superintendent. Four of the trustees are elected from each of the county commissioners precincts and one is elected at large. They serve for two years. The trustee elected at large serves as president.

PUBLIC SCHOOL FINANCING

In the 1970s, the system of financing the Texas public schools has come under severe attack in the courts and in other decision-making arenas.[21] A

---

[21]Before the controversy reached its peak in the 1970s, several groups had criticized public school financing in Texas. The Governor's Committee on Public School Education (COPSE), which completed a 1 million dollar research project on the public schools in 1968, was one of the most important of these groups.

review of the present system is necessary to understand why it is criticized.

State-Local Financing

The state of Texas relies upon two main sources of revenue for its share of public school costs: the Permanent School Fund, whose origins we have discussed, and taxes.[22]

State financing of public schools is almost entirely through the Minimum Foundation Program, which, as we have said, was established in 1949 by the Gilmer-Aikin School Laws of that year. The MFP provides over half of the total funds for the public schools in Texas, and 80 percent of the MFP cost is borne by the state government.[23]

The two principal purposes of the MFP are to provide for a minimum or basic quality of education for each school child in the Texas public schools and to force each school district to contribute to the program through taxes roughly in proportion to its ability to pay.

The minimum quality of education is principally defined in terms of three major components: (1) the number and salaries of teachers and other personnel; (2) maintenance and operating expenses; and (3) transportation costs. The MFP does not address itself at all to capital expenditures. Local schools must pay for their own school buildings and improvements.

The TEA computes the total cost of a minimum quality of education for each district in the state. The computation is complex, but an essential unit of measurement is the number of pupils in each district, which is determined by average daily attendance (ADA). For example, the number of teachers and other personnel required for a minimum education is determined by the school districts' ADA.[24]

After the total cost of the program for all districts has been calculated, each district must pay its share of the 20 percent collectively owed by all the districts. Called the "local fund assignment," the first step in its allocation is to divide the costs among the 254 counties. This is done on the basis of each county's assumed economic ability as measured by the so-called economic index. Though quite complicated, the index is based on three weighted factors: (1) the county's total assessed property

---

[22]The taxes are funnelled through various funds, namely, the Available School Fund, the Omnibus Tax Clearance Fund, the General Fund, and ultimately go mainly to the Minimum Foundation Program Fund. The Available School Fund, as we have seen, includes income from the Permanent Fund. In 1972, the income from the Permanent Fund was about 40 million dollars whereas the total value of the PF was almost 962 million dollars.

[23]*Texas Public School Finance, op. cit.,* p. 2.

[24]One classroom teacher unit is allowed for every 25 ADA in school districts over 488 ADA.

valuation; (2) the scholastic population; and (3) the income of the county. Although the "economic index" is supposedly a measure of each county's ability to pay, scholastic population has nothing to do with this, and the method of assessing property in Texas fails to give an accurate measurement of wealth.

The amount of the local fund assignment owed by each district in the county is determined by the proportion of its assessed valuation in relation to the total assessed valuation of the county.

To complicate things further, districts are eligible for credits to reduce their share, such as the presence of government-owned lands in the district. Also, the annual per capita distribution of the Available Fund (which was described earlier in the chapter) is subtracted from the amount the district would normally receive as its share of the MFP.

The local school district pays its share of the MFP from the local property tax. In general, about 98 percent of the local financing of public schools in Texas comes from this tax. The local school district is free to use its funds in excess of its MFP share for whatever it chooses. The extra amounts are called "enrichment" funds.

The Rodriguez Case

In December, 1971, a three-judge Federal district court ruled unconstitutional the Texas state-local financing system in the case of *Rodriguez v. San Antonio Independent School District*.[25] The court held that the Texas system discriminated on the basis of wealth in the manner in which public education was provided for its children. This violated the equal protection of the laws clause of the Fourteenth Amendment to the U.S. Constitution. Education, said the court, was a fundamental constitutional right the denial or abridgement of which required the state to prove that a compelling state interest was served.

The United States Supreme Court in March, 1973, reversed the decision of the lower court by a 5-4 decision.[26] Justice Lewis Powell, who wrote the majority opinion, held that education was not a basic constitutional right and that the Texas system of financing education was reasonably related to the goal of providing a minimum education for all public school children. Justice Powell did say, however, that the Texas school financing system was inequitable.

The inequities of which Justice Powell spoke are easy to document.

[25]299 F. Supp. 476 (1971). The lower court said that the "constitutional tend statutory framework employed by the State in providing education draws distinction between groups of citizens depending upon the wealth of the district in which they live."

[26]*San Antonio Independent School District v. Rodriguez*, 41 LW 4407 (1973).

For one thing, the market value of property of the school districts in Texas varies enormously, ranging in wealth per student from $1,000 to $10,000,000 or a 10,000 to 1 ratio.[27] This means that the resources available to each district for taxation for the schools are unequal. Also, the poorer districts must tax their citizens at a higher rate than richer districts, and yet their yield is less. ("Tax more, get less.") These disparities were well illustrated by the Edgewood School District in San Antonio, which was involved in the Rodriguez case. The district was the poorest in San Antonio, with an assessed value of property per student of only $5,429 in comparison with $49,000 in the Alamo Heights district, the richest of the San Antonio schools. Although it imposed the highest tax rate of any of the districts, the Edgewood district raised only $26 per pupil whereas the Alamo Heights district with the lowest rate raised $333 per pupil. Even with the addition of the funds from the Minimum Foundation Program, the amount available per pupil in the Edgewood district was far lower than that of the Alamo Heights school. (In 1967–1968 the total state-local expenditure per pupil in Edgewood was $248 and in Alamo Heights, $558.)[28]

Proposals for Reform

Following the 1971 Federal district court ruling in the *Rodriguez* case, numerous private and public groups began studies of how the state-local school financing system might be changed to eliminate the inequities highlighted by the court. The Texas Advisory Commission on Intergovernmental Relations served as a clearinghouse and coordinating body for the reports.[29] Five major proposals were examined by the TACIR.

Full State Funding   The Federal district court had held that the "quality of public education may not be a function of wealth, other than the wealth of the state as a whole." With this in mind, the proposal for full state funding is one alternative solution. It would be necessary, of course, to replace the approximately 200 million dollars contributed by the local governments to the MFP; and if all present local expenditures were to be replaced by state funds, another 800 million dollars or so. However, most

---

[27]"School Financing Is Good for You," *The Texas Observer*, Dec. 15, 1972, citing figures compiled by Peat, Marwick. Mitchell and Company, a consulting firm.

[28]In 1970–1971, the average state-local expenditure in Texas was about $700 per pupil, with a range from $418 to $3,363. *Public School Finance Problems in Texas: An Interim Report*, Texas Research League, p. 2, Austin, June, 1972.

[29]See *Texas Public School Finance: Resolving the Issue*, A Report of the Texas Advisory Commission on Intergovernmental Relations, Austin, 1973.

full funding proposals anticipate leaving for local school districts some measure of funding to permit "enrichment" and local controls. Also, the 800 million dollars includes capital expenditures, an item the state of Texas has to date not funded.

State Grant System By this plan, the state would provide a grant of equal amount or varying amounts per student based on differences in educational needs or the number of scholastics or some other factor. Local supplements of state aid would be allowed. One variation is simply to give the poorest districts in Texas an extra grant to bring them up to the average. Local differences in expenditures per pupil would continue but be narrowed.

Equalizing State Aid Equal revenues per student would be provided by state supplements of local revenues where needed. No local enrichment funds would be permitted. ("Equal dollars, equal scholars.")

Power Equalization The state would guarantee that each district would receive the same amount of revenue per student from the application of the same effective local property tax rate. Richer districts would probably have to remit tax collections in excess of set revenue.

School District Reorganization The idea behind this proposal is to redraw the school districts so that each would contain approximately the same amount of wealth or same property tax base per student.

Since the local property tax produces so much revenue for public schools, it is unlikely that the state would completely take over funding of the public schools. But if the property tax is to be continued as a major source of school funding, it must be reformed.[30] Uniformity in assessment practices from county to county; a uniform rate of taxation for school purposes; professional expertise in location, listing, and assessment of property; and a rational valuation system such as full market value—these are some of the reforms suggested by study groups.

Federal Financing

Federal financial assistance is over and above that received by each Texas school district from the Minimum Foundation Program and by other local

---

[30]The property tax has been the subject of more studies than any other in Texas. A critical approach to it as it applies to school financing is contained in *The Challenge and the Chance, op. cit.*

efforts. Proportionately, the amount from the Federal government is much less but hardly insignificant.

The first Federal grant-in-aid program for the public schools in Texas was for vocational education in 1917 for which matching state funds were required. Programs from that time until 1965 were rather specialized and generally required matching. The year 1965 marked a new era when the Federal Elementary and Secondary Education Act (ESEA) was enacted. The act provided funds on a large scale. For example, Federal aid to Texas increased three times from the 1966–1967 school year to 1969–1970 (from $45 million to $158 million). Also, matching was generally not required. Among the most important provisions was Title I, which provided for compensatory education programs. Funds were allocated to school districts on the basis of the number of children from families earning less than $2,000 annually as reported by the 1960 census.

The Texas Education Agency in its reports comments on the benefit from Federal aid in bringing about innovation in the public schools.

HIGHER EDUCATION

State-supported institutions of higher learning have experienced as dramatic a growth as have the public schools—in fact, more so in recent years. For example, in 1966 approximately 247,000 students were enrolled in public junior and senior colleges and universities. By 1972, the number had increased to 419,541, an all-time high. Among the reasons is the fact that more high school students are college-bound. About 32 percent went on to college in 1972 compared to 21 percent in 1960. For another, the college population is getting older, an indication that adults are returning to the campus for enrichment, for training, or whatever. But the most important reason is the desire for the opportunities, particularly in technical-vocational training, offered at the junior or community colleges. The sharpest rise in enrollment has been in these institutions.

To cope with increases in enrollment and demands for improvements and modernization, the legislature authorized a large number of new colleges and universities since the mid-sixties. In 1973 the Texas Senate declared a temporary moratorium on expansion of the higher education system pending a comprehensive study of needs by the Coordinating Board.

Generally speaking, the state's system of higher education is composed of two basic kinds of institutions—the four-year state-supported senior college and the two-year state-aided junior or community college. However, in the 1960s and early 1970s several upper-level senior institutions were authorized to provide instruction only to juniors and seniors. These new institutions are classified as senior colleges and universities. In addition, most of the upper-level and the traditional four-year colleges also offer graduate instruction. Finally, we may take note of the expansion of state-supported medical schools. In the 1970s there were six medical schools, two dental schools, and three medically related institutions—a Graduate School of Biomedical Sciences, a School of Public Health, and a School of Nursing, statewide.

Coordinating Board, Texas College and University System

The Coordinating Board is the highest administrative authority in the state in matters of public higher education. Created by the legislature in 1965 as the successor to the Commission of Higher Education, the board is composed of eighteen gubernatorial appointees who serve six-year overlapping terms. They appoint the commissioner of higher education who is the chief administrative officer of the agency.

The overall purpose of the board is to furnish leadership and coordination for the state's higher education system in order that Texas may achieve excellence in education. In carrying out its responsibilities, the board has considerable authority over state-supported institutions. It has drafted a master plan for the state system[31] and is currently studying the needs of the entire system. It initiates, consolidates, and eliminates, as may be, degree or certification programs; it approves or rejects course offerings; and it has budgetary powers. It prepares the budget for the entire system; and following its adoption by the legislature, it devises formulas for disbursing of the funds. For example, every general academic senior institution receives the same grant per student for given courses of instruction. The board also has authority over the community colleges—approving their creation, specifying the standards they must meet, and administering financial assistance. In addition, the board administers several student aid programs. The two most important are the Hinson-Hazlewood College Student Loan Program, which was authorized by constitutional amendment in 1966 and expanded in 1969 and the Tuition Equalization Grants Program (1971), which authorized grants to needy students at private colleges and universities. In 1972, the board was designated by the governor as the State Post-secondary Education Commission to receive and administer planning grants under the Federal Education Amendments Act of 1972.[32]

---

[31]*Challenge for Excellence: A Blueprint for Progress in Higher Education,* Austin, January, 1969.

[32]The new assignment requires planning and coordination of both public and private postsecondary educational resources so that all who desire postsecondary education may have the opportunity to receive it.

Senior Colleges and Graduate Institutions

In 1973, Texas had thirty-seven state-supported senior colleges and universities, including branches and medical facilities. The two major systems are The University of Texas and Texas A & M University, each of which is composed of several components. The institutions are listed in Table 10.

Governing Boards   The senior institutions are governed by nine-member boards of regents or directors appointed by the governor with Senate consent. Separate boards are provided for the University of Texas and the Texas A & M University systems and for the others except for four colleges, three of which were former teachers colleges, who are under the governance of the Board of Regents, State Senior Colleges.

State Financing   The senior colleges are financed from state appropriations, special funds dedicated for certain institutions, tuition and other user fees, donations, and Federal aid. In 1972, Texas ranked fourth among the states in total annual appropriations of state tax funds for the operation of higher education.[33]

The University of Texas and Texas A & M University are supported in part from income derived from the Permanent University Fund, whose historical origins we have already discussed. Two-thirds of the proceeds go to The University of Texas and one-third to Texas A & M. The fund was supplemented by additional grants in 1883; and today, they total 2,100,000 surface acres located in nineteen West Texas counties.[34] The discovery of gas and oil on the lands in 1923 eventually resulted in huge payments into the fund, which in 1972 amounted to about 636 million dollars. Only the income may be spent.

The constitution forbids legislative appropriations for university buildings; hence, most of the income from the Permanent University Fund has been expended on the construction of physical facilities, while current operating expenses are met largely by legislative appropriations. The University of Texas and Texas A & M have been allowed by constitutional amendment since 1947 to issue bonds secured by the expected revenue from a portion of the Available Fund for construction. As a result part of the Available Fund has been "mortgaged" to the year 2003.

To provide for the construction of buildings at other state-supported universities and colleges, a constitutional amendment adopted in 1947

---

[33]*Annual Report, Coordinating Board, Texas College and University System, 1971–72*, p. 14, Austin, 1972.
[34]*Statement to the Texas Constitutional Revision Commission*, UT Board of Regents, *op. cit.*

Table 10   Public Senior and Graduate Institutions and Their Branches

Institution	Date of establishment as a state school	Location
The University of Texas System		
The University of Texas at Arlington	1917	Arlington
The University of Texas at Austin	1883	Austin
The University of Texas at Dallas	1969	Dallas
The University of Texas at El Paso	1913	El Paso
The University of Texas of the Permian Basin	1969	Odessa
The University of Texas at San Antonio	1969	San Antonio
The University of Texas Medical Branch at Galveston	1889	Galveston
The University of Texas Southwestern Medical School at Dallas	1949	Dallas
The University of Texas Dental Branch at Houston	1943	Houston
The University of Texas Graduate School of Biomedical Sciences at Houston	1963	Houston
The University of Texas School of Public Health at Houston	1967	Houston
The University of Texas Medical School at San Antonio	1964	San Antonio
The University of Texas Dental School at San Antonio	1969	San Antonio
The University of Texas System School of Nursing	1967	Austin
Texas A & M University System		
Texas A & M University	1870	College Station
Texas Maritime Academy and Moody College of Marine Science and		

dedicated 5 cents per $100 valuation of the state ad valorem tax to be used as security for the issuance of bonds at enumerated institutions. Called the college building bond fund, the program was altered by amendments, as indicated in Chapter 11. At present seventeen institutions are served by the fund, which is secured by a 10-cent property tax.

Federal assistance to Texas colleges and universities supplements state funds. Probably the most important Federal act in this regard is the Higher Education Act of 1965 and its subsequent amendments. It is significant that Federal aid accounts for over half of all research funds at institutions of higher learning in Texas and well over half of the financial aid to college students.

Table 10 (*con't*)

Marine Resources	1931	Galveston
Prairie View A & M University	1876	Prairie View
Tarleton State University	1917	Stephenville
Texas A & I University		
Texas A & I University at		
Corpus Christi	1971	Corpus Christi
Texas A & I University at		
Kingsville	1925	Kingsville
Texas A & I University at		
Laredo	1969	Laredo
East Texas State University	1917	Commerce
East Texas State University at		
Texarkana	1971	Texarkana
University of Houston	1963	Houston
University of Houston at Clear Lake City	1971	Clear Lake City
University of Houston at Victoria	1971	Victoria
Lamar University	1951	Beaumont
Jefferson County Center	1971	Port Arthur
Orange County Center	1971	Orange
Midwestern University	1959	Wichita Falls
North Texas State University	1901	Denton
Pan American University	1965	Edinburg
Stephen F. Austin State University	1923	Nacogdoches
Texas Southern University	1947	Houston
Texas Tech University	1925	Lubbock
Texas Tech University School of Medicine	1969	Lubbock
Texas Woman's University	1902	Denton
Tyler State College	1971	Tyler
West Texas State University	1910	Canyon
State Senior Colleges		
Angelo State University	1965	San Angelo
Sam Houston State University	1879	Huntsville
Southwest Texas State University	1903	San Marcos
Sul Ross State University	1920	Alpine

Community Colleges

Community or junior colleges are comparative newcomers to Texas. Districts for the establishment of publicly supported junior colleges were first authorized by the legislature only in 1929. Since then, their growth has been little short of spectacular. Between 1960 and 1972 the number of junior colleges increased 50 percent. In 1973 there were 48 colleges with an enrollment in excess of 166,000 whereas in 1960 there were 32 colleges with an enrollment of only 39,000.[35]

[35] *Texas Almanac, op. cit.,* p. 550; *CB Report, Monthly Notes from the Coordinating Board, Texas College and University System,* November, 1972.

A reason for the growth is the changing concept of what a junior college should be. This is reflected in the name change to community college, authorized by the legislature in 1971 and reaffirmed in 1973.[36] The community college is designed to serve the needs of the entire community, providing for university parallel programs, occupational and technical training, and any course of interest to the people. An "open admissions" policy is the goal: Allow anyone to enroll who wishes to take courses at the college.

The Texas Education Code spells out in detail the methods by which community colleges are established, but in all instances the Coordinating Board must first give approval before the election, which is required, can be held. The procedures vary somewhat by the type of college to be created.[37]

The community colleges are governed by an elected board of trustees and are financed by local property taxes, per capita and other state aid, and Federal funds. The Texas Research League proposed in 1970 that the state undertake complete funding of all community colleges.[38] It was argued that local taxpayers in communities with public four-year colleges do not have to pay a special property tax to educate freshmen and sophomores whereas they do in community college towns. Also, the community colleges are needed in areas where the local taxpayers have refused to vote for them. The Coordinating Board has mapped out fifty-three community college regions; and perhaps in the future all communities where colleges are desirable will have them.

THE CHANGING EDUCATION SYSTEM

The revolution in technology and the knowledge explosion have produced vast changes throughout the Texas education system. Curriculum has undergone extensive revision, not only in mathematics and the sciences, but also in the social sciences and humanities. New methods of teaching, stimulated by technological advances, have been put in operation. Experimentation with new forms of educational administration and organization has occurred, although fundamental reorganization of the local school district remains for the future.

A greater awareness of and sensitivity to social problems have

---

[36]Texas Education Code, Section 130.005.

[37]There are six types: an independent school district junior college, a city junior college, a union junior college, a county junior college, a joint-county junior college, and a public junior college as a part or division of a regional college district.

[38]*Financing a Statewide Community College System in Texas* (Summary Copy), Texas Research League, Austin, 1970.

surfaced in the decade of the sixties and the seventies. The multiethnic population of the state is reflected in the school population, and disadvantages visited upon minorities have also been present in the school system. New programs have been instituted to provide for the special needs of Spanish-speaking children (bilingual education), migrant children, and children from low-income groups. At the college level, new courses of instruction in black and Mexican-American studies have been introduced.

The problem of dismantling the dual racial system of public education has not yet been resolved at the date of writing as desegregation issues continued to be litigated in the courts. It has been twenty years since the *Brown v. Board of Education* case was decided, but the issues have not yet been satisfactorily settled. Also, the small percentage of black and Mexican-American students on state-supported college campuses is a cause of concern.

The need to train students for jobs required in a science-based technological society has been more fully realized than ever before. Although vocational education has been available for years, a renewal and a resurgence have occurred in the late 1960s. The Vocation and Technological Act of 1969 was landmark legislation, and new institutions and programs have been accelerating at an unprecedented pace.

For the future, we can expect even more changes for which it is absolutely essential to plan now. Various planning programs are underway and, at the state level, are part of comprehensive planning.

Chapter 13

Public Welfare and Health

No governmental activity has undergone a more profound change in the twentieth century than that of public welfare. This change began about 1933 under the distressing economic and social conditions growing out of the Great Depression. No longer were welfare programs purely personal and local undertakings. They were now considered proper functions of the state and national governments, usually on a cooperative basis. Moreover, instead of such programs being conducted simply in the name of charity, they became synonymous with the democratic ideal of security and well-being for all. The acceptance of the idea of the welfare state has resulted in many positive governmental actions to promote economic security, health, and well-being. Public welfare, in all its various ramifications, is now one of the largest, most important, and most expensive functions of state government. As we have seen, public welfare is the second most costly item in the Texas state budget.

PUBLIC WELFARE

The assumption by the state of Texas of public welfare programs on a large scale was the direct result of the Social Security Act of 1935.[1] An omnibus law, the act contained among its provisions several public assistance programs for which Federal grants-in-aid were made available to the states on a matching basis. In order for Texas to participate in this venture in cooperative federalism, the Texas constitution had to be amended. Although not all have been in response to Federal pressures, sixteen amendments on welfare have been added to the Texas constitution during a forty-year period; three were rejected by the voters. As we shall see, Texas continues to curtail the welfare program by a ceiling on state welfare spending.[2]

It was also necessary for the state to develop administrative organization to administer welfare programs. For this purpose the Texas State Department of Public Welfare was established in the late 1930s. Legal responsibility for the department is vested in a three-member part-time citizen board appointed by the governor for six-year overlapping terms. The board appoints the commissioner of public welfare, who is the actual administrative head of the agency. At the county level, the county commissioners court has authority to appoint a county welfare board, which, as an agent of the state, exercises coordinating responsibility for state and local public welfare services. Not all counties have a welfare board, however.

Welfare Explosion

From their beginnings in the 1930s, public assistance programs have been among the most expensive in state budgets. However, from 1966 to 1972, the state welfare rolls and costs shot up all across the nation. In Texas, recipients of the basic assistance programs increased almost 100 percent during that time (from about 330,000 to 680,000); and total state costs more than doubled (from about 83 million dollars to 212 million dollars).[3]

The welfare increases have appeared paradoxical during a period of unprecedented prosperity. It has been difficult for working people in

[1]The Social Security Act is best known for the old age insurance program which, after numerous amendments, is currently called Old Age Survivors Disability Health Insurance (OASDHI), or simply "social security." This program is wholly administered by the national government and for that reason is not included in this chapter.

[2]The first welfare amendment was passed in 1933. It authorized bonds to be issued the proceeds of which were to be used for relief and work relief. The first amendment to take advantage of the Federal grants-in-aid for public assistance was adopted in 1935. The latest amendment at the date of writing was passed in 1969 and set the 80 million dollar ceiling on state expenditures.

[3]*Executive Budget, 1974–75 Biennium—State of Texas, Preston Smith, Governor of Texas,* pp. 20–21, Austin, 1973.

particular to understand why assistance to the needy is really necessary. "We work; why don't they?" Considerable misunderstanding or mythology surrounds the welfare programs. Two comprehensive reports, one by a Texas Senate Interim Committee on Welfare Reform[4] and the other by the Texas Office of Economic Opportunity,[5] published in 1971 and 1972 respectively, have shed considerable light on the reasons why public assistance is essential in Texas.

The Texas Office of Economic Opportunity report, based on a household survey, describes the meaning of poverty from many vantage points—illness, diet, housing, ignorance, and so on. Statistically, poverty is defined by an Office of Economic Opportunity sliding scale of income and family size. For example, the 1971 poverty threshold was a $3,800 income for a family of four. This amounted to $2.60 per person per day.

The research also points up the magnitude of poverty in Texas. Texas has more poor people than any other state. In 1971 there were 2.5 million poor Texans, or about 22 percent of the population. This was considerably higher than the national average of 13 percent.

Over half of the poor in Texas are children and old people. In 1971 some 33.7 percent were children fourteen years old or younger and 18.6 percent were persons sixty-five years of age or older. Although Anglos constitute the largest single poor group, the incidence of poverty among Mexican Americans and blacks was much higher. These two groups accounted for about 30 percent of the total population but 60 percent of the poor.

Contrary to popular impression, many poor people work. Texas in 1970 had the largest working poor population in the nation. About 38 percent of the poor in Texas are employed. These people comprised 55 percent of all family heads and 84 percent of male family heads in the working-age poor population. When we add the poor adults in Texas who are retired (they constitute about 31.1 percent of the adult poor) to the poor adults who are working, we get about 70 percent of the Texas adult poor either retired or working. This also adds up to 90 percent of poor adult males who are either retired or employed. Among those unemployed, 10.4 percent were seeking employment. Of those not seeking employment, 88 percent were female.

The public welfare programs represent the major state response to poverty in Texas. But they fall far short of coping with a very complex, multifaceted phenomenon. In fact, only about 27 percent of the poor are recipients of welfare in Texas. We shall turn to the programs next.

[4]*Breaking the Poverty Cycle in Texas*, Report of the Senate Interim Committee on Welfare Reform, Austin, 1971.
[5]*Poverty in Texas*, Report of the Texas Office of Economic Opportunity, Austin, 1972.

Categorical Public Assistance

Four Programs and Then There Was One   At the heart of the Texas welfare system from the 1930s to the mid-1970s was public assistance to four categories of the needy for whom Federal grants-in-aid were available. In other words, in order to receive aid, a person had to be needy *and* something else. It was not sufficient just to be poor. Texas does not have a general relief or residual program to catch those falling through the interstices of the net of categorical assistance.

The four categories of public assistance were: (1) Old Age Assistance (OAA); (2) Aid to the Blind (AB); (3) Aid to the Permanently and Totally Disabled (APTD); and (4) Aid to Families with Dependent Children (AFDC). The most expensive of the programs was the first (OAA) although the total number of recipients of the last (AFDC) was larger.

In January, 1974, the first three of the programs, the so-called adult programs, were taken over by the Federal government under a new program called "Supplemental Security Income" (SSI). It was authorized by an amendment to the Social Security Act and is administered by the Secretary of Health, Education and Welfare.[6] Eligibility requirements for recipients differ from those previously imposed by Texas. A majority of the recipients will enjoy higher payments than before. Persons without any income are guaranteed $130 a month and married couples, $195. It is anticipated that the persons receiving APTD will triple and those on the OAA rolls will increase 50 percent. The assumption of responsibility for the programs by the Federal government will lessen the pressure on the 80 million dollar constitutional welfare ceiling by about 10 million dollars in 1974 and 17 million dollars in 1979.[7] However, additional medical assistance costs for persons under SSI and social services will have to be absorbed by Texas.

Aid to Families with Dependent Children (AFDC)   Texas retains responsibility for administration of the AFDC categorical assistance program. However, the Federal government has borne about three-quarters of the cost and one-half of the administration expenditures; and this will continue.

The AFDC program is designed to keep needy children with their families rather than placing them in an institution. Payments are made to

---

[6]P.L. 92–603, Title III.
[7]*Executive Budget, op. cit.*, p. 20.

the parent or caretaker to provide necessities sufficient for health and wholesome living conditions. However, the actual payments are below what could be called adequate. The Public Welfare Department calculates a standard of need, and then it pays no more than 75 percent of that standard to the family. Income, if any, of the family is taken into account and the difference required to bring the payment up to 75 percent is made.

Payments are made only for children under eighteen or under twenty-one, if they are in school. To be eligible the child must have lost parental support but be living in his own home or that of a close relative and lack income to provide the necessities of life. He must be currently a resident of Texas and a U.S. citizen.

In 1972 there were approximately 120,000 families receiving assistance on behalf of 330,000 children.[8] The average monthly grant was around $40 and the average grant per family, $115. This was far below the national average, which was $187 per family. Only thirteen states made lower payments than Texas in 1972.

Social Services

Another public assistance program supported in large part by Federal grants is that of social services. Established by a 1967 amendment to the Social Security Act, the program encourages all manner of services to the needy and potential welfare recipients. In Texas it has been primarily a program of assistance to children and families, many of whom are on the AFDC rolls. As described by the Department of Public Welfare:

> The Department makes every effort to provide services to those who need them when they need them. The social service worker, for example, helps recipients find and use licensed day care facilities, learn about family planning, keep a child in school, get medical treatment, obtain job training or adopt a baby.[9]

In general, the department provides services for the protection and care of children without family or legal guardians; those whose families are unwilling or unable to provide the proper protection and care; children who are abused, neglected, or subject to improper surroundings; the child with behavioral difficulties; the child born out of wedlock, or any child who is in difficulty. Case workers from the department assist when a child is involved with the courts in such cases as custody in divorce cases, guardianship and adoption proceedings, and delinquency.

[8] *Annual Report*, Texas State Department of Public Welfare, pp. 4, 121, Austin, 1972.
[9] *Ibid.*, p. 17.

The Federal government drastically reduced its commitment to the social services assistance program by the State and Local Fiscal Assistance Act of 1972 (general revenue sharing). Texas cannot expect to receive again Federal payments as large as the 6 million dollars appropriated in 1972.

WIN

Another Federal grant-in-aid program is the Work Incentive Program (WIN) which is designed to assist AFDC recipients to achieve self-support by gaining employment. In Texas, the social services program has been used by the Department of Public Welfare to help WIN participants by providing child care, family planning, homemaker services, transportation, and so on. Amendments to the Social Security Act passed in 1971 required every AFDC recipient to register for the employment programs except those under sixteen or attending school full-time, the ill, mothers with children under six, and similar categories. To date the program has been a minor one in Texas.

Crippled Children's Service

One additional children's assistance program in Texas is the physical rehabilitation service for crippled children. It preceded the passage of the Social Security Act in 1935. The State Department of Health administers the program, which is jointly financed by Federal and state funds. To be eligible for rehabilitation, the child must be under twenty-one and his disability must be such that it is reasonable to expect that he may be improved through hospitalization, medical or surgical care, or artificial appliances. The child's parents must be financially unable to provide care and treatment. The Health Department uses approximately thirty-three hospitals and about the same number of orthopedic surgeons to provide services to some 13,000 children annually.

Other services for crippled children are furnished by two special state institutions, the Moody State School for Cerebral Palsied Children and the State Hospital for Crippled and Deformed Children. Both are located in Galveston and are operated by The University of Texas Medical Branch of Galveston.

Medical Assistance

In 1962, Texas began participating in a Federal grant-in-aid program of hospital and nursing home care for recipients of Old Age Assistance. The program became known as the Texas Medical Assistance Program. With the beginning of Medicare, the national social security health insurance program for persons sixty-five years of age and older, Texas had to expand its medical assistance to the needy. Today, medical assistance to the needy is known as Medicaid.

Under Medicaid, which is financed jointly by the Federal government and the state of Texas and administered by the Welfare Department, medical assistance is provided to those persons who receive Supplemental Security Income and to children on the AFDC rolls. Also covered are certain children under twenty-one years of age in some foster homes or private nonprofit institutions. A variety of medical services is provided, including physician, laboratory, and x-ray services; nursing home care; and inpatient hospital care. For each recipient of assistance under SSI and AFDC the state makes a contract with Group Hospital Service, Inc. (Blue Cross) for payment of medical services. In 1971 a new state drug vendor law was implemented under which prescribed medicines are furnished directly to the eligible needy person by pharmacists participating in the program.

The medical assistance program has become increasingly costly over the years and is now the most expensive of all the welfare programs. In 1972 the total cost was over 337 million dollars of which the state paid 35 percent.[10]

Vocational Rehabilitation

Since 1929, the state has had a Federal grant-in-aid program for those who are physically disabled to such an extent that they cannot support themselves by regular vocations. Through the years, the scope of the program has been broadened to include mentally retarded persons, the mentally ill, alcoholics, and public offenders. Such persons are offered whatever assistance is necessary to prepare them for work they can do successfully. They may receive financial assistance in securing training so that they may become economically self-sufficient. The training may be in schools, shops, or factories, or by correspondence. Assistance will be given them in locating suitable employment. If it appears that the physical or mental condition of the disabled person can be materially improved by medical, surgical, psychiatric, or other treatment to such an extent that his vocational possibilities are thereby increased, such treatment will be provided. Artificial appliances may also be furnished. The program for persons with handicaps other than visual is administered by the Texas

[10]*Ibid.*, p. 51.

Commission for Rehabilitation, which works with the Department of Public Welfare on some programs. The commission, which was established in 1969, is composed of six members appointed by the governor with Senate consent for six-year overlapping terms. The board appoints a commissioner to serve at its pleasure.

Food Assistance

The Commodity Distribution Division of the Public Welfare Department in cooperation with the U.S. Department of Agriculture and county governments administers two food assistance programs to needy Texans. The first and by far the largest is the Commodity Distribution Program. The Welfare Department distributes millions of dollars worth of food annually for school lunch programs, to eleemosynary institutions, and through city and county welfare agencies to needy citizens. Well over one million persons, mostly school children, benefit from this program each year.

The second food assistance program is the food stamp program. Participants purchase a portion of the food coupons for which they are eligible and then receive bonus coupons free of cost. The coupons are used to purchase food in participating stores. The needy have a much wider selection of food items in contrast to the commodity program. The program has been growing; and in 1972, over thirty counties had adopted it.

Evaluation of Public Assistance Programs in Texas

Public assistance programs and their administration in Texas have been subjected to searching criticism by several state committees. In 1973, a report of the House Interim Committee on Poverty summarized the most important of the objections and proposed corrective measures.[11]

The committee was greatly influenced by testimony of "insensitive, uncoordinated, and consequently inadequate" administration of services to the poor and of "the need for jobs paying wages above the poverty level." Guided by these criticisms and others, the House committee endorsed several recommendations, including some made by the Senate Interim Committee on Welfare Reform in 1970. We will review the more important of these.

1. The legislature must provide leadership to resolve the massive

---

[11]*Poverty: Time for State Policy*, Report of the House Interim Committee on Poverty to the Sixty-third Legislative Session, Austin, 1973.

problem of poverty in Texas. There is great need for a comprehensive state policy for human resources. To implement the policy, state agencies concerned with administering human resource programs should be required to submit annual performance reports to the governor and the legislature.

2. To remedy the uncoordinated delivery of services to the poor at the local level, the legislature should enact a law providing for multiservice centers in neighborhoods with large poverty populations. (The legislature in 1973 passed the law.)

3. To provide jobs paying wages above the poverty level, programs prepared by the Texas Office of Economic Opportunity and the Texas Industrial Commission should be funded.

4. The constitutional ceiling on state expenditures for welfare programs should be removed.

5. The Department of Public Welfare should be changed to the Department of Human Resources and entrusted with a wider range of responsibilities. It should be directed by a Secretary of Human Resources appointed by the governor with Senate concurrence.

6. Various educational programs—bilingual, community college, and adult education—should be promoted more vigorously.

7. The legislature should provide for greater consumer protection. (A new law was passed in 1973.)

PUBLIC HEALTH

An increasing proportion of the state's resources, greatly augmented by Federal funds, are being devoted to health care. In 1972, over 227 million dollars was expended, a sizable proportion of the state budget.

State Department of Health

The chief administrative agency for health programs in Texas is the State Department of Health. The department was established in 1879 and is under the control of a nine-member Board of Health, appointed by the governor for six-year overlapping terms. Six of the nine board members must be medical doctors. The board appoints the commissioner of health, who is the chief administrator of the department.

The department, aided by numerous local health centers which it partly finances, guards the health of the state in many ways, including enforcing meat and poultry offered for sale, approving plans for public water supplies and sewage-disposal systems, and prescribing the bacterial content of swimming pools. It licenses hospitals and nursing and convalescent homes.

The department's central laboratory makes thousands of complicated tests on specimens that are sent in, performs research on public health problems, trains laboratory workers for hospitals and local laboratories, and approves laboratories that perform the premarital and prenatal tests for syphillis required by Texas statutes. It is licensed by the National Institutes of Health to manufacture vaccines, toxoids, skin-test materials, silver nitrate ampules, and the like. These are distributed to local health officers and state institutions for use in immunization programs.

A recent development has been the establishment of public health regions for the purpose of delivering the Health Department's services to areas without organized health departments. The first of ten planned regions was set up in Tyler in 1970. Services provided include "programs in environmental health, medical services, maternal child care, family planning, immunization, venereal disease control, health education, tuberculosis control, dental health, and veterinary public health."[12]

The Federal government's Hill-Burton hospital construction program, which has involved an expenditure of over 230 million dollars from 1947 to 1972, is the largest allotted to any state.[13] It is administered by the Department of Health.

In 1965, the legislature further increased the department's responsibilities by transferring the state's four tuberculosis hospitals (located in San Angelo, Tyler, San Antonio, and Harlingen) to the department and authorizing it to establish regional TB control units, outpatient clinics, and laboratories.

Although not under the authority of the department, we should also take note of The University of Texas M. D. Anderson Hospital and Tumor Institute in Houston. It is one of the finest cancer research and treatment facilities in the nation. The hospital offers the only state-supported cancer treatment facility for the citizens of Texas.

The prevention of air and water pollution has also been a part of the Department of Health's responsibilities. The Texas Air Control Board, created to enforce the state's Clean Air Act, was until 1973 a part of the department. It is now an independent state agency. The department also performs services through its Division of Wastewater Surveillance and Technology for the Texas Water Quality Board.

Finally, in addition to its regular health activities, the department is

[12]*Executive Budget, op. cit.*, p. 33.
[13]*The Book of the States, 1972–73*, The Council of State Governments, pp. 372–373, Iron Works Pike, Lexington, Ky., 1972.

the vital statistics center for the state. Records of all births and deaths are kept here.

Mental Health

Since 1856, when the legislature established a hospital for the insane and schools for the deaf and blind (all of which were originally called asylums), Texas has provided care for certain types of persons who for various reasons are unable to care for themselves.[14] The most numerous of these groups are the mentally ill and the mentally retarded. The state now operates eight mental hospitals and geriatric centers, two intermediate or intensive treatment facilities with a third planned for El Paso,[15] and nine schools for the mentally retarded.[16] In addition, the state maintains the Houston State Psychiatric Institute, which is used for research and training. All these institutions are under the jurisdiction of the Department of Mental Health and Mental Retardation, which replaced the Board for Texas State Hospitals and Special Schools in 1965. It is composed of nine gubernatorial appointees who determine policy and serve in an advisory capacity to the commissioner whom they appoint.

Although institutional care will probably always be necessary for certain of the mentally ill and mentally retarded, emphasis is now being put on treating as many as possible in their home communities. This is frequently better than "shipping them off" to large, understaffed, and crowded hospitals and special schools. Accordingly, the department not only has outpatient clinics at Dallas, Fort Worth, and Harlingen but also assists in establishing community mental-health centers. In 1972, there were twenty-four of these centers.

Despite the growth in the state's population, the number of patients in the mental hospitals is not growing. This is the result of improved treatment, the development of outpatient services, contracting for care of patients in the community, and the discharge of many geriatric patients to nursing homes. This is not the case with the special schools for the mentally retarded, however, where the rate of admission is growing at a faster rate than the state's population. Over 300,000 Texans are mentally retarded to some degree, and it has been estimated that out of every

[14]The state educates blind and deaf children in two special schools on three campuses. All are located in Austin and are operated by the Texas Education Agency.

[15]The mental hospitals and geriatric centers are Austin State Hospital and Annex, San Antonio State Hospital, Terrell State Hospital, Wichita Falls State Hospital and Vernon Branch, Rusk State Hospital, Big Spring State Hospital, Kerrville State Hospital and Legion Annex, and Vernon Geriatric Center.

[16]Institutions for the mentally retarded are the Austin State School and Branch, Travis State School (Austin), and the State Schools at Abilene, Denton, Mexia, Lufkin, Richmond, Lubbock, Corpus Christi, and San Angelo.

thousand babies born each year three will remain below the seven-year intellectual level as adults. One out of every thousand will be so seriously retarded that he will never be able to care for his own needs in daily living. So far, there seems to be no solution to this major health, social, and economic problem.

Although great progress has been made in the last few years in care and treatment of the mentally ill and mentally retarded, especially the change from "warehousing" patients to treating them and returning as many as possible to society, several problems still exist. For example, there are many geriatric patients in the state hospitals who do not have serious psychoses and would benefit more from nursing-home care. But probably the greatest problem is the shortage of skilled medical and ancillary personnel. The supply of such people is limited, and state salaries are not high enough to attract and keep them. Another problem is lack of space and overcrowding, particularly in the schools for the mentally retarded where there is always a long waiting list for admission. Yet many improvements have been made in the care and treatment of the state's mentally ill and mentally retarded since 1965 when the present department was organized. Probably the most distinguishing feature of the new policies is the attempt to provide services at the community level.

CONCLUSION

State expenditures and programs for public welfare and health will continue to multiply in the years ahead. Nonetheless, it is very likely that much more of the total cost will shift to the national government. The Federal assumption of the three adult categorical public assistance programs in 1974 was a forerunner of things to come. The national government is under great pressure to take over all public welfare programs. Texas officials have already complained that the Federal rules and regulations are so extensive that state decision making has been reduced to the caretaker and delivery level. Also, the costs are heavy, many of them the direct result of Federal action.

National responsibility for public health is also likely to increase substantially in the future. It seems all but inevitable that some kind of compulsory national health insurance program for the entire population, probably patterned after Medicare, will be adopted. Such a program would relieve the states of a heavy burden of medical assistance costs.

Chapter 14

Highways

It would be difficult to overestimate the importance of public highways to the average citizen. Whether he is driving to work, putting his children on a school bus, moving livestock and farm produce to market, distributing factory products, or simply taking a Sunday afternoon drive in the family car, he cannot but be aware of the role of highways in our modern civilization. Highways are of especial importance in Texas, which ranks second in area but only thirty-third in population density. This means that many must travel considerable distances to get from city to city, from farm to market, or even from home to work. The Texas railroad system is not so extensive as that found in the more densely populated states; so this makes for still more dependence on the highways and has resulted in a highly developed system of truck and bus transportation. The motor vehicle on the highway is the only mode of transportation available to more than 1,176 Texas communities or 61.5 percent of the total.[1] Also,

[1] *Statement by Texas Highway Commission to the Finance Study Committee*, Texas Constitutional Revision Commission, Beaumont, June 14, 1973.

since transportation costs are reflected in the costs of goods, everyone is affected by the state's highways. Highways, then, play an important role in our complex modern life, and their planning, construction, and maintenance constitute one of the major and third most costly functions of state government.

In order to understand the administration of the present-day Texas highway system, it will be necessary to study past legislative and administrative developments out of which present policy has developed.

DEVELOPMENT FROM A LOCAL TO A STATE FUNCTION

For many years building and maintaining roads in Texas was considered a purely local affair, and for a long time no taxes for these purposes were levied. Every male taxpayer or his substitute was required to work a few days each year on the county roads. As the population of the state grew and dispersed and as subsistence farming gave way to commercial agriculture, a need developed for better roads, not only to connect the different parts of the state, but also to get agricultural goods to market. The legislature as well as the general public recognized this need, and in 1883 the Texas constitution was amended to allow the governing body of the county, the commissioners court, to levy a general property tax not to exceed 15 cents on the $100 valuation for the purpose of financing county roads and bridges. This was the first of several amendments concerned with county financing of roads.[2]

The early constitutional amendments were based on the premise that road building and maintenance were local government responsibilities. However, the inadequacy of locally financed and regulated roads, with no coordination between the road systems of the various counties, was becoming more and more evident as motor vehicular traffic grew. In 1913 the legislature passed a bill to create a State Highway Department, but it was vetoed by the governor.

As has been true of a number of other Texas programs, it took the stimulus of Federal government action to set up a state administration system for highways. Congress in 1916 passed the Federal Aid Highway Act under which generous Federal grants-in-aid were available to the states for the purpose of road construction. One of the conditions for receiving the assistance was that the state must have a highway department. The Texas legislature complied by passing the Highway Act of

---

[2]In 1887, the counties were allowed by amendment to issue bonds for the construction of bridges. In 1890, 1904, 1907, and 1909 still other amendments were passed. A county road financing amendment was adopted as recently as 1968.

1917, and the present Texas State Highway Department was born. With the enactment of the new law, Texas actively entered into planning, financing, and regulating designated highways.

Even after the creation of the Highway Department, road construction continued to be primarily a local responsibility until 1925. A 1921 amendment to the 1916 Federal Aid Highway Act required that after 1925, state highway departments were to have supervision over the construction and maintenance of federally aided highways as a condition of Federal aid. The Texas Highway Department was given this authority, and the legislature made money available for road construction by the state. Only non-Federal aid state highways remained partly financed by the counties.

In 1932 the state assumed the bonded debt of the counties and road districts which had been incurred in building roads that were now part of the state highway system. Finally, in 1939, the legislature removed the counties from highway financing altogether except for the acquisition of rights-of-way. With this enactment the present system of state control and operation of the highway system came into being.

THE TEXAS STATE HIGHWAY SYSTEM

Effectuating the legislative policy concerning highways calls not only for expenditures of vast sums of money, but also for administrative action on a very large scale. The routes must be planned, rights-of-way must be secured, roads and bridges must be designed, built, and maintained, and financing must be available. All of this necessitates a large administrative organization. The state agency responsible for state highway administration is, of course, the Texas State Highway Department.

Texas State Highway Department

The policymaking body of the Texas State Highway Department is the Texas Highway Commission, composed of three citizens appointed by the governor with Senate consent for six-year overlapping terms. The governor designates the chairman. The commission appoints the State Highway Engineer, who is the executive director.[3] He serves at the commission's pleasure. The department is organized into fifteen divisions, the head of which is directly responsible to the State Highway Engineer.

---

[3]For twenty-seven years Dewitt C. Greer was the State Highway Engineer. Greer enjoyed a national reputation for excellence as a highway administrator, and the development of the Texas highway system reflects his leadership. At the time of writing, Greer was a member of the State Highway Commission.

Because of the state's large size, there is considerable decentralization in the departmental organization. The department is organized into twenty-five semiautonomous district offices which are situated at key points throughout the state. Each of the twenty-five districts is headed by a district engineer. There is also an urban office in Houston which is headed by an engineer-manager.

Texas Highway Network

Three main systems make up the state-maintained highway network in Texas: interstate highways, United States- and state-numbered highways, and farm-to-market roads. Together, these facilities form a well-balanced, integrated transportation system serving all sections of Texas and every segment of the state's economy.

Interstate Highways   These are a portion of the national system of Interstate and Defense Highways. The system was authorized as early as 1944 but was not undertaken until the passage in 1956 of the Federal Aid Highway Act which set up a special trust fund for the program. The program has been described as the greatest public works program in history. When the system is completed in the 1980s, 90 percent of the nation's cities with populations of more than 50,000 will be linked with modern freeway facilities. Although this network will total only 1 percent of the national highway mileage, it is expected to bear more than 20 percent of the total traffic. The Texas portion of the 41,000 mile national network is 3,146 miles, most of which was completed by 1973.

United States- and State-numbered Highways   These primary highways, as they are also known, have long been the mainstays of the highway network. They will continue to serve as the prime routes for many relatively short trips, both inter- and intrastate. In addition, they will serve as feeder facilities to and from interstate highways for long-distance movements. More than 27,000 miles of these primary roads were included in the Texas State Highway Department Road Mileage Summary as of October 31, 1972.

Farm-to-Market and Ranch-to-Market Roads   These roads, known as secondary roads in other states, are primarily local service roads. Begun to provide all-weather roads for the movement of agricultural products from farm to market, this system now provides highway facilities for industrial development of small communities as well as furnishing access to recreational areas. In 1972, more than 40,000 miles of this system had been designated.

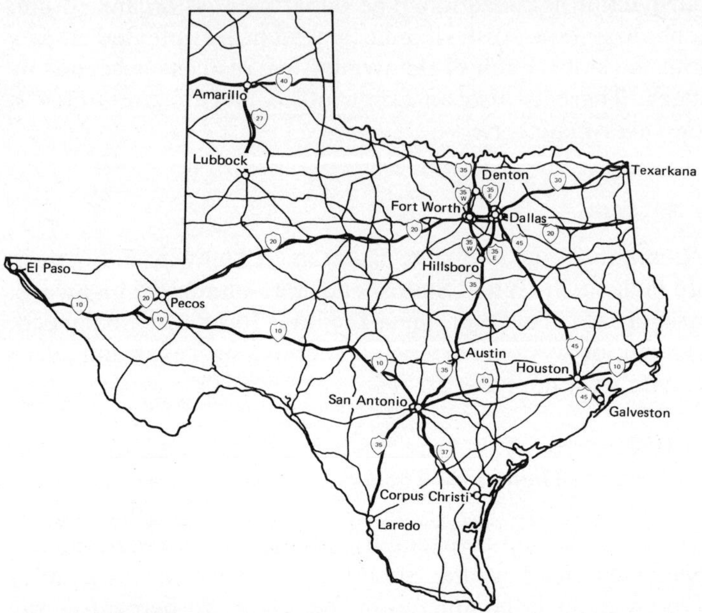

Source: Institute of Public Affairs, University of Texas,
and Texas Highway Department.

Financing

Texas highways are financed on a pay-as-you-go basis and on the principle that those who use the roads ought to pay for them—the user principle of taxation. The revenue comes from both Federal and state sources. The principal state source is the tax on motor fuels, which was authorized by a constitutional amendment in 1946, often called the "Good Roads Amendment." One-fourth of this gasoline tax goes to support public schools, but the rest goes to support highways.

The next most important state source of highway revenues are motor vehicle-license fees. All vehicles owned and operated in the state of Texas, except those of governmental units, must be registered by April of each year with the Motor Vehicle Division of the Highway Department. Registration fees are graduated according to vehicle weight and type.

The county tax officers collect the registration fees, and retain about 15 percent of the proceeds for the county road fund. The remainder is deposited in the State Highway Fund.

The Highway Department's revenue from the Federal government comes from the Federal Highway Trust Fund. About 36 percent or one-third comes from this source. This fund is composed of Federal levies connected with the operation of motor vehicles, including excise taxes, motor-fuels taxes, taxes on tires and tread rubber, and other items. The fund was established in 1956 concurrent with the beginning of the Interstate Highway System to finance all Federal-aid highway programs. Annual apportionments to the states are made from the fund according to

Texas State Highway Department Road Mileage Summary as of October 31, 1972

Highway System	Type of aid system	Miles designated as of this date	New mileage under construction	State-maintained mileage Rural	State-maintained mileage Urban	City-maintained mileage
Interstate	FAI	3,208	262*	2,189	754	0
	FAP	14,539	19	11,714	2,410	25
U.S. and state highways	FAM	342	0	15	253	59
	FAS	11,197	21	9,857	1,094	18
	Non-FA	928	5	474	302	33
	Total	27,006	45	22,060	4,059	135
Farm- or ranch-to-market and recreational roads	FAM	87	1	7	66	11
	FAS	30,571	272	28,410	1,414	12
	Non-FA	9,438	21	8,847	454	0
	Total	40,096	294	37,264	1,934	23
	FAI	3,208	262*	2,189	754	0
	FAP	14,539	19	11,714	2,410	25
All systems	FAM (State hys.)	429	1	22	22	70
	FAS	41,768	293	38,267	2,508	30
	FAP II	277	0	0	0	277
	FAM (City sts.)	63	0	0	0	63
	Non-FA	10,366	26	9,321	756	33
	Totals	70,650	601	61,513	6,747	498

*This 262 miles includes construction on new location and reconstruction on present traveled way to Interstate standards.

complex formulas based on land area, population density, highway mileage, and motor vehicle registration. Total allotments to the states cannot exceed receipts into the fund. No deficits may be incurred, and allotments from the trust fund are subject to matching by the states. On interstate construction, 90 percent comes from the Highway Trust Fund and 10 percent from the state. On other Federal-aid projects, the ratio has been 50-50. A 70–30 ratio is now common; and the Highway Beautification Program in Texas calls for about a 3–1 ratio of Federal-to-state funds. Allocation of trust-fund monies, as well as review of design and construction of Federal projects, is a function of the Federal Highway Administration, a part of the Department of Transportation.

Although Texas receives a large amount of Federal funds, not all highway construction projects involve money from this source. More than 10,000 miles of Texas highways have been constructed solely with state funds. Over 92 percent of Highway Department expenditures go toward construction or maintenance of the highway system of Texas. In 1972, 72 cents of each highway dollar was expended for rights-of-way and construction and 22 cents for maintenance.

Although the highway patrol is not a part of the Texas Highway Department, funds for its support come from the State Highway Fund. In 1972, 1.7 cents of each highway dollar went for this purpose.

Building and Maintaining Highways

The first step in construction of a highway is the selection of the route on the basis of studies showing traffic demand and other need factors. If the work is to be a Federal-aid project, an outline or a route map is submitted to the Federal Highway Administration. Detailed plans, including those for bridges and other structures, are prepared by field forces in the district, in consultation with engineers from the main office. On a Federal-aid-project, the Federal Highway Administration reviews the plans. Meanwhile, rights-of-way are secured by local governments. The state shares equally in acquisition of rights-of-way for United States–and state-numbered highways. Counties furnish all rights-of-way for farm-to-market roads, with the state assisting in preparation of the necessary deed. Rights-of-way for interstate highways are secured by the state, although the Federal government participates in the cost of purchase.

All highway construction contracts are let by competitive bidding. Bidders must show they have the necessary assets, equipment, and personnel to perform the job. In Federal-aid projects, the Federal Highway Administration reviews the contract. Construction is supervised by the district engineer in cooperation with the main office. The Federal

Highway Administration makes periodic inspection of Federal-aid projects. The contractor is paid monthly for the work completed during that month, with payments not exceeding 95 percent of the total cost of construction. The remainder is not paid until the project is completed and accepted.

Maintenance is one of the functions of the twenty-five Highway Department districts. Maintenance headquarters sections are located at strategic points throughout the district. Each section is responsible for the highways in a specific area and is organized and equipped to perform all types of normal maintenance. The district headquarters furnishes special equipment and technical and engineering assistance as well as shops for repair of heavy equipment and construction of signs. State maintenance extends into urban areas on many routes. Through cooperative agreements with the cities, the state performs a large portion of the maintenance on many state-designated highway routes in urban areas. This includes most urban freeway mileage.

FUTURE GROWTH

Texas highways are but one component of a much broader transportation system that encompasses rail, waterways, airways, pipelines, and urban rail transit. Nonetheless, it appears that for the immediate future, the highway will remain the mainstay of the Texas transportation system. This is true despite interest in urban mass rail transit, both intra- and intercity; concern by ecologists about automobile pollution and the location of highway routes; and challenges from urbanologists concerned about what expressways do to orderly urban physical, social, economic, and cultural development.

One reason why the highway will continue to carry most of the transportation load in Texas is the size of the state with its enormous sparsely populated areas. For a statewide system, truck, bus, and car travel is more economical and feasible than alternative forms, such as rail or air travel. Water transportation need not even be mentioned as an alternative for much of Texas. Second, the viability and popularity of urban mass rail transit have yet to be demonstrated in Texas. Densely populated urban centers are well served by urban rail transportation, but none of the Texas cities has yet approached the density of, say, New York, San Francisco, Philadelphia, or Chicago. Also, Texas cities have developed outward in a radial fashion, and only about 5 percent of travel is to the central business district. Furthermore, it is possible that many urban mass transit needs can be served by bus. Buses can cut across town and pick up passengers more easily than rail transportation. Exclusive bus lanes on highways can facilitate rapid transit. For example, express lanes reserved for buses on Shirley Highway in Washington, D.C., increased patronage by 230 percent in three years. Third, Texans are avid highway users. Between 1950 and 1970 while population grew 45 percent, the number of motor vehicles registered increased 143 percent.[4] In fact, Texas is approaching the "one man, one car" principle. In 1970, there were 1.69 persons per automobile.[5] It is estimated that by 1987 over 12 million motor vehicles will be registered in comparison with 7.8 million in 1971.

The anticipated growth of the Texas highway system will cause a financial strain on the resources devoted to highways. Already, Federal funding has become more and more uncertain. And the Texas segment of the 1972 National Transportation Needs Study, prepared at the instigation of the Secretary of Transportation, has projected the costs of the highways at 22.2 billion dollars in 1990 whereas only 15.7 billion dollars can be anticipated from present state and Federal sources. The gap will have to be made up somehow.

The competition for the transportation dollar will increase as time goes on. The "Good Roads Amendment" of 1946, based on the principle of a dedicated tax on gasoline for the highways, has come under attack for freezing out financing of other modes of transportation. It is imperative that a well-balanced transportation system be developed and financed and that it be consonant with other important values. To this end various planning programs have been established.

The Texas Highway Department has completed comprehensive transportation planning programs for all the SMSAs of the state as required by the Federal Aid Highway Act of 1962. These programs involve broad-scale, areawide surveys of many factors affecting community life in urban areas, including economic factors, population, land use, transportation facilities, travel patterns, terminal and transfer facilities, traffic-control features, zoning ordinances, subdivision regulations, building codes, and other regulations. Financial resources and social and community values, such as preservation of open spaces, park and recreational facilities, preservation of historical sites and buildings, environmental amenities and aesthetics, are taken into account. These studies complement long-standing Texas Highway Department policies aimed at integrating urban highway facilities into the communities they serve.

---

[4]*Executive Budget, 1974–1975 Biennium—State of Texas, Preston Smith, Governor*, p. 27, Austin, 1973.

[5]Charles P. Zlatkovich, "Texas in the Seventies: Transportation," *Texas Business Review*, April, 1970.

The Highway Department is represented on the Interagency Transportation Council in the Governor's Office together with such agencies as the Texas Railroad Commission, the Texas Aeronautics Commission, and the Texas Mass Transportation Commission. It was this agency that developed the Texas segment of the National Transportation Needs Study mentioned above.

Resolution of the transportation problems of the future will rank high among the priorities of the people of Texas. The groundwork is being laid to permit rational decisions, but much remains to be accomplished.

Chapter 15

Regulation of Business and Professional Activities

In the federal system, the responsibility for the regulation of business is shared between the national government and the states. Although the national government is the senior partner, the states retain the primary responsibility for protecting property rights, establishing organizational forms for business enterprise, and licensing professions and trades.[1] Also, the national government has voluntarily allowed the states either to dominate or to continue to exercise important regulatory responsibility over several industries. One of these is insurance. Quite clearly, the national government under the interstate commerce clause could assume the major regulatory tasks, but it leaves the basic authority with the states.[2] Another important field is banking. Unlike other developed nations, the United States has a dual rather than a centralized banking

[1]Daniel J. Elazar, *American Federalism: A View from the States*, pp. 53–61, Thomas Y. Crowell Company, New York, 1966.

[2]Congressional authority to regulate insurance was affirmed by the U.S. Supreme Court in *U.S. v. South-Eastern Underwriters Association*, 322 U.S. 533 (1944).

298

system.[3] National banks chartered by the national government and state banks chartered by the states coexist under a dual set of regulations although the national regulations are superior. The trend is toward an ever increasing national role in business affairs; but the states will continue to exercise responsibilities. In this chapter we shall look at the important areas regulated by the state of Texas.

Texas is no longer primarily an agricultural state. The development in commercial and industrial activities has made necessary a much broader program of state regulation of business, industry, and labor than was true during the earlier days. Such businesses as banking, insurance, oil and gas, and the sale of securities have been subjected to a higher degree of regulation than has business in general. Perhaps this is because of what seems to be a generally accepted doctrine that these activities affect the public interest more than other businesses do.

THE RAILROAD COMMISSION

The Railroad Commission was created during Governor James S. Hogg's administration in 1891 and was patterned in many respects after the Interstate Commerce Act of 1887. Its original purpose was the regulation of railroad passenger and freight rates and the enforcement of the state laws pertaining to railroads. Since the commission's inception, legislation has been enacted from time to time expanding its activities to include regulation of pipelines as common carriers, the enforcement of oil- and gas-conservation laws, the regulation of buses and trucks, and many other activities.

The Railroad Commission is composed of three members, elected for six-year overlapping terms. It has been the custom of the commission for the chairmanship to revolve each two years, the chairman always being the member who is next up for election. The chairman receives no added compensation.

The conservation of oil and gas resources is the chief function of the commission today. (See map, Texas Crude Oil Production, with insert of Railroad Commission Districts.) This is also the purpose of the Interstate Oil Compact Commission, of which Texas is a member. This agency was created in 1935 by the oil-producing states under authority of Article 1, Section 10, of the Federal Constitution, which permits states to make agreements among themselves with the consent of Congress. It is purely an advisory body with no regulatory powers, but it fosters exchange of

[3]See Emmette S. Redford, "Dual Banking: A Case Study in Federalism," *Law and Contemporary Problems*, pp. 749–773, Autumn, 1966.

TEXAS CRUDE OIL PRODUCTION

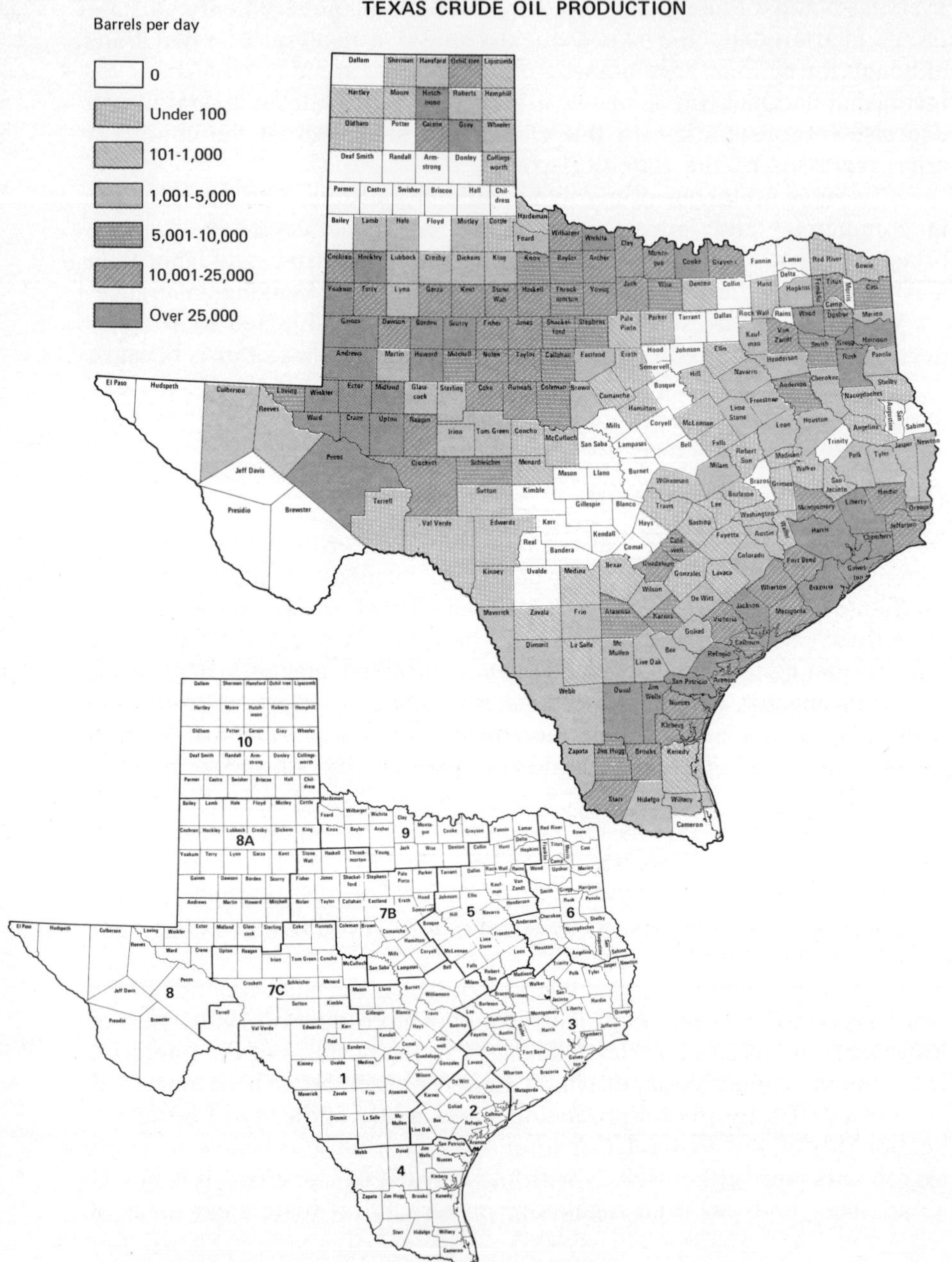

Small map indicates Railroad Commission districts.
Source: Texas Mid-Continent Oil and Gas Association.

ideas among the member states, collects and disseminates information, and proposes rules, regulations, and legislation concerning conservation of oil and gas. The actual regulation and control fall upon the regulatory agencies of the individual states. Texas' agent in this field is the Railroad Commission, which has been granted extensive powers to control almost all elements of the oil and gas industry. The main purpose of these broad powers is conservation, *i.e.,* the prevention of waste, both physical and economic, so that the maximum amount of oil, consistent with the existing economic environment, can be recovered from each reservoir.[4]

Conservation practices instituted by the commission have resulted in improved means of recovery and prevented wasteful overproduction. Their regulations have also stimulated the search for oil and gas by assuring each producer a share of the market and by stabilizing supply-and-demand factors of the market. Even though conservation regulations have a marked effect upon supplies of oil and gas, and consequently upon their prices, the primary purpose of the regulations is maximum recovery and prevention of physical waste.

Principal Conservation Regulations

Spacing A major aspect of the conservation of oil and gas is the spacing of producing wells. The goal of the spacing of wells is the optimum production of the resources consistent with the geological structure of the reservoir. Spacing control is exercised by the Railroad Commission through the granting of drilling permits. The two major factors considered are the optimum production characteristics and the rights of landowners to enjoy the benefits of their mineral rights. These two considerations are often in conflict in that the optimum production characteristics dictate that wells be allocated to larger tracts than are included in the holding of the landowner. The commission has adopted general rules that are employed in the solution of this problem. The statewide rule calls for one oil well per 40 acres. Tracts already subdivided into areas smaller than this may be awarded drilling permits as an exception to the rule, but tracts later subdivided are not eligible for exception. After production is begun and the field characteristics are known, the commission may adopt special field rules applicable to the spacing of subsequent wells. Also, for reservoirs discovered after March 8, 1961, the Railroad Commission has authority to provide for the pooling of mineral interests into prorational units for oil and gas wells.

---

[4]For an excellent discussion of conservation, see Philip E. Coldwell, *The Conservation of Southwest Oil and Gas*, Monthly Business Review, Federal Reserve Bank of Dallas, April, 1956.

Production Control   Both oil and natural gas are subjected to prorating production from common reservoirs. The Railroad Commission determines the total amount of oil, called the "allowable," which can be produced in the state each month. Every field is assigned a "Maximum Efficient Rate" (MER) of production, *i.e.,* the maximum production under which there would be no wastage of oil if the wells were operating every day. When setting the allowable, the commission first estimates the demand for Texas oil for the coming month. In determining this, the commission asks each buyer of Texas crude oil to submit his "nomination," *i.e.,* his expected purchase. The total nominations are then compared with the forecast of demand made by the U.S. Bureau of Mines. Current levels of stocks on hand, imports, and prospective economic conditions are also considered. After the commission has determined the total amount to be produced, it then calculates the percentage of the statewide market demand each field may produce. Thus production is equated with demand.

After the decision concerning the percentage of market demand that each field may produce has been made, the share of each individual well is determined automatically by allocation formulas adopted for each field. For any reservoir operating under rules of general application, the allowable for a well is determined by either the well MER or a yardstick standard based on depth of completion. The allocation formulas for fields operating under special rules are usually based simply upon acreage, thickness of the producing reservoir, and individual well factors. Occasionally gas-oil ratio (cubic feet of gas produced per barrel of oil produced), MER reservoir pressure, and other more complicated factors are used. In many cases production from wells is exempted from market-demand limitation. Marginal wells, *i.e.,* wells that by law are given an exempt status when they reach a certain producing status, may produce from 10 to 35 barrels daily depending upon the depth of completion. In addition, many wells in fields subjected to gas- or water-injection secondary recovery operations are exempted from market-demand limitation. Such wells are allowed to produce without limitation as a conservation measure. Exempt wells account for approximately 43 percent of the total allowable of the state.

Upon discovery of a new field, a "discovery allowable," which is considerably above the regular allowable, is assigned, on the theory that extra allowables stimulate exploration and compensate the operator for the heavy cost and risks involved in exploration. This discovery allowable remains in effect for twenty-four months following the completion of the first well or until the eleventh well is completed, if the field is onshore, or, if offshore, for a period of eighteen months or until the sixth well has been completed.

Production control is considered the cornerstone of conservation, for without it wells could produce at full capacity and wastefully deplete the field, as happened in the early days of the Texas oil industry. Unlimited production decreases underground pressure, thus reducing the total amount of oil that can be recovered. Even with present methods of recovery, it is estimated that only a little over 50 percent of the known oil reserves are recoverable. The commission does not allocate statewide demand for natural gas to the individual fields as is done for oil. Market demand for natural gas is determined on a reservoir basis by nominations from purchasers; the demand for natural gas from each such reservoir is then allocated to each individual gas well in the same manner that is used for oil.

Gas Flaring   Producing wells are classed as either oil or gas wells by a statutory formula based on the relative amounts of oil and gas produced from the well. There is a statutory prohibition of flaring gas produced from wells classed as gas wells, and the Railroad Commission has no discretionary power to grant exceptions to this prohibition so as to allow the production of the oil from the well under these circumstances. There will be some gas produced from wells classed as oil wells. Formerly it was the common practice to flare the gas produced, but now it is recognized that this practice is wasteful of an expendable natural resource and thus contrary to the public interest. The commission has the power to close a well to prevent this waste. Where there is an economic market for the gas produced, it is normally marketed by pipeline or processed as liquid hydrocarbons. Many wells employ the process of reinjecting the gas into the reservoir, which not only avoids the waste of the gas but also helps maintain reservoir pressure, thus increasing the amount of recoverable oil. The commission does have the discretionary power to allow the flaring of gas from an oil well if it finds that this is in the public interest after considering the production and market characteristics of the particular well. However, this is no longer a prevalent practice.

Abandonment of a Well   The Railroad Commission not only controls the drilling and production of wells but also regulates their abandonment. When a well owner decides to abandon a well, the commission must approve the method. If improperly done, underground liquids and gases may move into other strata; *e.g.,* salt water might move into pure-water sands, thus making the water unfit for human use.

All in all, the commission has taken many significant steps toward conservation of oil and gas. However, current controversies over nationwide gas and other fuel shortages increase the likelihood that Congress will nationalize the rules governing fuel conservation. Such a move would relieve the Railroad Commission of much of its decision-making responsibility.

Other Functions of the Commission

Among the other functions of the Railroad Commission is the one for which it was originally created, the regulation of transportation. All domestic common carriers must receive permits from the commission. It determines intrastate freight and passenger rates for railroads, trucks, and buses, and makes rules and regulations for transportation of both passengers and freight. Safety requirements, schedules, and services are prescribed. If the carrier fails to comply with any of these regulations, the commission may cancel its permit. Because of the primacy of the Interstate Commerce Commission of the Federal government, the commission has little actual control over railroads, but its control of intrastate trucks and buses is quite large.

Another function of the commission is enforcement of regulations concerning liquefied petroleum gases, such as butane and propane. This includes inspecting installations, investigating irregularities and accidents, licensing dealers, enforcing safety regulations, and setting standards for equipment and systems.

The Gas Utilities Division of the commission enforces regulations concerning fair rate charges of the utility companies and regulations for production, transportation, distribution, buying, selling, and delivery of natural gas by pipeline. In addition, its duties include apportionment of natural gas among the municipalities of the state, as well as regulation of gas odorization, construction and installation plan approval, and record keeping of all operations.

REGULATION OF BANKING

The Constitution of the Republic of Texas contained no reference to banking, and the state constitutions of 1845, of 1861, and of 1866 carried blanket prohibitions against the chartering of state banks. The constitution of 1869 was the first in the history of the state to omit the clause prohibiting the formation of banking corporations. However, the constitution of 1876 reinstated the ban against the chartering of banks, and it was not until 1903, when the constitution was amended, that the incorporation of state banks again became possible.

The original constitutional prohibitions against corporate banking in any form grew out of the people's unfortunate experience with uncontrolled banking. The restrictions which appear in our present constitution and laws prohibiting branch banking[5] were occasioned by the trend toward monopolistic control of business and finance which appeared at the turn of the last century. The result has been, with the exception of very brief periods, that the national and private banker dominated the entire field of banking in Texas until 1905, when the first state banking code was enacted by the legislature.

The Finance Commission

The banking laws are administered by the Banking Department, which is supervised by the Finance Commission. The commission is responsible for overseeing both the Banking Department and the Savings and Loan Department. The commission is composed of nine members and is made up of two sections. The Banking Section has six members, and the Savings and Loan Section is composed of three members. Each of these sections determines certain policies relating to its own institutions, while the commission as a whole formulates policy for state-chartered credit unions,[6] the Office of Consumer Credit Commissioner, and the regulatory activities relating to trust companies, money-order companies, and perpetual-care cemeteries. The commission is appointed by the governor with the concurrence of the Senate for six-year overlapping terms.

The Finance Commission appoints the banking commissioner to head the Banking Department and the savings and loan commissioner to head the Savings and Loan Department. Both these officials must be confirmed by the Senate.

The Finance Commission adopts general policies for the Banking Department and the Savings and Loan Department and is responsible for the financial needs of the two departments, including the adoption of their respective budgets.

The additional responsibility of supervising the administration of small-loan agencies was given the Finance Commission by the legislature in 1963. The Texas Regulatory Loan Act provided for the regulation of licensed agencies engaged in the business of making loans of $1,500 or less. In 1967, the legislature adopted a comprehensive credit code relating to all financial institutions and all credit transactions. The Office of Consumer Credit Commissioner was created to regulate all consumer

[5]"Branch banking" is defined as engaging in business in more than one physical location.

[6] Credit unions are private nonprofit investment corporations chartered by the Federal and state governments alike. Federally chartered credit unions may operate within the state as long as their operations are not inconsistent with state regulations.

finance companies, other than banks, savings and loan associations, and credit unions. Chapters of the code strictly regulate small loans, installment loans, second-mortgage loans, automobile sales finance, and retail sales finance. All lending institutions and companies subject to regulation by state or Federal agencies may operate under the code.

The Banking Department

This department is under the direct supervision of the banking commissioner. The duties of the department include supervision and regulation as provided in the State Banking Code, such as examination of banks and credit unions, trust companies, money-order companies, and perpetual-care cemeteries; the approval for mergers and reorganization of state banks; the removal, for cause, of directors, officers, and employees of state banks; and the closing and liquidation of insolvent state banks. The department also has the responsibility of reviewing the trust-fund investments of perpetual-care cemetery associations.

The Banking Department, since 1951, has been both self-supported and self-administered. It is the Finance Commission and not the legislature that fixes the salaries of the bank examiners and all other employees. Instead of being supported by state appropriations, the department's activities are financed by fees, penalties, and charges resulting from the performance of bank examinations and other services. The department is required to pay into the state's General Revenue Fund an amount sufficient to meet the cost of governmental services rendered to it by other state agencies.

Texas statutes require that state banks be examined twice each year and that credit unions be examined annually. The institutions pay a fee for these examinations. All corporations under the jurisdiction of the Banking Department are required by law to publish financial statements—state banks semiannually and credit unions annually. The law permits state banks to join the Federal Reserve System and the Federal Deposit Insurance Corporation but does not make this mandatory. Federally chartered banks may operate within the state as long as their operations comply with the Federal Banking Code and are not inconsistent with Texas statutes.

The Savings and Loan Department

The Savings and Loan Department performs functions with respect to state-chartered building and loan associations similar to those performed for state banks by the Banking Department. Under the direction of the savings and loan commissioner, the department charters, examines, and supervises building and loan associations. Whereas state banks can be chartered only upon approval of the State Banking Board, building and loan associations are chartered directly by the savings and loan commissioner upon compliance with certain statutory requirements. Periodic examinations are made of the operations and financial status of building and loan associations by examiners from the department. An association not meeting financial standards or legal provisions required by law may be ordered to meet such requirements by the commissioner, and if compliance does not occur, the commissioner has the power to annul its authority to do business and begin proceedings to revoke its charter. Revocation of charter and liquidation procedures are handled by the attorney general.

Like its banking counterpart, the Savings and Loan Department is self-financed through examination fees paid by savings and loan associations. These fees are set by statute and vary in amount with the gross assets of individual associations. The minimum fee is $100. Revenues from these fees are used to pay operating expenditures of the department in accordance with the budget adopted by the Finance Commission. Each association must file monthly and annual financial reports with the department, and the department publishes an annual report on the financial condition of all state-chartered associations as of December 31 each year.

The State Banking Board

This board, composed of the state banking commissioner, treasurer, and one gubernatorial appointee, serves as an adjunct to the Banking Department and functions as the licenser of state banks. State banks may be organized only with the approval of the board. The statutes outline the procedure to be followed and the capital necessary for organization. However, circumstances in each case are fully considered by the board in the action it takes. It also passes on the closing and liquidation of banks, on reopening of closed banks, and on bank reorganization and serves as a board of appeals for directors, officers, and employees of state banks.

Other Agencies Related to Banking

There are two additional state agencies whose duties relate to banking institutions. These are the Credit Union Commission and the State Depository Board. The Credit Union Commission consists of six members who are appointed by the governor with Senate consent for six-year overlapping terms. The commission appoints with Senate consent the Credit Union Commissioner who serves at the commission's pleasure. The commission is actually only an advisory board to the commissioner who charters credit unions in the state under the Credit Union Regulation Act. No credit union may transact business until formally certified by the commissioner. The State Depository Board, with the same membership as the State Banking Board,[7] is not a regulatory agency insofar as bank organization and operations are concerned. Nevertheless, this board has significant relationships with state banks that are depositories for state funds, because such depository banks must comply with the board's rules, regulations, and contractual provisions relative to state deposits and rates of interest paid by banks on such deposits.

In summary, the Banking Department and the Savings and Loan Department are the operating agencies carrying out the policies established by the Finance Commission with respect to banks and savings institutions, respectively. The departments are not autonomous, however, for the Finance Commission, aside from setting policy, acts as a check on the departments in that it holds the purse strings through its budget-making authority. The integrated relationship of the Finance Commission—with the banking commissioner functioning as ex officio chairman of the Finance Commission, as chairman of the State Banking Board, and as a member of the State Depository Board, and with coequal departments of banking and savings and loan associations under the commission—makes possible an integrated administrative structure for the effective regulation of state banking and savings institutions in Texas.

REGULATION OF INSURANCE

Insurance companies are regulated by the State Board of Insurance. The board is composed of three members who are appointed by the governor with the concurrence of the Senate. They serve six-year overlapping terms. The board's chief function is limited to the determination of "policy, rules, rates, and appeals." Administrative functions are left to the commissioner of insurance who is appointed by the board and serves during its pleasure. Appeals from decisions of the commissioner may be taken to the board and from the board to a Travis County district court.

The agency's functions fall into three main categories. The life insurance duties involve such matters as the chartering of life insurance companies, including stipulated premium companies, and investigation of their solvency and the fitness of their officers; approving policy forms for

---

[7]This board and the State Banking Board are the same for all practical purposes.

life, accident, and health insurance; the licensing of agents writing life, health, fire, casualty, and accident insurance; the investigation of complaints relative to life insurance; and the checking of fees, taxes, and deposits required of insurance companies. The fire insurance functions of the board include rate making for fire insurance, supervising the grading of cities and towns under the key rate schedule,[8] approving standard fire and windstorm policies and rates for inland marine, rain, and hail insurance, and promulgating rules governing the storage of flammable liquids. As a third major responsibility, the board administers state law regarding the writing of various kinds of casualty insurance, such as workmen's compensation, automobile, general liability, boiler and machinery, professional liability, fidelity and surety, burglary, theft, robbery, plate-glass, and title insurance.

In addition to life, fire, and casualty insurance companies and mutual assessment companies, the agency regulates burial associations. Two methods are used: (1) Statutes require board approval of all policies written by burial associations, and (2) the commissioner of insurance is a member of the Burial Association Rate Board.[9] The rate board establishes maximum and minimum rates to be charged by burial associations and, in addition, collects statistical data on the death rates, policy lapses, and other policy experiences of burial associations both within and outside the state.

As a result of much criticism pertaining to laws regulating insurance companies and their administration and the failure of several poorly organized and improperly managed companies, the legislature in 1955 and 1957 passed a number of acts aimed at improving conditions. One of the most important of these requires registration and supervision of insurance stocks with the securities commissioner.

Another major act tightened financial responsibility for insurance companies, making it more difficult to establish a company on a shoestring and requiring those on shaky financial ground to improve their conditions. This act established minimum capital and surplus of $200,000 to organize a life, health, or accident insurance company. A fire company is required to raise $150,000, and a casualty company must put up $225,000 in capital and surplus. To write all lines of fire, casualty, and marine insurance, a company must have $300,000 capital and surplus to organize.

---

[8] *Vernon's Annotated Civil Statutes*, Insurance Code, pp. xlvi–xlvii. The "key rate schedule" is the schedule of cities rated individually on their fire-prevention program. (See *Survey of Texas Laws on Fire Prevention and Control*, pp. 13–15, Institute of Public Affairs, University of Texas, Austin, 1953.)

[9] The Burial Association Rate Board was established by the legislature in 1947 and is composed of the insurance commissioner as ex officio chairman and six other members appointed by the governor and confirmed by the Senate for six-year overlapping terms. They receive $10 per diem compensation for attending meetings, plus travel expenses.

The examination of insurance companies has been improved, and the board's regulatory and examining facilities have been expanded. Another important piece of insurance legislation resulted in the betterment of policing regulations for health and accident insurance. Companies offering this type of insurance are required to use similar forms. This ostensibly removes the "fine print" from insurance contracts. Since 1965, all existing assessment associations must compute their reserves on a sound actuarial basis, a requirement now demanded of all insurance companies.

STATE SECURITIES BOARD

The State Securities Board regulates the sale of all stocks and bonds sold in Texas, with certain exceptions specified in the Texas Securities Act. It also regulates the persons and corporations who sell such securities and investigates alleged violations of the Securities Act. Securities exempted from provisions of the act include those listed on recognized stock exchanges and shares of nonprofit corporations, banks, and savings institutions. The board is authorized, however, to prohibit the sale in Texas of nationally traded securities if they fail to meet standards prescribed by the Securities Act.

The Texas Securities Act was passed originally in 1913, and a series of amendments culminated in 1957 with the establishment of a separate state agency to regulate the intrastate sale of securities—a function previously performed by the secretary of state's office and Board of Insurance Commissioners. The act created a nonsalaried board of three members appointed by the governor for six-year staggered terms. The board appoints the securities commissioner, who serves as head of the agency.

Before nonexempt securities may be sold in Texas, they must be registered by the commissioner, who issues a sales permit if he finds that they were issued in conformity with provisions of state law. The Texas Securities Act differs from the Federal Securities Act in that it requires a permit for the sale of securities to be based upon a finding that the sale price to public purchasers is "fair, just and equitable" in relation to the price paid by "insiders," in addition to the Federal requirement that the applicant for a permit make a full disclosure of material facts concerning the applicant's plan of business and finance.

If the commissioner determines that either the security itself or the method of sale would work a fraud upon the purchaser, the law requires him to deny a permit.

Securities dealers and salesmen must register annually with the commissioner, who may refuse to grant a license if the applicant is not of good moral character. The agency licenses approximately 6,000 individuals and corporations to sell securities. Applicants for a securities dealer or salesman license must pass an examination.

In 1972, the State Securities Board was processing annually for sale, in Texas, securities valued at more than one billion dollars and had become a major factor in the economic development of the state.

Violations of the Securities Act are punishable by a fine of not more than $5,000 and/or imprisonment for a maximum of ten years. Civil penalties also are provided.

THE TEXAS ALCOHOLIC BEVERAGE COMMISSION

The Texas Alcoholic Beverage Commission administers the state laws regulating the manufacture and sale of alcoholic beverages. The commission was formerly called the Texas Liquor Control Board, which was created in 1935 after an amendment to the Texas constitution repealed prohibition. However, the "open saloon" and sale of liquor by the drink were not permitted; and the sale of bottled liquor, beer, and wine was a matter of local option. In 1971, the voters approved a constitutional amendment repealing the "open saloon" provision the effect of which was to extend the local option to mixed drinks. Local option in Texas applies to a county, city, or even justice of the peace precinct. The people within any of these areas may decide for themselves whether to permit the sale of alcoholic beverages.

The commission is composed of three members, all appointed by the governor with Senate confirmation for six-year overlapping terms. The governor designates one member as chairman. Members serve in an advisory capacity on all matters of policy and procedure and have the power to pass various rules and regulations.

The commission appoints an administrator as the chief executive officer of the agency. He passes on the issuance of permits and licenses, cancellations or suspensions, and generally supervises enforcement of the law. The Alcoholic Beverage Commission is organized into six divisions under the administrator. They are: (1) the Administrative Division; (2) the Accounting Division; (3) the Audit Division; (4) the Enforcement Division; (5) the Hearings Division; and (6) the Ports of Entry Division.

The Administrative Division provides staff to the administrator and serves the entire agency.

The Accounting Division is responsible for accounting records, internal financial controls, issuance of permits and licenses, collection of fees, and the preparation of the board's annual reports and budgets.

The Auditing Division maintains district offices in Dallas, Houston, San Antonio, El Paso, Corpus Christi, and Odessa, for periodic audits of wholesale permits and licenses. This includes the processing of more than 4,000 reports each month.

The Enforcement Division operates through twenty district offices. It enforces various phases of the law related to the manufacturing, storing, importing, exporting, transporting, distributing, selling, possessing for sale, and possession of alcoholic beverages, including the proper labeling and advertising. The laboratory is a part of this division and conducts analyses of alcoholic beverages to determine the standards of quality and purity—thus safeguarding the public against sale and consumption of impure products. Violations of the law are submitted to the main office in Austin, in affidavit form, for final action. If court action is taken, the commission is represented by the attorney general's office, and hearings are before the board's administrator.

The Hearings Division prepares and processes noncriminal cases dealing with violations of the Liquor Control Act. When violations are noted, a hearing is held to determine whether to cancel or suspend a license or permit.

The Ports of Entry Division supervises the collection of taxes on alcoholic beverages imported into Texas from Mexico. There are seventeen ports of entry along the Texas-Mexico border which are manned by personnel of this division. Revenue from taxes collected at these ports exceed 1.5 million dollars a year.

The Texas Alcoholic Beverage Commission is self-supporting from revenue derived from the sale of tax stamps and the beer excise tax. The license and permit fees, liquor and beer taxes, and funds derived from the sale on confiscated liquor and equipment constitute the bulk of state revenue collected by the commission. During the 1972 fiscal year, the agency collected more than 95 million dollars in taxes and fees.

The board faces many problems in the control of the manufacture and the sale of alcoholic beverages. The most frequent violations in the wet areas are sales to minors and to intoxicated persons. The passage of legislation in 1973 giving eighteen to twenty year olds full rights of majority has relieved somewhat the problem of sales to minors. In the dry areas, individual and organized bootlegging is a problem of major concern.

REGULATION OF PROFESSIONS AND OCCUPATIONS

The rapid growth in population and the expansion of the business and industrial life of the state have necessitated the establishment of certain rules and regulations regarding private industry to protect the general welfare. In the professions and occupations affecting the public interest, general standards have been established by law. The state recognizes it has a responsibility to protect its citizens from imposters, quacks, shysters, and fly-by-night operators. Consequently, regulatory agencies have been set up for the various professions and occupations or trades to examine and license qualified practitioners in order that the untrained and unscrupulous be barred from practice. Regulatory agencies not only protect the public, but also guard members of the professions and occupations from unethical competition of persons who are not qualified to practice.

Texas has over thirty-one professional and vocational licensing boards.[10] The usual term is six years. Members are usually individuals experienced in their particular vocation or profession.

Except for rare instances, the boards are self-supporting, and some contribute certain percentages of their income to the General Revenue Fund. The legislature sets the fees for examination, certification and/or registration, and renewal fees. License fees range from $10 to $150; annual renewal of licenses ranges from $2 to $100. In some cases, they are the same as the original fee. There is considerable variation in the fiscal control of the individual boards. Some operate primarily on appropriations from the General Revenue Fund, whereas others maintain essentially independent financing and expenditure operations with auditing control by the state.

Written examinations are the general rule for most boards, but in some instances practical or oral examinations are offered instead of the written examinations. In other cases, examinations are waived where diplomas from accredited schools and institutions are presented. In still other instances, the examination gives consideration to character and citizenship. In all cases, the examinations are prepared and administered by the various boards. The time and place of these are set by the boards. Examinations vary from once a year to monthly or more often as the board may deem necessary. Only in a few instances are boards regulated by statutes covering how often examinations or reexaminations may be offered.

In almost every agency, licensing by reciprocity[11] is recognized.

---

[10]Although there are thirty-one boards which may be classified strictly as licensing boards, about ten other agencies, basically regulatory in nature, also issue licenses to practice a particular trade or profession. For example, the Board of Insurance licenses insurance agents, the Securities Commission licenses dealers in securities, and the commissioner of agriculture licenses dealers in agricultural products.

[11]In other words, Texas will recognize licensed persons from states which recognize those licensed by Texas.

Reciprocity is most easily established in the professional fields where there is a national accrediting agency of one form or another. In the nonprofessional fields reciprocity is a matter of policy determination for the board, if it is not provided for in the statutes. All but ten of the boards have provisions for reciprocity in their enabling acts.

Mention should be made at this point of the Basic Sciences Board and its role in examining and licensing in the healing arts. The State Board of Examiners is composed of six members learned in the basic sciences. This board is appointed by the governor for six-year overlapping terms. All persons applying for licenses to practice the healing arts, which include chiropractors, medical doctors, osteopaths, and others are required to pass an examination in the basic sciences. The laws list the basic sciences as anatomy, bacteriology, chemistry, pathology, physiology, hygiene, and public health. Exceptions are made for chiropodists, dentists, nurses, optometrists, masseurs, and commissioned or contract surgeons of the United States Army, Navy, public health, or Marine hospital services. The board offers examinations in each of the categories and licenses those who qualify. A passing grade of 75 was established by the act. Those applicants who have acquired sixty semester hours (with a grade of 75 or better) in the above fields will have the examinations in these particular areas waived, provided The University of Texas will accept the college credits on a par with their own courses in the same fields. Those applicants not having such requirements in the basic sciences must pass the board's examination before being examined and licensed in their own particular field of the healing arts.

CONCLUSION

It may be said that the state may regulate a lawful business, industry, or profession. But the power to regulate is not usually construed by the courts as conferring upon the state the power to prohibit. The state possesses no power to prohibit a useful business. The state's power to regulate includes the power to provide for reasonable examinations to test the knowledge of those who desire to pursue certain professions or occupations, or to require medical examinations on the grounds of public health. All occupations are subject to reasonable regulation by the state in the exercise of its police power. However, discriminatory or unreasonable use of the police power is forbidden.

Chapter 16

Labor

The states and the Federal government share responsibility under the Federal system for the protection and regulation of labor. In general, the national government exercises the principal responsibility, but in some areas, such as workmen's compensation, the states have traditionally dominated.[1] From a constitutional point of view, the Federal government has increased the scope of its labor legislation by means of the broadening definition of Federal power under the interstate commerce clause of the U.S. Constitution. However, insofar as intrastate commerce is concerned, state power continues to be primary. Probably about one-half of the laboring people of Texas are employed in concerns largely regulated by state law.

[1]For a table which assigns relative state and national governmental authority over given labor subjects, see Daniel J. Elazar, *American Federalism: A View from the States*, pp. 55–56, Thomas Y. Crowell Company, New York, 1966.

With regard to interstate commerce (and labor is a part of commerce), a state law is applicable if it does not conflict with the United States Constitution or a Federal statute. It is also a recognized principle of constitutional law that, if the Federal government has not exercised control in a certain area of interstate commerce, the state may do so as long as there is no unconstitutional burden on interstate commerce. In areas where both the Federal and state governments have legislated on identical phases of labor relations, the state statute will also be valid unless it is in conflict with the national law or deals with subject matter which has been preempted or made the exclusive jurisdiction of the national government.

State control of contractual relationships, whether such transactions are incidental to intrastate or to interstate commerce, is usually a valid exercise of state power, as are laws enacted by virtue of the state's police power. In both instances, however, the Fourteenth Amendment to the national Constitution concerning due process and the equal protection of the laws must be considered. The area of labor legislation remaining with the states is, therefore, still quite large.

So far Texas has lagged behind some states, particularly those in the industrial East and Northeast, in adopting laws designed to protect the laborer.[2] Certain fundamental rights affecting the individual worker are guaranteed in the state constitution, in that it provides for freedom of speech and assemblage and gives protection against search and seizure, imprisonment for debt, and impairment of liens. Persons engaged in mechanical or agricultural pursuits are given assurance that they shall not pay an occupation tax. Wages are not subject to garnishment, and contracts, other than those made by licensees under and pursuant to the Interest-Consumer Credit-Consumer Protection Act of 1967, for a rate of interest greater than 10 percent are deemed usurious. Laborers are given the right of lien against property for the value of labor done by them. Provision is made to protect a certain portion of the personal property of the heads of families or unmarried adults. Finally, homesteads are protected from forced sale except for payment of debts incurred in purchasing or improving the homestead and for nonpayment of taxes.

PROTECTIVE LABOR LEGISLATION

A variety of Texas labor laws may be described as protective in nature. Their major purpose is to prevent exploitation of working people and to

---

[2]For an excellent brief treatment of Texas' early labor laws from the employer's point of view, see *Labor-Management Relations in Texas,* prepared for the Texas Pharmaceutical Association, Austin, 1947. Parts of this discussion have been adapted from that monograph.

assure certain minimum standards of employment. Among the oldest, which date back to the early days of this century, are laws protecting women and children in the labor force.

Child and Female Labor Laws

Texas laws establish a minimum of fifteen years of age for employment in a factory, mill, workshop, or laundry or in messenger service in towns and cities having more than 15,000 population. This provision does not apply to the employment of boys for the purpose of distributing newspapers. There is no minimum age for work in communities under 15,000 population or for nonfactory work, but in hazardous occupations where explosives are used, a minimum of seventeen years is required. However, if the earnings of a child under the age of fourteen who has completed the seventh grade in school are needed to support himself, his mother, invalid father, or younger children in the family, a special work permit may be obtained from the county judge, but the child may not work where dangerous machinery or explosives are used. There must also be a physician's certificate stating that the child is physically able to perform the work assigned.

Texas laws set a maximum of eight hours a day or forty-eight hours a week for working minors under fifteen years of age. Further, children under fifteen are prohibited from working between the hours of 10 P.M. and 5 A.M. Girls over sixteen years of age are governed by the Nine Fifty-four Hour Law for Women.

The Nine Fifty-four Hour Law, enacted in 1915, was intended to prevent women, with certain exceptions, from working more than nine hours a day or fifty-four hours a week. However, in 1971 the law was amended to permit women who desire to do so to work for longer hours. The amendment also exempted "female employees employed in any bona fide executive, administrative, professional, or outside sales capacity."[3] In addition, a female employee who is required to work more than forty hours a week is entitled to a rate not less than one and one-half times the regular rate in excess of nine hours a day. She must work more than forty-eight hours a week to qualify for the time and a half overtime pay.

Several Texas laws have been passed to protect the health, morals and safety of women workers, including the requirement of rest periods and special seating. These and the maximum hours laws have been attacked by women's liberationist and similar groups on the grounds that they discriminate rather than protect. The Federal Equal Pay Act of 1963,

---

[3] *Vernon's Annotated Texas Civil Statutes*, Art. 5172a.

Title VII of the Civil Rights Act of 1964 (which barred discrimination on account of sex in employment), and similar legislation have in the 1970s been interpreted to prohibit labor laws applicable solely to women.[4] Texas laws of this nature will probably have to be changed.

Wage and Hour Laws

Wages The Texas Minimum Wage Act of 1970 was the first to provide for a state minimum wage for private employment in Texas. The minimum wage was initially set at $1.25 an hour and then increased to $1.40 an hour after February 1, 1971. This is still far below the Federal minimum wage rate established by the Federal Hour and Wage Law (Fair Labor Standards Act of 1938, as amended). The latter, of course, is based on the interstate commerce power and does not apply to all employees in Texas.

In general, the 1970 act applies to employers liable for contributions to the Texas Unemployment Compensation Fund, to be described later in the chapter, and to employers of agricultural workers. But there are numerous exceptions to the law, including all employers who are already regulated by the Federal Fair Labor Standards Act.[5]

The law is quite complex. Insofar as agricultural workers are concerned, they are generally entitled to receive a wage not less than 20 cents an hour below that set by the Federal Labor Standards Act. The law recognizes the use of piece rates in agriculture and provides for a rate generally equivalent to the minimum hourly wage rate for other agricultural workers.

Employees who receive tips as part of their remuneration are covered. The tips may be deemed part of their wages by an amount determined by their employer, provided they do not exceed 50 percent of the applicable minimum wage rate. The 1970 act contains many more provisions as well.

Prior to the Minimum Wage Act, state regulation of the amount of wages in Texas was limited to employees on public works, including highway construction crews, who were to receive the local "prevailing wage." On projects supported in part or in whole by Federal grants-in-aid, the same requirement was imposed.

---

[4]*The Book of the States, 1972–73,* pp. 513, 514, 512–526, The Council of State Governments, Iron Works Pike, Lexington, Ky., 1972.

[5]The exceptions are indeed numerous. They include firms with retail sales below $150,000 annually; members of a religious order; switchboard operators for an independently owned public telephone company with no more than 750 stations; domestics in private homes; persons under eighteen years of age who are not high school or vocational training graduates and persons under twenty who are enrolled in high school, college, or for vocational training; employees of dairy farmers; and many others too numerous to mention.

Another Texas law of long standing requires wages to be paid semimonthly by corporations and certain other types of private business.

Hours   Texas has no maximum hour law of general application to workers in private industry. The laws are directed at special groups. In addition to the laws governing the hours of work of women and children, the hours of railroad crews and drivers of carriers licensed under the Texas Railroad Commission, such as truck and bus drivers, are also regulated. As for public employment, the Texas laws set a maximum of eight hours a day for most public employees. Firemen and policemen, because of the special nature of their work, have special standards, which vary according to the size of the city concerned.

Health and Safety Laws

Texas has for years legislated on the subject of health and safety of workers at their place of employment, but the laws have been either limited in application or not well enforced. A number of specific industries and situations, for example, the operation of mines and steam boilers, are covered by detailed civil and criminal statutes, concerning the maintenance of working conditions free from health and safety hazards. Of general application to all business or industrial establishments is the Health, Safety, and Morals law, which empowers representatives of the commissioner of labor and standards to close those places of business not complying with its standards of humidity, air pollution, safety, comfort, and morality. The State Department of Health has also regulated occupational health under authority of the Texas General Sanitation Law of 1945.

However, perhaps the most important law of all is the industrial safety law of 1967, which is concerned with occupational safety in Texas industries. The law set up within the State Department of Health a division administered by an Occupational Safety Board. This board consists of the commissioner of health, the commissioner of labor and standards, and a third member appointed by the governor to represent the public. The board in turn appoints a state safety engineer whose responsibility it is to direct the activities of the division. He appoints industrial subcommittees, representing employees and employers, to advise on safety standards and regulations for approval by the Safety Board.

Another development of note is the participation of Texas in the landmark Federal Williams-Steiger Occupational Safety and Health Act of 1970. The law enables Texas to enforce "standards relating to any job safety and health issue covered by a federal standard" and includes "enforcement of state safety and health standards which are at least as effective as counterpart federal standards."[6] A state plan approved by the Secretary of Labor is a prerequisite for participation.

An effective practical factor in encouraging industrial safety by employers is the operation of the variable-rate scheme of the Workmen's Compensation Law, to be discussed in the next section.

Workmen's Compensation

Texas was one of the first states to enact a workmen's compensation law. Adopted in 1913, the purpose of the law was to establish an insurance plan, mutually beneficial to employees and employers, to pay workers injured on the job and death benefits to survivors of workers killed in industrial accidents.

The 1913 law created an Employer's Insurance Association, which continues today. Employers of one or more employees are eligible to become subscribers to the association upon payment of the necessary premiums. (The law does not apply to employers of domestic servants, farm or ranch workers, or common carriers.) The association (or insurance carrier) then assumes responsibility for payments for work-related injuries and death of employees. Employers not joining the association are subject to civil suits by employees or their survivors for on-the-job injuries and deaths, which may be ruinously costly. They are also barred from relying on any of the three common law defenses against employee suits—the doctrine of contributory negligence, fellow-servant doctrine, or assumed risk doctrine. The doctrines do not apply to members of the association, and the economic liability of the employer is limited to the weekly benefits provided in the act. The common law doctrines still exist for valid nonsubscribers to the association.

Initially, the Employer's Insurance Association was expected to write insurance policies inasmuch as no private insurance companies had indicated an interest in providing this type of coverage. Experience demonstrated the profitability of covering the risks, and numerous insurance companies have obtained authority to provide the insurance under rules and regulations promulgated by the Texas insurance commissioner and the Industrial Accident Board.

Prior to 1973, several state agencies had procured voluntary workmen's compensation coverage for their employees, including The University of Texas at Austin, Texas Tech University, and the Texas State Highway Department. Amendments to the workmen's compensation law in 1973 required workmen's compensation for all state employees. The

[6] *The Book of the States, op. cit.,* pp. 507–508.

legal processing for statewide agencies not already covered by special provision are administered by a division in the Attorney General's Office.

Also, municipalities and other political subdivisions could adopt workmen's compensation on a permissive basis before 1973, but they are now required to do so. Municipalities may be self-insured (the city sets up its own insurance fund and makes payments from it), or they may contract for insurance from an approved private insurance company, or they may enter into an inter-local cooperative agreement.

The exact amount of compensation for on-the-job injuries is based on the type of injury and the worker's average weekly wage. Schedules determine payments for specific injuries—so much for the loss of an eye, the loss of a thumb, and so on. Benefits for general injuries, such as "temporary total disability" (the most common payment to job-injured workers) or for "total and permanent disability," extend for a maximum of 401 weeks. Benefits for "partial" incapacity, whether "temporary" or "permanent," are paid for a maximum of 300 weeks. The maximum benefits were raised from $49 to $63 a week in 1973. The minimum was $15. The minimum-maximum ranges will be raised to $16–$70 in 1974. Thereafter, the payment range will be linked to a moving base. The minimum will automatically increase $1 and the maximum, $7, for every average weekly wage increase of $10 for manufacturing production workers in Texas.

Death benefits for widow and widowers, which are now based on $66^2/_3$ percent of the employee's average weekly wage (it was formerly 60 percent), are continued until death or remarriage. Upon remarriage, a lump sum is paid. Weekly benefits paid a dependent child are continued until the age of eighteen, or beyond if actually dependent, or until the age of twenty-five years if a full-time student in an accredited educational institution.

Insurers of workmen's compensation are required by the 1973 amendments to provide for accident prevention facilities. They may employ consultants for this purpose to conduct safety engineering surveys, or whatever is deemed appropriate. The new requirement complements the variable rate scheme of the workmen's compensation law which benefits the employer with a good safety record.

The Industrial Accident Board to be described later in the chapter administers the workmen's compensation law.

Unemployment Compensation (Insurance)

Texas also has an unemployment compensation or insurance law which provides payments to insured workers during a temporary period of unemployment. It is designed to be a cushion to fall back on while the worker is looking for another job. The Texas law is a direct result of the U.S. Social Security Act of 1935, as amended. Under the Federal law, employers who hire one or more workers as often as one day a week for twenty weeks in a year are subject to a Federal tax of 3.2 percent of their total payroll. In computing the payroll, only the first $4,200 of the worker's salary or wage are considered. (Certain employers are exempt from the tax, such as churches and employers of agricultural workers.) If, however, a state has an approved system of unemployment compensation, employers may deduct up to 2.7 percent of the Federal tax. Putting it another way, the Federal government says to the states, "We are going to take a 3.2 percent payroll tax from your employers, but if you will adopt an unemployment compensation system of which we approve, the employers who pay into your fund are exempt from a large percent of the Federal tax. If you do not adopt such a program, we will take the full 3.2 percent, otherwise only 2.7 percent."

Under the stimulus of this "encouragement," Texas and all the other states have an approved program of unemployment compensation. The full cost of administration is borne by the Federal government. State funds accumulated for paying the benefits are held by the Federal government, which sets up a separate trust account for each state. As money is needed to meet the benefit payments, the individual state requisitions its account in the Federal treasury for the necessary funds.

The unemployment insurance system is administered by each state, and the variations among the systems are numerous, including the range of the tax rates on employers, the size of the worker's weekly benefit, the kinds and number of employers added to those subject to the Federal tax, and so on.

In Texas, there are five classes of "subject employers" who come under the law. They are employers who: (1) pay "as much as $1,500 in wages in any calendar quarter *or* had in employment at least one individual for some portion of the day in each of 20 different days"; (2) "acquired the organization, trade, or business, or substantially all the assets of a subject employer"; (3) are "non-profit organizations as described in Section 501(c) of the Federal Internal Revenue Code which is exempt from the income tax and had as many as four or more individuals in employment for some portion of 20 days"; (4) are "subject to the Federal Unemployment Tax Act and had employees in Texas"; and (5) "have elected to become a subject employer."[7] (The state of Texas has elected to become a subject employer.)

---

[7]Texas Employment Commission, *Unemployment Insurance and Tax Information*, p. 8, Austin, n.d.

In Texas, there are also twenty classes of workers who are exempt from the unemployment compensation law. They include agricultural workers, domestic servants, newsboys under eighteen, ordained ministers, employees of the United States government, and employees of churches.

The basic tax rate for each employer is 2.7 percent until he becomes eligible for an experience tax rate—that is, as soon as his account has been chargeable with benefits to workers for four calendar quarters. His tax may then range from a low of 0.1 percent (one-tenth of 1 percent) to a high of 4.0 percent. The variable tax rate is designed to provide enough money to pay the benefits and to reward an employer who maintains a high employment level.

Certain employers, such as the state of Texas and its political subdivisions and nonprofit organizations (which elect to do so), do not pay taxes as such; they pay reimbursements.

Let us now see how the worker is benefited by the system. Bill Brown, an employee in a "covered" industry, *i.e.,* one participating in the program, is out of a job. He then goes to the nearest local office of the Texas Employment Commission and registers for work.

The commission will interview Bill Brown and get a complete picture of his employment history, the reason for his being unemployed, his skills, amount of wages earned, etc. They will then make every effort to find him a job commensurate with his skills, abilities, and past earnings.

At the time Bill Brown went to the commission's local office to register for work, he also filed a claim for unemployment compensation.[8] The employer may protest the claim, for if it is a valid one it would hurt his employment record and thus affect his tax rate. The claim will not be paid if it can be proved that the employee is not able to work or not available for work, has voluntarily quit his job without good cause or for the purpose of attending school (although he is not disqualified for taking approved training), was discharged for misconduct, is receiving wages in lieu of notice, or is unemployed because of a labor dispute in which he is participating or which he is helping finance.[9] Or the employer may protest the claim on the grounds that the worker's unemployment was caused by a work stoppage due to a labor dispute at another unit of the concern, and that the worker was indirectly assisting the dispute in that he belonged to the same union.

The employer has ten days in which to file the protest. As soon as

[8]The commission has been authorized by the legislature to make reciprocal arrangements with other states whereby an employee with accumulated benefits in one or more states may receive unemployment compensation either from Texas or from one of the other states in which he has worked. (*Vernon's Revised Civil Statutes,* Art. 5221*b*–15*a*, 1945.)

[9]In this connection, the failure to cross a picket line or resume customary work at the establishment where he is employed is considered as participating in a labor dispute against the employer.

this period is over, and Bill Brown's claim can be processed (a total time of from twelve to fourteen days has now elapsed since he filed his claim for unemployment compensation), the payments start, as of the second week. The first week is called a "waiting period," and there is no compensation for it unless the worker is unemployed for four consecutive weeks. The laid-off employee must also be actively seeking a job. It is not enough to be registered with the commission.

Payments are made every week and vary from $15 to $63, depending on the worker's former earnings. The maximum period that unemployment compensation may be drawn in any twelve-month period is twenty-six weeks. If the worker draws benefits for the entire time for which he is eligible, his benefits are exhausted for one year from the date of the initial claim; otherwise, he may receive compensation during subsequent periods of unemployment, but never for more than twenty-six weeks in any twelve-month period. Provision is also made for partial unemployment payments for partial employment.

Congress in 1970 enacted emergency legislation providing for extended benefits because of high unemployment rates. The law, which has been continued on a more or less yearly basis, authorizes additional unemployment payments amounting to 50 percent of the weekly benefit to eligible employees whose regular benefits have been exhausted. The additional benefits are paid for a designated period of time (it has varied from thirteen to fifty-two weeks) when the national unemployment rate among insured workers is 4.5 percent or more for three consecutive months or when the unemployment rate within a state is 4 percent among insured workers for thirteen consecutive weeks with certain qualifications. In the latter case, the payments are applicable only to the state affected. The Federal government pays half of the extended benefits and the "experienced rated" employers the other half.

Texas Employment Service

An important free employment service is provided to workers and employers alike by the Texas Employment Commission, which operates over ninety centers throughout the state. Employers of all types register their employee needs with the agency, and when the demand for labor cannot be met locally, the Texas Employment Commission will help find workers from other parts of the state or nation. From data compiled in the central offices, employers can learn where various types of workers can be found and job seekers can learn the most likely opportunities for employment. The employment service includes a farm labor placement service on both a permanent and seasonal basis. During parts of the year when agricultural labor is in no great demand in Texas, workers may be referred to jobs in other states.

LAWS REGULATING LABOR UNIONS

When the Texas economy was still overwhelmingly agrarian, there was little need for laws regulating organized labor as we now know it. The laws that were passed were generally favorable. For example, a law of 1899, which is still on the statute books, declares lawful trade unions and associations. It was not until the rapid strides of industrialization in the 1940s, stimulated in great part by the needs of World War II, that Texans really became conscious of organized labor. In general, this consciousness took the form of antagonism. There seemed to be a natural antipathy between the traditional frontier, agrarian individualism, and the newer philosophy of labor unions. This attitude is changing, however, as the state becomes more highly industrialized and more accustomed to organized labor.

O'Daniel Antiviolence Law

The first of the labor union laws enacted in the 1940s was the O'Daniel Antiviolence Law of 1941 which made it a penal offense for any person to use force or threats of force to prevent one from engaging in a lawful activity, or to assemble at or near a place where a labor dispute is in progress to prevent, by force or violence, anyone from engaging in a lawful vocation. Punishment for violation was from one to two years in the penitentiary. Organized labor attacked this law in the courts and in the marketplace of public opinion, contending it was discriminatory. In 1967 the legislature amended the law by making it an offense to use any such means to prevent a person from engaging in peaceful and lawful picketing and reduced penalties for all violations to confinement in the county jail for from thirty days to two years or a fine of from $25 to $2,000.

To prevent employment of professional strikebreakers, armed detectives or other persons who are not residents of the state may not be hired in Texas, but this prohibition is not meant to prevent employers from defending themselves and their property.

Manford Act

The second of the laws of the 1940s was the Manford Act of 1943. This statute regulates the internal activities of labor unions, and in purpose is similar to the U.S. Labor Management Reporting and Disclosure Act of

1959 (the Landrum-Griffin Act). The major provisions of the act are as follows:

1 Labor unions must file an annual report with the secretary of state showing the name and address of any state, national, or international organization with which the union is affiliated and a statement concerning property owned by the union. In addition, a copy of the union constitution must be filed.

2 An alien or one convicted of a felony may not serve as a labor-union officer or organizer.[10]

3 Unions may not make financial contributions to a political party or to campaign expenses of a candidate for political office.

4 Union organizers must receive an organizer's card from the secretary of state before soliciting members or funds. The United States Supreme Court held this section a violation of the Federal guarantees of freedom of speech and assembly when applied to a national labor organizer without an organizer's card who, in addressing a public gathering of employees, invited one person specifically and all his hearers generally to join the union but made no solicitation of funds. It appears certain, then, that the act of informing people concerning the advantages of a labor union, without registering, is permissible.

5 The collection of fees, assessments, etc., by a labor union as a prerequisite for work is unlawful. This does not, however, prohibit the collection of union initiation fees or the charging of nominal fees of apprentices employed in shops or schools operated by unions.

6 Itemized accounts of all receipts and expenditures must be kept by a labor union and made available for examination by any member of the union at any reasonable time.

7 A member of a union cannot be expelled without good cause. Reinstatement may be ordered by the courts.

8 Penalty for a labor union's violating the act is a fine not exceeding $1,000. Penalty for a labor organizer or union officer who violates it is a fine of up to $500 or sixty days in jail, or both.

The right of workers to organize unions and to bargain collectively is specifically recognized; however, Texas courts have held that state law does not create a correlative duty on employers to recognize and bargain with unions. Unions and workers have the right to engage in peaceful strikes and picketing but must not invade or trespass on premises of the employer or any other person without his consent.

---

[10]This does not apply to convicted felons who have had their "citizenship rights" restored by pardon.

The 1947 Laws

The peak of antilabor union sentiment in Texas was reached in 1947. It was paralleled at the national level by the enactment of the well-known Taft-Hartley Act. A postwar wave of strikes was one reason for the hostility to labor unions throughout the country. Indignation over what some considered the ruthless tactics of labor unions was expressed in the legislature by the enactment of several major labor bills imposing rather stringent regulations upon labor unions. The major provisions of the most important of these laws will be reviewed.

Anticheckoff Law   This statute prohibits contracts which permit or provide for the checkoff, or reduction of an employee's wages to pay union dues or assessments, except upon the individual employee's written consent, which must be given to the employer. Any contract providing for the checkoff made after the law became effective is void.

Anti-Closed-Shop (Right-to-Work) Law   Neither applicants for employment nor employees may be denied employment on account of membership or nonmembership in a labor union. Any contract which requires that workers shall or shall not be or remain members of a labor union is contrary to public policy and null and void. In other words, all forms of what labor unions regard as contractual "union security" are prohibited, including provisions for a closed shop, union shop, maintenance of membership, and the like. A closed shop is one in which only members of the contracting union may initially be employed. A union shop is an arrangement between an employer and union in which the employer may hire whomever he desires, but every employee must become a member of the contracting union after a specified period of time, usually thirty or sixty days after being hired. Maintenance of membership does not require any employee to become a member of a union but does prescribe that every employee who is a union member when the contract becomes effective, or subsequently becomes one, shall remain a member during the contract term. However, because the National Railway Labor Act expressly permits a union-shop arrangement, the courts have held this state law inapplicable to contracts between railroads and unions to that extent.

This so-called right-to-work law was later amended so that violations on the part of either employers or labor unions are considered conspiracies in restraint of trade, thus violative of the state's antitrust laws. The courts may assess fines up to $1,500 a day against any person or group that conspires to violate the act.

Anti-Mass-Picketing Law   When picketing is being conducted, the use of force, violence, and conduct dangerous to the health and general welfare of the people is prohibited. The act further prohibits "mass picketing," which is defined as placing more than two pickets within 50 feet of the entrance to the picketed premises or within 50 feet of another picket. Placing obstacles to prevent persons from entering or leaving picketed premises is also prohibited. Threatening or insulting workers entering a strike-bound establishment, defamatory statements, using placards or handbills containing false statements, and picketing to secure the breach of a valid contract are also outlawed by the act. The penalty for violation is a fine of $25 to $500 and/or ninety days' imprisonment. Picketing which does not violate the provisions of the statute may be considered "peaceful," although peaceful picketing may still be prohibited by the Secondary Boycott Act, the Utility Anti-Picketing Law, or the Union Antitrust Acts.

Secondary Activity Law   Labor unions may not use secondary economic weapons to bring pressure to bear on a primary employer with whom they have a dispute. Nor may they use primary economic weapons upon a secondary employer with whom they do not have a legitimate dispute. The idea is to preclude coercive conscription of any neutral secondary employer into a dispute for the purpose of causing him to cease dealing with the primary employer. To this end the state law undertakes to proscribe many forms of secondary activity. Since, however, it was enacted before the full development of the concept of picketing and related peaceful activities as being elements of communication protected by the free-speech and assembly provisions of the Federal Bill of Rights, several of its prohibitions are of doubtful validity. Those that are based on existence of a "labor dispute" as is defined in the act—"any controversy between an employer and the majority of his employees concerning wages, hours or conditions of employment"—are probably invalid because the very definition has been held to be unconstitutional by the courts. Thus, the law's prohibitions against a "secondary strike" by two or more employees against an employer with whom there is no "labor dispute" or against "secondary picketing" at premises of any employer where no "labor dispute" exists are virtually meaningless. However, the objective of conduct proscribed by "secondary strike" and "secondary picketing" provisions is usually that of inducing the secondary employer to take action detrimental to the primary employer and is, therefore, part of an unlawful "secondary boycott." For instance, a union may not picket or instigate a strike against a secondary employer in order to force him to cease dealing with a primary employer with whom there is a lawful dispute; nor may it boycott him because he uses or handles products of that primary employer.[11] And a "sympathy strike" by employees of a neutral employer for any similar purpose is unlawful—not because of number of employees involved but because of the strike's objective. An employer damaged by any such unlawful conduct may apply to the courts to recover damages and to obtain immediate relief by injunction. Persons found guilty of violating the law are subject to fine of up to $500, to confinement in county jail for up to six months, or both.

Utility Anti-Picketing Law   Picketing a plant, premises, or property of a water, gas, or an electric utility is prohibited if the intent in picketing is to disrupt service or prevent maintenance of the utility or if it has that effect. In case of actual or threatened violation of the law, a district court may issue an injunction restraining the unlawful action. A strike against a public utility is not prohibited. Persons who willfully damage or destroy utility property or equipment to disrupt service or prevent maintenance, or who enter into a combination to persuade others to do so, are guilty of a felony and subject to imprisonment from two to five years.

Union Antitrust Laws   Two measures make labor unions amenable to the state's antitrust laws. The measures take from the unions their exemptions from the operation of laws prohibiting monopolies and conspiracies in restraint of trade. A conspiracy in restraint of trade is an agreement by persons, firms, or corporations to refuse to handle, deliver, receive, or work with the goods or products of another. For example, refusal by the employees of a warehouse to store goods belonging to another employer would be a conspiracy in restraint of trade, as would a union directive for its members not to do business with a firm. However, it is lawful for employees to agree to end their employment or refuse to work with the goods of their immediate employer, unless such action is to induce him to cease purchasing the goods of another employer. The right of organized labor to engage in peaceful strikes against an employer for the purpose of securing wage increases or improved working conditions is not affected. Penalties for violation of the union antitrust laws include forfeiture of corporate charter, fine of $50 to $1,500, or confinement in the penitentiary from two to ten years.

[11]The secondary picketing law, insofar as it denies the right to picket an employer with whom the employees have no direct conflict, was held to be unconstitutional by the Texas Supreme Court in *Dallas General Drivers, Warehousemen and Helpers v. Wamix, Inc., of Dallas,* 156 T. 408, 295 S.W. (2d) 873 (Tex. Sup. Ct. 1957).

Equal-Responsibility Law   Labor unions are liable for damages resulting from picketing or striking in the event that such activity is held by the courts to be a breach of contract. Unions or their members engaging in lawful strikes or picketing are not affected by the statute, for it applies only to those who engage in illegal acts as defined by law. If a union should call a strike before the termination of its contract and the company suffer a loss, the union would then be liable for the full amount of the loss if the courts found that the union had breached its contract.

Later Laws

Although most laws regulating labor unions in Texas were enacted during the 1940s, other statutes, mostly in the nature of amendments, have been passed since that time. One of the more important of these was a 1955 law directed at jurisdictional strikes and picketing, which are called to force an employer to recognize a particular union as the bargaining agent for his workers. Under the law, a suit may be brought in district court after the strike has begun to force an election to determine the workers' choice for bargaining agent. If a majority of the workers in the plant favor the striking union, it is certified as the bargaining agent. If not, the strike is unlawful and may be stopped by court order and damages assessed if the strike continues.

ADMINISTRATION OF LABOR LAWS

In Texas, the authority for the administration of labor legislation is so diversified that it is difficult to attach responsibility for enforcement to any agency of state government. Some of the laws which concern labor are not assigned to any administrative agency for execution; thus little, if any, protection is afforded the worker with respect to some statutes.

Department of Labor and Standards

Of the several administrative agencies obliged to enforce the various labor statutes, the Department of Labor and Standards, formerly called the Bureau of Labor Statistics, which was created in 1909, is given most of the responsibility. The administrative control of the agency is vested in a commissioner who is appointed biennially by the governor with Senate confirmation.

The most important duty of the department is to enforce some thirty labor laws and to assist local governments with their enforcement. The department is also entrusted with the responsibility to: (1) collect industrial statistics; (2) license and collect fees from domestic and out-of-state employment agents; (3) license and collect fees from persons engaged in boxing and wrestling; (4) promulgate and enforce a code of rules for the construction and operation of steam boilers; (5) investigate and certify union charters; and (6) enforce standards for mobile homes as set by the American Standards National Institute.

Texas Employment Commission

The Texas Employment Commission is another important state labor agency. It administers the Texas Unemployment Compensation Law and operates over ninety employment service centers, both of which have been discussed in this chapter.

In the course of its operation, the commission collects a wealth of labor statistics, which are published in its reports. As a result, the function of the Department of Labor and Standards as originally conceived is now carried out in large part by the Employment Commission.

The commission is also a Federal agency for various Federal manpower programs. It has nonlabor responsibilities also, such as its appointment of the Merit System Council.

The commission is composed of three members appointed by the governor with the consent of the Senate. One member must represent employers, one employees, and the third, who is chairman and executive director, the general public. The commission operates through district and local offices scattered throughout the state.

Industrial Accident Board

A third important agency is the Industrial Accident Board whose main duty is to administer the Workmen's Compensation Law. The board is composed of three members appointed by the governor with Senate consent who serve six-year overlapping terms. One must be an employee, one an employer, and one a lawyer, who serves as legal adviser and chairman of the board.

In administering the Workmen's Compensation Law, the board decides whether an injured employee needs medical treatment or hospitalization; it determines the amount of compensation (within the limits set by law) to be awarded injured employees, or their beneficiaries in case of death; and it supervises the payment of claims. Parties dissatisfied with the board's decision on claims may sue in a court in the county where the injury occurred. All compromise agreements between an insurance company and the injured employee must be approved by the board.

Records are kept of all accidents reported, the amount of compensation paid on each claim, and the employers who carry insurance.

Railroad Commission

The Railroad Commission inspects to see that railway companies fulfill the requirements of the full-crew law, which provides that carriers must operate with a designated number of crewmen. The commission is also required to see that all structures or projections on the track right-of-way leave the clearance specified in the statutes. In nearly every instance, Texas laws with reference to laborers working on railroads are duplicates of Federal statutes which are administered by the Interstate Commerce Commission.

Texas Industrial Commission

The original purpose of the Texas Industrial Commission, which was established in 1920, was to help the governor resolve labor controversies. He was authorized to refer them to the commission if it was in the public interest. However, the commission's primary responsibility since 1959 has been to attract new industries and promote the expansion of the old. It was not until 1962 that money was appropriated to the agency.

In pursuance of its original purpose the nine-member commission is composed of two employers and two employees as well as five citizens from the public at large. The governor with the Senate's consent appoints all members, each of whom must be from a different geographical area of the state. The members serve six-year overlapping terms.

CONCLUSION

In many states the Labor Department administers all the labor laws. In addition, several advanced industrial states give the department power to issue and enforce rules, especially in the fields of child labor, minimum wages and hours, health and safety, and the employment of women. Also, provision is made for recourse to the courts should it be necessary.

Texas has several administrative agencies performing various functions of interest to labor. Most of these functions could be consolidated and placed under the stewardship of a department of industrial relations, with the rule-making power and the necessary provisions for enforcement delegated to it by the legislature. The Department of Labor and Standards whose head is currently appointed by the governor would be a logical core of such a consolidated agency. A substantially increased appropriation commensurate with the increase in responsibility should be provided.

Chapter 17

Units of Local Government: The County

In addition to the state government, the Texas political system includes political subdivisions or local governments.[1] The three kinds of local governmental units in Texas are the county, the municipality, and the special district. The school district is a special district but is usually separately classified. In 1972, the number of local governmental units in Texas was as follows:[2]

Counties	254
Municipalities	981
Special districts	1,215
School districts	1,174
Total	3,624

[1]One ambiguity concerns the exact status of regional planning councils or councils of governments. Texas law classifies them as political subdivisions, but it is doubtful that they are local units of government. Questions are also raised about river authorities.

[2]U.S. Bureau of the Census, *Governmental Units in 1972*, p. 8, U.S. Government Printing Office, Washington, D.C., 1972. The figure given in the text excludes two school systems counted by the Census Bureau. Figures for 1973 indicate that there are 999 municipalities and 1,149 school districts.

Texas ranked fifth among the states in the total number of local units.[3]

All local governments in Texas are legally creatures of the state. In contrast to the federal relationship between the states and the national government, the state-local relationship is unitary. All powers not delegated by the states to the local governments are reserved to the states. Also, the delegated powers of local governments are strictly construed under the Dillon Rule.[4]

The Texas constitution of 1876 is less than satisfactory as a basic framework for local governments. It appears that the drafters "just assumed the existence of the entire local governmental structure and put into the constitution only such odds and ends as occurred to them."[5] For example, the structure of county government is set forth in the document, but county powers have to be implied from it or granted by the legislature. Also, in order to find out what the constitution has to say about Texas counties, it is necessary to look at six different articles. Article IX, which is entitled "counties," is concerned more with hospital districts.

We will discuss the county, the special district, and the municipality in this and the next two chapters.

TEXAS COUNTIES

Basic Geographical Subdivision

The basic geographical subdivision of all the states is the county.[6] (However, Connecticut and Rhode Island lack organized county government.[7]) There are over 3,000 counties. The number by state varies from 3 in Delaware and Hawaii to 254 in Texas. (See map, pp. 336–337.) The number seems to bear some relation to the size of the state and its population; it is well known, however, that in many states counties are too numerous.

---

[3]*Ibid.*, p. 1. Illinois ranked first with 6,386; Pennsylvania was second with 4,936; California, third, 3,820; and Kansas, fourth, 3,716.

[4]The "creature concept" of local government is of nineteenth-century origin. Very influential in its adoption was Iowa supreme court justice, John F. Dillon, whose court opinions and *Treatise on the Law of Municipal Corporations* espoused the doctrine of strict construction of local governmental powers as well as its basic premise: Local governments are created, altered, and abolished by the will of the state in which they are located.

[5]George D. Braden, *Citizen's Guide to the Texas Constitution*, p. 49, prepared by the Institute for Urban Studies, University of Houston, for the Texas Advisory Commission on Intergovernmental Relations, Austin, 1972.

[6]Section 1 of Article XI of the Texas constitution reads: "The several counties of this State are hereby recognized as legal subdivisions of the State."

[7]U.S. Bureau of the Census, *op. cit.*, p. 1. Connecticut and Rhode Island retain the county as a name for a geographical area, but there is no county government. In limited portions of a few other states there are no organized county governments. In Louisiana the county is called the "parish" and in Alaska, the "borough."

The county was originally designed to extend state services to rural areas. As the nation became urbanized, people looked to the city or municipality to serve their local needs. In Texas, however, the county remains important as a local unit. Although 80 percent of the people live in urban areas and 50 percent live in the four largest SMSAs, the state is still rural in many respects. This is largely the result of the geographic and economic nature of Texas and its vast land area, much of which is still sparsely populated. Over 200 counties are not in any of the twenty-four SMSAs, and 106 counties have fewer than 10,000 people. The county is the only local government in some of these areas.

History

The real history of the Texas county begins in 1836 with the establishment of the Republic of Texas. (The influence of the Spanish and Mexican periods on the development of the modern Texas county was negligible.) Counties were set up which were similar to those in the states of the South, from which most of the "Texians" had come. The chief governmental agency was the county board, called variously the county commissioners, commissioners court, and county court. At first it was composed of the county judge and the justices of the peace, but in 1845, just before Texas became a part of the United States, the membership was changed so that it was composed of the county judge and four commissioners, all elected, just as at present. There were a number of other officers, including a county clerk, sheriff, and tax assessor, corresponding to those of the modern Texas county.

This form of county government served with very few changes throughout the periods of the Republic, early statehood, and the Confederacy. During the Reconstruction period following the Civil War, local self-government was, for all practical purposes, abolished, and the counties were dominated by officers appointed by the governor. But with the overthrow of the radical element in the state government in 1873, county government was restored to about what it had been previously. When the present state constitution was adopted in 1876, the old forms of county government, almost unchanged, were incorporated into the new document.

Legal Position of the County

As a legal entity, the county may best be described as a body corporate and politic, a quasi corporation. It is in no sense a business or private corporation. It exists largely for the convenience of the state, is its

COUNTY MAP OF TEXAS

functionary, and has only those powers given to it by the state. In the absence of constitutional restrictions, the legislature has absolute power over the organization, dissolution, powers, and liability of counties. With regard to liability, it is a general principle of law that a state may not be sued in its own courts without its consent. Since the county is viewed by the courts as a portion of the state, created for the more conve-

nient administration of state policy, a suit against the county would be, in effect, a suit against the state. A county, therefore, is immune from suit unless a state statute expressly allows the maintenance of action against it.

Although it is true that the law grants to counties an immunity from suit for wrongful acts of public officials, some tendency to modify this rule has appeared in recent years. Particularly has this been true in cases where negligent acts of a county in the use of its property or in the performance of its functions have caused property damage to landowners. For tort[8] liability, the Texas rule seems to be that counties are not liable for injuries resulting from neglect by their officers or agents unless such liability is imposed by statute.[9] However, some courts have held counties liable for their torts when they were acting not in a governmental capacity but in a private capacity or where they were performing some function voluntarily assumed.[10] It should be noted that such cases are rare and that in most instances the county still holds its position as an agent of the state, performing only governmental functions, for which there is no liability in tort.

As a rule, there is a greater liability to suit on contracts on the part of the county than is true of the state. In other words, the immunity of the state from suit for breach of contract does not generally apply to the county.

The county has a dual nature. It is the state's agent in carrying out certain functions, such as conducting elections, levying and collecting taxes, maintaining law and order, dispensing justice, and the like. But it is also a unit of local government, exercising those powers and providing those services permitted by the state, and has its own governmental structure which includes numerous *locally* elected officials.

STRUCTURE OF TEXAS COUNTY GOVERNMENT

The governmental organization of the 254 counties is spelled out in great detail by the Texas constitution. Much of this lengthy document and

---

[8]The word "tort" is used to describe that branch of law which treats of the redress of injuries which are neither crimes nor arise from the breach of contracts. See Bouvier's *Law Dictionary,* Vol. III, p. 3285.

[9]In the leading Texas case on this point, *Heigel v. Wichita County,* 19 S.W. 562 (1892), the court in applying the rule stated that the grounds for it were not uniform. Some courts have held that counties are quasi corporations, brought into existence by the state for the purpose of government, and that the powers conferred upon them are duties rather than privileges; thus the county is not liable. Other courts have argued that the county is an arm of the state and for this reason not liable to suit. On the other hand, since the state may by statute permit itself to be sued in certain cases in its own courts, it may also place liability upon counties in certain instances. See *Harris County v. Gerhart,* 283 S.W. 139 (1926).

[10]*Comanche County v. Burke,* 166 S.W. 470 (1914).

many of its amendments deal with the subject. Each county is provided with the same form of government, the same powers, and practically the same officers. Each has a commissioners court composed of the county judge and four commissioners, a tax assessor-collector, a county clerk, a state's attorney, a county health officer, a county treasurer, constables, justices of the peace, a surveyor, and a sheriff. The county health officer is statutory.

There are a few variations in this rigid system. In counties of 8,000 population or more, there is a clerk of the district court, whereas in the smaller counties a single officer may perform the duties of clerk in both county and district courts. In those counties with 10,000 population or more, the office of the assessor and collector of taxes is separate from the sheriff's office, while in counties of less than 10,000, the sheriff, in addition to his other duties, may serve as assessor and collector of taxes. In those counties having 3,000 scholastics or more, a superintendent of schools is elected (unless the office has been abolished by special act of the legislature or by vote of the people of the county), while in counties with a smaller scholastic population or total populations of not less than 30,000 and no common-school districts, the county judge usually acts as school superintendent. In counties with 35,000 population or an assessed valuation in excess of 15 million dollars, the office of county auditor has been established. In counties of 70,000 population, there may be a juvenile probation officer. Any county may have one or more adult probation officers. In counties of 120,000 population or more, there may be a medical examiner to serve as coroner. Finally, counties of 74,000 population or more may appoint a purchasing agent.

Although numerous powers and duties and a few officers have been added by the legislature, county government is still basically that given in the constitution. With a few exceptions, all county officers are elected and serve for four years, the terms having been increased from two years by a series of constitutional amendments in 1954. In the discussion that follows, the constitutional officers will be considered first and then those created by statute.

Constitutional Officers

County Commissioners Court   The county commissioners court, which is the most important agency in county government, is composed of the county judge, who is elected at large and serves as the presiding officer, and four commissioners, elected from precincts. Like all elective county and precinct officers, they serve for a period of four years.

Each commissioner is also the road commissioner for his precinct.

Under the general supervision of the commissioners court, he is responsible for the construction and maintenance of county roads (those not in the state system) in his particular precinct.

If it can be said that the county has a policy-determining body, it is the commissioners court. Its most important functions are in the field of finance, in that it approves the county budget and sets the county tax rate. The state constitution authorizes the court, on its own authority, to levy a total county tax of 80 cents on the $100 valuation, to be distributed among the four constitutional funds of the county—the General Fund, Road and Bridge Fund, Jury Fund, and Permanent Improvement Fund. Formerly, when the court met to levy the tax rate, it had to state the specific rate for each fund, but a constitutional amendment voted on and adopted in November of 1967 allows the commissioners court to place all tax receipts into one general fund. The total county tax rate, including debt services, cannot exceed the 80-cent limitation. In addition, the taxpaying voters may authorize a special levy of 15 cents for road and bridge maintenance and 30 cents for farm-to-market roads and flood-control purposes. Also, counties along the Gulf of Mexico may levy, with consent of a majority of the voters, a tax for seawall construction, breakwaters, or sanitary facilities. The constitution sets no limit on the tax.

Other financial powers of the commissioners court include letting contracts in the name of the county, authorizing all payments from county funds, and serving as a board of equalization for state and county tax assessments.

The commissioners court is also responsible for constructing and maintaining the courthouse and jail, appointing the county health officer and numerous minor officials, filling vacancies in county offices, administering the county's public-welfare services, and dividing the county into justice precincts. In addition, the commissioners court may establish county hospitals, health centers, libraries, parks, airports, and other public works authorized by law and cooperate with the A & M University System in providing demonstration work in agriculture and home economics.

County Judge   The county judge is the presiding officer of the commissioners court. He is responsible for preparing the county budget and presents it to the commissioners court for their approval.[11] With regard to elections, he has numerous duties, including the posting of election notices, allocating supplies, receiving the returns, and transmit-

---

[11]In counties of over 225,000 population, the budget is prepared by the county auditor. In some counties with smaller populations the auditor, either by custom or special law, also prepares the budget.

ting them to the secretary of state. He is the judge of the county court, which also has general jurisdiction as probate court, including the appointment of guardians, the probation of wills, and the settlement, partition, and distribution of estates. In "wet" counties he issues licenses for the sale of beer and wine. In addition, he is a notary public and may perform marriage ceremonies. In counties having less than 3,000 scholastic population, the county judge also serves as ex officio county superintendent.

Sheriff　The major duties of the sheriff are to serve as conservator of the peace and to act as executive officer of the county and district courts, serving their writs, subpoenas, processes, and the like. In addition he has charge of the jail and prisoners. He selects his own deputies. In counties of less than 10,000 population, he is also ex officio tax assessor and collector unless the voters have approved a separate office of assessor-collector.

Assessor and Collector of Taxes　Those counties having 10,000 or more population are required to elect a tax assessor-collector. In the other counties the sheriff serves ex officio unless the property-taxpaying voters of the county have authorized a separate office of tax assessor-collector. The major duties of the officer are to assess and collect the ad valorem (general property) tax for both state and county purposes and to issue and collect fees for license plates and certificates of title for motor vehicles. He also serves as the registrar of voters.

County Treasurer　The chief function of the county treasurer is to receive and pay out all county funds under the direction of the commissioners court. In addition, he examines the books of county officials who receive any county money, and makes quarterly reports to the commissioners court on the condition of the treasury.

County Attorney　A county attorney is elected in each county where there is not a resident criminal district attorney. His main duties are to serve as legal adviser to county and precinct officers, represent the state in criminal cases in the county and justice of the peace courts, and represent the county in civil cases, such as suits for the collection of taxes.

District Attorney　Although a constitutional officer, the district attorney is not required in every county. The legislature may require the office as it deems necessary. "However, a county must have either a

TEXAS COUNTY GOVERNMENT

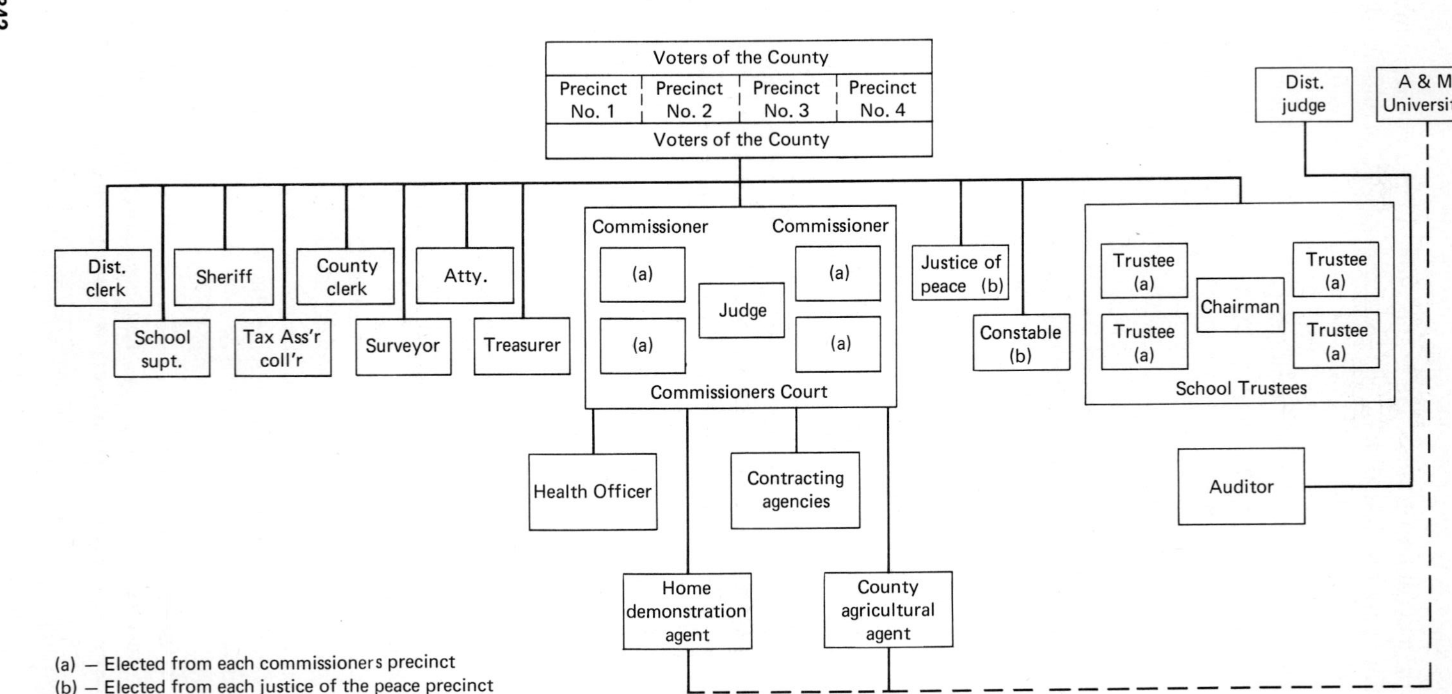

342

county attorney or a criminal district attorney; it may have both, or it may have a county attorney and a district attorney."[12] In counties where both a county attorney and a district attorney hold office, the district attorney usually represents the state in the district court(s) and the county attorney in the county and justice of the peace courts.

County Clerk The county clerk serves as clerk of both the commissioners court and the county court and, in counties of less than 8,000 population, as clerk of the district court. He is also the recorder and custodian of legal documents and instruments, such as deeds, mortgages, contracts; and he issues marriage licenses. If there is no county auditor, he has certain functions in regard to periodical statements on the financial condition of the county. As we explained in Chapter 3, he is the major election officer of the county.

District Clerk In counties of 8,000 or more people, there is a separate clerk of the district court. He is the recorder for the sessions of the district court and has power to administer oaths and to take depositions of witnesses.

Justice of the Peace The constitution requires that the commissioners court divide the county into not less than four or more than eight justice of the peace precincts and that one justice of the peace be elected from each such precinct. If a precinct contains a city of 8,000 or more population, a second justice of the peace is elected. The major function of the justice of the peace is to preside over the justice court, which has jurisdiction over minor civil and criminal cases. He also serves as coroner except in Dallas, Harris, Tarrant, and Bexar counties, where the commissioners court appoints a medical examiner. In unincorporated towns of less than 2,500 population, the justices of the peace are registrars of vital statistics for the Bureau of Vital Statistics in the State Health Department. (In incorporated cities of 2,500 or more population the city clerk or city secretary is the registrar.)

Constable A constable is elected by the qualified voters of each justice precinct. He serves processes, attends the sessions of the justice court, and in general performs the customary duties of the peace officer.

County Surveyor The constitution provides for the election of a county surveyor in each county, but with the disappearance of open land,

---

[12]Robert E. Norwood, *Texas County Government: Let the People Choose*, p. 26, Texas Research League, Austin, 1970. This monograph must be regarded as the most definitive work on county government in Texas. The authors of this text have relied upon it extensively.

the importance of the office has declined, and in numerous counties the office is now vacant. His duties still pertain primarily to making surveys of public lands.

Inspector of Hides and Animals   Another of the county officials mentioned in the constitution is the inspector of hides and animals. The office is optional. The duties of the office are actually performed by private groups or U.S. Department of Agriculture officials in counties where they are needed.

Statutory Officers

Some county officers have been created by statute, for example, the county superintendent of schools and the county school trustees. Since their duties have already been described elsewhere, they will not be considered here. Other statutory officers are optional, for example, county librarians, purchasing agents, welfare directors, and parks directors. A discussion of a few of the major statutory officers follows.

County Auditor   By legislative enactment, all counties with a population of at least 35,000 or tax values in excess of 15 million dollars are required to have an auditor, and other counties may have one if the commissioners court so orders. All county auditors are appointed by the district judge having jurisdiction in the county[13] and serve for two years. The major duty of the auditor is to oversee the financial books and records of the county, including countersigning all warrants drawn on the county treasury (except those for jury service), approving all claims against the county, inspecting the treasurer's reports,[14] and advertising for bids on county supplies.

County Health Officer   The legislature has required that the commissioners court appoint a county health officer biennially. He is charged with giving medical care to the prisoners in the county jail and those on the pauper rolls of the county. In addition he must discharge certain duties required of him by the State Board of Health, including matters relating to quarantine, inspection, disease prevention, general

---

[13]The more populous counties often comprise a judicial district in themselves and may have several district courts. In that case the auditor is selected by majority vote of all the district judges in the county.

[14]Any county may have a special "outside" audit of all county records upon petition of 30 percent of the qualified voters of the county who voted at the last general election. The district judge appoints the auditor. Counties of 350,000 population or more must have such an audit. In this case the auditor is appointed by the commissioners court.

sanitation, and the presence of epidemic diseases. If the county health officer does not carry out the duties prescribed by the State Board of Health, removal proceedings may be instituted in the district court.

County Agricultural Agent and Home Demonstration Agent

Beginning with a legislative act in 1911, the commissioners court in most counties have appointed agricultural agents and home-demonstration agents who serve during the pleasure of the court. They work under the supervision of the Extension Service of the Texas A & M University System which pays half of their salaries. The agents' primary function is to assist farm men and women in scientific farming and modern home-making.

Texas County and District Retirement Plan

Each county or other political subdivision in the state, except school districts and incorporated municipalities, may, if it wishes, become a member of the Texas County and District Retirement Plan, which provides retirement and disability benefits for elective and appointive county employees. If the political subdivision, through its governing body, elects to enter the system, it must deduct from 4 to 7 percent of the first $3,600 of the employee's salary and contribute a like amount. Those who are covered by the system may retire and receive an annuity at age sixty if they have twelve years' service or at any age with thirty years' service. This system was created by the legislature in 1967.

Administrative control is vested in a nine-member board appointed by the governor from among the participating employees for six-year overlapping terms.

At the option of the commissioners court, county officers and employees are also covered by social security. The necessary payroll taxes from both the county and the employee are paid to the State Department of Public Welfare which transmits them to the Federal government.

COUNTY EXPENDITURES AND REVENUES

Expenditures

The Texas county performs many services for the state and for its local citizens. The kinds and their relative cost can be determined by looking at county budgets. Available data for all counties at the date of writing indicate that Texas counties depart from the national county expenditure

Table 11   Five Highest Texas County Expenditures Compared with National County Averages (In Percentages of Total Budgets)

Texas		U.S.	
Highways	33.1	Public welfare	21.4
Hospitals	12.3	Education	17.9
General control	12.3	Highways	15.7
Financial administration	7.3	Hospitals	10.2
Police	6.1	General control	6.0

Source: Based on Robert E. Norwood, *Texas County Government: Let the People Choose*, pp. 51, 103, Texas Research League, Austin, 1970. The data were compiled from the U.S. Bureau of the Census, *Census of Governments, 1967*, Vol. 4, *Finances of County Governments.* The percentages do not include the entire budgets and do not total 100 percent.

pattern in several respects.[15] This can be seen by comparing the five most costly services of Texas counties with those of all counties. See Table 11.

Texas counties have much less to do with welfare and education, which in Texas are largely financed from state funds (and Federal particularly in the case of welfare) than counties in other states and have a great deal more to do with roads, which accounted for one-third of the total Texas county budget. The education expenditures of Texas counties were below the 1 percent level, and welfare accounted for only 3.3 percent of the total.

Revenues

The Texas county revenue pattern also differed from that of counties in other states. Table 12 demonstrates this very well.

Texas counties raised about 50 percent more in taxes than counties in the other states and close to twice as much in charges and miscellaneous. The sharpest contrast was in intergovernmental general revenue. Texas counties do not receive significant sources of revenue from the state as do most counties. Federal assistance has also been small. However, the general revenue sharing program enacted in 1972 will give Texas counties about 373 million dollars over the five-year life of the Federal program.

The only tax available to Texas counties is the ad valorem or general property tax. Some 531 counties in twenty-three other states levied a sales tax in 1972.[16] If Texas counties should expand their functions in urban

[15]The data available at the time of writing were compiled in 1967. New data will be available in 1974.

[16]"News in Review," *National Civic Review*, p. 205, April, 1972.

Table 12   Sources of Revenues for Texas Counties Compared with National County Averages (In Percentages)

Source of revenue	Texas	U.S.
Taxes	69.3	45.7
Charges and miscellaneous	24.1	14.0
Intergovernmental general revenue	6.6	40.3
Total	100.0	100.0

Source: Based on Robert E. Norwood, *Texas County Government: Let the People Choose*, pp. 51, 103, Texas Research League, Austin, 1970. The data were compiled from the U.S. Bureau of the Census, *Census of Governments, 1967*, Vol. 4, *Finances of County Governments*.

areas, the county sales tax might be permitted some time in the future inasmuch as cities have the option of the tax at present.

CRITICISMS OF COUNTY GOVERNMENT

County government is probably the most criticized local unit of government in Texas although the special district would place a close second. A basic reason is that the Texas constitution of 1876, which provides the basic framework for county government, was designed for an almost entirely rural and agricultural state. The county government provided for in the constitution met the needs of the day, but social and economic conditions have changed so rapidly that this is no longer true. Let us look at some of the reasons why the county has been criticized.

Frozen Governmental Structure

Governmental structure of the county is frozen in the constitution. Although a few variations are allowed from county to county, there can be no real adaptation of the government to meet local needs. Loving County with 164 inhabitants and Harris County with 1.7 million have essentially the same form of government. This is also true of Rockwall County with its 147 square miles and Brewster with 6,208, and so on.

The constitution and statutes also limit the counties' powers so much that they, particularly the urban counties, cannot provide effective government without constantly seeking legislative action.

No Chief Executive

There is no chief executive officer for the county. Under the present organization, practically every officer is his own boss. Division of authority and the lack of administrative control characterize the entire organizational setup.

Too Many Elective Officers

With voters electing approximately fourteen county and precinct officers, the Texas counties have the long ballot with a vengeance. It is exceedingly difficult for the voters to know the qualifications of all the candidates for these offices, and as a result, there is much "blind" voting.

No Merit System

The spoils system reigns supreme in the Texas county. The accepted way to get a job at the county court house is to support the right, *i.e.*, successful, candidate. County service is evidently considered too unimportant to require the services of the specially trained. However, some county officials are opposed in principle to the merit system, believing that they can appoint qualified personnel without it.

No Coordinated Road System

There is usually no coordinated road system. In most counties, the road money is divided four ways among the various commissioners without regard to need. There is no overall coordination or supervision, and poor administration is common. In 1947, the legislature passed an optional county road law allowing the voters to adopt the county-unit system which would abolish the precinct boundaries for roads and make possible the employment of an engineer who would have supervision of all the county roads. Only a few have done so. The county unit system should result not only in a great financial saving but also in better roads. At present, approximately 80 percent of all county roads are built and maintained by amateurs.

Precinct Representation Shortcomings

Before 1968, the commissioners precinct boundaries were not required to be equitably drawn. The constitution merely said that the commissioners court was to determine the boundaries "for the convenience of the people" and did not mention "population." When originally set up, most of the precincts were approximately equal in population, but then population shifted drastically without a corresponding redrawing of precinct boundaries. Then, in 1968, the U.S. Supreme Court ruled that county commissioners precincts must conform to the "one man, one vote" principle.[17] Many counties have still not redistricted to provide for substantially equal representation for all its citizens. Most citizens are not interested enough in county government to spend the time and money to bring a suit in their county forcing reapportionment.

In addition, various county ills can be attributed to precinct representation. Redrawing districts, even if equal in population, can be gerrymandered, as we saw in Chapter 5. Also, precincts contribute toward a precinct-first, county-last point of view in the administration of roads, as we have already seen, and other functions. Insofar as determining policy is concerned, the precinct system has much to recommend it because all parts of the county are represented. But when it comes to administration, which is the province of the county commissioners court, then it has its drawbacks. The county judge is elected countywide, of course, but his is only one voice among five.

Inadequate Financial Systems

Counties have inadequate financial systems. There is too little investigation of budget requests or budget needs except in the best run counties. Rarely is there centralized purchasing. Money may be wasted, but because of the headless nature of county government, no one is responsible for doing anything about it. Furthermore, the financial reports are frequently inadequate if not unintelligible.

Inadequate Compensation

Although county commissioners and judges are well paid in most of the large metropolitan counties, receiving much higher salaries than state legislators or city councilmen, for example, the general salary levels in most counties is not high. This is particularly true of employees. Also, far too frequently county officers have been paid on a fee basis. However, all district officers are now paid on a salary basis as well as all county officers in counties of 20,000 or over.[18] Counties with less than 20,000 population must compensate all sheriffs, deputy sheriffs, county law enforcement officers, and their deputies, and since 1972, the justices of the peace, on a salary basis only. Similarly the commissioners courts in all counties may

---

[17] *Avery v. Midland County*, 390 U.S. 474 (1968).
[18] The fees are still collected but are paid into the county's "salary account."

determine whether precinct officials will be compensated on a fee or salary basis, except for constables, deputy constables, and precinct law officers, who must be paid only by salary.

Too Many Counties

Some counties are too small in population and resources to provide the services that should be provided. It is not at all unusual for three-fourths of the taxes in such counties to go for salaries of officers, leaving little for anything else. With distances shrinking and population declining, many rural counties do not make much economic sense today.

Inadequate State Supervision

State supervision over important state functions performed by the counties is slight. This is particularly true of financial functions. There is little state supervision of tax collection and none over assessment, with the result that similar pieces of property in different counties vary widely in assessed valuation. Locally elected county assessors like to keep assessment as low as possible, thereby lowering the amount of state property tax the property owners of the county must pay.

Accounting and auditing systems are set up very much in accord with the ideas of local officers, and the state has no control over them. Although the state attorney general must pass on the legality of all bonds issued, no inquiry into the county's economic capacity to retire these obligations can be made. All in all, state supervision over county finance is practically nil.

COUNTY REORGANIZATION

In Texas as well as in other states, reform of county government has been very slow, perhaps more so than at any other level. Several reasons have been given for this. By and large, it would seem that those who have personal or political interest in county government tend to resist any major changes. Individuals who aspire to an elective office prefer a system that provides a great many offices; a number of taxpayers do not relish the idea of scientific assessing methods; and those whose stock in trade is patronage see little good in a personnel system based on merit. Most important, the people of the state have never shown any great concern about efficient county government. Certainly if county government is to play its proper role, it must set its own house in order and perform more efficiently the functions now assigned to it, but any thoroughgoing revision of county government will require substantial constitutional change. Let us look at some of the proposals for reform.

County Home Rule

We saw earlier how all Texas counties have basically the same constitutionally prescribed form of government. Home rule would allow the people of the county to draw up and adopt their own charter provided nothing in it violated the Texas constitution or laws, thus allowing them to better tailor the county's government to their needs. It would also permit them to adopt county ordinances, provided they were not contrary to their own charter, the state constitution, or state laws.

The Texas constitution was amended in 1933 to provide for county home rule. However, the amendment was so ambiguous, conflicting with other parts of the constitution, and procedurally unworkable that it is highly doubtful that any valid charter could have been passed under it. Although in several counties some action toward home rule was attempted under the amendment, only El Paso, Delta, and Bexar counties actually drew up proposed charters. The El Paso charter was the only one to be voted upon, and it was defeated. Although a majority of the voters on a countywide basis approved, it failed to get a majority of the rural vote which, under the dual majority provision, was necessary. At any rate, the voters in 1969 repealed the county home rule amendment.

Although home rule is a firmly established American principle of government, and prevalent at the municipal level, it has won only grudging acceptance for counties. In the nation as a whole there are only about fifty counties with home-rule charters. Nonetheless, the idea is not dead. Home rule was proposed by the Texas Constitutional Revision Commission of 1967–1968 and the Texas Constitutional Revision Commission of 1973–1974.

Optional Charters or Plans

Another avenue toward reforming Texas county governmental structure is to provide for county optional plans. In New York, Montana, North Dakota, North Carolina, and other states offering the plans, the legislature enacts a statute describing the available forms of government for counties. The voters of a given county may, according to procedures outlined, select the plan they prefer. The range of choice is not as great as under a county home-rule charter, but it is better than no choice at all, which is what Texans have now. The Texas Research League and the 1967–1968 Texas Constitutional Revision Commission both proposed optional plans for Texas counties.

County Executive Proposals

It is common to refer to Texas county government as headless, as we have done in this chapter. Several proposals have been advanced to provide for a county executive.

County Manager Plan The manager plan of government has proved successful in Texas cities as well in many other cities throughout the country, and it should receive careful consideration in the reconstruction of county government.

The county-manager form has two major characteristics: (1) a board of three, five, or seven members elected by the voters of the county, which formulates county policies and selects a manager, and (2) a manager chosen for an indefinite term by the county board, who is to serve as the chief administrative officer of the county.

The plan calls for the election by the people of only a few county officials, preferably only the county board. The manager selects the heads of the various administrative agencies and is charged with the preparation of the budget and responsibility for all other administrative matters.

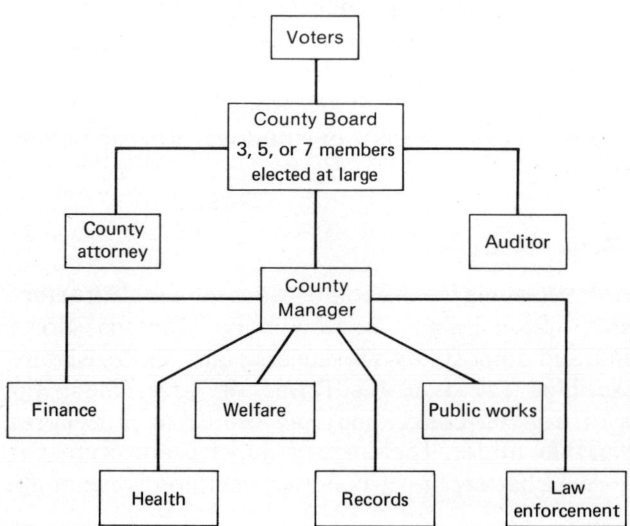

The proponents of the plan argue that it is efficient and businesslike and that it will tend to eliminate partisan politics from county government. Yet it is doubtful that the manager plan can be adopted by Texas counties without careful constitutional change. During the life of the 1933 county home-rule amendment, the attorney general ruled that should a county adopt a home-rule charter providing for a county manager, the manager could not be authorized to appoint or remove subordinate officers, since such authority would be an unconstitutional delegation of power by the commissioners court. Furthermore, the charter could not abolish the offices of county tax assessor-collector, district clerk, sheriff, justice of the peace, constable, or the commissioners court, since each of these is a state functionary exercising powers and charged with duties of statewide importance as distinguished from purely county affairs.[19] In effect, the opinion seems to say that although a constitutional amendment authorizes home-rule charters under which a manager plan could be provided, the amendment itself is unconstitutional, as it is inconsonant with many other parts of the constitution! It is highly essential, therefore, that another constitutional amendment clarifying the situation be proposed before the county-manager plan can make any headway in Texas unless a new constitution is adopted.

County Administrative Officer   There has been objection to the vesting of such broad powers in an appointive chief executive as is proposed in the county-manager plan. To meet such opposition, a county administrative officer has been suggested. Under this plan, as in the county-manager plan, the county administrator is selected by the county board and holds office at its pleasure; the board is responsible to the people for the conduct of county government. It differs from the manager plan in that the county board retains the power either to choose the department heads directly or to appoint and remove them upon the recommendation of the administrator. This form has found acceptance in certain counties in North Carolina, California, and Virginia. A somewhat similar plan has been used successfully in school organization for many years.

Elective-Executive Plan   Some fear that, by the adoption of a plan which provides for an appointive chief executive, the local community loses control of its government. This fear is no doubt unfounded, but nevertheless it is a very real one in the minds of many citizens. To satisfy such opinion, the elective-executive plan has been proposed. This

---

[19]Tex. Attorney Gen. Op. V–723, Nov. 20, 1948.

plan generally corresponds to the strong mayor-council form of city government; it is certainly a step in advance of the current headless condition of most county governmental structures.

The provisions concerning the composition and election of the county board are the same in this as in the preceding two plans. The board is the policymaking agency of the county, but it does not have the power to appoint and remove the chief executive or his major subordinates. The county executive is elected by the voters and is responsible to them for the conduct of the county administration. He appoints and removes the heads of the several departments and through them controls departmental operations. Examples of this plan are found in Wisconsin and in several New York counties.

City-County Separation or Consolidation

Different from the proposals we have been discussing for reorganization of county governmental structure are suggestions for changing the jurisdiction of county government in relation to other units of government within its boundaries. The purpose of the plans is to provide county government or some kind of government with the areal and financial powers to serve the people.

One old device is to separate the county from the city on the premise that the city would then finance and otherwise handle urban problems and the county, rural. Except for Virginia, where any city reaching 10,000 in population is automatically separated from the county, all but one of the city-county separations occurred in the nineteenth century—Baltimore, St. Louis, San Francisco, and Denver. Today, the idea is unpopular because urban sprawl is no respecter of strict urban-rural divisions.

City-county consolidation is another old device. The city government is absorbed by the county or vice versa in order that one government shall govern the entire area. There are variations on the theme as well. City-county consolidation has provided one government for Boston, New York, New Orleans, Honolulu, and Philadelphia. In modern times, modified city-county consolidation has been accepted by Baton Rouge, Louisiana (1947); Miami and Dade County (1957); Nashville and Davidson County (1967); Columbus and Muskogee County, Georgia (1970); Indianapolis and Marion County, Indiana (1970); and a few others.

Although each plan is designed for the needs of the particular county in question, in general a government elected from the county and city is authorized to make some, most, or all the decisions for the countywide area. The Miami-Dade County consolidation is one of the best known. It is actually a kind of federation of governments in which certain areawide functions are delegated to the commission-manager county government while the twenty-six municipalities in the county retain authority over local affairs to the extent there is no conflict with the county charter.

Recent Texas Amendments

Although progress toward structural reorganization of Texas counties or city-county consolidation or separation has been zero to date, three constitutional amendments are directly of relevance to county improvement. The first, passed in 1966, authorized counties with at least 1.2 million people (Harris County only at the time) to consolidate some county functions and enter into contracts with other local governments. Legislative authorization and local voter approval were prerequisites for consolidation. In 1968, the voters approved a more broadly worded amendment applicable only to El Paso and Tarrant counties; and finally, in 1970, they approved the same language for all counties.

A careful examination of the last two amendments by the Texas Research League suggests that only a limited consolidation of functions and offices would be possible under the amendments. A principal reason is that state functions performed by the county can be neither abolished nor consolidated. However, a limited consolidation of functions of a local nature might be possible under the commissioners court. The Texas Research League regarded the intergovernmental contract portion of the amendments to be more significant; and suggested that various services could be offered by the county to the political subdivisions within its boundaries, including public health, parks and recreation, library services, waste disposal, planning and engineering, and so on.[20]

County contracts with local governments to provide county services have seen their greatest development in Los Angeles County. More than fifty municipal-type services may be purchased by cities from the county, including election services, tax assessment and collection, housing of prisoners, emergency ambulance service, library service, and many more.[21] This is one way of delivering services economically and efficiently by a county government to the people in the area. However, if Texas should go this route, it will be necessary to provide the counties with a broader tax base.

---

[20]Norwood, *op. cit.*, pp. 79–83.
[21]*Ibid.*, pp. 119–124.

REBIRTH OF THE COUNTY

As we noted at the beginning of this chapter, the county has been regarded as a rural government. But times are changing. There has been a rebirth of interest in the county as an urban government. With the advent of urban sprawl, duplication and conflict among numerous municipalities, densely populated unincorporated areas, and the interrelatedness of needs within a single area, the county offers many possibilities for urbanites. It is an established general-purpose areawide government, encompassing within its borders an entire SMSA in many instances. It is a responsible government, elected by the voters. It has taxing authority coterminous with the entire county. And it is there. It is not necessary to create it. We shall return to this subject in the last chapter.

Chapter 18

Units of Local Government: The Special District

Special districts are the fastest growing, most numerous, and least understood units of government in the United States.[1] They are found in every state,[2] in both rural and urban areas, and range in size from the minute nontaxing district to the colossal multimillion dollar authority.[3] The functions they perform include nearly all those commonly thought of as governmental and many not normally included in that category.

Practically every resident of this country lives in some kind of special district. In fact, he may come under the authority of three or more,

[1]Much of the material for this chapter has been adapted from Woodworth G. Thrombley, *Special Districts and Authorities in Texas*, Institute of Public Affairs, University of Texas at Austin, 1959. The authors wish to express their indebtedness to Professor Thrombley and also to David W. Tees, who wrote "A Fresh Look at Special Districts in Texas," in *Governmental Organization and Authority in Metropolitan Areas*, report of the Texas Urban Development Commission, Arlington, 1971.

[2]Alaska has school districts but not other kinds of special districts.

[3]A unit meeting the specifications of the special district is often called an "authority," *e.g.*, the Lower Colorado River Authority. Some writers have maintained that the authority is a self-liquidating enterprise which is financed through service charges only, while the special district generally has the power to tax. This distinction is, however, largely superficial, and for our purposes the terms are considered synonymous.

but he could probably identify less than half of them. Only the school district is generally well known.[4]

SPECIAL DISTRICTS IN THE UNITED STATES

What is a special district? How can it be identified? How is it like or unlike other units of government? Definitive answers to these questions are not possible, for the one overriding feature of the special district is its great diversity. For example, some districts may tax; others may not. Some may incur debt; some may not. Some are governed by elected officials, others by appointed officials. Many possess police powers, but many do not. Most districts are intrastate, but several are interstate. Some districts are far removed from public control, while others are highly responsive to the popular will. Many are staffed by unpaid amateurs, many by highly paid professionals. Some are informal, personal, and intimate; and some are formal, impersonal, and autocratic.

Moreover, districts are equally diverse from a functional standpoint. The functions they perform deal with such services as water supply, water power, flood control, fire prevention, housing, schools, sanitation, hospitals, soil conservation, irrigation, cemeteries, highways toll roads, street lighting, libraries, parks, airports, ports, harbors, beach erosion, noxious weeds, grasshopper suppression, predatory animal control, mosquito abatement, and so on. The special district, then, appears in an almost infinite number of guises. It is foremost, however, an independent unit of local government.

Governmental Characteristics

Special districts, like all units of government, must possess certain essential characteristics in order to be classed as governments. In other words, there is something about the species "government" which differentiates it from, say, a labor union, a business, or a branch of the U.S. Department of Agriculture. The U.S. Bureau of the Census defines a unit of government as "an organized entity which, in addition to having governmental character, has sufficient discretion in the management of its own affairs to distinguish it as separate from the administrative structure of any other governmental unit."[5] Thus in order to be counted a

---

[4]The school district meets all the specifications of a special district. However, because a chapter of this text is devoted to public education and because school districts are generally well known, as opposed to nonschool districts, this chapter will be concerned solely with nonschool districts. All references to special districts, unless otherwise noted, refer only to districts in the nonschool category.

[5]U.S. Bureau of the Census, *Governmental Units in 1972*, p. 3, U.S. Government Printing Office, Washington, D.C., 1972.

government, an entity must possess (1) organized existence, (2) governmental character, and (3) substantial autonomy. Each of these is, of course, subject to further explanation and limitation.

Organized Existence   Obviously, mere existence is not sufficient to fulfill this requirement. The entity must, in addition, possess some corporate powers, such as the power to make contracts, acquire and dispose of property, sue and be sued, the right of perpetual succession, and so on. A designation in the law such as "a public corporation" or "a public body corporate and politic" (the latter is used to describe Texas soil conservation districts) is always an indication that the unit described is an independent organized entity, although not all independent units are so designated.

Governmental Character   The attribute of governmental character is the key provision. Corporations, farm cooperatives, and baseball teams have an organized existence, and a high degree of autonomy, but none of these possesses governmental character. Governmental character is attributed to any unit with the power to tax, the right to incur debt the interest on which is exempt from Federal taxation, or the responsibility for performing a function commonly regarded as a governmental function. Police powers are perhaps the best example of the latter, although it is not unusual for nongovernmental institutions to possess certain police powers. Likewise, governmental character exists where officials are popularly elected or are selected by other public officials and where a high degree of public accountability is present.

Substantial Autonomy   Substantial autonomy is the most difficult of the three qualities to define. Generally speaking, this requirement is met where an entity has considerable fiscal and administrative independence from other units of government. Fiscal independence is usually present when an entity is authorized to make its own budget, set its own tax rates, fix its own charges, and incur debt, without detailed review and revision by other local governments. Administrative independence is largely determined by the methods of selecting the entity's governing body. Such independence is indicated where the district's governing body is elected by popular vote or is appointed for fixed terms of office.

The usual prerequisites of "area and population" are not included among the essential attributes of government. This is because not all special districts operate within a defined geographic area for which a population can be determined, *e.g.,* toll-road and bridge districts.

Number of Districts

In 1972, there were 23,886 nonschool special districts in the United States, accounting for 30.5 percent of all units. This represented a 30 percent growth in their number in the space of ten years. However, over the same ten-year period, the number of governmental units in the United States declined from 91,237 to 78,268, or 16.6 percent. The strange result is mainly explained by the sharp decline in the number of school districts, which dropped from 34,678 to 15,780, or 54 percent. See Table 13.

Rural and Urban

The special district has a long history in rural areas. Most districts are probably still devoted to rural purposes, such as reclamation, drainage, soil conservation, irrigation, and similar functions. However, the use of the district device as a means of coping with urban problems began to gain momentum in the latter part of the nineteenth century, although Philadelphia established a prison district as early as 1790. Since World War II, heavily urbanized communities have turned more and more to the use of the special district in an attempt to solve some of their most pressing metropolitan problems.

Functions of Districts

The vast majority of special districts performs only one major governmental function. Some districts, however, are multifunctional. Water is

Table 13   Governmental Units in the United States: 1962–1972

Types of government	1962	1972
U.S. government	1	1
State governments	50	50
Local governments	91,186	78,217
Counties	3,043	3,044
Municipalities	18,000	18,516
Townships	17,142	16,991
School districts	34,678	15,780
Special districts	18,323	23,886
Total	91,237	78,268

Source: U.S. Bureau of the Census, *Governmental Units in 1972*, U.S. Government Printing Office, Washington, D.C., 1972.

Table 14 Governmental Units in Texas: 1962–1972

Types of government	1962	1972
Federal	1	1
State	1	1
Counties	254	254
Municipalities	866	981
School districts	1,474	1,174
Special districts	733	1,215
Total	3,328	3,626

Source: U.S. Bureau of the Census, *Governmental Units in 1962*, U.S. Government Printing Office, Washington, D.C., 1962; and *Governmental Units in 1972*, 1972. The 1972 total is 3,625 in the original table.

the most frequent common denominator in multifunctional districts and is usually found in combination with sanitation, fire protection, irrigation, or flood control.[6]

In 1972, nearly one-half of all special districts were found among four types: fire protection (16.2 percent); soil conservation (10.7 percent); urban water supply (10.4 percent); and housing (9.5 percent).

TEXAS SPECIAL DISTRICTS

Of the 3,626 units of government in Texas in 1972, more than one out of three was a special district. If school districts are included, two-thirds were special districts. Moreover, the rate of growth of special districts has been a dramatic 66 percent over the past ten years. See Table 14.

Collectively, these districts spend millions of dollars every year, incur more millions in debt (close to one billion dollars in 1971), and in one way or another have a profound effect on every citizen in the state.

Like all local government, special districts must look to state law for their creation and survival. Nonetheless, no single state agency is charged with keeping count of these districts, much less knowing anything about their financial activities, or their relations with other governments. However, local water districts are subject by law to continual supervision by the Texas Water Rights Commission, and soil conservation districts are under limited supervision by the State Soil and Water Conservation

---

[6]School districts have the single function of providing education and are, therefore, classed as unifunctional districts.

Board, which is the only state agency devoted exclusively to special districts.[7]

Texas Districts by Function

There are over twenty-two different kinds of districts that can be created by general law and an unlimited number by special law. Some of these, of course, perform identical functions, but because they are organized under loosely written or separate state laws (or are embodied in the constitution itself) they bear different titles and possess different degrees of power and authority. For example, there are at least sixteen different varieties of water districts, which account for about 50 percent of all Texas districts.[8] They are as follows:

Water control and improvement
Water improvement
Fresh-water supply
Municipal water
Conservation and reclamation
Underground water conservation
Flood control
Recreation
Drainage
Water supply
Levee
Navigation
River authorities
Watershed
Improvement
Water-power control

A seemingly endless maze of legislation covering water-related districts reveals practically nothing with respect to the activities of individual districts. For example, some water-related districts collect refuse, some build dams, some build lakes, some are wholly promotional (they supply no services), and at least one dispenses natural gas. Most

[7]Critics argue that neither the Texas Water Rights Commission nor the State Soil and Water Conservation Board exercises really effective supervisory powers over the special districts entrusted to each. The 1969 legislature gave the Texas Water Rights Commission the right of continuing supervision of water districts created under Article XVI, Section 59, of the Texas constitution (*Vernon's Annotated Civil Statutes*, Art. 7477d), but staff is lacking for effective control.

[8]Water districts are created under both general and special laws by the Water Rights Commission, the legislature, or the county government. Further, many of the districts fail to meet the requirements of registration with the commission. These factors make it difficult to determine the exact number of such districts.

districts retail directly to consumers, but many operate on a wholesale basis only. One, the Red Bluff Water Power Control District, is a "master district," that is, a sort of superdistrict set up to serve other districts. Moreover, in addition to those which contain the word "water" in their titles, many districts which are not so named, such as conservation and reclamation districts, drainage districts, and navigation and river districts, have a distinct water function.

Texas Districts by Geographic Class

Another way of classifying special districts is according to the areas in which they are established—metropolitan districts, urban-fringe districts, coterminous districts, rural districts, and school districts.[9]

Metropolitan Districts   A metropolitan district is one which covers all or a substantial part of a metropolitan area; thus not all special districts in metropolitan areas are metropolitan districts. A district may be termed "metropolitan" only if it performs an urban function and includes the central city (and it may contain more than one central city) and a major portion of the remaining territory of a metropolitan area.

In spite of the fact that Texas has a number of heavily urbanized areas, only a few metropolitan districts have been established in the state. Among these are several hospital districts,[10] several airport authorities, and the Gulf Coast Waste Disposal Authority, which was set up by a special legislative act in 1969 to control pollution in three Gulf Coast counties, all heavily industrialized. Liberal annexation laws and the relative youth of Texas cities account, in large part, for the relatively small number of metropolitan districts. However, as the already intense finance, service, and jurisdictional problems of the state's metropolitan areas increase, we may expect the number of metropolitan districts to increase.

Urban Fringe Districts   Urban fringe districts, sometimes called "suburban" or "satellite districts," are districts that ring or border on the legal boundaries of an incorporated city. The city may or may not be within a metropolitan area. By definition, an urban fringe is substantially populated land bordering a city that has need for urban services but lacks a general-purpose government to provide them. In the absence of such a

[9]John C. Bollens, *Special Districts in the United States,* University of California Press, Berkeley, Calif., 1957.

[10]These include districts in Bexar, Dallas, El Paso, Harris, Potter, Wichita, Jefferson, and Tyler counties.

government, the fringe resident is forced to make other arrangements for water, sewerage, garbage collection, and the like. More often than not, he, in union with other property owners in his neighborhood, elects to create a special district to supply the needed service.

One of the most publicized urban fringe districts is the Municipal Utility District (MUD), also referred to as the water or water control and improvement district. "More than 140 of these districts, spawned by almost as many special acts of the state legislature, ring the City of Houston, while more than 50 others have been annexed to make way for mushrooming expansion of the city's corporate limits."[11] The districts may be created under general or special laws, with the latter being the most prevalent method in recent years.

Coterminous Districts   Districts which are coextensive in area with earlier established governments are sometimes called coterminous districts. Public-housing authorities account for nearly all such districts in Texas. Until 1937, the Federal government participated directly in the construction of municipal public housing. However, partly as a result of a lower Federal court decision that the national government did not possess the authority to condemn land for housing purposes, the Congress passed the United States Housing Act of 1937. This act provided for Federal financial assistance to local governments willing to undertake housing projects. Because most cities which desire to provide public housing for their lower-income residents were financially unable to do so through existing city agencies, a public authority was created. The practical effect of the Federal court decision, together with the unrealistic constitutional and statutory tax and debt limitations on Texas city finance, virtually compelled cities to choose between doing without Federal housing assistance or circumventing state law by creating a new unit of government. The 379 public-housing authorities in Texas attest to the fact that the latter course proved very tempting indeed.

Rural Districts   Rural districts are still the most numerous class of districts in the state. Special districts designed to improve the land and conserve natural resources through irrigation, flood prevention, better farm methods, land drainage, and so on, were among the first districts to be organized. The outstanding single example of a rural district is the soil and water conservation district. These districts cover nearly 100 percent of the land area in the state. The soil conservation district is unique among special districts in that it may not tax or incur debt. Moreover, these

[11]Tees, *op. cit.*, p. 52.

districts receive very little financial help from the state government. As with housing authorities, the motivating force behind the creation of soil conservation districts came from the Federal government. From the creation of the first soil conservation district in the "dust bowl days" of the late 1930s up to the present time, the Federal Soil Conservation Service has served as the local soil conservation district's unofficial guardian angel. This exceptional agency maintains an average of from three to four professional soil conservationists in every Texas soil conservation district.

The rationale behind the creation of rural special districts is much less difficult to explain than is the case with their counterparts in the city. The simple fact is that county government has ceased to correspond with the social, economic, and political realities of rural living. The county is, for the most part, still geared to the days when the rural resident lived in relative isolation, when travel was hard and infrequent, and when governmental functions were few, simple, and strictly local. The twentieth-century technological revolution in agriculture, together with such knotty problems as waste disposal, water supply, river control, and so on, has forced the rural constituent to look elsewhere for solutions. In part he has looked to the Federal government, in part to the state government, but most of all he has turned to the use of the special district.

WHY SPECIAL DISTRICTS ARE CREATED

A common complaint is that there are altogether too many local governments, too many local officials, too many taxing jurisdictions. Students of government are likewise familiar with the charge that one of the causes for the apparent lack of citizen interest in local affairs is the confusing multiplicity of local governments. Why, then, if the citizenry is virtually smothered by layers of complicated, expensive government, do we continue to create more government in the form of special districts? There is, of course, no single, all-inclusive reason for the proliferation of special districts. In a general way, however, it is possible to identify several of the more important reasons for their creation.

Unsuitability of General-Purpose Governments

Probably the most potent reason has to do with the inability of existing local government to perform a wanted service. This inability is sometimes real, sometimes fancied, and sometimes a convenient disguise for less noble motives.

A lack of geographic comprehensiveness has accounted in large measure for the spread of special districts in both rural and urban areas, but particularly so in rural areas. The rural special district was early designed to fill a governmental need that the county was not able to fill. Thus, for example, a proposed flood-control project might overlap three or four counties and a dozen cities. The advocates of such a project are generally confronted with three governmental choices. They may petition the state for help; they may attempt to find a remedy through the cooperative action of the several governments involved; or they may form a special district. The first alternative runs contrary to well-established concepts of local government: local problems can best be solved through local effort. All too frequently, the second has resulted in nothing but bitterness, selfishness, and frustration. Almost by default, then, the organization of a special district becomes the only feasible solution.

Often existing governments cannot readily undertake an additional function, or expand a service, because of the rigid financial and legal limitations imposed upon them by state constitutions and state legislatures. These restrictions have become more or less sacrosanct with age, and their removal and/or modernization is very difficult. It is easier, quicker, and less disruptive of the status quo to satisfy the need for a new service by creating a special district.

Special districts, however, are not always created to perform new functions. Such time-honored governmental services as water supply, waste disposal, refuse collection, and indigent hospitalization, for example, are increasingly being turned over to district jurisdiction. In many instances, the formation of a special district is instigated by regular governments in order to circumvent tax and debt limitations, or as a convenient means of freeing themselves of a thankless and burdensome service. There are often legitimate reasons for transferring certain traditional services from regular governments to special districts, but one should be wary of accepting the attractive, but fanciful, argument that the transfer somehow substantially increases the number of taxpayers who support the service in question. For the most part, the tax burden remains as before "on the same old taxpayers." The chief difference is that they pay to one more level of government—and at a higher total rate.

Politics and Authority

Regular governments are sometimes deemed unsuitable to perform certain functions for reasons other than physical, legal, or financial limitation. Any number of well-meaning people will work for the formation of a special district in an effort to get a governmental function "out of politics." This basic distrust of regular governmental authority is most often evidenced on the state level with the establishment of semiautonomous boards and commissions, but it plays a prominent role in the establishment of special districts as well.[12] The school district remains the classic example. There is the presumption that a better, more public-minded class of people than may be found at the city hall or the county courthouse is needed to administer the most vital functions of government. Too often the result of this view of the political process has been the wholesale substitution of visible public politics for the politics of the obscured special interests.

Private Government

Some people who have studied the development of special districts seem to believe that their rapid growth is due, in some measure, to the desire for financial gain on the part of selfish groups and individuals. They use government to serve private ends. A good example of this is the Municipal Utility District (MUD). Although there is a legitimate need for districts of this type, they can be abused. This has been particularly true of the "bald prairie" or "predevelopment" type of district. In some instances, its purpose has been to enable a real estate developer to build a subdivision with proceeds from bonds issued by a municipal utility district. The homeowners who eventually buy residences in the subdivision become liable for the bond obligations. The district may initially have been established by the vote of as few as two voters who have been moved into the area for this purpose by the developer. They live in tents or trailer homes temporarily and then depart.[13] Annexation of the development by the nearby city results in the assumption of the district's debt obligations by the city taxpayers. The legislature has taken note of abuses of the "MUD" and various proposals have been offered for protection of the homeowner and the city.[14]

SPECIAL DISTRICTS: PRO AND CON

In spite of the apparent widespread popularity of the district device among locally elected officials, it is almost universally condemned by those who write in the government field. This dichotomy of opinion

---

[12]The American Assembly, *The Forty-eight States: Their Tasks as Policy Makers and Administrators,* p. 119, New York, 1955.

[13]*Ibid.,* p. 53. For other kinds of sharp practices, see pp. 54–59.

[14]For two interesting articles on this subject, cf. "See MUD Run: A Primer," *Texas Observer,* p. 7, Sept. 22, 1972; and "More on MUD," *Texas Observer,* pp. 10–11, Oct. 6, 1972.

reflects a basic difference in approach to the problems of government. The local official is forced to deal with the demands of his constituents on a more or less immediate basis. The public is seldom satisfied with long-range solutions. To the local official, the special district is an easy and politically acceptable way of getting things done. He is not too receptive to the argument that the extensive creation of special districts can only lead to further governmental confusion and complexity.

Advantages

The principal justification for the creation of special districts is to fill an unmet service which existing governments are unable or unsuited to perform. This is most applicable to rural areas where legal, financial, and administrative inadequacies of existing units make *ad hoc* government a practical necessity. It has some merit in highly urbanized fringe or suburban developments, particularly if state laws allow districts to be annexed by expanding cities. A number of large-scale metropolitan districts also provide services which otherwise would be unmet, or provided only at great cost to the governments involved. For example, the bistate Port of New York Authority has received wide acclaim. So also has the Metropolitan Water District of Southern California, which provides water from the Colorado River to water agencies in a three-county area running from Los Angeles to San Diego.

The special district also has certain financial advantages over regular governmental units. State constitutional debt and tax limits often make it impossible for a city or county to undertake new or expanded functions. Formation of a special district is often an easy method of circumventing these restrictions.

An important advantage of the district device from the locally elected official's point of view is that the creation of a district does not disturb the existing structure of government. Thus existing political loyalties are not strained or destroyed. Nor are jobs abolished or transferred. In short, it is possible to provide a new service or expand an old one and maintain the political status quo at the same time.

Finally, the special district is sometimes considered the "nearest thing to business in government" that has been devised. This claim is generally made only with reference to the large and well-financed districts and authorities which can afford to employ top administrative and technical help. This claim also implies that the relative insulation of these governments from public scrutiny, and therefore political pressures, makes for a more businesslike operation of a public enterprise.

Disadvantages

Undemocratic The real and alleged disadvantages of special districts are so numerous that no exhaustive listing can be made here. One of the most frequent criticisms is that they are undemocratic. That is to say, their activities are obscured from the public eye by infrequent and little-publicized meetings, little or no public reporting, disguised tax and service charges, the smallness of their operations, and the omnipresence of their numbers. According to a report by Public Administration Service, "the most revealing evidence that districts are not the democratic device they are often thought to be is that the average citizen (in metropolitan Sacramento) does not know what district(s) he is in."[15] The result of these shortcomings is that the public is effectively barred from influencing district operations. Although the district may be efficient, competent, public-spirited government, it is not self-government.

Now it is unquestionably true that some of the districts in the United States fit this general characterization, but it does not necessarily follow that district government is per se undemocratic. There is nothing inherently undemocratic about the Lower Colorado River Authority, the Dalworth Soil Conservation District, or the Lower Neches Valley Authority. If the general public is uninformed about their operations, it is not because they are conducted in secrecy or otherwise secluded from public view. It is perhaps because the nature of their operations is such as not to command general public attention in an age when competition for such attention is at fever pitch.

Too Complex Another widely cited weakness of the special district is its tendency to confuse and complicate the local-government picture. This view equates number with confusion and complexity; that is, the more government we have, the more complex and confused is our government. At first glance, one is intuitively inclined to accept this judgment. Yet is it really a valid generalization? If so, what is the optimum number of governments for a given area? Is it one, fifty, or a hundred? Obviously, this line of questioning is absurd and unanswerable, for it completely ignores the great variations across the country—in geography, climate, population, economics, politics, mores, wealth, existing government, and so on. Is it not more accurate to say that the use of the special-district device can be overdone, but whether or not it has been depends upon an analysis of particular situations?

[15]Public Administration Service, *The Government of Metropolitan Sacramento,* p. 55, Chicago, 1957.

Ironically, many people who endorse the notion that the less government we have the better also expound the philosophy of grass-roots government.[16] If we define grass-roots government as little government—"government where the grass grows," the smaller the better[17]—then it is clear that the two doctrines largely cancel each other. For this argument against special districts is not that they perform services, but that they fragment local-service performance. There are too many of them. However, if districts were suddenly abolished, some existing unit of government would have to undertake the services they provide. Thus, government would become larger, not smaller in keeping with grass-roots philosophy.

Too Costly   A third criticism of special districts is that they are costly and uneconomic. This is a telling criticism, for the great majority of districts in the United States are very small units. For example, less than 10 percent of the special districts in Texas employed more than twenty full-time employees, and nearly half had no professional staff. Also, in terms of area, more than one-third were under four square miles. It can be demonstrated that their small scale results in uneconomical operations.[18] Small governments do not generally benefit from the financial advantages which accrue from such tested administrative practices as central purchasing, personnel pooling, and machine operation. Nor are they generally able to employ personnel of the caliber available to larger governments. In addition, in Texas the interest rates charged for special district bonds may be considerably above those for general-purpose governments.

Decentralizing Effect on Administration   The chief disadvantage of the special district is not, however, that it is undemocratic, confusing, or costly, but that it grossly decentralizes administration. Each service performed by the special district is exalted to a status it probably does not deserve, and the officers in charge of it tend to lose their sense of proportion. Furthermore, regular local-government units are stripped of the power and responsibility they ought to have.[19]

Picture, if you will, a typical American metropolitan area, one in

---

[16]For a critical commentary on grass-roots government, see Roscoe C. Martin's collection of essays in *Grass Roots,* University of Alabama Press, University, Ala., 1957.

[17]What, for example, could be "more grass roots" than soil conservation districts—government on the land, run by and for working farmers?

[18]Tees, *op. cit.,* pp. 48–51. For example, the average cost for treating sewerage in two small water districts near Dallas is about 46 cents per 1,000 gallons whereas it is only 19 cents per 1,000 in Dallas.

[19]See Kirk H. Porter, "A Plague of Special Districts," *Capitol Courthouse and City Hall,* p. 223, Houghton Mifflin Company, Boston, 1954.

which only the central city and county governments are present. Superimpose upon this picture a dozen single-purpose special districts, and to make the problem more difficult, a dozen suburban municipalities. The effect is to transform what was once a recognizable political, social, and economic entity into twenty-six separate, independent ones. Now the harm is not that the twenty-six governments confuse the public or that they produce irresponsible, grafting politicians. The overriding cause for alarm is that there no longer exists a metropolitan government capable of dealing with the problems of the metropolitan area. In other words, there is almost complete administrative decentralization. And this is why many of the country's metropolitan areas are moving toward some form of metropolitan government or at least new forms of cooperation.

CONCLUSION

No matter how one views the case for or against special districts, they exist in large numbers; and they are increasing. Local-government services must go on and, it would appear, at higher and higher costs. It is not likely that they will decrease, nor will our population shrink. The future will bring a greater demand for water, sewer systems, hospitals, roads, public education, river control, soil conservation, mosquito abatement, and the like.

The challenge for order and reasonableness in local government is great. It is important that we develop an aggressive, responsible political leadership in this area of government. Local officials in the past have not been given much opportunity to provide this kind of leadership. We may give it to them, or we may continue down the same old road—trusting that partial and makeshift arrangements will somehow maintain inadequate and obsolete governments. The latter course is almost certain to fail in time.

Chapter 19

Units of Local Government: The Municipality

The basic unit of local government in Texas today is the municipality. Almost 80 percent of all Texans live in urban areas served by approximately 1,000 cities, towns, and villages.[1]

The Texas municipality enjoys a long history, which reaches back to Spanish rule. The Spanish municipality, an early form of local-provincial government, included not only the urban settlement itself but also large areas of surrounding territory, which might cover thousands of square miles. Under Mexican rule, these settlements continued to serve as nuclei of local government. Prior to 1836, there were no incorporated cities of the kind we know today. But with the advent of the Republic, municipalities began to incorporate, and by 1845, when Texas entered the Union, there were fifty-four incorporated places.

[1]According to the Texas Municipal League, there were 999 active incorporated municipalities in Texas as of May, 1973.

By 1850, the year in which the population of Texas was first enumerated, there were 212,000 people in the state, but only two incorporated places of over 2,500 people—Galveston and San Antonio.[2] By 1900, the urban population had more than doubled to 520,000, which was 17.1 percent of the total population; and the number of urban places had increased to fifty-six. Even though the rural population exceeded 80 percent of the total, there were several cities which showed considerable growth potential. San Antonio had the largest population with over 50,000 people, whereas Houston and Dallas had both passed the 40,000 mark. Four other cities exceeded 20,000—Galveston, Fort Worth, Austin, and Waco.

By 1920, the year the United States officially became an urban nation, four Texas cities had over 100,000 people—San Antonio, Dallas, Houston, and Fort Worth, in that order. These cities constitute the "Big Four" to this day, although their rank order has changed. The Texas urban population in 1920 was 30 percent of the total.

By 1940, there were 2.9 million people living in 196 urban places, constituting 45.5 percent of a total of 6.4 million. However, over half of the rural population was classified as "rural non-farm," meaning that they did not live on farms although in rural areas. Texas was rapidly approaching urban status.

Finally, in 1950 Texas became urban with 62.7 percent of her people residing in the urban areas. The urban population had reached 4,800,000. The 1960 census revealed some new urban developments, one of which was the growth of the suburban cities around the central city. This was very evident in the Dallas and Houston areas. Also, Houston had by this time become the state's number-one city in population with almost 1,000,000 people. Dallas, San Antonio, and Fort Worth were the next in rank, which is their order today. There were eleven cities with over 100,000 at this time.

The story since 1960 has been told in Chapter 1. Texas in 1970 was overwhelmingly urban and metropolitan as well. The very largest cities continued to grow, but so did their suburbs, and at a faster pace. Some cities in the 100,000 and above range actually lost population. Growth was concentrated in the very largest SMSAs.

A summary of growth in Texas urban population from 1850 to 1970 appears in Table 15 on page 374.

---

[2]Galveston had a population of 4,177 and San Antonio 3,488. Before 1950, urban population was defined by the U.S. Bureau of the Census as population in incorporated places of 2,500 or more. All else was rural population. In 1950, the urban classification was changed to include both incorporated and unincorporated places of 2,500 or more.

Table 15   Texas Urban Population from 1850 to 1970 in Number and Percentage of the Total Population

| | | Urban population | |
Year	Population	Number	Percent
1850	212,592	7,665	3.6
1860	604,215	26,615	4.4
1870	818,579	54,521	6.7
1880	1,591,749	146,795	9.2
1890	2,235,527	349,511	15.6
1900	3,048,710	520,759	17.1
1910	3,896,542	938,104	24.1
1920	4,663,228	1,512,689	32.4
1930	5,824,715	2,389,348	41.0
1940	6,414,824	2,911,389	45.4
1950	7,711,194	4,838,060	62.7
1960	9,579,677	7,187,470	75.0
1970	11,196,730	8,920,946	79.7

Source: Texas Urban Development Commission, 1971.

THE LEGAL POSITION OF THE MUNICIPALITY

The Texas municipality, in common with other units of local government, is a creature of the state and comes under the Dillon Rule.[3] There is one important difference, however, from other units. This is the option granted to cities having over 5,000 population to adopt a home-rule charter.

Most of the incorporated Texas communities which came into existence during the nineteenth century were probably created by special legislative act. Before the adoption of the constitution of 1876, the legislature was free to incorporate by either special charter or general law. The first general law providing for the incorporation of cities and towns was passed in 1858,[4] but it is not known how many communities took advantage of this act. Probably only a few did so.

The constitution of 1876 provided that cities and towns having a population of 10,000 or less could be chartered only by general law, while cities with more than 10,000 inhabitants might have their charters granted and amended by special act of the legislature. Thus the first step was taken toward the elimination of the special legislative charter. The constitution was amended in 1909 to provide that cities of 5,000 or less were to be restricted to the use of general laws.

[3]See Chapter 17.
[4]*Gammel's Laws of Texas*, Vol. IV, pp. 941–946.

In 1912, a home-rule provision was added to the constitution. Under this amendment, cities with populations of over 5,000 might frame their own charters and include anything they wished not inconsistent with the constitution and general laws. Before an enabling act making this amendment effective was passed, twenty-four cities drafted charters. All these were later validated by the legislature. However, the home-rule amendment did not immediately stop the legislature from granting charters and charter amendments by special law. The same legislature that passed the enabling act amended three charters, and others were amended or granted until a court decision in 1920 held such action unconstitutional.[5] Another case in 1929 emphasized the fact that all power to grant or change a city charter by special law had been withdrawn from the legislature by the home-rule amendment.[6]

Apparently the underlying thought of the various Texas legislatures has been the creation of two types of communities, in name at least, if nothing more. According to the general laws of the state, there are, on the one hand, the city and town and, on the other, the town and village. This general plan permeates the statutes of the state; nevertheless, in many instances the two groups enjoy similar powers and privileges. To draw a sharp line of demarcation between cities, towns, and villages becomes virtually an impossibility. In addition to the general-law cities, there are, as we have seen, home-rule cities.

It is relatively simple, therefore, to classify various communities by using the terms "general-law cities" and "home-rule cities." Cities under 5,000 population have no choice but to operate under the general laws, although in some few instances they may have special charters. As stated above, according to the Texas constitution, cities of over 5,000 population may adopt a home-rule charter. Such cities may ". . . adopt or amend their charters, subject to such limitations as may be prescribed by the legislature, and providing that no charter or any ordinance passed under said charter shall contain any provision inconsistent with the Constitution of the State, or of the general laws enacted by the legislature of this State. . . ."[7]

THE FORMS OF MUNICIPAL GOVERNMENT

Three forms of government have constituted the basic structural pattern of municipal organization in the United States. These three are the

---

[5] *State v. Vincent,* 217 S.W. 402, Tex. Civ. App. (1920).
[6] *Ex parte Norton,* 21 S.W. (2d) 663, Tex. App. (1929).
[7] The Constitution of the State of Texas, Art. XI, Sec. 5.

mayor-council, the commission, and the council-manager forms. All have undergone many varying adjustments, depending upon the time, place, and circumstances under which they happened to operate. Although there appears to be little conformity to exact patterns, most cities can be classed roughly as belonging to one or the other of these three major types.[8]

The Mayor-Council Form

The traditional form is the mayor-council, still used in a majority of the cities of this country, both large and small.[9] Two general types of the mayor-council form have evolved in American cities: One is known as the strong mayor-council, and the other as the weak mayor-council. The most distinguishing difference is the position of the mayor. In the strong-mayor plan, the mayor has important administrative duties, including the selection and removal of most or all of the department heads and preparation of the budget. He has the power to veto acts of the council. In other words, the mayor is the responsible head of the administration; in addition he has important legislative powers. The primary function of the council is that of legislation and policymaking.

Briefly stated, the characteristics of the strong-mayor form are

1 A mayor elected at large
2 A council elected at large or by wards
3 A mayor with the power to appoint and remove most department heads
4 A mayor responsible for the preparation of the budget for council consideration
5 A mayor with the veto power

A few large cities, including Houston, have adopted an interesting variation of the strong-mayor form, which involves the appointment of a chief administrative officer by the mayor. The role of this administrative assistant has yet to be clearly defined—it varies from city to city. Nevertheless, as cities increase in size and the demand for both political leadership and professional administration increases, this combination form may gain in popularity and use.

The mayor-administrator form embodies the characteristics of the strong-mayor form and includes the following:

[8]Several pamphlets relating to the forms of municipal government are obtainable from the National Municipal League, New York. Among these are *Forms of Municipal Government—How Have They Worked? The Story of the Council-Manager Plan;* and *Who's Boss?—Story of the Manager Plan in Twenty Pictorial Charts.*

[9]Approximately 44 percent of the incorporated cities with over 5,000 inhabitants operate under the mayor-council form. See *The Municipal Year Book,* p. 15, 1972.

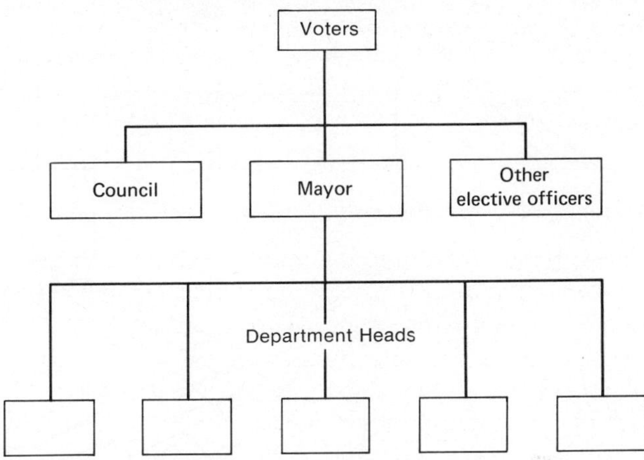

1   A mayor with the power to appoint an administrative assistant
2   An administrative assistant who has the power to appoint and remove "line" and some "staff"[10] department heads and to assist the mayor in coordinating the budget

In the weak-mayor form, the administrative powers of the mayor are severely restricted and the council exercises more direct control over administration, often through committees. If the mayor is given the veto, it usually may be overridden by a simple majority vote of the council. The weak-mayor plan was in vogue during the nineteenth century; however, the modern tendency is toward its abandonment in favor of either the strong-mayor or the council-manager form.

The most common characteristics of the weak-mayor type are

1   A large council elected by wards
2   An elected mayor with limited administrative authority
3   Elected administrative heads, including the city attorney, treasurer, and various others
4   Elected administrative boards

Of the 195 cities in Texas which have adopted home-rule charters, 39 provide for the mayor-council form of government.[11]

---

[10]Line agencies are operating agencies which come in close contact with the people—police, fire, health, and public-utility departments. Staff agencies are concerned with the routine or housekeeping activities of government—such things as planning, budgeting, purchasing, personnel, and the like.

[11]According to information obtained from the Texas Municipal League for 1971.

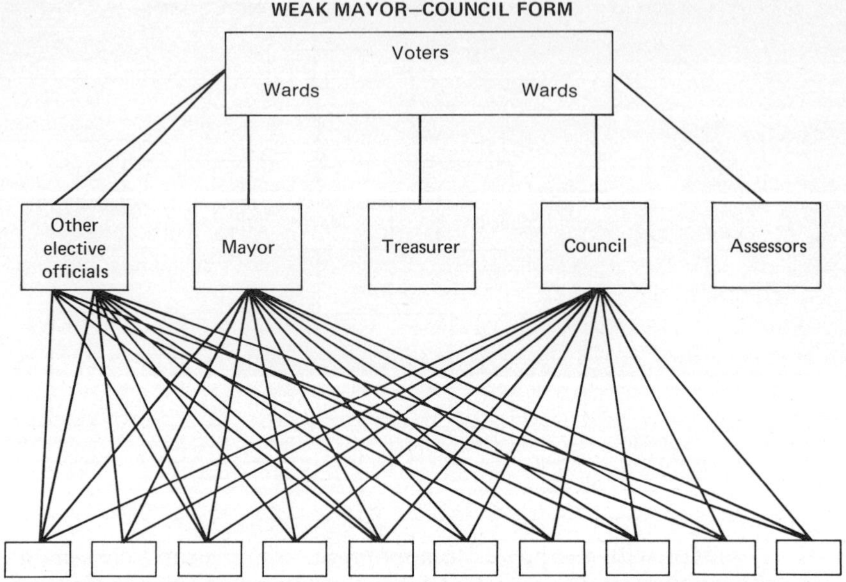

Historically, the trend in Texas municipal government has been to strengthen the position of the mayor. However, in a home-rule city the decision concerning whether the office of mayor is to be strong or weak is a local matter to be settled at the time of charter adoption or amendment.

The general laws relating to municipal government provide for the incorporation of "cities and towns" and "towns and villages." The aldermanic, or mayor-council, form of government is available to either class at the time of incorporation. There is, however, some difference in the details of organization.

The general-law city or town has a government consisting of a city council composed of a mayor elected at large and two aldermen elected from each ward. If the city is not divided into wards, the council consists of a mayor and five aldermen elected at large. In addition, the statutes provide for the election or appointment of a treasurer, an assessor and collector, a secretary, a city attorney, a marshal, and a city engineer. However, these officers may be dispensed with by ordinance, and their duties conferred upon others. Even the office of marshal in cities below 5,000 population may be abolished by the council, and the duties imposed upon a police officer of the city to be appointed as the council directs. The council may designate additional officers and agents.

Because of the powers provided in the statutes, the office of mayor in a general-law city or town may be one of considerable prestige and authority.[12] However, in practice, the position is frequently not a particularly strong one. The existence of a number of important elective officials and others appointed by the council, together with the almost total absence on the part of the mayor of the power of removal, serves to restrain him from exercising effective administrative control. In addition, any act of the council may be repassed over the mayor's veto by a simple majority of the total number of aldermen. Despite the limitations of his authority, the mayor may, through personal influence and judicious use of his powers, direct the city's administrative affairs in a very real sense and play a leading role in the shaping of municipal policies.

The only officers for a general-law town or village mentioned by the statutes are the mayor, five aldermen, and a marshal, who are to be elected for one-year terms. However, the board of aldermen is authorized to appoint other necessary officers and define their duties. In the smaller communities, most of the routine administrative duties are commonly handled in the city clerk's office. The mayor's authority is even more circumscribed than in the city or town.

Of the approximately 1,000 active incorporated municipalities in Texas, more than 500 have the mayor-council form of government. On a percentage basis, mayor-council government is much more popular with general-law cities than with home-rule cities.

The Commission Form

The commission plan was the second basic type of government to gain considerable favor among our American cities. Although Galveston did not originate the idea, it did adopt the commission form at a highly critical time in the city's history and demonstrated to the country the possibilities of commission government. After the disastrous storm and tidal wave in 1900, the mayor-council government in Galveston failed to cope with the urgent problems of relief and reconstruction. A group of interested citizens succeeded in securing legislative approval of a new charter which provided for a government by five commissioners, three appointed by the governor and the remaining two elected. All legislative and administrative power was concentrated in these five men; although one was designated mayor, he merely served as chairman of the body. Owing to conflicting court decisions by the highest civil and criminal courts of the state, the charter had to be amended in 1903 to provide for the election of all the commissioners.

[12]For an enumeration of these powers, see *Forms of City Government,* 7th ed., Institute of Public Affairs, University of Texas, Austin, 1968.

COMMISSION FORM

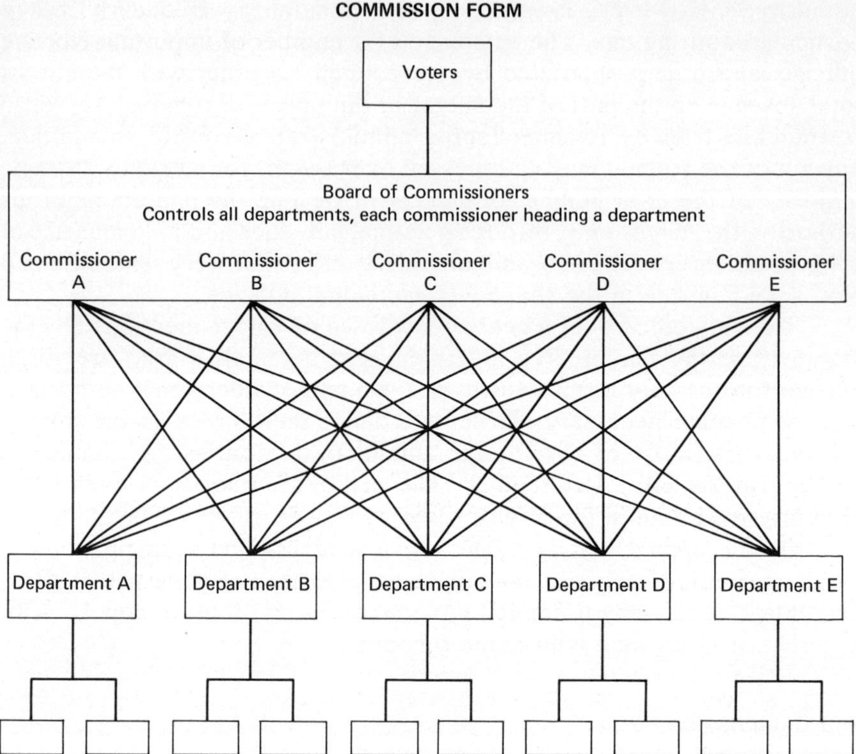

The commission plan has developed along lines laid down in the Des Moines charter rather than those first found in the Galveston charter. The framers of the Des Moines charter took the Galveston charter and superimposed upon it initiative, referendum, and recall; a nonpartisan ballot for primaries and elections; and a merit system. Commission government today is commonly characterized by a small body of commissioners, elected at large by a majority vote. The commissioners serve as the legislative body, and at the same time each commissioner heads an administrative department. The apparent simplicity of the plan, coupled with its success in Galveston, gave it a quick vogue. By 1917, about 500 cities throughout the country had adopted commission charters.[13] Its two outstanding characteristics are

1 A small commission, elected at large, which serves as the legislative body

---

[13]Austin F. Macdonald, *American City Government and Administration,* 6th ed., p. 203, Crowell-Collier Publishing Co., New York, 1956.

    2   Each commissioner acting as head of an administrative department

From the beginning the plan worked remarkably well in Galveston, and other Texas cities began to study seriously the possibilities of commission government. Houston, the second city to adopt the plan, secured legislative approval of a commission charter in 1905. The next session of the legislature granted commission charters to five other Texas cities, and the following legislature, that of 1909, approved five more. By 1915 there were at least forty commission cities in Texas; today there are about 110.[14] However, the consensus among students of municipal affairs is that the popularity of the plan is waning and that few cities will adopt it in the future.

There are only two home-rule Texas cities using commission government, but the general laws make it possible for a city or town or a town or village to incorporate under this form. It is also possible for a community that has been incorporated under the mayor-council plan to adopt the commission plan if the change is approved by a majority of those voting upon the proposition. Once this change has been effected, the municipality may again return to its original form if approved by the voters.

The governing body provided by the general laws is known as the board of commissioners, and it is composed of a mayor and two commissioners elected at large. These three are the only elective officers. The board of commissioners is directed to appoint a clerk, who acts as treasurer, assessor, and collector; in addition, it is authorized to appoint a city attorney, police officers, and such other officers as may be deemed necessary. The board has the authority to discharge any officer, clerk, or employee whom it appoints.

It appears to be the intent of the statutes that the board of commissioners perform the functions of legislation, appointment and removal of officers, and general oversight of the administration. The statutes do not direct that the mayor and the commissioners are to be elected to head specific administrative departments as is sometimes done in home-rule cities with commission charters. In practice, however, the mayor often devotes much of his time to city administrative affairs, and the commissioners may also give considerable attention to the administration of particular activities.

It will be noted that under the general laws the commission form differs from the mayor-council form in these respects: (1) Fewer officers are elected under the commission plan than under the mayor-council plan,

---

[14]According to information obtained from the Texas Municipal League.

and (2) the commission plan concentrates legislative and administrative authority in the board of commissioners, while in the mayor-council plan these two functions are divided among the mayor, the council, and elective administrative officers.[15] The statutes extend practically identical powers to the two types of government.

The Council-Manager Form

The newest development in city government is the council-manager form. Staunton, in the Shenandoah Valley of Virginia, was the first to use the term "manager" in 1908, where the office of "general manager" was created by ordinance as a rather novel adjunct to an old-fashioned city government consisting of a mayor and council. Three years later, the council-manager plan appeared in a proposed charter drafted by the Board of Trade of the city of Lockport, New York. Although the New York legislature failed to approve this charter, much publicity was given to the idea. Sumter, South Carolina, in 1912 became the first city to operate under a charter provision providing for council-manager government, and an amendment to the charter of Dayton, Ohio, made it possible for this form of government to go into effect there in January, 1914. Dayton's adoption gave wide publicity to the plan. There are now over 2,100 cities and counties operating under manager government in the United States.

In general, this plan unifies municipal legislative and policymaking powers in a small elective council and concentrates administrative authority in a manager appointed by and responsible to the council. Although a mayor is usually designated, either by the voters or by the council from its membership, he is not charged with administrative responsibility as under the strong-mayor plan; his duties are customarily those of presiding over council meetings, representing the city on formal occasions, and participating in the determination of policy. It is intended that only members of the council shall be elected, that the manager shall be appointed by the council, and that all other officers shall be appointed, in general, by the manager without dictation by the council. Although the council may request the manager to give advice on policy matters, the final determination of policy is the council's responsibility. Once the plans

[15]Many home-rule cities designate their governing body as a "commission," although the form of government actually employed is mayor-council or council-manager. The basic criterion for classification as a commission city is the concentration of legislative and administrative authority in the board of commissioners. Home-rule charters are thus sometimes misleading in providing for "legislative supervision of administrative activities." This provision is found in many charters by virtue of the legislative body's position as the main policymaking branch of municipal government; it does not provide for true commission government.

and policies have been laid out, however, it is the manager's job to see that they are put into operation and to report thereon to the council. Insofar as the voter is concerned, the council is responsible not only for policies but also for the administrative record of its own appointee, the manager.

Briefly stated, the outstanding characteristics of council-manager government are as follows:

1 A small council is elected at large.

2 Legislation and policymaking are located in the council.

3 The council employs a professionally trained city manager who is subject to dismissal by the council at any time.

4 The manager is responsible for administration, having the power of appointment and removal subject to civil-service rules.

5 The manager is responsible for the preparation and presentation of the budget to the council.

The adoption of the home-rule amendment to the Texas constitution in 1912 made possible the introduction of council-manager government in

COUNCIL—MANAGER FORM

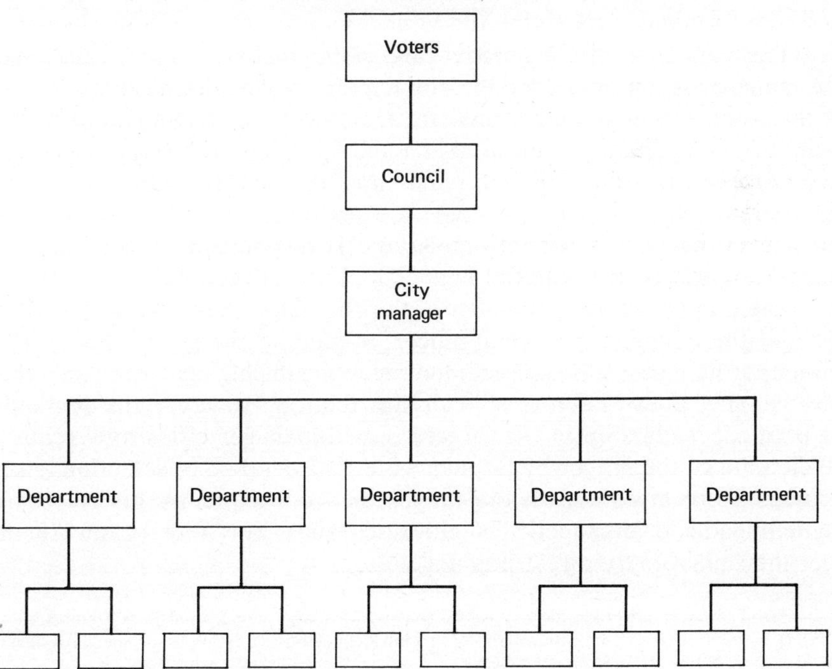

the state.[16] Amarillo, in 1913, was the first Texas city to adopt council-manager government. Except for the decade of the 1930s, acceptance of the plan has moved steadily ahead. Today it is the most popular form of government in home-rule cities, and there is no evidence to indicate a loss of popularity.

Before 1943, there was no explicit provision in the statutes for the adoption of council-manager government by cities operating under the general laws. In a number of instances, however, general-law cities provided for the manager form by ordinance. In 1943, the legislature authorized any municipality incorporated under the general laws and having a population of less than 5,000 to adopt the council-manager form by vote of the local electorate.

Since the beginning of the council-manager plan in Texas, six cities have abandoned it—Athens, Denton, Houston, Gainesville, Waco, and Rosenberg. However, Athens, Denton, Gainesville, and Waco later readopted the plan and are now operating under it.

In general, council-manager government in Texas follows the commonly accepted characteristics of the plan. The governing body is composed of from three to nine members, usually five. The members are ordinarily elected at large. In some of the larger cities, candidates run for specific numbered places on the council. Where the place system is not used, the candidates receiving the largest number of votes are elected.

The council is the legislative and policymaking body of the city. The manager is appointed by the council and serves during its pleasure. As the chief executive and administrative officer, he is responsible to the council for all affairs placed in his hands. He appoints and removes the heads of departments, although sometimes the city attorney, city clerk, and judge of the corporation court are appointed by the council. The manager is the chief financial official and is responsible for keeping the council advised concerning the financial affairs of the city.

The mayor, who is a member of the council, is the titular head of the city and the council's presiding officer. Sometimes he is selected by the council, or he may be the councilman receiving the highest vote. Only in a few instances does he run specifically for the job. However, the demands for political leadership in the larger council-manager cities may require the election of the mayor by popular vote. This method of selection tends to focus more attention on the mayor, and consequently his role as a political leader is enhanced. The cities of Dallas, Fort Worth, and Austin elect their mayors by direct popular vote.

[16]In Texas the governing body may be known either as a commission (hence commission-manager) or as a council (council-manager). The term "council-manager" is used here to designate city-manager government in Texas regardless of the official title of the governing body.

There is no doubt that the commission and mayor-council forms of government are steadily losing favor, especially with home-rule cities, for most of them now operate under the council-manager plan.

TERMS OF OFFICE

Historically all elective and appointive city officials in Texas have served two-year terms, but a constitutional amendment adopted in 1958 allows both home-rule and general-law cities to provide for terms of office not exceeding four years. The voters in each municipality determine by majority vote whether to adopt a two-, three-, or four-year term for their city officials.

If the term is increased beyond the customary two years, three requirements must be accepted: (1) When an elective or appointive officer with more than one year remaining in his unexpired term announces for another public office, his candidacy is considered as an automatic resignation from the city government. (2) Cities adopting a term longer than two years must elect the officials of their councils by majority vote. (Many home-rule cities now elect their officials by a plurality.) (3) Vacancies in the city council must be filled by majority vote at a special election called within 120 days after the vacancy occurs.[17]

MUNICIPAL EXPENDITURES AND REVENUES

Data permitting a comparison of Texas municipalities with those in other states reveal some interesting similarities as well as contrasts with respect to expenditures and revenues.[18]

Expenditures

Table 16 indicates the relative cost of the eight programs for which the most money is spent by Texas municipalities and by municipalities of all the states as measured by the United States average.

In Texas as well as in municipalities elsewhere in the United States, police protection, highways (streets, lighting, etc.), fire protection, and sewerage are among the most costly programs. However, in contrast to Texas, education, public welfare, and hospitals are among the programs for which most money is expended in other states. One reason for the

---

[17]All general-law cities were already required to fill vacancies on the council by special election.

[18]The data comparing all Texas municipalities with all municipalities in the United States were available only for the year 1967. New data will be ready early in 1974, after the date of writing. Limited data for some cities are more recent.

Table 16   Distribution of General Expenditures of Texas Municipalities for Eight Functions Compared with U.S. Averages in Percentages*

| Texas | | U.S. | |
Function	Percentage	Function	Percentage
Highways	18.6	Education	16.6
Police protection	12.5	Police protection	10.6
Sewerage	11.2	Highways	10.5
Fire protection	9.5	Other	9.6
Sanitation exclusive of sewerage	7.0	Fire protection	6.8
Parks and recreation	6.4	Public welfare	6.6
Other	6.3	Sewerage	5.8
Interest	6.1	Hospitals	5.4

*The percentages do not add to 100 because only eight of the total number of functions were selected for the tabulation.

Source: U.S. Bureau of the Census, *Census of Governments, 1967*, Vol. 4, U.S. Government Printing Office, Washington, D.C., 1969.

high priority of education is that in some large cities, most notably New York City, schools are controlled and financed by the city rather than by independent districts.

Revenues

The contrast between Texas and other states is much sharper when we examine the sources of revenue for municipalities.[19]

As Table 17 shows, general revenues make up a much smaller percentage of income for Texas cities and revenues from utilities much more (twice as much) as in other cities. But perhaps of most significance is the very small percentage of intergovernmental revenue received by Texas municipalities (4 percent compared with 21 percent) and the extremely small proportion flowing from the state government (under 1 percent compared with 17 percent). Intergovernmental revenue includes funds from other local governments and the Federal government, but for municipalities generally, the state is the largest provider.

The revenue picture in Texas has changed since the data were collected for the table. A very important change for Texas has been the widespread adoption of the optional 1 percent sales tax, first authorized for cities in 1967. The voters in over 600 cities had approved of the tax in the early 1970s. Statistics based on the total general revenue of the

[19]As was true of expenditures, data for revenues allowing a comparison of all Texas municipalities with all municipalities were from the 1967 Census of Governments.

twenty-three largest Texas cities in 1970–1971 indicate that 15.3 percent is derived from the sales tax.[20]

The ad valorem or general property tax continues, however, to be the principal tax at the city level. Constitutional and statutory provisions limit the tax to $2.50 on each $100 valuation in cities with populations over 5,000 and to $1.50 on each $100 valuation in cities with populations of 5,000 or less. However, neither class of city need levy the full rate and most do not. (A constitutional amendment on the November, 1973, ballot, which failed to pass, would have removed debt service from the tax limits.) The rate of assessed value of property and the taxation rate vary considerably from city to city.

Another important development for municipal finance in Texas and in the other states was the enactment by Congress of the State and Local Fiscal Assistance Act of 1972 (general revenue sharing). It has been estimated that Texas cities will receive about 57 percent of the Federal money allocated to local governments in Texas during the five-year life of the program. During the calendar year 1972, about 93.5 million dollars went to the cities. (The twenty-seven Texas cities over 50,000 in population received 70.5 percent.) In 1976, it is anticipated that the annual amount will increase to 114 million dollars. During the five-year period, the total amount received will probably be about 494 million dollars. As we have already explained in Chapter 11, the cities may spend the money

---

[20]Derived from data in U.S. Bureau of the Census, *City Government Finances in 1970–71*, Series GF 71-No. 4, U.S. Government Printing Office, Washington, D.C., 1972.

Table 17   Revenues of Texas Municipalities Compared with the U.S. Average in Percentages

Source	Texas percentage		U.S. percentage	
General revenues		65.0		80.0
Taxes	39.5		43.6	
(Property 35.1)			(30.5)	
Intergovernmental	4.0		21.1	
(From state .09)			(16.6)	
Charges and miscellaneous	21.0		15.0	
Utilities and liquor		33.0		17.0
Liquor	0.0		.04	
Insurance trust		1.5		2.0
Total		100.0		100.0

Source: U.S. Bureau of the Census, *Census of Governments, 1967*, Vol. 4, U.S. Government Printing Office, Washington, D.C., 1969.

only in seven high-priority areas enumerated in the law, capital expenditures, and financial administration. Also, numerous nonprogram strings are attached to the use of the money. The minimum sum dispensed by the U.S. Treasury will be $200. The general revenue sharing program sets no population limit on the size of the city or town to receive aid.

Long before the general revenue sharing program was launched, Texas municipalities had been receiving Federal grants-in-aid. The Great Depression of the 1930s witnessed the first use of the Federal grant-in-aid device as a way of aiding cities on a large scale. Since that time, pressing financial problems resulting from urban sprawl, urban blight, and increased population densities have contributed toward more Federal financial assistance for local programs.

In order for a city to receive Federal grants, permissive state legislation is required directly or indirectly. Even though the state grants cities general permission to participate in Federal programs, the initiative has usually rested with the local government to request the funds. In some cases, such as urban renewal programs, it has been necessary to submit the issue to the people for voter approval before the Federal funds could be used.

Federal grants-in-aid have covered a wide spectrum, including grants for air pollution control; projects in cancer research and other public health projects; in transportation, such as construction and maintenance of local airports; public works; urban development, including low rent housing, which is one of the oldest urban development programs; and community action programs in connection with the War on Poverty initiated under the Lyndon B. Johnson administration in 1964.

Municipalities are obliged to go into debt in order to finance capital improvements and certain other programs. In financing capital improvements or public works facilities, the principal source of revenue is from bonds. There are three basic types of municipal bonds: general obligation, revenue, and special assessment. General obligation bonds are repaid through regular municipal income, such as the property tax; revenue bonds are self-retiring in that they are sold to obtain money for construction of a municipally owned property that returns a revenue, such as a water system; special assessment bonds are retired by a special tax levied against the citizens who require the service, such as street paving or sidewalks.

FUNCTIONS OF MUNICIPAL GOVERNMENT

As we have seen from the review of municipal expenditures and revenues, municipalities are engaged in a wide variety of services for their citizens. Municipal functions are extremely numerous and also of vital concern to most citizens inasmuch as they affect the quality of life in a most immediate sense. For example, they concern the water we drink, the streets we drive on, the parks and playgrounds we enjoy, and the sanitation facilities upon which we depend. Police, fire, and health protection are among the oldest functions assumed by cities and remain among the most important for us today. In addition, many new functions have been added, including some resulting from the carrot of Federal grants-in-aid. For clarity and simplicity, let us treat municipal functions under a few general headings.

Protective Functions

Foremost among the responsibilities of city government has been the protection of the health, life, and property of its citizens. Thus, the protective functions of the city include those duties performed by the police, fire, and health departments. Policing certainly presents a serious problem to any city administration. Every police force is obligated to face both criminal and traffic problems, and both are of constant concern to the public. The fire department's function was originally only that of fire fighting, but today this department is a fire prevention agency as well. In addition the modern fire department is responsible for salvage work, and is frequently called upon to provide first aid in cases of drowning, shock, and other accidents. Many departments also share with the police the regular duty of arson investigation and other activities.

The field of public health has been the scene of some of the most notable achievements in municipal administration, despite the fact that the city health department usually receives only a small portion of the tax dollar. Today, the municipal health department protects health by both sickness-prevention and sickness-treatment functions. Prevention work usually includes control of communicable disease, registration of vital statistics, protection of child health, and promotion of sanitation through inspection of food, milk, water supply, and sewage. Curative work is usually limited to venereal-disease clinics, laboratory analyses, treatment of minor illnesses by public health nurses, and treatment of tuberculosis cases. In larger municipalities the city health service often provides educational programs in maternity care, home nursing, and nutrition.

There has been a growing concern among Texas officials about air and water pollution, both of which pose serious health threats. Today the cities in the Houston area appear to be particularly threatened by air pollution, and the city of Houston has taken certain steps to control it. Other areas in the state are also concerned, for pollution is no longer confined to one or two large cities. Almost all cities try to prevent stream pollution by the maintenance of adequate sewage-treatment facilities and the enforcement of municipal regulatory ordinances which are designed to control industrial pollution. In addition, the Texas Water Quality Board was created in 1967 to establish and enforce minimum standards of water quality for the state's rivers, lakes, and streams. The Water Quality Board replaced the older and less effective Water Pollution Control Board.

Welfare Functions

"Welfare" is a rubbery term capable of being stretched to include many municipal functions. We have been using it primarily to refer to public assistance programs to the needy, but it may be applied more generally.

Texas has provided continuing as opposed to temporary public assistance mainly through Federal-state matching programs under the Social Security Act of 1935. (See Chapter 13.) The role of the municipality has been comparatively minor, certainly in a financial sense, in these programs. The cities provided some general relief during the Depression of the 1930s for persons not qualifying for categorical assistance. But perhaps the major contribution of the cities insofar as continuing programs are concerned has been in providing hospitals to which charity patients may be sent. However, even in this area, hospital districts and city-county cooperation have been common; in short, the municipality has not assumed the sole or even the major responsibility for this function.

The municipality has played an important role in the temporary programs (which may not be so temporary) launched during the antipoverty campaigns of the 1960s and early 1970s. At the date of writing, Federal programs administered by the U.S. Office of Economic Opportunity (OEO) were being phased out; but many of the programs have been transferred to other departments or agencies.

One antipoverty program of particular interest to municipalities is the Community Action Program. The Economic Opportunity Act of 1964 provided for grants to support a local community action council or agency (CAA) whose purpose was to coordinate local antipoverty efforts. Community action agencies were created in many Texas cities and counties, but considerable opposition to them arose. For one thing, it was argued that they were performing governmental functions, although many were private organizations, and were bypassing regular governmental agencies. In 1966, their number was frozen by the Federal government in all states, appropriations for the program were reduced, and eventually all planning grants were stopped. In 1972, CAAs were still functioning in

Texas.[21] They were predominantly intergovernmental rather than municipal only, and many were private.

A municipal function different from public assistance but classifi-
able as a welfare function is the provision for public libraries. The public
library is historically a local institution and has local functions. Many
municipal libraries today are providing such important services and
programs as circulation of reading lists to the public, service for the blind
through special books and phonograph records, and expansion of service
through traveling units and extension libraries. Public libraries also
provide adult-education programs in such varied fields as great books,
general literature, music, art, and foreign languages. Often the library
collection contains materials of special interest to the city and county.

An active municipal recreation department is a "must" in the
modern city. A complete list of its activities would require several pages,
but the reader should be aware of the emphasis which the average city
places upon organized recreation, realizing that the chief function of the
recreation department is to promote these various activities and to furnish
leadership for their organization. Illustrative of the services offered are
the provision and maintenance of parks, playgrounds, water-sports
facilities, and recreation centers where arts and crafts, sports, and useful
social skills such as dancing and games are taught. Recreation facilities
may include city-owned theaters, auditoriums, and convention centers. A
modern recreation department provides programs for every age group
within the city.

Physical Services

One of the functions of any city administration is the orderly development of the external and physical aspects of the city. This end can be
attained only through planning. The purpose of city planning is to
promote public order, safety, health, and welfare in the broadest sense,
including convenience, comfort, attractiveness, economy, and efficiency
of operation. The legal basis for these activities is the so-called "police"
powers of the city. The emphasis in city planning has gradually shifted
from the "city beautiful" to the "city practical." As city planning became
of primary importance, most cities established city planning as a separate
department, although formerly the planning function had usually been
carried on by the public-works department. The city planning department
is concerned with both the immediate and the long-range needs of the

[21]For a list of the CAAs and a map showing their location in Texas, see *The Texas Front . . . In
the Nation's Struggle against Poverty, 1972*, p. 133, Annual Report of the Texas Office of Economic
Opportunity, Austin, 1972.

city's development, such as those involving business and industrial expansion, home sites, school and recreational facilities, protective and physical services expansion, traffic patterns, and city appearance.

Planning is concerned with land use, and one of the key requirements for a well-planned city is that it be properly zoned. Zoning refers to the division of a city into districts, or zones, for the purpose of applying different regulations to the property within each district. It is actually the first step in city planning. Originally, zoning was merely a means of preventing "nuisances" from being established in residential areas; today proper zoning allows the necessary municipal services to be supplied more easily, aids in stabilizing values, prevents the formation of slums and low-value areas, and reduces migration to areas outside the city limits. Of the cities in Texas with over 50,000 population, only Houston remains unzoned.[22] Actually, most Texas cities with over 25,000 population have zoning ordinances. A comprehensive zoning ordinance usually includes many categories of zones, ranging from one-family residential to heavy industrial, although some smaller cities use a simplified plan with only the categories of residential, business, and industrial. The zoning ordinance of a city, necessary and vital though it is, is a complex procedure, allowing a person certain grievance rights when a rezoning classification would work a hardship upon him and also allowing him rights of petition for zoning classification changes.

One of the most recent aspects of planning is regional planning involving two or more municipalities, usually two metropolitan areas located in separate counties. Consideration is given to matters of such area importance as water supply and development, air pollution, and airports. Regional planning is underway in a number of Texas urban communities. Recent Federal requirements demanding areawide planning as a prerequisite for the receipt of certain Federal funds has encouraged the formation of voluntary councils of governments and regional planning commissions. These organizations are designed to perform areawide planning functions for their member governments.[23] Regional planning commissions will be considered in greater detail in the next chapter.

Housing is also a matter of public concern, for poor housing is known to have a direct bearing on delinquency, dependency, and health, with a consequent effect upon the cost of maintaining city government. Especially in larger cities there is a constant problem of maintaining

---

[22]A referendum was held in Houston in November, 1962, to decide the issue of a comprehensive zoning ordinance. It was defeated by the voters of that city.

[23]Philip W. Barnes, *Metropolitan Coalitions: A Study of Councils of Governments in Texas*, Institute of Public Affairs, University of Texas at Austin, 1969.

standards in the central city area because surrounding residential areas tend to decline as a result of the fact that they are the older areas of the city. Some cities in Texas have taken advantage of Federal funds through the urban-renewal plan to clear slum areas and erect new public housing.

Along with planning and housing, modern "mechanized" civilization considers the construction and maintenance of good thoroughfares, boulevards, freeways, and streets to be among the most important functions of a municipal administration. The boulevards and streets of any city perform many services. In addition to carrying traffic, they are the location of many public installations such as water mains, subways, sewers, gas pipes, and wire conduits. Light and air may reach shops and dwellings through these channels. Thus in planning highways and streets, the city must combine utility with attractive appearance in order to provide the citizens with a roadway that meets many diverse requirements. It may be noted that a trend in modern municipal street thoroughfare planning is the routing of traffic away from the congested central city area through the use of extensive freeway networks and also through the use of multistory parking garages, which are encouraged by the city government but usually privately financed and owned. Some of the larger cities have considered the use of malls, or green areas for pedestrian traffic only, in the central shopping district; although this plan has been successfully employed elsewhere, no Texas city has undertaken a full program of stopping downtown vehicular traffic and creating pedestrian malls.

Public Utilities

Public utilities include all those enterprises, either publicly or privately owned, which render a necessary public service and at the same time are a natural monopoly by virtue of certain privileges granted by some governmental agency. Public utilities, in a narrow sense, include water, gas, electricity, communication, and transportation services. Others might include airports, abattoirs, sewers, markets, bridges, tunnels, and auditoriums. The services rendered by these various utilities have one thing in common: They are of such primary importance that regulation is imposed by some level of government to protect both the rights of the consumers and the interests of the utility owners. Municipal ownership of utilities in Texas is confined for the most part to water and sewer systems. Of the remaining major public utilities, airports and cemeteries rank highest on the public-ownership list. A few Texas cities now own and operate their own bus systems. One of the most lucrative of all utilities, that of electric generating and/or distributing, is mostly privately owned. The means by which a private company is designated to perform a function of public utility is a franchise, which is a contract, usually exclusive, issued by the city. Privately owned companies also secure construction contracts through competitive bidding to build the facilities for municipally owned public utilities.

AN IMPROVED CITY GOVERNMENT

Municipalities in the United States hold a reputation for efficiency, more so than any other unit of government. This has not always been so. In fact, quite the contrary was the prevailing view in the nineteenth and early twentieth centuries. Charges of bossism and machine politics, corruption and inefficiency, dirt and filth, and others along similar vein were levelled against the city. The tremendous improvement since the early 1900s has been due in part to various citizens' groups which were organized for the purpose of "throwing the rascals out." Many of these have long ago disappeared, but others have taken their places and continued to work toward the goal of more efficient and responsible government. During the Depression years, as well as during the years that followed, more attention has been directed toward the many economic and social problems faced by cities.

Certainly one of the most important historical periods for municipalities was the decade of the 1960s, when riots broke out (in some instances simultaneously) in numerous cities. Hard questions were asked about city government and its democratic responsiveness, particularly to its black citizens. It was argued that cities had grown too large and too professional to be responsive to the people. Municipal institutions were criticized for not representing all sections of the city and for failure to communicate with people where they lived—in the neighborhood.

Texas was spared the large-scale rioting of Detroit, Newark, Los Angeles, and other cities. But questions have been raised in Texas also about the responsiveness of Texas municipal institutions. One question has concerned the electoral systems used in Texas cities. Are they really designed for fair representation of the citizens in all parts of the city?[24]

The prevalent method of electing city councilmen (or commissioners) in Texas is at large with the place system. At-large elections mean that unless the candidate for the city council can win a plurality (or majority) throughout the entire city, he will lose. Formerly, most cities

---

[24]A study of city election systems is provided by Philip W. Barnes, "Alternative Methods of Electing City Councils in Texas Home Rule Cities," *Public Affairs Comment*, Institute of Public Affairs, University of Texas at Austin, May, 1970.

operated under a ward system from which the derogatory phrase "ward politics" is derived. A city councilman had only to win a majority (or plurality) of a portion or section or neighborhood, not the entire city. The place system as used in Texas usually simply requires candidates to declare for a given place, *e.g.*, place 1, 2, 3, etc. The candidate does not have to reside in any given area represented by the place. (However, this is a feature of some systems.) With the at-large system without a residency requirement for each place, there is no guarantee that the entire membership of the city council cannot reside in a single block of the city. The place system simply pits candidates against one another by chance or design. (It takes fast political footwork to select a place for which the candidate feels secure or for which he desires to wage battle; some candidates wait until the last possible moment to file for office in order to "look over the lay of the land.")

There is some evidence that at-large systems are actually less responsive to community demands in given situations.[25] City councilmen are only human and tend to see the public interest from their own perspective, which may very well deviate from that of others in the community. Hence, a representation system that allows various areas of the city to be represented in decision making has much to recommend it. On the other hand, critics doubt that there is sufficient evidence to support the proposition that one kind of electoral system produces different results from another in terms of performance of government or in policy output. Nonetheless, the creativity of reformers of city government could well be brought to play on current electoral institutions.

Cities face other problems as well. There is abundant evidence of the need for planning the reorganization of the cities and their closer integration with the countryside. In many communities a deliberate decision has been made to guide, insofar as possible, the currents of community life. This will require close and continuing cooperation of private enterprise and governmental and civic groups.

Numerous studies have indicated a causal connection between the physical conditions of city life and such problems as social disintegration, a high incidence of delinquency and crime, and high infant-mortality rates. Planning programs must be based, therefore, on a recognition of such relationships in order that cities can be made healthful, comfortable, and convenient environments for living.

[25]See Robert L. Lineberry and Edmund P. Fowler, "Reformism and Public Policies in American Cities," *American Political Science Review*, pp. 701–716, September, 1967.

Chapter 20

Governing Metropolitan Texas

One of the most important developments affecting the Texas political system has been the growth of the metropolitan areas. Virtually all the population increase from 1960 to 1970 took place in the Standard Metropolitan Statistical Areas (SMSAs), where over 73 percent of the people of Texas now live.[1] In other words, Texas is not only an urban state but a metropolitan one as well. As we have seen, Texas has more SMSAs (24 in 1973) than any other state.

[1]On April 27, 1973, the Office of Management and Budget announced that there were 269 SMSAs in the United States and Puerto Rico. The Texas number was reduced from 25 to 24 with the consolidation of the Dallas and Fort Worth SMSAs. The definition of the SMSA has changed from time to time since it was first employed by the OMB some twenty years ago. A memorandum from the OMB dated January, 1972, defines an SMSA as follows: "Each SMSA must include at least (1) one city with 50,000 or more inhabitants, or (2) a city with at least 25,000 inhabitants, which, taken together with contiguous places having a population density of at least 1,000 persons per square mile, constitutes (for general and social purposes) a single community with a total population of at least 50,000. In addition, the county or counties in which the city and places are located must have at least 75,000 inhabitants."

TEXAS SMSAs

An obvious reason for the growth of the Texas metropolitan areas is that they offer more opportunities than the non-SMSAs for most people. On virtually every measurement of economic or educational achievement, the SMSAs score higher than the other areas.[2] For one thing, average income is greater. This comports with the well-known fact that wealth is heavily concentrated in the metropolises of the nation. The average graduate of Texas metropolitan public schools scores higher on standardized tests. Most of the new housing built from 1960 to 1970 was in the SMSAs. Employment opportunities were much greater during the last

[2]Many of the figures used in the text are from Joe B. Harris, *Urban Texas: Past - Present - Future*, a report prepared for the Texas Urban Development Commission, Arlington, 1971.

THE 24 METROPOLITAN AREAS OF TEXAS—1973

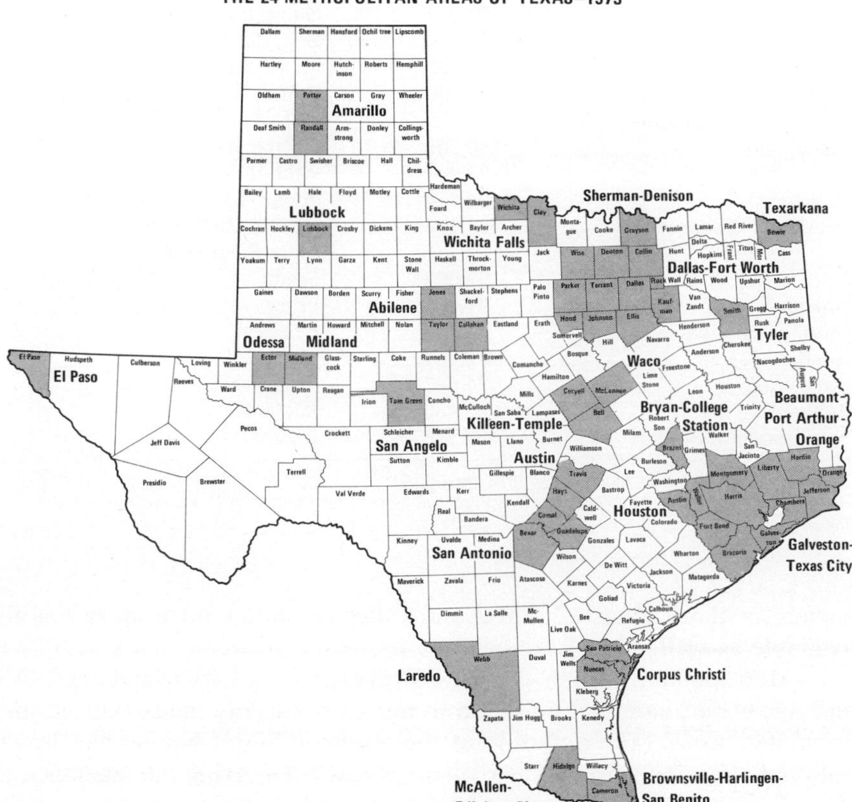

Table 18   Standard Metropolitan Statistical Areas of Texas–1973

Name	1970 population*	County area
Dallas-Fort Worth	2,377,979	Collin, Dallas, Denton, Ellis, Kaufman, Hood, Rockwall, Wise, Parker, Johnson, Tarrant
Houston	1,999,316	Brazoria, Fort Bend, Harris, Liberty, Montgomery, Waller
San Antonio	888,179	Bexar, Guadalupe, Comal
El Paso	359,291	El Paso
Beaumont-Port Arthur-Orange	345,939	Jefferson, Orange, Hardin
Austin	323,158	Travis, Hays
Corpus Christi	284,832	Nueces, San Patricio
McAllen-Pharr-Edinburg	181,535	Hidalgo
Lubbock	179,295	Lubbock
Galveston-Texas City	169,812	Galveston
Killeen-Temple	159,794	Bell, Coryell
Waco	147,553	McLennan
Amarillo	144,396	Potter, Randall
Brownsville-Harlingen-San Benito	140,368	Cameron
Wichita Falls	129,941	Wichita, Clay
Abilene	122,164	Jones, Taylor, Callahan
Texarkana (Texas-Ark.)	101,198	Bowie, Miller (Ark.), Little River (Ark.)
Tyler	97,096	Smith
Odessa	91,805	Ector
Sherman-Denison	83,225	Grayson
Laredo	72,859	Webb
San Angelo	71,047	Tom Green
Midland	65,433	Midland
Bryan-College Station	57,978	Brazos

*County populations based on the 1970 Census.

Source: Based on information from the Executive Office of the President, Office of Management and Budget.

decade in these areas. Cultural and other amenities were more readily available as well.

Metropolitan growth is not, however, without its drawbacks. We find air, water, and land pollution in the more heavily industrialized and populated areas. (The pollution of the Houston Ship Channel has drawn national attention.) Solid waste disposal has been taxing the ingenuity of metropolitan area dwellers. (A self-destruct beer can would be a great help.) The incidence of crime and other social problems is higher in the SMSAs. Traffic snarls plague the urban dweller. Also, governmental costs are higher with a correspondingly heavier tax burden. Imbalances exist between the central city and the surrounding areas (OCC or outside the central city). Many suburbanites work in the city but live in the outlying areas and escape the city property tax. Within the central cities, there are disparities in physical facilities—streets, parks, lighting, and so on—between the richer and the poorer districts. The plight of the poorer school districts was well documented in the *Rodriguez* case discussed in Chapter 12.

The ills of the city have been widely broadcast and diagnosed in the United States. The urban crisis has become a household word. Yet, there are those who say we are better off than ever before; it is only our expectations for city living that have been outstripped.[3]

Texas metropolitan areas have serious problems, but they have not yet become as grave as those in the older urbanized parts of the nation. Texas cities are younger and developed after the automobile became the dominant mode of transportation so that streets and highways could be better planned. Also, Texas has had frontier elbow room in which to expand. Texas annexation laws were for many years very liberal, as we shall see in the next section, and they permitted control of growth around cities to avoid some of the worst cases of urban sprawl and governmental complexity.

LOCAL GOVERNMENT IN THE TEXAS SMSAs

The Standard Metropolitan Statistical Area is an urban region characterized by economic, social, and physical interdependence. It is not a unit of government. In fact, the most outstanding feature of the SMSAs insofar as political structure is concerned is the proliferation of local governmental units. There are literally hundreds of them in the larger SMSAs around the country. (The average in the nation is about eighty-seven units per SMSA.) Texas does not have as many as the older areas, but the number within the largest SMSAs is not insubstantial. The 1970 census showed the Dallas SMSA with 192 units of government; Houston with 214; Fort Worth, 83; and San Antonio, 59.[4]

Unfortunately, the metropolitan regions have problems that cannot be solved by individual governments acting alone. The problems straddle the limits of villages, towns, cities, counties, school districts, special

---

[3]See Edward C. Banfield, *The Unheavenly City*, Little, Brown and Company, Boston, 1970.

[4]The 1967 Census of Governments, the latest available source of data for all SMSAs at the time of writing, showed 1,096 units of government in the Texas SMSAs.

districts, state lines, and even international boundaries. For example, fumes from industrial plants do not recognize city limits as they blight vegetation or congest the lungs of people in neighboring communities. Most assuredly, factory wastes that pollute streams do not turn back at the next political subdivision. Problems of airport development, hospitals, public health, traffic control, fire and police protection, sanitation, and rapid transit have also spread beyond the boundaries of existing governments in many parts of Texas. They are really areawide problems, yet in most instances there is no areawide government with the authority to deal with them.

Valiant attempts have been made to reform local governmental structure, particularly the county, to provide for regional authority to handle areawide problems of concern to citizens. However, as we have seen, fundamental reform has been rare in the United States and nonexistent insofar as county structure is concerned in Texas. Opponents usually refer to proposals for regional organization as "metro," which to them is about as popular as cholera.

Nonetheless, in Texas as well as elsewhere, we muddle through with what we have. One of the most important devices available to Texas cities has been annexation, which we will turn to next. Other methods of handling areawide problems will follow.

Annexation

Annexation has been described as perhaps the most important "tool" Texas cities have had to control urban sprawl.[5] Among twenty-two cities described as national leaders in annexation between 1950 and 1960, eight were Texas cities. Seven of the Texas cities had at least doubled their size during this period; by 1970, all had doubled and two quadrupled in area as a result of annexation of adjacent territory.

Before 1963, there were virtually no restrictions on the annexation powers of Texas home-rule cities, but in that year a statute severely limited these powers. This statute provides for the establishment of extraterritorial jurisdiction by a municipality over unincorporated land contiguous to its corporate boundaries. These extraterritorial districts may extend from $^1/_2$ to 5 miles from the corporate limits, with the area being dependent on the population of the city. The annexation powers of a city are limited to territory within its extraterritorial jurisdiction. Furthermore, a municipality may not annex yearly new areas in excess of

[5]Homer D. Reed, *Texas Urban Government Profile*, paper prepared for the Texas Assembly, The State and the Urban Crisis, Austin, 1970.

10 percent of the total land area of the city as of January 1, of that year, except by the request of a majority of the landowners and qualified voters of the territory annexed. Also excluded from this 10 percent maximum is land annexed which is owned by the city, the county, the state, or the Federal government and is used for a public purpose; territory annexed at the request of the owner; and territory annexed at the request of a majority of the resident voters of that territory. If a city fails to annex the amount of land authorized by the statute, such unused allocation may be carried over and used in subsequent years up to a maximum of 30 percent of the total land area of the city.

As the boundaries of a city are altered to conform with annexations, the extraterritorial jurisdiction expands in conformity with the new boundaries. This will create the problem of overlapping areas of extraterritorial jurisdiction between cities within close proximity. These areas will be apportioned between the two cities either upon their agreement or by the courts. New cities may not incorporate within the extraterritorial jurisdiction other than by the consent of the existing city unless the existing city refuses to annex the territory of the proposed city within six months after a majority of the landowners in the territory request such annexation. A city may extend the operation of its ordinances relating to plats and the subdivision of land to its extraterritorial jurisdiction, but the city's remedy for enforcement in these areas is limited to injunctive, rather than penal, relief. Cities may also establish industrial districts in these areas and may enter agreements pursuant thereto, but the term of such districts is limited to a period of seven years, although the agreements or contracts may be renewed on the agreement of the city and the other party.

Once an area has been annexed, it must be provided with water and sanitary sewer service equivalent to that in similar areas in the rest of the city within three years or the residents and property owners may petition for disannexation under court order. After one year, a municipality may reannex an area which has been disannexed, provided it is still unincorporated, but it must provide the required services within one year.

Intergovernmental Contracts

Generally speaking, the most widely used form of cooperation in Texas is the intergovernmental contract which has been available to Texas local governments for 100 years. These contracts permit governmental units to conduct, jointly or cooperatively, a service or activity. Often, the contract is for a specific service or performance, such as sewage treatment or the sale of water. In other instances, the contract may provide for direct services to the residents of another community, as in police and fire protection agreements. A 1972 survey revealed that contracts for water supply, fire services, sewage treatment, tax assessment and collection, police services, solid waste disposal, and library services were most common.[6] The possible area of intergovernmental contracts was widened somewhat in 1967 by a legislative enactment allowing cities, independent school districts, or any political subdivision in the same or adjacent counties to establish and operate joint recreational activities. Also, authorization was given for two or more counties to enter into cooperative agreements to provide probation, detention, and diagnostic services for juvenile delinquents. A 1971 law greatly enlarged the scope of the contracts by giving blanket authority to all governmental units to contract for any service.

The interlocal contract is flexible and responds more readily to prevailing political pressures than forms of consolidation or reorganization which require major reconstructions of existing government patterns. Even though the contractual device is usually considered an *ad hoc* solution, its wide acceptance and continued use give it a character of permanence as an effective approach to some regional problems.

Special districts

Special districts, which we discussed at length in Chapter 18, are widely used in the United States to provide areawide functions in metropolitan areas. However, in Texas, except for hospital services, the special district has been more of a device for fragmentation than coordination.

Urban County

Some Texas counties have assumed municipal-type functions. Ector County has complete responsibility for the park system; Ector and Tom Green counties finance the libraries; Jefferson County operates the airport for the area; Orange County has a county housing authority; Tarrant County built a 14 million dollar convention center; and Harris County broke precedent when it built the world's first domed stadium.[7] However, as we have seen, the Texas constitution will have to be changed before Texas can rely heavily on the county for areawide urban functions. Also, there will have to be a political desire to allow the county to perform these functions.

---

[6]David W. Tees and Jay G. Stanford, *Handbook for Inter-local Contracting in Texas*, prepared by Institute of Urban Studies, University of Texas at Arlington, 1972.
[7]Texas Research League, *Metropolitan Texas: A Workable Approach to Its Problems*, pp. 56–57, Austin, 1967.

Regional Planning Councils

The most important development of all for handling problems in the metropolitan areas has been the rise of the regional planning councils. (In Texas, the term "regional planning council" is used interchangeably with "councils of governments" (COGs), "development councils," and "associations of governments.") Texas has gained national recognition for its regional planning councils which were first authorized in Texas in 1965. The legislation has been compared in significance to the municipal home-rule act of 1913.[8] The first council created in pursuance of the law was the North Central Texas Council of Governments (NCTCOG). Today there are 24 COGs serving 97 percent of the people of Texas and to which all but 30 of the state's 254 counties belong.

The regional planning council is a voluntary association of governments for purposes of cooperation and planning the orderly development of the area over which the member governments have jurisdiction. Although legally a political subdivision, the council has no powers of taxation, eminent domain, zoning, or any of the traditional governmental powers. However, it may enter into contracts with other governments and perform services.

The COG is usually governed by two bodies, the General Assembly, which represents all members and has policymaking authority, and the Executive Committee, composed of officers of the General Assembly, which meets more frequently than the Assembly. Every COG has an Executive Director and several advisory committees. The statutes require that at least two-thirds of the governing body be composed of local elected officials.

Texas COGs are financed from local, state, and Federal funds. Texas was the first state to provide for state aid. In 1971 and 1972, state funds amounted to 3.2 million dollars, which represented a 250 percent increase over the preceding biennium. However, Federal funds accounted for the greatest amount of revenues.

Regional planning councils perform a variety of functions in Texas. These have been growing in importance. "More and more federal, state, and local programs in health, education, childhood development, manpower, transportation and other areas are being provided by and through regional councils."[9] The 1972 Directory of Regional Planning Councils discusses ten functions, which we will turn to next.

---

[8]*Regional Directory '72*, Office of the Governor, Division of Planning Coordination, p. 8, Austin, 1972. For a definitive work on COGs in Texas, see Philip W. Barnes, *Metropolitan Coalitions: A Study of Councils of Governments in Texas*, Institute of Public Affairs, University of Texas at Austin, 1969.
[9]*Regional Directory, loc. cit.*

Table 19   Regional Councils in Texas (September, 1973)

Organization	Central city
Alamo Area Council of Governments	San Antonio
Ark-Tex Council of Governments	Texarkana
Brazos Valley Development Council	Bryan
Capital Area Planning Council	Austin
Central Texas Council of Governments	Belton
Coastal Bend Council of Governments	Corpus Christi
Concho Valley Council of Governments	San Angelo
Deep East Texas Council of Governments	*Diboll
East Texas Council of Governments	Tyler
Golden Crescent Council of Governments	*Victoria
Heart of Texas Council of Governments	Waco
Houston-Galveston Area Council	Houston-Galveston
Lower Rio Grande Valley Development Council	McAllen-Brownsville
Middle Rio Grande Valley Development Council	*Del Rio
Nortex Regional Planning Commission	Wichita Falls
North Central Texas Council of Governments	Dallas-Ft. Worth
Panhandle Regional Planning Commission	Amarillo
Permian Basin Regional Planning Commission	Midland-Odessa
Southeast Texas Regional Planning Commission	Beaumont-Orange
South Plains Association of Governments	Lubbock
South Texas Development Council	Laredo
Texoma Regional Planning Commission	Sherman
West Central Texas Council of Governments	Abilene
West Texas Council of Governments	El Paso

*Nonmetropolitan.
Source: Office of the Governor.

1. Technical Assistance   The COGs provide their member governments with advice on how to apply for Federal aid; they furnish the services of such experts as engineers, physical planners, and others as needed; and they help prepare model codes. For example, the Panhandle Regional Planning Commission provided help on the matter of devising a building code to discourage burglary of residences.

2. Criminal Justice   With the enactment of the U.S. Omnibus Crime Control and Safe Streets Act of 1968, Federal grants have been available to the state and local governments for the purpose of improving law enforcement. The Texas Criminal Justice Council, created by executive order in pursuance of the act, provides funds to COGs as well as to local governments for planning and action grants. For example, COGs have played a role in police training. It is recognized that crime is no respecter of local government boundaries and is an appropriate subject for regional action.

3. Alcoholism   The Texas Commission on Alcoholism has designated eleven regional planning councils as Regional Alcoholism Authorities for the purpose of developing programs relating to treatment and rehabilitation.

4. Information Systems   The COGs compile and disseminate great quantities of information to their member governments. The Houston-Galveston Area Council has established a computerized information retrieval system called RIM.

5. Health   The utilization of COGs in health planning was made possible by the Partnership for Health Act of 1966. The Federal law required areawide as well as statewide health planning. The first areawide comprehensive health planning organization was established within the Alamo Area Council of Governments (San Antonio). In 1972, there were five organizations.

6. Human Resources and Manpower   Regional planning councils have been called upon to play a role in several human resources and manpower programs. For example, the councils administered funds under the Emergency Employment Act in 1971–1972.

7. Comprehensive Planning Services   The oldest function assigned to the COGs has been to make comprehensive areawide plans under the Federal government's 701 program. (The name is derived from Section 701 of the Housing Act of 1954, as amended.) Among the planning services in which COGs participated in 1971–1972 was the Texas segment of the national Transportation Needs Study, to which reference was made in Chapter 14. The regional planning programs under the 701 authority are diverse and include such functional areas as environmental quality, water and sewer needs, open space, land use, and solid waste management.

8. Economic Development   Economic planning to aid depressed areas was performed by six regional councils in 1972.

9. Land Use   The COGs have been cognizant of the lack of a coordinated land use planning program in Texas. They have for years been engaged in preparing regional land use plans. Projects "have centered on the inventory and evaluation of regional land resources. The Concho Valley Council of Governments' remote sensing project, for example, will provide cities with detailed aerial photography of urban and land use trends."[10]

10. Review and Comment   One of the best-known and oldest of the functions performed by the regional planning councils is that of review and comment. Authorized by Federal legislation, such as the Demonstration Cities and Metropolitan Development Act of 1966 and

----

[10] *Ibid.*, p. 12.

OMB Circular A-95, the councils review applications for more than 100 separate Federal and state grant-in-aid programs providing for water supplies, sewage disposal, highways, public facilities, and so on. The purpose of the review and comment procedure is to estimate the impact of the requested projects upon the orderly development of the area. The projects include water and sewer, highways, public facilities, and so on. The comments are attached to the applications for the grants and are taken into account by the Federal or state agency. They may result in the rejection of the project. By the end of 1972, Texas COGs had reviewed projects totalling 4.1 billion dollars. Texas COGs have engaged in the review and comment procedure more extensively than COGs in other states.

In Texas there are other regional units of one kind or another with planning functions.[11] The Planning Division in the Governor's Office has issued policy statements expressing concern that the initial purpose of the COGs may be circumvented by these agencies. It was intended that the COGs would be umbrella organizations to coordinate all regional or areawide planning in Texas. In other states, considerable confusion and conflict have arisen from a proliferation of multijurisdictional and multifunctional planning agencies. It is hoped that this can be avoided in Texas.

STATE GOVERNMENT ROLE IN METROPOLITAN AREAS

Considerable amounts of ink have been spilled over the question of the role of state governments in resolving the so-called urban crisis.[12] The state possesses an awesome array of legal powers over its own local governments. It could, if it wished, force a consolidated or federated metropolitan government; it could redistribute tax burdens and benefits in the metropolitan areas; it could transfer local functions to the state; and so on. There is, however, a gap between legal and political reality. States have generally relied upon the local populace for decisions on basic local reorganization and reforms.

Nonetheless, throughout the country, the states are taking on more responsibilities toward their local governments in the metropolitan areas.

---

[11]These are Economic Development Districts (EDDs); Resource Conservation and Development Projects (RC&Ds); Regional Manpower Planning Systems (CAMPs); and Community Action Agencies (CAAs), multicounty.

[12]See Alan K. Campbell (ed.), *The States and the Urban Crisis*, prepared for the American Assembly, Prentice-Hall, Inc., Englewood Cliffs, N. J., 1970; Richard I. Hofferbert and Ira Sharkansky (eds.), *State and Urban Politics*, Little, Brown and Company, Boston, 1971.

This has coincided with the modernization movement and revival of the states to which reference was made in earlier chapters. Texas has been recognized nationwide as a leader in developing better state-local relations for greater coordination and delivery of services in the urban areas.

State Planning

We have already seen how the state of Texas took the lead in support of councils of governments. The same 1965 law authorizing COGs also authorized state planning. In 1967, the governor was designated by statute as the chief planning officer of the state. The Division of Planning Coordination was established in his office and several interagency planning agencies to assist him.[13] The Planning Division and the agencies all have responsibilities toward the metropolitan areas of the state. It is almost impossible to separate state and regional planning. In fact, in a report entitled *Texas' Urban Challenge*, the Planning Division has compiled a list of urban programs planned or already in operation by numerous state agencies many of whom are also members of one of the interagency planning agencies.

Under Governor John B. Connally, twenty-one state planning regions were set up in 1968. Their boundaries have been revised since then, but their major purpose remains. It is to provide for master planning regions for better coordination of state plans and programs with one another and with Federal, regional, and local plans. The Federal government has recognized the regions for the administration of its programs affecting Texas. In 1973, Texas had twenty-four state planning regions.

Texas Urban Development Commission

In 1970, Governor Preston Smith established by executive order the twenty-two-member Texas Urban Development Commission. During the two-year life of the commission, significant recommendations were made for improving state-local relations and the state's response to urban problems. Unlike many commissions of this type, most of the recommendations were implemented. Perhaps the most significant fact of all was that the state saw the need for a commission to reexamine the state's role in the urban and metropolitan areas.

---

[13]In the 1970s the following interagency councils were in the Governor's Office: Interagency Council on Natural Resources and the Environment, Interagency Human Resources Council, Interagency Transportation Council, Texas Criminal Justice Council, and Interagency Health Council.

Texas Advisory Commission on Intergovernmental Relations

One of the recommendations of the Texas Urban Development Commission that bore fruit was the establishment of the Texas Advisory Commission on Intergovernmental Commissions, one of the few of its kind in the nation at the time. Patterned after the highly successful U.S. Advisory Commission on Intergovernmental Relations, the twenty-four-member commission is composed of representatives of all levels of government and the private sector. A significant innovation in membership was the inclusion of two Federal government officials. The 1971 statute setting up the commission directed it to give careful and continual attention to the interrelationships between and among governments. Intergovernmental relations in metropolitan areas have been studied by the commission.

Department of Community Affairs

Another of the successful Texas Urban Development Commission's recommendations was the establishment of the Department of Community Affairs, which was formerly the Division of State-Local Relations in the Governor's Office. By the creation of the new independent agency in 1971 Texas joined other states in the institutionalizing of its concern for local problems.

The new department performs many duties directly bearing upon the metropolitan areas. Among its duties is to provide for housing codes, to administer the 701 comprehensive planning programs for cities and counties, to coordinate early childhood development programs, to coordinate Model Cities programs, and to act as the governor's Youth Secretariat in coordinating programs for young people. The 1973 legislature added several new responsibilities, including supervision of the multiservice delivery of programs for the poor in low income neighborhoods.

THE ROLE OF THE FEDERAL GOVERNMENT

The Federal government has played a leading role in the metropolitan areas, particularly in encouraging the regional planning councils by funding and by requiring review and comment on Federal grant-in-aid applications. In addition, numerous Federal programs have an impact upon the metropolitan areas, intended or not. The Federal government has recognized their potential impact, which is the reason for requiring areawide planning as a prerequisite for grant-in-aid programs. The significance of Federal action in the metropolitan areas is apparent from the fact that between 1962 and 1973 Federal aid to urban areas increased from 3.9 billion dollars to 315 billion dollars, an 800 percent growth.[14]

Throughout this and the preceding chapters we have made frequent references to specific Federal programs of concern to the metropolitan areas. Suffice it to say that virtually all domestic programs—be they concerned with the environment, poverty, planning, health, education, or whatever—have an impact upon Texas and other metropolitan areas of the nation. Laws such as the Intergovernmental Cooperation Act of 1968 and the Intergovernmental Personnel Act of 1970 help to improve intergovernmental relations in the metropolitan areas. The ultimate effect of the U.S. State and Local Fiscal Assistance Act (general revenue sharing) upon metropolitan problems cannot yet be determined. The provision of assistance without the usual program strings means that there is less Federal direction of the programs undertaken by the local governments in these areas. Also, revenue sharing does not address itself to governmental reorganization and may contribute to further proliferation.

COOPERATIVE FEDERALISM

The metropolitan areas of Texas illustrate very well the need for intergovernmental cooperation in the Federal system. The many programs we have considered should be evaluated on the basis of whether they are directed toward achieving the common goal of a better quality of living for citizens by cooperation and coordination among all levels of government.

---

[14]*The 1973 Municipal Yearbook*, International City Manager's Association, p. 11, Chicago, 1973.

Appendix

Section Outline of the Constitution of the State of Texas*

ARTICLE 1

Bill of Rights

Sec. 1.   Freedom and Sovereignty of State.
Sec. 2.   Inherent Political Power; Republican Form of Government.
Sec. 3.   Equal Rights.
Sec. 3a.   Equal Rights for Women.
Sec. 4.   Religious Tests.
Sec. 5.   Witnesses Not Disqualified by Religious Beliefs; Oaths and
            Affirmations.
Sec. 6.   Freedom of Worship.

*The Section Outline of the Texas Constitution has been reproduced with permission from the following source: George D. Braden, *Citizens' Guide to the Texas Constitution*, prepared for the Texas Advisory Commission on Intergovernmental Relations by the Institute for Urban Studies, University of Houston, Austin, 1972. The *Citizens' Guide* and the complete text of the Texas Constitution may be purchased from the Texas Advisory Commission on Intergovernmental Relations, 55 North Interregional, Austin, Texas 78702. The Section Outline has been changed from the original to incorporate amendments adopted in November, 1972.

ARTICLE 2

Powers of Government

ARTICLE 3

Legislative Department

ARTICLE 4

Executive Department

ARTICLE 5

Judicial Department

ARTICLE 6

Suffrage

ARTICLE 7

Education

The Public Free Schools

Asylums

University

ARTICLE 8

Taxation and Revenue

ARTICLE 9

Counties

County Seats

Hospital Districts

ARTICLE 10

Railroads

ARTICLE 11

Municipal Corporations

Sec. 6.   Taxes to Pay Interest and Create Sinking Fund to Satisfy Indebtedness.
Sec. 7.   Counties and Cities on Gulf of Mexico; Tax for Sea Walls, Breakwaters and Sanitation; Bonds; Condemnation of Right of Way.
Sec. 8.   Donation of Portion of Public Domain to Aid in Construction of Sea Walls or Breakwaters.
Sec. 9.   Property Exempt From Forced Sale and From Taxation.
Sec. 10.   City or Town as Independent School District; Maintenance of Institution of Learning. (Repealed Aug. 5, 1969.)
Sec. 11.   Maximum Four Year Terms of Office for Elective and Appointive City Officials Authorized.

ARTICLE 12

Private Corporations

Sec. 1.   Creation by General Laws.
Sec. 2.   General Laws to be Enacted; Protection of Public and Stockholders.
Sec. 3-7.   (Repealed Aug. 5, 1969.)

ARTICLE 13

Spanish and Mexican Land Titles

(Repealed, Aug. 5, 1969.)

ARTICLE 14

Public Lands and Land Office

Sec. 1.   General Land Office.
Sec. 2-8.   (Repealed Aug. 5, 1969.)

ARTICLE 15

Impeachment

Sec. 1.   Power of Impeachment.
Sec. 2.   Trial of Impeachment of Certain Officers by Senate.
Sec. 3.   Oath of Affirmation of Senators; Concurrence of Two-Thirds Required.
Sec. 4.   Judgment; Indictment, Trial and Punishment.
Sec. 5.   Suspension Pending Impeachment; Provisional Appointments.
Sec. 6.   Judges of District Court; Removal by Supreme Court.
Sec. 7.   Removal of Officers When Mode Not Provided in Constitution.

Address

Sec. 8.   Removal of Judges by Governor on Address of Two-Thirds of Each House of Legislature.

ARTICLE 16

General Provisions

ARTICLE 17

Mode of Amending the Constitution of the State

INDEX